An Introduction to Psycholinguistics

LEARNING ABOUT LANGUAGE

General Editors:
Geoffrey Leech & Mick Short, Lancaster University

1894 Chautaugua, New York
Alexander Graham Bell (47 years), who was a teacher of the deaf before
he invented the telephone, with Helen Keller (14 years), seated, and Anne
Sullivan Macy (28 years), standing. Helen Keller became deaf and blind at
19 months due to an illness. At the age of 7 years she learned language
through a system of touch by her teacher, Anne Sullivan.

An Introduction to Psycholinguistics

Second edition

Danny D. Steinberg and Natalia V. Sciarini

PEARSON
Longman

Harlow, England • London • New York • Boston • San Francisco • Toronto • Sydney • Singapore • Hong Kong
Tokyo • Seoul • Taipei • New Delhi • Cape Town • Madrid • Mexico City • Amsterdam • Munich • Paris • Milan

PEARSON EDUCATION LIMITED

Edinburgh Gate
Harlow CM20 2JE
United Kingdom
Tel: +44 (0)1279 623623
Fax: +44 (0)1279 431059
Website: www.pearsoned.co.uk

First published 1993
Second edition published in Great Britain in 2006

© Pearson Education Limited 1993, 2006

The rights of Danny D. Steinberg and Natalia V. Sciarini to be identified
as authors of this work have been asserted by them in accordance
with the Copyright, Designs and Patents Act 1988.

ISBN-13: 978-0-582-50575-9
ISBN-10: 0-582-50575-5

British Library Cataloguing in Publication Data
A CIP catalogue record for this book can be obtained from the British Library

Library of Congress Cataloging in Publication Data
Steinberg, Danny D.
   An introduction to psycholinguistics / Danny D. Steinberg and Natalia V. Sciarini.—2nd ed.
      p. cm. — (Learning about language)
   Includes bibliographical references and indexes.
   ISBN 0-582-50575-5 (pbk)
   1. Psycholinguistics.   I. Sciarini, Natalia V.   II. Title.   III. Series.

P37.S77 2006
401'.9—dc22

2005051529

10 9 8 7 6 5 4 3 2 1
10 09 08 07 06

Set by 35 in 10/12.5pt Palatino
Printed by Malaysia

The Publisher's policy is to use paper manufactured from sustainable forests.

To our sons Kimio, Will, and Artem, who brought us joy and furthered our understanding of language.

Contents

Contents

Preface

A little more than a decade has passed since the first edition of this book appeared. Since then the field of psycholinguistics has grown so much that it is necessary to update the earlier materials.

This book is directed towards readers who wish to understand the psychology of language as it relates to learning, mind and brain as well as various aspects of society and culture. Although the topics that are presented are dealt with in depth and involve current issues and research, no specific knowledge of any topic is presupposed on the part of the reader; basic terms and concepts are generally presented and discussed before more complex or abstract matters are considered.

The knowledge presented in this volume is intended to bring the reader to the highest level of understanding of the topics considered in an engaging way. Students, lecturers and researchers from a variety of fields – psychology, linguistics, philosophy, second-language teaching, speech pathology – can all benefit from the wide range of important knowledge and theory that are considered.

The book is divided into three parts, each with a number of chapters:

Part 1, First-language learning: Chapter 1, How children learn language; Chapter 2, The deaf and language: sign, oral, written; Chapter 3, Reading principles and teaching; Chapter 4, Wild and isolated children and the critical age issue for language learning; Chapter 5, Animals and language learning.

Part 2, Second-language learning: Chapter 6, Children vs. adults in second-language learning; Chapter 7, Second-language teaching methods; Chapter 8, Bilingualism, intelligence, transfer, and learning strategies.

Part 3, Language, mind and brain: Chapter 9, Language, thought and culture; Chapter 10, Where does language knowledge come from? Intelligence, innate language ideas, behaviour?; Chapter 11, Natural Grammar mind and speaker performance; Chapter 12, Language and the brain.

Of particular note in this book is the presentation of a radically new theory of grammar, *Natural Grammar*. Such a grammar conforms to the primary acquisition process of speech comprehension, where comprehension develops prior to production in normal children and it develops without production for mute-hearing children. Production is considered as a secondary process deriving from comprehension. Natural Grammar is the only current grammar that can account for the psycholinguistic processes of speech comprehension and speech production.

We are indebted to Professor Hiroshi Nagata of Kawasaki University of Medical Welfare, Japan, Professor David Aline of Kanagawa University, Japan, and to Mr Jeff Matthews, Naples, Italy, who not only made substantial contributions to various chapters of the book but were instrumental in providing us with many source materials. We would like to thank Professor Steven Davis of Carleton University, Canada, for his enlightening discussion on mind and philosophical functionalism, Professor Richard Schmidt of the University of Hawaii for his important comments on morpheme learning, and Professor Julia Herschensohn of the University of Seattle for her insightful suggestions on aspects of Chomsky's Universal Grammar, as well as Professor Jun Yamada of Hiroshima University for his useful comments on the new theory of grammar, Natural Grammar. These scholars, it must be noted, do not necessarily agree with the views expressed in the chapters.

Our appreciation is extended to the editors, Professor Geoffrey Horrocks, Ms Casey Mein, and Mr Philip Langeskov for their encouragement, help and patience in bringing this book to publication.

DDS
West Vancouver, British Columbia

NS
Guilford, Connecticut
15 January, 2005

List of tables

List of figures

Publisher's acknowledgements

We are grateful to the following for permission to reproduce copyright material:

Frontispiece: Library of Congress, Prints & Photographs Division, Gilbert H. Grosvenor Collection of Photographs of the Alexander Graham Bell Family, LC-G9-Z1-137, 816-A; Figure 2.2 from Crystal, D., *The Cambridge Encyclopedia of Language* (Cambridge University Press, 1987); Figure 2.3 from Liddell, Scott K., *American Sign Language Syntax* (Mouton de Guyter, 1980); Figure 12.2 adapted from Tortora, G. J. and Grabowski, S. R., *Principles of Anatomy and Physiology* (Biological Sciences Textbooks, Inc., A & P Textbooks, Inc. and Sandra Reynolds Grabowski, 1993).

In some instances we have been unable to trace the owners of copyright material, and we would appreciate any information that would enable us to do so.

Part 1

First-language learning

Chapter 1

How children learn language

We have minds and in our minds we have the means for producing and comprehending speech. But how did we come to have such abilities? At birth we cannot comprehend speech, nor can we produce speech. Yet, by the age of 4 years we have learned vocabulary and grammatical rules for creating a variety of sentence structures including negatives, questions, and relative clauses. And although 4-year-olds still have passives and some other elaborate syntactic structures to learn, along with a never-ending stock of vocabulary items, they have already overcome the most difficult obstacles in language learning. This is true of children the world over, whatever the language may be.

Indeed, the language proficiency of the 4- or 5-year-old is often the envy of the adult second-language learner, who has been struggling for years to master the language. It is one of the fundamental tasks of psycholinguists to explain how children learn language.

For reasons that will become apparent later, we will separate language into two distinct, but related, psychological processes: *speech production* and *speech comprehension*. We will deal with each in turn and then consider how they are related.

1.1 The development of speech production

1.1.1 From vocalization to babbling to speech

1.1.1.1 Vocalization to babbling

Prior to uttering speech sounds, infants make a variety of sounds – crying, cooing, gurgling. Infants everywhere seem to make the same variety of sounds, even children who are born deaf (Lenneberg *et al.*, 1965). The ability and propensity to utter such sounds thus appear to be unlearned. Later, around the seventh month, children ordinarily begin to babble, to produce what may be described as repeated syllables ('syllabic reduplication'), e.g. 'baba', 'momo', 'panpan'. While most of the syllables are of the basic *Consonant + Vowel* type ('baba' and 'momo'), some consist of closed syllables

of the simple *Consonant + Vowel + Consonant* variety ('panpan'). This structure of babbling as repeated syllables has been found to be produced by
children in all studied languages.

The sounds that infants make involve many but not all of the speech sounds
that occur in the languages of the world. For example, English sounds like
the 'th' in 'though' and the 'th' in 'thin' are rare, as are the click sounds
common in various African languages such as Zulu. In time, however, such
vocalizations take on the character of speech. From as early as 6 months of
age infants from different language communities begin to babble somewhat
distinctively, using some of the intonation of the language to which they have
been exposed (Nakazima, 1962; Lieberman, 1967; Tonkova-Yampol'skaya,
1969). Research seems to indicate that in languages where the intonation
contours are quite distinctive, native speakers can tell the difference between
the babble of infants who were learning their (the native speakers') language as opposed to the babble of infants learning other languages (de
Boysson-Bardies *et al.*, 1984).

The production of sounds using the intonation contours of the first language is obviously a learned phenomenon because when infants babble
they follow the intonation contours of the language which they hear. This is
something that deaf infants deprived of hearing speech do not do. While
such infants are able to vocalize and cry, they do not progress to babbling.
Interestingly, deaf infants who have been exposed to sign language from
birth do the equivalent of babbling – *with their hands* (Petitto and Marentette,
1991)!

1.1.1.2 Babbling to speech

It is from the advanced stage of babbling that children move into uttering
their first words. Often this occurs at around 1 year of age but can occur
much earlier or much later. When children begin to utter words, somewhat
surprisingly only some of the sounds that they have uttered in babbling
appear in speech. The other sounds must be reacquired.

And there may be some order to the acquisition of speech sounds. For
example, sounds like /x/ (as in Ba*ch*), /k/, and /l/ that commonly occurred
in vocalization and babbling prior to speech may now tend to occur later,
after the acquisition of such phoneme sounds as /p/, /t/, /m/, /a/ 'fall',
and /o/ 'tall'. A phoneme, it should be said, represents a class of speech
sounds in a language. For example, in the word 'pep' the individual sound
/p/ can represent the sound at the beginning of the word '*p*ep' as well as
the sound at the end of the word 'pe*p*'. (Incidentally, the letters surrounded
by slashes (//) indicate that a phoneme sound is identified. A phoneme
sound is a single discrete sound of a language.) Phonetically, the two sounds
are different, with /p/ in the final position having a large amount of aspira-
tion (puff of air). Nevertheless, they are regarded as the same phoneme.
There is, then, some discontinuity between babbling and meaningful speech

where the kinds of sounds that occur in babbling are not always immediately realized in meaningful speech.

While some studies show some continuity between babbling and early speech (Vihman *et al.*, 1985), most research shows a lack of continuity, e.g. Oller and Eilers (1982), Stoel-Gammon and Cooper (1984), and Kent and Bauer (1985), in that advanced babbling seems to approach the consonant–vowel combinations of later meaningful speech. The relationship, however, is not a strong one.

Why is there some degree of discontinuity from babbling to the production of speech sounds? In our view, the discontinuity issue involves, as Jesperson (1933) noted many years ago, the distinction between intentional and non-intentional vocalization. Babbling is non-intentional in the sense that particular sounds are not under central cognitive control; the infant does not intentionally make the particular babbling sounds that occur. They seem to happen by the chance coordination of *speech articulators* (various parts of the body that are used to create speech sounds: mouth, lips, tongue, vocal cords, etc.). The case of meaningful speech is quite different. Here, sounds must not be uttered at random but must match previously heard sounds that are conventionally associated with certain objects, needs, and so forth. In order to accomplish this feat, it is necessary that the child discover which sound is created by which speech articulators. It is this knowledge that the child must acquire in order to speak meaningfully. Speech *is* dependent to some degree on babbling, however, for it is in engaging in babbling that the child will chance on many of the various articulatory mechanisms for producing speech and give practice to the use of those articulators.

1.1.1.3 Explaining the acquisition order of consonants and vowels

In the meaningful speech phase, it appears that consonants are acquired in a front-to-back order, where 'front' and 'back' refer to the origin of the articulation of the sound. Thus, /m/, /p/, /b/, /t/, and /d/ tend to precede /k/, and /x/. Conversely, vowels seem to be acquired in a back-to-front order, with /a/ (ball) and /o/ (tall) preceding /i/ (meet) and /ʌ/ (mud). Jacobson (1968) devised a theory based on his distinctive feature theory of phonological oppositions that attempts to predict the order of the acquisition of speech sounds. In the main, however, empirical studies have not supported his predictions (Velten, 1943; Leopold, 1947; Braine, 1971; Ferguson and Garnica, 1975). There is much more variation in the order of acquisition than the theory predicts. Actually, this may well be expected, since there could be a great deal of chance involved when a child searches for the proper articulators of speech with which to make a sound.

As far as the establishment of intentional connections is concerned, our opinion is that two variables dominate this process: *visibility of articulators* and *ease of articulation* (first proposed by Steinberg, 1982). When the child becomes motivated to produce meaningful speech (this occurs after the child has learned to understand some words spoken by other people), the child begins to seek ways to produce the desired sounds. The child then becomes alert to clues that relate to the articulation of the speech sounds.

The child observes where speech sounds come from and notes the relationship between the sounds and the position of noticeable speech articulators, particularly the mouth and lips (Kuhl and Meltzoff, 1988; Legerstee, 1990). It is mainly movements that the child observes and imitates. Since noticeable mouth and lip movements are primarily involved in the articulation of certain consonants, it is not surprising, therefore, that children tend to produce these consonants, such as /m/, /p/, and /b/, before the others. Consonant sounds like the stop /k/ and the fricatives /s/ and /z/, which involve the movement of non-visible articulators, are generally learned later.

As for vowels, since most involve the use of largely unseen articulators, children get little aid from direct observation. Rather, they must indulge in a lot of trial and error in order to secure the proper positions for articulators. It seems that those sounds that are closest to the resting position of articulators, e.g. back vowels such as /a/ (watch), are easier to create and are learned earlier while those sounds that require more motor control to create, e.g. a tensed front vowel such as /i/ (feet), are learned later.

However, over and above the operation of these variables of ease and visibility, there is (as first mentioned above) the important one of *chance*. It seems that children may discover by chance a particular articulator–sound connection, e.g. the daughter of Leopold (1953), Hildegard, was able to pronounce the word 'pretty' with precision yet she was unable to pronounce other words composed of similar sounds. Interestingly, although the word 'pretty' was pronounced accurately at first, over time, as her pronunciation of words developed, the pronunciation of that word deteriorated. It seems that if a word is to be retained, the chance discovery of an articulator–sound connection must be followed by its incorporation within the overall developing sound system.

1.1.2 Early speech stages: naming, holophrastic, telegraphic, morphemic

1.1.2.1 Naming: one-word utterances

When do children start to say their first words? It may surprise you to learn that research on this basic question is not at all conclusive. This is not only because there is a very wide range of individual differences but also because the precise determination of just when a word has been learned is not easy to make and is not standardized.

The mere uttering of speech sounds by the child, e.g. 'mama', may or may not indicate word knowledge. Children can be said to have learned their first word when (1) they are able to utter a recognizable speech form, and when (2) this is done in conjunction with some object or event in the environment. The speech form may be imperfect, e.g. 'da' for 'daddy', and the associated meaning may be incorrect, e.g. all people are called 'da', but, as long as the child uses the speech form reliably, it may be concluded that the child has acquired some sort of word knowledge.

First words have been reported as appearing in children from as young as 4 months to as old as 18 months, or even older. On average, it would seem that children utter their first word around the age of 10 or 12 months. Some of this variability has to do with physical development, such as the musculature of the mouth, which is essential for the proper articulation of sounds. Certain brain development is also involved since the creation of speech sounds must come under the control of speech areas in the cerebral cortex (Bates *et al.*, 1992).

It appears that children first use nouns as proper nouns to refer to specific objects (Moskowitz, 1978), after which they may or may not extend the meaning correctly for common nouns (Clark, 1973). For example, while 'dada' may first be used to identify one particular person, it may or may not be extended to include all men or all people. Or, 'wow-wow' may be used to refer to one dog, and then be extended to refer to all animals, soft slippers, or people in furs. In time, of course, the proper restrictions and extensions are learned.

1.1.2.2 Holophrastic function: one-word utterances

However, children do not only use single words to refer to objects; they also use single words to express complex thoughts that involve those objects. A young child who has lost its mother in a department store may cry out 'mama', meaning 'I want mama'. Or a child may point to a shoe and say 'mama', meaning 'The shoe belongs to mama'. Research has shown that the young child can express a variety of semantic functions and complex ideas by the use of single words (Bloom, 1973; Greenfield and Smith, 1976; Scollon, 1976). In such cases, the child uses a single word to express the thought for which mature speakers will use a whole sentence. It is because of this whole sentence function that this aspect of one-word speech is often referred to as 'holophrastic', where 'holo' indicates whole, and 'phras' indicates phrase or sentence.

Actually, it is quite remarkable how inventive children can be in the use of single words. Researchers have noted that children may describe a complex situation by using a series of single-word holophrases. For example, 'peach, Daddy, spoon' was used to describe a situation where Daddy had cut a piece of peach that was in a spoon (Bloom, 1973), and 'car, go, bus' was used to describe a situation in which hearing the sound of a car reminded the child that she had been on a bus the day before (Scollon, 1976). These strings of words are not yet sentences, because at the end of each word the child pauses slightly and uses a falling intonation of the sort that is used by mature speakers to signal the completion of a sentence.

It is often not easy, of course, to interpret what a child is intending to convey by the single word. And, while knowing the child, the child's previous experiences, and elements of the present situation will serve to aid in the interpretation of an utterance, even the most attentive parents are frequently unable to interpret utterances that their children produce. Incidentally, we often use the traditional term 'utterance' rather than 'sentence' in order to avoid disputes as to whether what the child says is truly a sentence or whether it is grammatical. The advantage of the term 'utterance' is that it describes what the child says without having to worry about assigning sentencehood or grammaticality to what was said.

1.1.2.3 Telegraphic speech: two- and three-word utterances

Children do not proceed as rapidly to two-word utterances as one might expect. Why this should be the case is a matter of conjecture, although it is our view that children must first become aware that adding more words will improve communication, e.g. 'tummy hurt' is more effective than just 'hurt' or 'tummy'. In any case, around 2 years of age or so children begin to produce two- and three-word utterances.

Table 1.1 lists a number of typical two-word utterances along with what a mature speaker might say in the same circumstances. The possible purpose of each utterance is indicated, as are some of the semantic relations involved.

Variety of purposes and semantic relations

The most striking features about the dozen and a half or so very ordinary utterances shown here are the *variety of purposes* and the complexity of *semantic relations* that they exhibit. Regarding purpose, the child uses language to request, warn, name, refuse, brag, question, answer (in response to questions), and inform. In order to gain these ends, the utterances involve such semantic relations and concepts as agent, action, experiencer,[1] receiver, state, object, possession, location, attribution, equation, negation, and quantification.

Low incidence of function words

A second feature of the child's utterances is the low incidence of function words such as articles, prepositions, and the copula 'be'. Rather, it is nouns, verbs, and adjectives which mainly appear in the utterances. This is not surprising when one considers that these are the most informative classes of

---

[1] The term *experiencer* is used differently from many theorists here. We use it as indicating a sentient being that experiences states or ideas. A *receiver* is an experiencer who is affected by an action.

Table 1.1 Two-word child utterances and their semantic analysis

Child utterance	Mature speaker utterance	Purpose	Semantic relations (expressed or implied)
Want cookie	I want a cookie	Request	(Experiencer)–State–Object
More milk	I want some more milk	Request	(Experiencer)–State–Object; Quantification
Joe see	I (Joe) see you	Informing	Experiencer–State–(Object)
My cup	This is my cup	Warning	Possession
Mommy chair	This chair belongs to Mommy	Warning	Possession
Mommy chair	This chair belongs to Mommy	Answer to question	Possession
Mommy chair	Mommy is sitting in the chair	Answer to question	Location
Big boy	I am a big boy	Bragging	Attribution
Red car	That car is red	Naming	Attribution
That car	That is a car	Naming	Equation
No sleep	I don't want to go to sleep	Refusal	Experiencer–State–Negation
Not tired	I am not tired	Refusal	Experiencer–State–Negation
Where doll?	Where is the doll?	Question	Location
Truck table	The truck is on the table	Informing	Location
Daddy run	Daddy is running	Informing	Agent–Action
Joe push	I (Joe) pushed the cat	Informing	Agent–Action–(Object)
Push cat	I pushed the cat	Informing	(Agent)–Action–Object
Give candy	Give me the candy	Request	(Agent)–Action–Receiver–Object

words and would be the first that children would learn to understand. The meanings of function words, *to* John, *with* Mary, *the* car, candy *and* cake, could never be determined if the meanings of nouns, verbs, and adjectives were not known. Given knowledge of the words 'toy' and 'table', a child could guess what function a preposition like 'on' might signify when hearing the sentence 'The toy is *on* the table' in a situational context where a toy is 'on' a table. In other situations the idea 'under', for example, may be suggested.

Close approximation of the language's word order

The final feature of the child's utterances that should be noted is the close correspondence of the child's word order to that of proper sentences. The child learning English tends to say 'My cup' rather than 'Cup my', 'Not tired' rather than 'Tired not', and 'Daddy come' rather than 'Come Daddy' when describing the arrival of Daddy. Thus, even with two-word utterances, the child exhibits some learning of the word order of the language. This is not to say that the child does not produce significant deviations, nor is this a sufficient basis for claiming that the child realizes that different word orders signal different semantic relations. Yet it does show that the child has acquired a significant aspect of the grammar of English that will later enable the child to comprehend and produce appropriate utterances.

1.1.2.4   Morpheme acquisition

Once two- and three-word utterances have been acquired, children have something on which to elaborate. They start to add function words and inflections to their utterances. Function words like the *prepositions* 'in' and 'on', the *articles* 'the', 'a', and 'an', the *modals* 'can', and 'will', and the *auxiliaries* 'do', 'be', and 'have', begin to appear, together with *inflections* such as the plural /s/ on 'cats', and /z/ on 'dogs', and tense markings such as the /t/ past tense form on 'worked'.

A morpheme, it should be noted, is a root word or a part of a word that carries a meaning. Thus, for example, the single word 'elephants' consists of two morphemes, 'elephant' and Plural (s), as does the single word 'ran', which consists of 'run' and Past. Incidentally, 'elephants' consists of eight phonemes /e/, /l/, /ə/, /f/, /ə/, /n/, /t/, and /s/ (the symbol ə, schwa, represents a sort of reduced vowel). Clearly, the orthography often does not adequately represent actual speech sounds.

The Brown morpheme acquisition research

The most notable piece of research on morpheme acquisition to date is that done by the noted psycholinguist Roger Brown (1973). In a long-term and detailed study with three children, Brown focused on the acquisition of different function words and inflections in English. He found that children acquired the morphemes in a relatively similar order.

Brown's order of morpheme acquisition

Table 1.2 shows the list of morphemes and the general order in which they were acquired. Other studies have generally confirmed Brown's results. Even though other researchers have found some variation among children in terms of the speed in which they learned the morphemes, nonetheless the order was generally the same (Lahey *et al.*, 1992). A similar acquisition order of these English morphemes has also been found for children with language disorders (Paul and Alforde, 1993).

Morphemes towards the top of the table are acquired before those towards the bottom. Thus, we see that Present Progressive,[2] Prepositions ('in' and 'on'), and the Plural were learned well in advance of morphemes like the Article, Third Person (Regular and Irregular), and the Auxiliary 'be'.

Why this order of acquisition?

That the morphemes should have been acquired in this order has been the subject of much speculation. Brown checked the frequency of occurrence of the morphemes in adult speech to see if more highly used morphemes were learned faster by the child. He found no relationship. He then considered that the order reflected an increasing order of semantic or grammatical complexity. For example, Plural is learned early because it only requires the idea of 'number', whereas the copula 'be' is more complex because the child needs to apply both number and tense to select which form of the copula to use (see Kess, 1992, p. 294). Undoubtedly, these are contributing factors. More contentious is the view of Dulay *et al.* (1982), who suggest that there is a sort of predetermined order in the child's mind that is governed by as yet *unknown* mechanisms, and that the morphemes appear in the order they do because of such mechanisms. We do not agree. A less metaphysical explanation is available.

Our explanation of the order of acquisition

Although it has been nearly three decades since Brown's theory of morpheme acquisition was first presented, no theory to date other than that of Steinberg (1982, 1993) and Steinberg *et al.* (2001) has adequately explained that order. The order of morpheme acquisition can be explained directly and simply by applying psychological learning principles, principles that are universal and accepted. As such, they will hold for children learning the grammatical morphemes of any language. The three variables that we posit to explain the general order of acquisition, according to the first author, are: (1) *Ease of observability of referent*, (2) *Meaningfulness of referent*, and (3) *Distinctiveness of*

---

[2] Regarding Brown's naming of the first morpheme acquired as Present Progressive, it should probably be termed simply Progressive because only the '-ing' suffix appears. However, the Present is implied in the child's utterance because the child usually talks about the here and now. The auxiliary 'be' that goes along with the Progressive does not appear until much later. It is for this reason that the Present is marked off with parentheses in Table 1.2.

Table 1.2 How psychological variables explain order of learning of morphemes

Morpheme name and concept	Examples	Learning variables			Summary		
		Observability of referent	Meaningfulness of referent	Sound signal for referent			
1. **(Present) Progressive**: continuing action	Mary playing	High	High	High	H	H	H
2. **Prepositions**: location	in, on	High	High	High	H	H	H
3. **Plural**: one vs. more than one object	/s/, /z/, /iz/	High	High	Low	H	H	L
4. **Past Irregular**: past time	came, went, sold	Low/Medium	High	High	L/M	H	H
5. **Possessive**: possession	/s/, /z/, /iz/	High	High	Low	H	H	L
6. **Copula 'be' Uncontractible**: connector with tense	What is it?	Low	Low	High	L	L	H
7. **Articles**: one; previous reference	a, an, the	Low	Medium	High	L	M	H
8. **Past Regular**: past time	/t/, /d/, /id/	Low/Medium	Medium	Low	L/M	M	L
9. **Third Person Regular**: third person present singular	/s/, /z/, /iz/	Low	Low	Low	L	L	L
10. **Third Person Irregular**	does, has	Low	Low	High	L	L	H
11. **Auxiliary 'be' Uncontractible**: tense carrier	Is Mary happy?	Low	Low	High	L	L	H
12. **Copula 'be' Contractible**: connector with tense	Mary's hungry	Low	Low	Low	L	L	L
13. **Auxiliary 'be' Contractible**: tense carrier	Mary's playing	Low	Low	Low	L	L	L

the sound signal that indicates the referent. The three variables are further based on the principle that generally what the child first understands will be that which the child first produces. These variables affect second-language learning as well.

- **Variable 1: Ease of observability of referent.** Whether an object, situation, or event is or is not easily observed by the child is essential for learning. The more easily a child can see or hear or otherwise experience the referent, e.g. seeing a dog, smelling a cookie, hearing a car, feeling hungry, the more likely are such referents – in conjunction with the speech sounds spoken by others – to be stored in memory. For example, if someone were to say 'The dog is barking' as opposed to 'The dog barked' or 'The dog will bark', the referent in the first sentence will be more saliently observable because it involves a present ongoing action, and this difference will affect learning.
- **Variable 2: Meaningfulness of referent.** Referent objects, situations, and events that are of interest to the child and about which the child desires to communicate will be learned faster than those that lack such interest. It is only natural that the child will remember the more highly meaningful referents.

  Child utterances reflect the concepts that the child wishes to communicate, e.g. 'Car table', 'Car going', 'Doll sitting', 'Doll walking'. When these highly meaningful items are compared to such grammatical function items as the Article, Auxiliary 'be', Copula 'is' with the auxiliary contractible 's, and Third Person marker, it is clear that function items have little inherent meaning for a child who is just beginning to learn the language. These are not, therefore, items that we would expect a child to learn quickly.
- **Variable 3: Distinctiveness of the sound signal that indicates the referent.** In order to learn a morpheme, besides the observability and meaningfulness of the referent, it is essential that the child be able to identify the speech sound that signals that morpheme. The greater the sound distinction involved, the easier it will be for a morpheme signal (consisting of one or more phonemes) to be learned. For example, compare the Incontractible Copula 'be' in 'What *is* it?' with the Auxiliary 'be' Contractible in 'Mary's playing'. The former case with 'is' is more distinctive from a hearing point of view because it is a separate word with a vowel, and, as a separate word, it receives some degree of stress in a phrase or sentence. This gives prominence to the sound. In contrast, -'s is merely a consonant that is manifested as a suffix and does not receive stress.

Rating the morphemes on these variables

Let us rate the morphemes in the Brown study on each of these variables, assigning a value of High (H), Medium (M), or Low (L) depending on the degree to which we estimate the morpheme to manifest that variable.

Thus, for example, for the child's utterance of No. 1, 'Mary play*ing*', we assign a High on Observability (the continuing action is easy to see), a High on Meaningfulness (the whole event is of great interest to the child), and a High on Sound Signal because the '-*ing*' suffix is easy to distinguish ('play' vs. 'play*ing*') when the child hears this spoken.

Thus, in the Summary column this morpheme receives a H–H–H pattern. In contrast, for number 13, Auxiliary 'be' Contractible, we assign a Low on Observability because even without the -'s the child probably assumes that the '-ing' in 'playing' already implies present time in addition to continuing action. Until the child learns to understand and wants to express ideas of the past that involve a continuing action, like 'Mary *was* playing', the child will not be interested in such a morpheme. A Low is also given on Meaningfulness for the same reason. Since the -'s is barely discernible at the end of a noun, it is assigned a Low on Sound Signal. Thus, in the Summary column, this morpheme receives an L–L–L pattern.

Looking at the top of the Summary column, we see three Highs for number 1, (Present) Progressive, and number 2, Prepositions. As we proceed downwards in the order, the number of Highs decreases on the Observability and Meaningfulness variables; there is H–H–L for number 3, Plural, until at the bottom we see L–L–H for number 11, Uncontractible Auxiliary, and L–L–L for both number 12, Contracted Copula, and number 13, Contractible Auxiliary. Clearly, the more Highs there are for a morpheme, the faster is the learning, and, conversely, the more Lows, the slower the learning.

The data are remarkably uniform with respect to the postulated variables. This could hardly be otherwise, on reflection, *given the strong psychological drive that motivates the child in its search for meaning in speech*. Thus, morpheme referents that are more observable and carry more meaning will be more quickly learned than those that are not; this is why we find morphemes whose referents are less observable and less meaningful, generally the so-called grammatical function morphemes, towards the bottom of the list.

The morphemes in the top third of the table are undoubtedly qualitatively different from the morphemes in the bottom third of the table. The summary ratings reflect that intuition. This being the case, we can conclude that the three variables provide a good general explanation for the learning order of morphemes.

Explaining the order of some morphemes by the three variables theory

Let us now look in some detail at how the variables operate with one another so as to provide the learning outcomes that they do. In this regard, it will be instructive to consider three questions on morpheme acquisition order that highlight the operation of these variables. They are: (1) Why are Progressive and Prepositions 'in' and 'on' learned earliest?; (2) Why is Plural and Possessive learned before Third Person?; (3) Why is Past Irregular learned before Past Regular?

1. **Why are the Progressive and Prepositions 'in' and 'on' learned earliest?**
   Objects in the child's world are of great importance to the child. The Progressive (continuing action) morpheme involves the *action* of those objects, while prepositions involve the physical *location* of those objects. The Progressive morpheme relates to the action of objects, where the action continues through present time. A cat jumping, a car moving, a baby crying, for example, all involve objects in action. A mother says, 'The dog is barking' or 'The car is coming'. The events that interest the child stimulate the child's interest in what the mother is saying.

   However, not all verbs are used with -ing at the same time. The Progressive tends to appear first on verbs involving durative, non-completed, events such as 'play' and 'hold' (Bloom *et al.*, 1980). This would serve to increase the meaningfulness of the Progressive morpheme, since durative action would tie in with the meaningfulness of the words that the child has learned; these are usually associated with *continuing* events such as 'playing' or 'running'. The Progressive is used on non-durative verbs such as 'break' and 'spill' later in the child's speech development.

   Not only are children interested in the actions of objects, they are interested in their location as well. The prepositions 'in' and 'on' are highly meaningful because they signal the locations of objects, objects which are important in terms of meaning and communication, e.g. 'Doll *on* box' as opposed to 'Doll *in* box'. The prepositions 'in' and 'on' are learned prior to other prepositions for two reasons. (1) They are linearly sandwiched between two concrete nouns (e.g. *'doll* in *box'*), the referents of which are meaningful and easily observable in the physical environment. (2) The referents remain stationary in physical space with respect to one another, thus allowing for ease of observability. Such clearly observable object-plus-object relations make these particular prepositions relatively easy to learn. On the other hand, other prepositions such as 'to', 'at', and 'with' often involve more complex semantic constructions, e.g. Action + Relation (preposition) + Object: 'walk to the school', 'stand at the door', 'go with Daddy'. The greater the semantic complexity, the slower will be the learning (all other things being equal).

2. **Why are Plural and Possessive learned before Third Person?** Since all three regular morphemes of the Plural, Possessive, and Third Person Singular are suffixes that have exactly the same sound forms, for example, 'dog/z/' (Plural), 'Bob/z/' (Poss.), and 'sing/z/' (Third Person), all end with /z/. In fact, the three forms of each suffix for each of these three morphemes are exactly the same, /s/, /z/, and /iz/. The selection of these suffixes is governed by the same sound conditions (the final sound of the word). Since the three different morphemes have exactly the same sound

pattern characteristics, the reason for their differential acquisition order must be due to factors *other than* their sounds, these factors are Observability and Meaningfulness.

The Plural and Possessive are much more involved with observable and meaningful referents for the child than the Third Person Singular. These two morphemes involve physical events, situations, and objects that are readily observed in the environment, e.g. for the Plural the child can easily distinguish one cookie versus two cookies and one cat versus two or more cats, while, for the Possessive, the child can easily distinguish his or her toys from another child's toys. Thus these are morphemes whose referents are easily noticeable and, in addition, involve referents that are highly meaningful to the child.

The Third Person morpheme, on the other hand, involves the noting of a singular Third Person referent, a much less obvious kind of object, being defined by a more abstract relationship. The child typically must pick up the use of the abstract first and second person (speaker–listener) relationship (I and You) before making the Other (non-speaker, non-hearer) distinction. We call this an 'abstract' relationship because the 'I' changes on the basis of who is speaking, and the 'You' changes according to who is listening. The Person role is more abstract than the unchanging concrete objects that are named in the Plural and the Possessive.

3. **Why is Past Irregular learned before Past Regular?** Since the idea of past is involved with both the Past Irregular and Regular forms, the explanation for the order of acquisition of these two types of past forms must lie other than in Observability, i.e. noting that a certain sound indicates that what is being said concerns an event that occurred in the past. That leaves the other two variables: Meaningfulness and Sound Signal. Before we focus on these variables, it will be instructive to compare the verb forms of the present tense with those of the past, for both Irregular and Regular verbs:

Irregular in Present/Past: come/*came*, go/*went*, eat/*ate*, break/broke, fall/fell, run/ran, sing/*sang*
Regular in Present/Past: jump/jump*ed*, jog/jogg*ed*, want/want*ed*

If one says these pairs aloud it will be obvious that the sound changes from Present to Past are much more noticeable for the irregular verbs than for the regular ones. The sound suffixes of the Regular Past forms are /t/ (jump*ed*), /d/ (jogg*ed*), and /id/ (want*ed*), with the first two (/t/ and /d/) being especially hard to hear. Since a sound difference must first be noticed and brought to attention before it can be learned, we would expect the very noticeable irregular forms to be learned faster, and that is the case. So, the Sound Signal is a crucial variable here.

However, meaningfulness is also at work here because, although the regular verbs are more numerous, the irregular verbs tend to be highly important ones in everyday life. These are the so-called 'strong' verbs of

English. This extra meaningfulness gives the irregular forms an additional boost in the process of learning, which is why in Table 1.2 the Past Irregular is given a High on Meaningfulness but the Past Regular is only given a Medium. But this is not the whole story. Because the irregular verbs are the most common ones in everyday life, they tend to occur more frequently (as individuals) than the regular verbs. This *higher frequency of occurrence* of irregular verbs would also serve to make these verbs easier to learn.

From the examples given above, it is clear that the three common psychological learning variables of Referent Observability, Referent Meaningfulness, and distinctiveness of Sound Signal go far in explaining the learning of various morphemes and the order in which they are learned. Frequency of occurrence operates too but only within the confines of the three determining variables.

1.1.3 Later speech stages: rule formation for negatives and other complex structures

With the production of longer utterances, simple structures are elaborated to yield more complex ones. Negative sentences, question forms, passives, and relative clauses are just a few of the many complex rules that children acquire in their first five years. (Rules are used here in a general sense and may be interpreted as principles, parameters, limits, etc. Chomskyan theory is by no means necessarily implied by the use of these terms.) Although many other rules are also being acquired, we will select for consideration the complex rules used in forming negations, questions, relative clauses, and passives. Since this is the general order of acquisition of structures, we will use this order in presenting these constructions. It should be borne in mind, however, that the learning of some of these constructions sometimes overlaps, such as in the case of negation and question, which share a number of grammatical features.

1.1.3.1 Negation formation

Negation development

Before presenting some of the acquisition data concerning negation, it may be useful to review some of the features of the negation process.

Let us consider some sentences and their negations.

1a.	Affirmative:	Kim is hungry.
1b.	Negative:	Kim is not hungry.
1c.	Negative Contraction:	Kim isn't hungry.
2a.	Affirmative:	Kim wanted some candy.
2b.	Negative:	Kim did not want any candy.
2c.	Negative Contraction:	Kim didn't want any candy.

Features of negation

In learning to produce these negations, the child must learn a number of different things. In considering these features, let us make negative the affirmative sentence of:

Kim wanted some candy.

1. Where to *insert the negative marker*.
   (a) If the verb is 'be', then NEG is placed *after* the Copula 'be' form. Thus, 'Kim is NEG happy' becomes 'Kim is not happy'.
   (b) If the verb is not 'be', then 'not' is placed *before* the verb. Thus,

   Kim not want + PAST some candy.

2. When and where to *insert auxiliary 'do'*.
   Insert 'do' when the verb is one other than 'be' ('have' is a special verb, e.g. 'Kim did not have any money' and 'Kim had no money', which will not be considered here). Thus, we get

   Kim do not want + PAST some candy.

   'Do' is not inserted if there is a modal (will, can) or auxiliary (be, have) present, as in 'Kim *will not want* to go'.

3. When auxiliary 'do' is used, then *the tense from the verb is shifted to the auxiliary 'do'*. Thus, from 'Kim do not want + PAST . . .', we get

   Kim do + PAST not want some candy.

   Then, lexicalization (the asterisk here and elsewhere indicates ungrammaticality):

   * Kim did not want some candy.

4. In English, *Lexical Concordances* must be made in the case of the negative, e.g. 'some' must change to 'any' so as to yield the grammatical

   Kim did not want any candy.

5. Optionally, AUX + NEG ('did' + 'not') can be *contracted* to 'didn't'. This would provide us with

   Kim didn't want any candy.

The above features of negation must be taken into account by any theory of grammar. While in the above example, for simplicity's sake, operations were applied to an affirmative *sentence*, a semantic or conceptual representation of such a sentence can (and should) be the point of origin. Negation features therefore may include meaning terms. The surface string of words must be the same whatever theory of grammar is being considered, as must be the features of negation.

Negation is one of the earliest sentence structure rules acquired by children. According to the classic research of Klima and Bellugi (1966) and others who later replicated their work, there is a consistent pattern in this, with negation being acquired in three main periods. Sample sentences and their analysis follow below for each period. Incidentally, these data are taken from the same three children whose morpheme acquisition was described above in the Brown study.

Period 1

> 'No money'; 'Not a teddy bear'; 'No play that'; 'No fall'; 'No the sun shining'; 'No singing song'

In this, the earliest period, a negation marker (NEG), in the form of 'no' or 'not', is placed at the front of an affirmative utterance (U). Thus we see utterances typically of the form, Neg + U ('No fall'). Children everywhere seem to use much the same pattern in early acquisition of negation. French children place *non* or *pas* before U (Grégoire, 1937), while Japanese children place the Japanese negative marker *nai* after the U (U + Neg) in accordance with the structure of their language (McNeill and McNeill, 1968).

Period 2

> 'I don't want it'; 'I don't know his name'; 'We can't talk'; 'You can't dance'; 'Book say no'; 'Touch the snow no'; 'That no Mommy'; 'There no squirrels'; 'He no bite you'; 'I no want envelope'

In this second period, the negative marker tends to appear internally within the utterance rather than outside it as in the previous period, and the auxiliaries 'do' and 'can' appear with the negation marker. Klima and Bellugi believe that children treat 'don't' and 'can't' as single words and do not analyze them as Aux + Neg. That the uncontracted forms of 'do' and 'can' do not appear in the data is one telling argument that they present in support of their view. Utterances are still of a rather crude nature, though, and negative imperatives, 'Touch the snow no' ('Don't touch the snow'), are as poorly formed as they were in the previous period ('No play that' ('Don't play with that'), 'No fall' ('Don't fall', in one interpretation)).

Period 3

> 'Paul can't have one'; 'This can't stick'; 'I didn't did it'; 'You didn't caught me'; 'Cause he won't talk'; 'Donna won't let go'; 'I am not a doctor'; 'This not ice cream'; 'Paul not tired'; 'I not hurt him'; 'I not see you anymore'; 'Don't touch the fish'; 'Don't kick my box'

In this third period, the period before which perfect negatives are formed, the Copula 'be' ('am not') and the modal 'will' ('won't') appear with negation and imperative negatives are formed with 'do' rather than the simple negative ('Don't touch the fish' as opposed to 'Touch the snow no' in earlier periods). The child now has a good idea of when 'do' must be inserted

('You didn't caught me', 'I didn't did it', 'Don't kick my box') and when 'do' is not inserted ('I am not a doctor', 'Donna won't let go'). The child still makes errors but seems to grasp the basic notion that 'do' is not added when there is a modal ('can', 'will': 'This can't stick [adhere?]', 'Donna won't let go') or when 'be' is the verb ('I am not a doctor'). The children's mastery of negation at this period is nearly complete. Only a number of relatively minor problems, such as the re-assignment of tense from Verb to AUX ('You didn't caught me', 'I didn't did it'), remain to be resolved.

After this period, in a matter of months or a year, most of the problems in negative marking are successfully dealt with, although children may make occasional mistakes for years after. (The first author recently observed such occasional errors in the speech of his 5-year-old son along with errors in other morphemes involving exceptions. See Steinberg *et al.* (2001) for a consideration of their learning of other complex syntactic structures).

1.2 The development of speech comprehension

Thus far, we have been focusing on the child's development of *speech production*. Now we would like to focus on the child's development of *speech comprehension*. When, for example, does the understanding of speech begin and how does it relate to production?

1.2.1 Fetuses and speech input

Before dealing with newborns, let us look at research that is concerned with stimulating language development even *before* the child is born. Can speech sounds reach the fetus while it is still in the uterus? Benzaquen *et al.* (1990) put a microphone inside the uterus of a pregnant woman to see if speech sounds could reach the ear of the fetus over the background sounds of the women's heartbeat and blood flow. The mother's speech sounds *were* found to be able to reach the ear of the fetus above the background sounds. However, whether the ear of the fetus is developed enough to send such significant sounds to the brain is in dispute.

In another study where loudspeakers were placed next to pregnant women, two experimental groups were presented with sound sequences in different orders: one group was exposed to /babi/ + /biba/ while the other received the reverse order /biba/ + /babi/ (Lecanuet *et al.*, 1989). Later, after a number of presentations, the two sound sequences were played in varying orders to both groups of women and measurements were taken. Measurements of the fetuses' heart rates showed a differential effect for the two groups during the testing period. The heart rate of the fetus was higher when the sequence they were trained on was played. The effects of the mother's voice on the fetus's intrauterine listening thus may explain post-birth listening preferences of the neonate (newborn baby) for the mother's voice and for the language the mother spoke while pregnant.

DeCasper and Fifer (1980) recorded mothers reading a story to their newborns. Then their 3-*day*-or-younger infants were given a pacifier connected to a computer that would play recordings of the mother's voice or of another woman's voice. A high rate of sucking on the pacifier would activate the playing of a mother's voice. Comparing changes on the sucking rate with the infant's baseline rate, the researchers found that the infants sucked more in order to activate the tape with their mother's voice than to hear the voice of another woman!

The requirement was then changed so that the infants had to suck at a *lower* rate than normal in order to hear their mother's voice. The infants quickly changed to slower rates, thus demonstrating that they could distinguish the sound of their mother's voice and that of another woman. Locke (1993), however, suggests that the learning of the mother's voice may actually have occurred, not prenatally, but within the first 12 hours after birth when the mother was talking to the newborn. Since the measurements were taken after the 12-hour period, this could well be the case. If so, then there may not have been any prenatal learning.

It is worth mentioning that even if a fetus could hear sounds from the outside world, those sounds would have to be through the medium of a liquid in the fetal sac. That being the case, *speech* sounds are difficult to distinguish. How much, for example, in terms of speech sounds, can one hear when one is underwater in a pool? General sounds are all that come through. While this may be enough of a basis for a fetus later to distinguish among different voices according to pitch or loudness, it is certainly insufficient for identifying speech sounds.

1.2.2   Speech comprehension occurs *without* speech production: the case of mute-hearing children

While the ability to utter speech in appropriate situations is a good indicator of language knowledge, the absence of the ability to produce speech may *not* indicate a lack of language knowledge. There are many hearing persons who are born mute. People may be born with cerebral palsy or some other abnormality that prohibits them from articulating speech. Yet such persons may learn to comprehend all that is spoken to them. Let us consider some actual cases here so as to better understand this important phenomenon. Following this we shall consider the development of speech comprehension in normal children, which, we shall see, also relates to this phenomenon.

Christopher Nolan

Christopher Nolan is an Irish writer of some renown in the English language. Brain-damaged since birth, Nolan has had little control over the muscles of his body, even to the extent of having difficulty in swallowing food. He had to be strapped to his wheelchair because he could not sit up by himself. Nolan cannot utter recognizable speech sounds.

Fortunately, though, his brain-damage was such that Nolan's intelligence was unimpaired and his hearing was normal; as a result he learned to understand speech as a young child. It was only many years later, though, after he had reached 10 years, and after he had learned to read, that he was given a means to express his first words. He did this by using a stick that was attached to his head to point to letters. It was in this 'unicorn' manner, letter by letter, that he produced an entire book of poems and short stories, *Dam-burst of Dreams* (Nolan, 1981), while still a teenager (he was born in 1965). This was followed some years later by an autobiographical book, *Under the Eye of the Clock* (Nolan, 1988), also written in the letter-by-letter mode. Nolan's writing is of such quality that it has been compared to the works of Yeats and Joyce.

Anne McDonald

The first author came across another case similar to Nolan's while reading *The New Yorker* magazine. It was that of Anne McDonald (Specter, 1999), another remarkable person. She was born in Australia in 1961. Due to brain-damage during birth McDonald has never been able to control her muscles and speech articulators. Her hearing has always been fine though. Like Nolan she too had to be strapped to a wheelchair; she uses an elaborate computer device on her lap for issuing recorded messages.

At 16 years of age McDonald weighed only 28 pounds (about 13 kg), but it was at that time that her life changed. Friends took her to an art gallery, where for the first time she discovered art and was 'transfixed by the Matisses', her friend said. Despite her handicaps, this woman was motivated to study the Philosophy of Science and Fine Arts at the University of Melbourne. She later published a book and continues to write by the use of print devices.

Rie

Rie was a little Japanese girl whom the first author had the opportunity to study while he was a visiting professor at Hiroshima University. From birth Rie was mute, except for being able to utter two weakly whispered sounds, roughly /i/ and /a/. Such sounds were not used in any communicative fashion. In contrast to the conditions of Nolan and McDonald, however, Rie's other motor skills appeared normal. She could run and jump and, when the first author met her at the age of 3 years, could even ride a tricycle. While Rie probably had some sort of brain damage to the motor area of speech, the exact cause of her muteness was not known.

On being tested for her ability to comprehend speech, Rie could respond appropriately to such complex commands (in Japanese) as 'Put the red paper under the table' and 'Bring me the little doll from the other room'. Her level of speech comprehension was similar to that of other 3-year-olds. She was even able to learn basic reading by comprehending 100 different *kanji* (Steinberg and Chen, 1980).

Clearly, like Nolan, Rie learned to comprehend speech and even to read in the absence of any ability to produce speech.

Conclusion

Persons who are mute but hearing can develop the ability to comprehend speech *without* their being able to produce speech, so long as their basic intelligence is intact. But how are such people able to comprehend the sentences that they do, given that such sentences reflect the essential characteristics of language, i.e. comprehension of an unlimited number of novel grammatical sentences, recognition of synonymy, of ambiguity, etc.? The answer must be that these mute persons developed a grammar, *a mental grammar based on speech comprehension*; that enabled them to understand the speech to which they were exposed! This is the same grammar that normal children develop.

1.2.3 In normal children speech comprehension develops in advance of speech production

That children are unable to utter words or sentences for the purpose of communication without first gaining an understanding of speech could hardly be otherwise. If children did not first learn to understand the meaning of words and sentences, they would not be able to use words or sentences in a meaningful way. They observe what others say and how what is said relates to objects, situations, and events.

To say that comprehension of a language necessarily precedes production does not mean a child must understand all of the language before being able to produce something. Rather, progress goes bit by bit. As the comprehension of some word, phrase, or grammatical form is learned, some of that learning may be produced in speech (Ingram, 1974). That speech understanding always precedes production is the pattern that continues throughout the acquisition process (Ingram, 1989) whether it be for first words (Clark and Barron, 1988), elaborate syntax such as passives (Golinkoff and Hirsch-Pasek, 1995), or the later acquisition of idioms and figurative speech (Levorato and Cacciari, 1995).

It should also be noted that the two systems of comprehension and production do not develop separately for the normal child. As the child acquires an aspect of grammar for comprehension, the child will then try to figure out how to use it in production. Thus, the child attempts to coordinate production to conform to the system that the child has developed for comprehension (Clark and Hecht, 1983).

Pre-speech normal infants

Babies can recognize words as early as 6 months of age. Tincoff and Jusczyk (1999) had 6-month-old babies watch two TV monitors, one with a picture of the baby's mother and the other with a picture of the baby's father. While being held, and facing one of the images on the TV, a synthesized voice said 'mommy' or 'daddy'. After a number of presentations of voice and picture, the baby then heard the voice say one of the words. More often than by chance, the baby would turn to look at the picture being named. Thus, when the voice said 'mommy' the child would look at the video image of the mother, and when the voice said 'daddy' the child would look at the video image of the father.

Understanding at 6 months is earlier than most researchers had previously supposed. As Tincoff and Jusczyk note, 'Most of the previous work on comprehension indicated it was eight or ten months of age when kids started to attach language labels to particular objects.' Whatever the case, it is clear that the *comprehension and production processes develop in a parallel mode with production always trying to keep up with comprehension.*

1.2.4 Speech production lags behind speech comprehension

1.2.4.1 The Huttenlocher study

Huttenlocher (1974) studied four young children, aged 10 to 13 months, over a six-month period and found that they were able to comprehend speech at a level beyond that to which they had progressed in production. The children were able to select familiar objects such as 'bottle' or 'diaper' that were named for them and were able to respond appropriately to commands even though they did not use such words and structures in their own speech. One boy, for example, responded appropriately to such distinctions as 'baby's diaper' and 'your diaper', and 'baby's' bottle' and 'your bottle' (the 'baby' referred to here is the boy's younger sister). Even if, as Ingram (1989) notes, a scrambled word order should also have been tested, this would not change the interpretation of the outcome. For it is a fact the boy did give appropriate responses to combinations, combinations that involved complex possessive distinctions that he himself had never used in speech.

1.2.4.2 The Sachs and Truswell study

In another important study, Sachs and Truswell (1978) found that children who could only produce single-word utterances (they were at the one-word stage of speech production) nevertheless could comprehend syntactic structures composed of *more than one word*. Words for the testing were selected from the children's own productions, e.g. the verbs 'kiss' and 'smell' and the nouns 'ball' and 'truck'. These words were placed together in novel combinations in the imperative form, for example, 'Kiss ball' and 'Smell truck'. The children did what they were told: they kissed the ball and smelled the truck! Obviously the children's level of speech comprehension was well in advance of their level of speech production.

1.2.4.3   A Reading before Speaking study

Parents have always noted that children are able to understand more than what the children are able to say. Steinberg and Steinberg (1975) went one further. They taught their son to read (understand the meaning of) many written words, phrases, and sentences even before he was able to say them. Thus, he was able to respond appropriately to words and sentences, e.g. 'Open the door,' whether they were in speech or in writing and *even when he himself did not say those words*. The items that he had been taught to read were only those items that he could comprehend when such items were spoken to him. Later he was able to comprehend novel combinations of those written items.

1.2.5   Relative plaucity of comprehension studies

Unfortunately, although speech comprehension plays a crucial role in language acquisition, comparatively few studies have been devoted to its investigation. Most of the language acquisition studies have been concerned with the development of speech production. The reason for this is simple: production studies are easier to do. The product of the speech production process, the child's utterance, is something that can be directly observed while the product of the comprehension process, meaning, cannot. Comprehension can only be inferred on the basis of relevant behaviour. Needless to say, this is very difficult.

1.3   The relationship of speech production, speech comprehension, and thought

1.3.1   Speech comprehension necessarily precedes speech production

In learning any of the world's languages, children must first be able to comprehend the meaning of the language before they themselves can produce it. Though children may at times appear to speak an occasional word or phrase intelligibly, these are usually instances of echoed sounds spoken without knowledge of their meaning. The basis of all language is meaning, and without having had the opportunity to hear and understand words, phrases, and sentences within meaningful contexts, children could not begin to produce language meaningfully.

Children first need to be exposed to utterances with a clear connection to the articles referred to before they themselves can begin to say such utterances. Since children are not born with the knowledge of any particular language, e.g. English or Chinese, it is necessary that they be exposed to a language in order to learn it. However, simple exposure is not enough for language acquisition to occur. It is also necessary that the speech to which children are exposed be related to objects, events, and situations in their physical environment, and to subjective events in their minds such as pain, hunger, desire. Children will not learn language if all that they are exposed to is speech sound, no matter how many times it is uttered. Thus, for example, even if one heard the speech sound /neko/ a hundred times, one would have no way of knowing that it means 'cat' (in Japanese) unless there was some environmental clue.

Children may sometimes repeat words or phrases they hear, but this is not evidence for learning unless the sounds are used in a meaningful context that is suitable for those sound forms. Only when speech sounds are used appropriately in situations is there a basis for imputing language knowledge to the utterer. There are birds, for example, that can imitate the words of the language very clearly but generally they cannot do so in a meaningful context.

Speech comprehension precedes and is the basis of speech production. How could it be the other way? It is unimaginable for a person to have the ability to produce speech without having the ability to comprehend speech (or any other physical mode of expression – sign, touch, writing). While we know of people who can comprehend speech without being able to produce it (the cases of Nolan, Rie, etc. above), the reverse situation does not exist. This is *necessarily* so and could not be otherwise for two reasons: (1) A learner must first hear speech sounds before the person knows what sounds to make, and (2) A learner must hear the speech sounds in coordination with the experience of objects, situations, or events in the environment or the mind before the person can assign a meaning to the speech sounds.

1.3.2 Thought as the basis of speech comprehension

The meanings that underlie speech comprehension are concepts that are in a person's mind. Speech does not provide such concepts. Speech sounds initially are simply sounds signifying nothing. The contents of thought are provided by the child's *experience of the environment,* i.e. dogs, cats, people, food, and events concerning those objects, and the child's *experience of its own feelings, emotions, desires, and conceptual constructions (thoughts).* Without such contents of thought, the child would have nothing to assign as the meanings of words and sentences. Thought necessarily precedes language. For example, while we can find cases of persons who have no language (deaf people and children raised in isolation without language: Chapters 2 and 4), we cannot find cases of persons who have language but no thought. Language is a system that allows for the labelling of thoughts in terms of physical sound so that the thoughts may be communicated to others. Thought, however, is independent of language, including as it does ideas, feelings, percepts, emotions, etc. (see Chapter 9 for details). As such, thought provides the basis for speech comprehension, which in turn provides the basis for speech production.

In learning the meaning of syntactic structures, simply hearing the speech sounds 'John chased Bill', and knowing the meanings of the individual words 'John', 'chased', and 'Bill' is insufficient information for determining who is doing the chasing and who is being chased. One must hear sentences in conjunction with related events in the world in order to learn that English has an Agent–Action–Object sequence. Thus, by hearing the sentence 'John chased Bill' along with an experience of the event of John having just chased Bill, the child is provided with a basis for learning that it was 'John' who did the chasing and that it was 'Bill' who was being chased.

1.4 Parentese and Baby Talk

1.4.1 Parentese

During the 1960s, Chomsky's theorizing about innate language knowledge had a dampening effect on the study of experiential input, both language and environmental, with respect to the learning of language. A sort of mystical aura dominated the field. Language was not 'learned' but somehow mysteriously 'acquired'. Research has since shown, however, that the nature of the speech and environmental input which children receive is essential for language learning. For example, children who have the misfortune to have been exposed to limited and impersonal language such as through television or by overhearing adults' conversations do not acquire significant language knowledge (Todd, 1972; Snow *et al.*, 1976).

Parentese (coined by the first author in Steinberg, 1993, p. 22) is the sort of speech that children receive when they are young. Parentese is also referred to as 'Motherese', 'caregiver speech', 'Adult-to-Child Language' (ACL) (Reich, 1986), and as 'Child-Directed Speech' (CDS) (Pine, 1994). All of these terms take into consideration the fact that the child receives input from many sources – mother, father, siblings, relatives, friends, etc. (Nwokah, 1987; Bavin, 1992) – and that such input has special linguistic characteristics.

1.4.2 Characteristics of Parentese

Immediacy and concreteness

The speech that parents and others use in talking to children has a number of distinctive characteristics that evidently aid language learning. For example, parents generally talk to their children about what is happening in the immediate environment and not about abstract or remote objects and events (Phillips, 1973; Slobin, 1975). A sentence like 'The dog wants water' and not 'Speech comprehension precedes speech production in language learning' is what a 1- or 2-year-old is likely to hear even from these two authors!

Grammaticality of input

Generally, the speech directed to children is highly grammatical and simplified. Ungrammatical sentences are found to occur but rarely. Newport (1975, 1976), for example, in a long-term study with 15 mothers, reports an incidence of only one ungrammatical utterance in 1500 in their speech. Such grammatical consistency undoubtedly is useful to the child who is searching to discover the structures that underlie sentences. These research findings are not perhaps surprising, and they lend evidence against Chomsky's claim that children learn language despite being exposed to a high proportion of 'degenerate' sentences (Chomsky, 1967b).

Short sentences and simple structures

Speech directed to children by adults also tends to consist of short sentences with simple rather than complex structures (Snow, 1972; Seitz and Stewart, 1975; Garnica, 1977a), such as 'The dog wants water' as opposed to 'The dog which has been running a lot wants to drink some water'.

Vocabulary: simple and short

The vocabulary typically used by adults is simple and restricted (Phillips, 1973; Seitz and Stewart, 1975), e.g. 'see' instead of 'notice', 'hard' rather than 'difficult', and has simplified phonology and structure (Ferguson, 1964, 1977; DePaulo and Bonvillian, 1978). For example, consonant plus vowel word patterns such as 'mama', 'wawa', and 'byebye' are used rather than the more complex sound patterns of 'mother', 'water', and 'goodbye'.

Exaggerated intonation, pitch, and stress

Furthermore, adults exaggerate intonation and use a slower tempo (Drach, 1969; Cross, 1977; Garnica, 1977b), and frequently repeat or rephrase what they or their children say (Brown and Bellugi, 1964; Kobashigawa, 1969; Snow, 1972; Newport, 1975). For example, adults tend to use higher pitch, slower speech, with more and clearer pauses between utterances, and they place more distinctive stress on words than they do when speaking with other adults. Additionally, adult speech to children refers more to the context of the conversation (Snow, 1972; Phillips, 1973), and often serves to clarify the children's utterances (Cross, 1977). These changes will vary depending on the age of the child the adult is talking to (Snow, 1972; Garnica, 1977b); the speech addressed to 2-year-olds will be different in modifications from that addressed to 10-year-olds.

Older children, too, adapt their speech

It is interesting that not only adults but children, too, tend to use simplified speech in talking with younger children. For example, 4-year-old children produced simplified speech when talking to 2-year-olds but not when talking to adults, even though some of the 4-year-olds did not have younger siblings (Shatz and Gelman, 1973). It seems, too, non-parents also simplify speech (Sachs *et al.*, 1976). The simplification of speech may well be a universal phenomenon (Blount, 1972; Snow *et al.*, 1976).

1.4.3 Baby Talk

Baby Talk is a form of Parentese but with its own characteristics. While Parentese uses vocabulary and syntax, though simpler than that addressed to other adults, Baby Talk involves the use of vocabulary and syntax that is *overly* simplified and reduced. Curious, though, from a psycholinguistic view, is the fact that most of the features that Baby Talk adopts are those that have their basis in the early speech of children. Parents and others evidently believe that those features, when reintroduced back to the child, serve to foster communication. However, it should be remembered that Baby Talk is something that parents learn from other adults and involves standardized vocabulary. It is 'standard' in the sense that such vocabulary is culturally transmitted over generations.

Vocabulary

Most Baby Talk involves modifications in vocabulary. There are already established words like 'bow-wow' (dog), 'pee-pee' (urine), and 'choo-choo' (train) in English and, in Japanese, 'wan-wan' (dog: the standard word for which is *inu*), 'shee-shee' (urine: the standard word is *nyoh*), and 'bu-bu' (car: the standard words for which are *jidosha* or *kuruma*). From such examples, we can see that the main sound structure of such words tends to be dominated by a Consonant + Vowel syllable unit that is often repeated (reduplicated). Sometimes it involves a closed syllable as in 'wan-wan'. Thus, the sound structure of Baby Talk words, $[C + V + (C)] \times N$ (where N can be any number, but, usually, 1 or 2), is common to languages around the world.

Another construction principle for many Baby Talk words is that they are supposed to represent the sounds that various things make, i.e. they are onomatopoeic. Thus, English 'bow-wow' and Japanese 'wan-wan' are apparently simulations of the barking of dogs, Japanese 'bu-bu' is supposed to be the sound made by a car engine, and English 'choo-choo' the sound made by a train. The fact that such a sound as 'choo-choo' in English is meant to approximate to the largely extinct steam locomotive bothers neither parent nor child. Here the word has become an entry in the standard Baby Talk vocabulary.

Syntax

Syntax plays a less prominent role in Baby Talk than does vocabulary. Parents seem only occasionally to use standard syntax in Baby Talk. When they do, their utterances are strikingly similar to those in the children's telegraphic stage of speech production, with the focus being on word order. A mother might say, for example, something like 'Mommy give Tony banana' instead of the syntactically proper 'I will give you a banana'. In such an utterance, neither the modal 'will' nor the article 'a' has been included. And the names 'Mommy' and 'Tony' have been substituted for the more difficult personal pronouns 'I' and 'you'. Substituting proper names for personal pronouns is a common feature of Baby Talk that is not usually found in speech between adults (Elliot, 1981). Certainly, fixed proper nouns are easier for the young child to understand than are items involving shifting speaker–listener relations. It is later that the child learns to cope with the speaker–listener complexities of 'I' and 'you'. Such proper name substitutions, it should be noted, also occur in Parentese and thus are not solely features of Baby Talk.

1.4.4   The effect of Parentese and Baby Talk in language learning

Do Parentese and Baby Talk facilitate language learning? The studies done on these questions demonstrate a positive but small effect (Newport *et al.*, 1977; Furrow *et al.*, 1979; Kemler-Nelson *et al.*, 1989; Murray *et al.*, 1990). Other research also provides evidence that Parentese may be effective but only for children who are very young (Gleitman *et al.*, 1984). It seems to us that the fact that Parentese and Baby Talk occur gives strong weight to the notion that they are beneficial.

1.5   Imitation, rule learning, and correction

1.5.1   What is learned by imitation

Many people believe that language is learned by imitation. By imitation it is meant that the child copies and repeats aloud the words that he or she hears. Through imitation, children learn how to pronounce sounds and words and they seem to enjoy imitating the sounds that they hear (Masur, 1995). All this is fine. However, it must be kept in mind that there is an obvious limitation, which is that *imitation can apply only to speech production and not to speech comprehension*. Since we know that speech comprehension precedes speech production, we can say that imitation cannot be involved in the primary process of language learning, comprehension. A further limitation is that even in the domain of production, imitation is *not* involved in the construction of sentences. Abstract rules cannot be imitated for the simple reason that rules do not exist in the physical world. Of course, the output of rules, speech, exists in the world but not the rules themselves; rules are formulations that involve observable entities. This is not to say that imitation is not important. It is, but it is limited to the development of the articulation of speech sounds and the sound pattern of sentences.

1.5.2 Productivity by rule

The child's production of certain novel words and sentences cannot be explained by imitation. Children commonly produce ungrammatical words like:

1. 'sheeps', 'mouses', and 'gooses', regarding the PLURAL, and
2. 'goed', 'comed', 'falled', and 'breaked', regarding the PAST.

Why do they utter such words? It *cannot* be because of imitation because rarely would anyone say such words for them to imitate. Similarly, why do children utter such ungrammatical sentences as:

1. 'No heavy' and 'No the sunshine', regarding the Negative, and
2. 'When we can go?' and 'He is doing what?', regarding the Question.

They cannot be imitating such speech because no one says these things for the child to copy.

Clearly, children have formulated *rules* in their minds from which they construct novel utterances. They learn the PLURAL morpheme and the PAST tense morpheme and then apply those to new cases. This works when the new words are regular, such as hat/hats and fish/fishes, and carry/carried and push/pushed. However, when the new word is an exception, the child must learn that it is an exception and not apply the rule. This explains why the child produces PLURAL words like 'sheeps' and 'mouses'.

What are especially interesting are the creations that the child makes with the PAST regular rule: 'goed', 'comed', 'falled', 'breaked'. Typically before the PAST rule was learned, the child had already learned many of the PAST irregular forms, especially go/went and come/came. The power of the PAST rule is so strong that the formerly learned irregular past forms of 'went' and 'came' are disregarded or confused. Sometimes the child will even produce forms like 'wented' and 'camed'. Thus, the child typically slips and loses some of the earlier learned past irregular forms. The child has then to relearn them. The child develops rules in the mind and then uses those rules to make these novel creations. These rules are so powerful that they strongly control the child's output.

Morpheme and structure rules are learned by children and, when they are, they may strongly affect production. Undoubtedly the proper forms can be understood when such forms are spoken to the child. It is a different matter, however, for the child to learn the restrictive application of such rules. There are always exceptions.

1.5.3   The frequent futility of correction

It used to be thought by many that the correction of children's speech is essential to improvement. Research has shown, though, that such is not the case, with parents typically paying little attention to the grammatical correctness of their children's speech (Brown *et al.*, 1969; Brown, 1973). When parents do attempt to correct their children's speech, the results are often fruitless and frustrating.

Undoubtedly, there are cases where parents' corrections, particularly with older children, may directly result in improvement. However, because grammatical corrections are relatively rare with respect to the number of deviant utterances that a child actually produces, it is reasonable to conclude that correction does not play an important role in grammar learning. Eventually, the child does notice his or her own incorrect speech and then makes the necessary revision.

It is worth noting that 'correction' typically takes the form of a corrected repetition of the child's utterance. This may not be helpful because, in order to improve, the child must: (1) note the difference between the child's own utterance with that of the parent, (2) determine what the nature of the error is, and (3) figure out a way to permanently change his or her grammar or strategies so that it yields the parent's utterance in the future. This is quite a burden for a child, so much so that the child typically ignores the attempt at correction. The alternative of telling the child what the nature of the problem is often worse, e.g. 'add *do* when you are making a Negative with a Verb rather than *be* and place *do* in front of the Verb'. Most parents are more interested in the truth value, social appropriateness, or cleverness of what their children say than they are in the ungrammaticality of the utterances of their children. A child who says, 'I no broked it' when she did commit that act may not receive a grammatical correction such as 'You should say, "I didn't break it" ', but more likely will receive a scolding if she is lying. Similarly, a child who says to a visiting aunt, 'Mommy no like you' will be given a scolding not for grammaticality but for good manners.

1.6   Learning abstract words

When acquiring the meanings of words, children begin with the concrete and go on to the abstract. They begin with *physical objects* ('mama', 'dog', 'ball', 'table') and *direct activities* ('run', 'jump', 'play', 'give') then move to relations and statives ('on', 'sitting'). Soon following will be words involving *mental experiences and relations* ('hungry', 'hurt', 'happy', 'want'), which then yield such utterances as 'Mary hurt', 'John thirsty', and 'Kitty want eat'. Later come *complex abstract ideas* ('I', 'you', 'truth', 'lie', 'honest', 'guess', 'hope', 'idea', 'thought').

But how are these words learned, especially the complex and abstract ones? While simple association is sufficient for an item such as 'dog' where the speech sound 'dog' is associated with the object 'dog', complex hypothe-sizing needs to be employed for learning the words for feelings and con-cepts, since these are not in the physical environment for the child to directly observe. The child must make inferences from what people say, and on the basis of what happens in the environment and the mind. Such learning at first glance seems to be so mysterious as to be almost magical, yet the fact is that children *do* learn such words. The first author offers the following ideas to explain how such learning occurs.

For example, how might the words 'hungry' and 'hurt' be learned? First the child must take note of when such words are spoken by others and the situ-ations in which they occur. The child might cry and the mother might then say, 'Are you hungry?' The mother says this because the mother guesses what the child's internal state might be, based on when the child last ate, for instance. If the child has the feeling of hunger, the child may then guess (after some repeated instances) that 'hungry' refers to what he or she is feeling. Or, the child might point to a banana and the mother might say in response, 'Do you want a banana?' and the child might get the meaning of 'want'. Consider 'hurt'. Perhaps the child falls and is bruised on the knee. The father might say, 'Poor girl. Does it hurt?' The child's feeling of pain might then be associated with the word 'hurt'. Or, on receiving an injection with a syringe, the child cries, and the father says, 'It hurts, doesn't it? Poor child.'

It is up to the child to remember what words were spoken, e.g. 'hungry' and 'hurt', and to relate them to particular feelings that the child has experienced in the mind, 'hunger' and 'pain'. After a number of such instances where certain words (spoken by others) and certain feelings are experienced together, the child will have enough information to make a guess at which sound form relates to which feeling. When the child then experiences further instances, the child can test whether he or she is correct, i.e. whether the sound form of 'hungry' relates to the feeling of hunger and the sound form of 'hurt' relates to the feeling of pain. (See Gillette *et al.*, 1999, for a considered discussion on how verbs of mental experience, e.g. 'think', 'know', and 'like', can be learned.)

Words like 'lie' (falsehood) and 'guess' must also have particular envir-onmental situations and mental states for the child to bring together. These will be more difficult to identify than feelings because they involve pure (non-feeling) ideas. The child will have to make logical inferences from complex situations in order to extract such ideas. For example, suppose after telling his mother something that he knows is untrue, 'I didn't hit her', the little boy's mother might say angrily, 'That's a lie!' What the little boy must do to discover the meaning for this sound form of 'lie' is to recall the intention and what he knew in his mind before he said what he said. He knows that what he said ('I didn't hit her') did not correspond with what had actually happened before in the world (he *did* hit her). Once he has this situation in mind, the boy can assign a meaning to the sound form of 'lie', thereby learning the meaning of the word 'lie'. He comes to realize that the discrepancy between what he says and the situation or event in the world is the meaning of the sound form /lai/, and then assigns this concept to the sound form. Whether this hypothesis is accurate or not is something the child will test when he hears the word 'lie' again.

The use of metaphor too will help children to comprehend abstract concepts. Metaphoric language extends a child's experience of the world by exposing hidden meanings of already familiar words and phrases. The book by Lakoff and Johnson (1980), *Metaphors We Live By*, is very suggestive as to how children could learn abstract meanings by hearing metaphorical usage, although this is not the intent of the book. For example, a child hears his father tell him, 'I'm glad you saw the light', after the child has told the truth about something he had been lying about. The child hears the word 'light' used in this special way for the first time and tries to guess at the intended meaning. Considering the situation and the ordinary meaning of light, the child hypothesizes that it may mean something like the right way or the correct thing to do. Thus, as Holme (2004) argues, metaphors can also be a powerful tool in second-language learning and teaching.

1.7 Memory and logic in language learning

1.7.1 Memory

Underlying all of the remarkable accomplishments of the child in language learning is one crucially important psychological factor, that of memory. For, in the course of learning to identify the words of the language, devising rules for their use, and relating speech to the environment and mind, the child utilizes a phenomenal memory capacity. The child must remember a multitude of particular words, phrases, and sentences, along with the contexts, both physical and mental, in which they occurred. Such data provide the basis for structural analyses and vocabulary learning.

If children did not remember many of the words, phrases, and sentences they heard, they would have little basis for discovering abstract meanings and rules. The various syntactic structures that were mentioned and discussed earlier, negation for instance, require that the child remember previously experienced negative sentences. If the child could not remember negative sentences that had been experienced previously, the child would have nothing with which to compare a presently occurring sentence, and thus could not make significant inferences as to its structure.

Without a good memory, language learning would not be possible. Some recent studies of patients with semantic short-term memory deficit demonstrate that such persons are unable to comprehend and produce structures that involve more than one word meaning; for example, they can not produce an Adjective–Noun phrase, or process grammatical relations (Martin and Freedman, 2001; Martin and He, 2004).

Aside from the common observation that children often remember, word for word, stories that they are told, children also learn a host of idioms in phrase and sentence form. There is no reason, therefore, not to believe that children also store in memory a multitude of ordinary phrases and sentences, which can serve them for analysis later. Children as young as 8 months can begin to remember speech sounds. This was demonstrated by the infants' preferential listening patterns to words heard in children's stories that were read to them (Jusczyk and Hohne, 1997). The infants turned their heads more towards the sound of the words that had occurred in the stories than towards unfamiliar words. Such a prodigious memory capacity, it is worth noting, is not unique to language. For in many other areas of life – in remembering faces, objects, music, past events, and vast quantities of knowledge in a variety of domains – the extent of a child's memory is similarly remarkable.

1.7.2 Logic

In learning language, the child must use both induction and deduction in the analysis of words and sentences and the formulation of grammar and strategies.

Young children use INDUCTIVE logic

Even in the early grammatical phase of learning basic morphemes, e.g. Progressive, Plural, and Third Person, children must use an inductive analysis. Taking the Plural as an example, children must scan the sentences uttered by mature speakers and then note that a suffix is added when two or more objects are being talked about. The children then formulate a rule in their minds. This rule is tested when the children hear other sentences uttered by the mature speakers. This type of analysis, where (1) there is a search for characteristics in speech, and then (2) those characteristics are related to objects, situations, and events, represents the essence of the use of inductive logic. An abstract rule or principle is gleaned on the basis of actual data.

Young children use DEDUCTIVE logic

The child's production of speech, even in the early years, reflects a great deal of conceptualization and thinking on the part of the child. Suppose one 4-year-old child (Rose) says to another child (Tom), 'You have more than me!' This is said in a situation where an adult has put down a plate of cookies in front of the two children and the children have made a grab for them. Then suppose that, after Rose has said this, Tom, the child with the greater number of cookies, gives some to Rose, the child with the lesser number.

Now we may ask, why did Tom give Rose some cookies? What was it about what Rose said that persuaded him to behave the way that he did? Rose must have implied the following logical argument:

> *Premise 1* You have more cookies than me.
> *Premise 2* We should have an equal amount.
> *Conclusion* You should give me some of your cookies to make it equal.

The fact that Tom responds to Rose's simple declaration, 'You have more than me!' by giving her some cookies indicates that Tom understood her argument. He did not consider her sentence as simply stating a fact. Both children understood the logical argument implied by Rose's statement.

Such an advanced level of conceptual development may surprise many of us, especially some Piagetian theorists, who, relying on such limited notions as 'conservation', believe that deductive logic develops after the age of 6 years (Piaget and Inhelder, 1969). A proper language analysis, such as the one above, demonstrates that age norms for the development of deductive logic must be drastically revised downwards. As for inductive logic, norms have yet to be established, but they surely would have to be below the child's second or first year.

Then, too, according to Piaget, intelligence has its basis in the child performing actions with respect to objects in the world. Here, also, Piaget was mistaken. Such actions are not essential to the development of intelligence or language. As we noted earlier with the cases of virtually paralyzed persons like Nolan and McDonald, their inability to perform such actions did not prevent them from developing high levels of intelligence and language.

The 1- and 2-year-old child is quite an intellectual marvel whose thinking powers should not be underestimated.

Chapter 2

The deaf and language: sign, oral, written

2.1 Sign language: a true language without speech

2.1.1 What is a true language?

By now most of us have had the opportunity to experience sign language, if only to see it occasionally in the corner of our TV screens. There we can see a person translating speech into sign for the benefit of deaf and severely hearing-impaired viewers.

You may wonder whether those signs truly are part of a language or are just a collection of gestures that lack the sophistication of a language based on speech. How can we judge whether persons who use 'sign language' truly have language? First, a sign language is a true language because the language system allows a signer to comprehend and produce an indefinitely large number of grammatical sentences in signs. This feat can be accomplished with a limited number of signs (vocabulary) and a system (syntax and semantics). Secondly, a signing person has a true language if that person can communicate by sign whatever can be communicated by speech. This is reasonable because we can all agree that people who communicate in speech do have language.

2.1.2 Language based on speech compared to language based on signs

There is, of course, a difference in the *physical* means of communication: signing involves light and speech involves sound. But a particular physical mode is not an essential aspect of language. Of course, language must depend on some physical mode for its use and learning but that mode need not be limited to sound. The mode can be visual, as in signing, or even touch as in languages used by the deaf-blind (Helen Keller's is one such case in point: see Chapter 4).

Thus, what we are really interested in here is, for example, whether an abstract sentence like 'If the weather had been fine, then Mary's uncle could have come and given her money' can be conveyed through signing. It can. Such a sentence is a good test, since it expresses a variety of complex semantic functions and relations and involves a number of events and situations, none of which, interestingly enough, had occurred. According to the sentence, the weather was not fine, Mary's uncle did not come, and the uncle did not give money to Mary. A person who could comprehend and produce communications such as this, through sign rather than speech, surely can be said to have language.

2.1.3 Complete and incomplete sign language

Research on sign languages seriously began for the most part in the 1960s when linguists and psycholinguists addressed themselves to this newly discovered area. The findings showed that signers of such sign languages as American Sign Language, French Sign Language, British Sign Language, and others, can indeed communicate in sign whatever is expressed in speech (Stokoe *et al.*, 1965; Klima and Bellugi, 1979; and, more recently, Siple and Fischer, 1990). A sentence like that shown at the end of the previous section can be expressed through all of these languages.

Other sign languages may be incomplete syntactically or limited in terms of vocabulary. Such incomplete sign languages are typically found in developing countries, although in even some developed nations, sign language may suffer from deficiencies. In Japan, for example, where the national government until recently prohibited the teaching and use of sign language in public schools, standardization and vocabulary are problems. (The rationale for this anti-sign position is considered in a later section of this chapter.)

2.1.4 Speed of signing and speaking sentences is comparable

Not only can a fluent signer of a complete sign language such as American Sign Language (ASL) sign whatever a speaker can say, but the signer communicates at about the same speed as a speaker does. The speed at which signers produce sentences (more precisely the ideas that underlie sentences) in a signed conversation tends to be similar to that at which speakers produce sentences in a spoken conversation (Bellugi and Fischer, 1972). This occurs even though a signer, as does a speaker, has the ability to exceed this speed. There seems to be an optimum speed at which humans are comfortable in processing language information, whether that information be in the form of speech or sign.

2.1.5 Dialects and foreign accents in sign language

There may even be strong dialectic differences within a language from region to region within a country. For example, signers from Paris have difficulty in understanding signers from Lyon, and vice versa. The reader may be surprised to know, too, that American Sign Language and British Sign Language (BSL) are not mutually intelligible. American Sign Language actually has more in common with French Sign Language than with British Sign Language because ASL was derived from French Sign Language early in the nineteenth century. British Sign Language had its beginnings before the seventeenth century, with the first deaf schools opening in Britain in the late eighteenth century. Some BSL vocabulary is depicted in Figure 2.1.

2.1.6 There is no universal sign language

This might be a good place to emphasize that, contrary to common belief, there is no universal sign language. There are some similarities among languages, but not many. There is a multitude of sign languages, complete and incomplete. If there were a campaign for an artificial sign language to be adopted by signers everywhere, it would run into the same opposition that Esperanto has met in its quest to serve as a universal speech-based language. Like speech-based languages, a sign language is part of a culture. It may be useful to learn a foreign (or second) language but to give up one's native language, be that speech or sign, is something that people are not eager to do.

2.2 Gestures of hearing people are signs but do not form a language

Before considering the essentials of sign language, it will be useful to examine a related means of communication that is used by hearing persons: gestures. Once the role of such gestures is understood, they will not be confused with the signs of a sign language. It is necessary for the reader to make this distinction. For, although gestures may be complex, they are only collections of signs that are limited in scope and do not form a true language. There is little or no syntax with which gestures may be combined to form the equivalent of sentences, except those of the most rudimentary Tarzan sort ('You come', 'I hungry'). Nevertheless, gestures *do* play an important part in the communication of hearing persons and they occur both with and without speech.

Gestures using arms, head, torso

We use gestures to communicate a variety of types of messages, as, for example, in indicating: *greetings*: hello, goodbye – by moving the hands

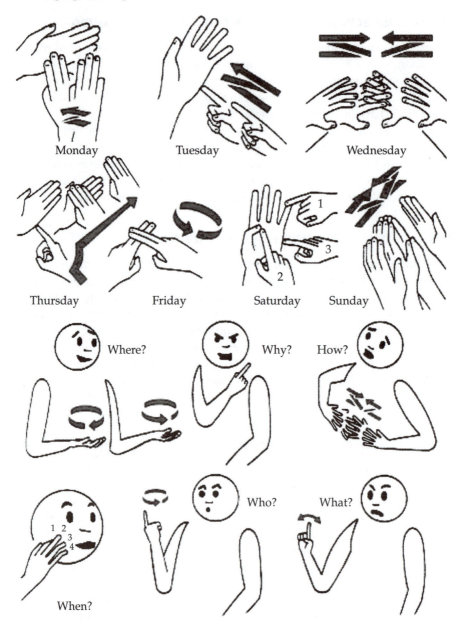

Figure 2.1 Some British Sign Language vocabulary

and arms; *requests/commands*: come, go, stop – by moving the hands; *insults*:
the sticking out of the tongue by children, the raising of the middle finger
by adults; *answers*: yes, no, I don't know – by moving the head; *evaluations*:
good/perfect – by making a circle with the thumb and index finger; *success/
victory*: by making the V letter with two fingers; *descriptions*: tall, short, long

– by use of the hands and arms; and referring: to self, others, this one, that one – by pointing with a finger. These are only some of the categories for which we have gestures that may be used for communication, independently of speech.

Gestures are often similar but seldom universal. Most gestures are specific to cultural, linguistic, or geographic areas. To indicate 'self' (I/me), most Westerners point to their chest with their index finger. Chinese and Japanese, however, point to their nose with that finger. The meaning of such pointing is readily understandable, though, to the outsider.

Facial gestures

Facial movements are used everywhere to convey a wide range of emotions and feelings. Some of these gestures are natural and universal. We do not actually need to utter a sentence like 'I am . . . (happy, surprised, disgusted, disappointed, excited, angry, etc.)' when we have in our non-verbal repertoire the amazing flexibility to smile, laugh, sneer, roll our eyes in exasperation, or contract our brow in consternation. States of confusion, attention, distress, love, annoyance, admiration, belligerence, doubt, bewilderment, determination, and so on, can all be conveyed in context by facial expressions, supplemented, or not, with hand movements and body posture.

Gestures with speech

Every speech community has its own distinctive gestures that are co-ordinated *with* speech. While alone these gestures do not indicate a meaning, with speech they generally do serve some function such as to emphasize a meaning or to indicate new information. To construct in gesture a sentence like 'John will go tomorrow if the car is fixed' is an impossible task.

2.3   Speech-based sign languages

Sign languages use hand, face, or other body movements in a three-dimensional space as the physical means of communication. Principally, there are two types of sign language: one that relates to ordinary speech-based language and one that is independent of ordinary language. *Speech-based sign languages* represent spoken words (or their spelling) and the order of these words or morphemes as they appear in ordinary spoken languages, such as Swedish, English, and French. This contrasts greatly with such sign languages as American Sign Language and British Sign Language, which are not speech-based and not mutually intelligible. These sign languages are independent of the ordinary spoken language, having developed their own words and grammatical systems for the production and understanding of sentences. We shall call these *Independent Sign Languages* (ISLs).

Sign language based on the speech of ordinary language can be of two different kinds: one that represents the morphemes of speech and one that represents spelling (orthography). Let us begin with the latter, which is easier to explain and which, by the way, every signer of whatever system must learn so as to be able to express proper nouns such as the names of people or places.

2.3.1 Finger spelling: letter by letter

According to this system words are represented by spelling them out letter by letter in terms of individual signs, where each sign represents a letter of the alphabet. Hand and finger configurations are used to indicate letters, such as making a V with the index and middle fingers or an O with the thumb and index finger. Thus, a word such as 'enough' would be signed letter by letter, e, n, o, u, g, and h. Words and entire sentences can be communicated in this letter-by-letter method. The order of letters is exactly the one that occurs in the writing of the ordinary language. Thus the sentence 'The boy coughed' is expressed as the series of individual letter signs: t, h, e, b, o, y, c, o, u, g, h, e, and d.

There are both one-hand and two-handed systems of finger spelling (Figure 2.2). The Americans and Swedes, for example, use one hand, while the British use two. Users of both systems can sign relatively quickly but both processes are rather laborious. The two-handed system, however, is faster

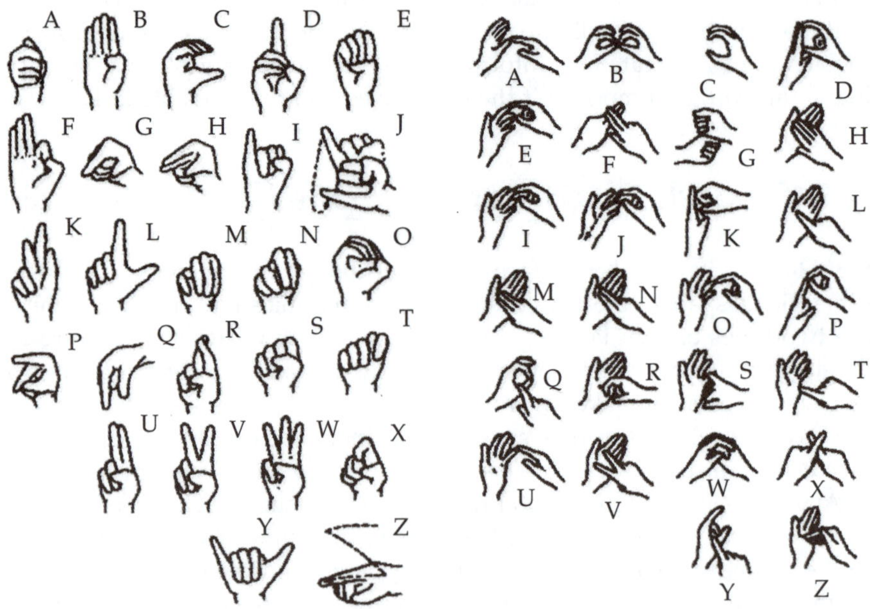

Figure 2.2 One-handed and two-handed signs

and provides more easily identifiable letters. The downside is that it does not allow a hand free for other uses. Few, if any, deaf schools in America rely wholly on finger spelling as a language to express all communications. The Rochester School for the Deaf was perhaps the last school to use this method and that was some years ago. It was called the *Rochester Method* and was typically used in conjunction with speech (Scouten, 1963, 1967).

Signers of all systems, though, must learn to use finger spelling, since many place and person names like Manila, Kensington, Sheldon, and Francine may not have their own individual signs, as do such frequent words as London, New York, Mary, and John. Infrequent and novel names must be finger spelled letter by letter.

2.3.2 Morpheme by morpheme (MnM) sign languages: 'Signing Exact English' and 'Seeing Essential English'

Some deaf schools advocate a sign system that uses a whole sign for each speech word or meaningful part, i.e. a morpheme. Such systems are directly based on the spoken form of the speech-based language. Since these systems represent the morphemes of true speech-based languages, they therefore can be said to be true languages.

Signing Exact English was developed by Gerilee Gustason in the 1970s. This, and *Seeing Essential English* (Anthony, 1971) are typical of this type of sign system, most of which were created in the USA around the 1960s, before the interest in and widespread acceptance of ASL. These language systems follow in sign the exact linear flow of spoken words. Thus, for 'coughed', for example, there would be one sign for 'cough', and another sign for the past tense. For 'I asked John for the cards', there would have to be a sign for each English morpheme in the sentence. These would be signed in the same order as the spoken sentence: I + ask + PAST + John + for + the + card + PLURAL.

The learner learning such a system need not know the speech-based language on which the system was created in order to learn it. The learner learns the signs in context as would be done by the learning of an independent sign language such as American Sign Language. The fact that such signs reflect the morphology of a speech-based language is not a piece of information that is necessary for its use.

Advantages of MnM systems

1. **Learner simultaneously acquires the morphology and syntax of both the sign and related speech-based language.** A morpheme-by-morpheme system, which the first author has dubbed MnM, has certain important advantages for the learner. By learning the system, not only will the person be able to communicate with other hearing-impaired persons who also know the system but he or she will have acquired knowledge in terms of

syntax and word structure that will be useful in learning the ordinary speech-based language (English, in this case) as well. An ordinary language such as English would then not have to be learned as a remote second language since by learning MnM the learner would have acquired the morphology and syntax of English. This is important because deaf persons whose native language is an independent sign language like American Sign Language (ASL) will have a hard time learning English. There is little commonality between English and ASL. Because of the similarity between an English MnM and actual English, such a situation is avoided.

2. **Easier for an adult hearing person to learn an MnM than an ISL.** The system has the advantage of being easier for *adult hearing* persons to learn than would an independent sign language (ISL) since the grammar of the MnM system is based on the grammar that the hearing person already knows through speech. This is of particular advantage to hearing parents of deaf children who naturally want a means with which to communicate with their child as quickly as possible. Hearing parents who want to learn an independent sign language like ASL must, as adults, devote years to the task; learning an MnM sign system is much less difficult.

It should be pointed out that about 90 per cent of deaf children are born to hearing parents. Of these, 30 per cent have a genetic cause while most are born deaf through some factor in their fetal development. Contracting rubella (commonly known as German measles) during early pregnancy on the part of the mother is one major cause. For the most part, though, the etiology for about half of the cases is unknown. Only about 5 per cent of deaf children are born to deaf parents due to an inherited gene. The remaining percentage involves children who become deaf after birth due to disease, e.g. scarlet fever, other streptococcal infections, or some other cause.

Serious disadvantages

1. **Children do not learn MnM easily.** Research shows children do not readily acquire these languages (Supalla, 1990). As a result, the use of these devised systems often tends to be confined to classrooms where their use is required.

2. **MnM is not preferred by the deaf community.** Despite its advantages, MnM systems are not preferred by deaf signers and the deaf community. Such people generally prefer an independent sign language like ASL. MnM is considered to be more cumbersome and more wearying to use over long periods than ASL, which is more comfortable and flexible. ASL is a natural sign language that has evolved on its own from its parent, French Sign Language, over the past 150 years in the deaf community in America. Through the extensive use of signing during this time, ASL has developed into an optimal means of signing for its users.

2.4 Independent Sign Languages (ISLs) such as American Sign Language (ASL)

2.4.1 Some characteristics of ISLs

The signs of an Independent Sign Language (ISL) can be analyzed into three basic components: (1) *hand configuration*: the shape that the hand forms; (2) *place of articulation*: where in space the hand is formed; and (3) *movement*: how the hand moves.

Word structure (morphology)

At the word level of an ordinary language, there are not only words that differ completely in meaning from one another, but also words that are very much related, differing only in morphology, i.e. their component and derived morpheme forms. English derives many words from 'compare', such as 'compared', 'compares', 'comparing', and 'comparison'. Such morphological changes also have their equivalents in an ISL such as American Sign Language. Adjusting the movement of a sign by changing the speed or tension or rate of repetition gives ASL signers the ability to derive nouns from verbs, such as 'comparison' from 'compare', as well as to produce derivations that are unique to ASL.

There are, then, uninflected forms of signs that can be defined by the features of place, configuration, and movement, with variations in movement providing the means for morphological variation and changes in aspect. ASL words and morphemes are manipulated in much the same way as are spoken words so as to provide variation in grammatical classes and meaning.

Linguistic analyses of (natively acquired) ASL have revealed that it is a language with quite a different type of structure from that of English, but one that is found among other spoken languages: for example, it shares certain typological similarities with Navajo. According to Elissa Newport and Ted Supalla (1980), structure in ASL is quite complex, particularly for verbs. Typical verbs are marked morphologically for agreement in person and number with both subject and object, and for temporal aspect and other features. Word order in ASL is relatively free, with an unmarked Subject–Verb–Object order.

2.4.2 The syntax of a typical ISL: American Sign Language

The greatest amount of linguistic and psycholinguistic research on independent sign languages has been conducted on American Sign Language (Stokoe *et al.*, 1965; Klima and Bellugi, 1979; Siple and Fischer, 1990). Accordingly, most of our material will involve ASL.

ASL began with the initiative of one man, Thomas Gallaudet, an American educator of the deaf who, after the study of deaf education in France, wanted to bring French Sign Language to America. He did so by convincing a French teacher of the deaf, Laurent Clerc, to return with him. Gallaudet opened his first school in Hartford, Connecticut, in 1817, where he and Clerc, in effect, established American Sign Language. They used French Sign Language along with some indigenous American signs (particularly from the island of Martha's Vineyard). Since that time, ASL has had nearly two hundred years to evolve on its own, separate from French Sign Language.

In a speech-based language, individual words are structured together into sentences according to syntactic rules, the heart of the grammar of a language. ASL, too, has rules that govern the relationship between individual signs in a sentence. While the words and morphemes of sentences in languages such as Signing Exact English are signed in the air on a sort of imaginary two-dimensional blackboard and in a word-by-word linear sequence, ASL sentences are radically different. They are not linear sequences but three-dimensional creations (see Figure 2.3 for examples). A signing space allows for combinations of meanings and the simultaneous blending of a number of meaning elements that cannot be produced linearly. As a result, signed sentences can be produced quickly and with a minimum of effort. Violation of the rules that govern the relationship between signs will lead to confusion, with the resulting occurrence of poorly formed and ambiguous sentences; very similar to what happens in speech when rules of grammar are broken.

The parallels between the acquisition of language through speech and sign language are very striking. In acquiring ASL as a first language, deaf children go through stages of language acquisition which are similar to those of hearing children. Their signing goes through a single-sign stage and even a telegraphic stage of simple sign productions where inflections and function signs are not included. However, there are linguistic problems that deaf children must face and overcome that are unique to ASL, such as the proper indexing of space. While young signers at the age of 3 will not yet have fully differentiated their signing space correctly, this will have been accomplished by the age of 5. It is by this age that all of the essentials of the formal language system will have been acquired.

2.4.3 The process of learning ASL

A highly unusual feature of signing communities is that native users are relatively rare; 95 per cent or more of deaf signers are first exposed to their language *after* infancy, and sometimes not until late childhood or even adulthood. These demographics result from the fact that most deaf children are born into hearing families, and also from the fact that, until recently, hearing parents were often discouraged from learning sign language. Advocates of

(a) The sequence of signs 'woman–forget–purse' is used as a statement, *The woman forgot the purse* (the articles are not separately signed).

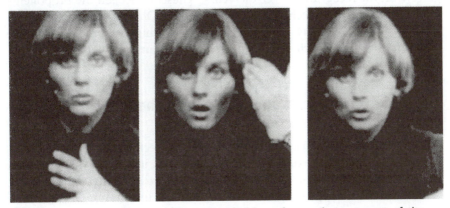

(b) The same sign sequence is accompanied by a forward movement of the head and shoulders, and the eyebrows are raised: this would express the yes–no question, *Did the woman forget the purse?*

Figure 2.3 Making sentences in American Sign Language

the Oral Approach (see next section) denounced sign language, arguing that it would reduce the effectiveness of speech training.

Research does not show, however, that the avoidance of sign languages improves speech abilities. In fact, the contrary is the case. Evidence shows that, among the profoundly deaf, native signers do better in speech, speechreading, and reading abilities (Meadow, 1966, 1980). The most potent variable in the ability to produce speech, unsurprisingly, is the degree of hearing loss (Jensema, 1975; Quigley and Paul, 1986). In recent years it has therefore begun to be more common practice to encourage hearing parents of deaf children to learn to sign, and to expose deaf children to sign language as early in life as possible.

Bonvillian *et al.* (1983) investigated the sign language and motor development of 11 young children born of deaf parents who were studied across a 16-month period. The participants showed accelerated early language development, producing, on average, their first recognizable sign at $8^1/_2$ months, their tenth sign at about 13 months, and their first sign combination at 17 months. The structure and content of the participants' 50-sign vocabularies closely resembled those for children at the same stage in previously published studies of spoken language acquisition.

2.5 The Oral Approach and Total Communication

The general public aside, who is it that the ASL people have been struggling with for recognition over the years? These have been the proponents of the teaching of speech, the view called the Oral Approach. The Oral Approach has a worthy aim, to teach the hearing-impaired to produce and comprehend speech so that they can communicate with the hearing community.

2.5.1 Oral Approach successful with the less hearing-impaired

The Oral Approach focuses on the teaching of speech *production*. Its secondary focus is on speech comprehension. Be that as it may, in this approach children from the age of 2 or 3 years onwards are specially trained in the skill of articulating speech sounds. Also, it is not uncommon nowadays to have some computerized equipment that displays sounds and assists in the teaching. Many children do respond and do acquire a fair ability to speak. For the most part, however, the successes are with children who have only a moderate hearing loss. Those with more severe impairment typically fare poorly.

2.5.2 Oral Approach fails with the severely hearing-impaired

As was just noted, a great problem with the Oral Approach is that it tends only to work for a portion of the hearing-impaired population. Research shows, unsurprisingly, that the less people can hear, the less they will be able to produce and comprehend speech. Thus, relatively few children who are born with a severe or profound hearing loss (over 75 or 80 decibels in their better ear) acquire any significant degree of speech. Even those with a lesser hearing loss often do not acquire sufficiently clear pronunciation to be understood by ordinary hearing persons.

There is a good reason that persons who are severely hearing-impaired do poorly in producing speech. Simply put, in order to produce speech sounds, one first must hear the sounds that someone else is making. One must have a target. Without having heard the target sounds, one would have no basis for comparative judgement.

Speech teachers of the deaf are trained to assist the deaf person in articulating speech sounds. The task is exceedingly difficult for the deaf and severely-impaired, as one might expect, and most deaf speakers produce speech that is largely unintelligible to ordinary hearing persons who haven't had any familiarity with such speech. Most deaf persons are not mute because of any physical defect with the articulatory system, but mute because they do not know how to utter appropriate speech sounds.

2.5.3 Speechreading (lipreading) is not easy

The comprehension of speech is usually fostered through both exploiting any residual hearing that learners may have and the teaching of speechreading, commonly known as 'lipreading'. With speechreading, an adept person can interpret about half of what is said, which, given the great amount of redundancy in ordinary speech, is enough to guess most of the content. The better the deaf person is in hearing, the better that person will be in both speaking and speechreading.

2.5.4 A sensible approach: Total Communication

Because of the large number of failing cases as a result of the application of the Oral Approach, many hearing-impaired persons were not only unable to communicate with the hearing community but were unable to communicate adequately with their hearing-impaired friends and colleagues. It was this tragic situation in many places that convinced educators of the deaf to include sign language in their curriculum along with speech training. These programmes, which generally go by the name of *Total Communication*, spread in the 1970s in the United States, Canada, and other countries. While Total Communication is now widely accepted in many countries, there is still resistance in many to admitting sign language into the educational curriculum for the hearing-impaired.

We believe, too, that in addition to Total Communication an additional type of language, Written Language, must be taught. This is the written form of the speech-based language that is prevalent in the deaf person's country, e.g. Britain, France. Such a language should be considered as distinct from reading because *reading* involves persons who *already* know their language. The written language approach will be discussed later in the chapter.

2.6 The sign language vs. Oral Approach controversy

It was in the 1880s that the Oral Approach advocates defeated Sign Language advocates. Subsequently, in the United States and other countries, it was the Oral Approach that dominated deaf education in the schools. Such domination, which included a ban on sign language, lasted for nearly one hundred years. ASL was proscribed for communication even among deaf persons. (See Lou, 1988, for a good history of methods in the United States.)

2.6.1 Rationale of Oral advocates in excluding sign language

While Oral Approach advocates, such as Daniel Ling and the Ewings (Ewing and Ewing, 1964), may reluctantly admit that sign language is a language, they argue not only that the learning and use of sign language negatively affects the acquisition of speech but that without speech production there will be defective thinking. The teaching of reading and written language are attacked for similar reasons, which is why the teaching of reading in so many deaf schools was – and often still is – delayed until children are beyond the second or third grade. These contentions, which have no basis in empirical observation or psycholinguistic theory, are false. If anything, knowledge of ASL and reading *facilitates* the acquisition of speech (Meadow, 1966; Steinberg *et al.*, 1982). And, as far as thought is concerned, deaf people without speech are found to test nearly as highly in intelligence as hearing people despite their typically lower level of formal education (Furth, 1971). It is unfortunate that such erroneous and detrimental ideas continue to be held in so many places.

2.6.2 One formidable advocate of the Oral Approach: Alexander Graham Bell

Alexander Graham Bell comes to America

One of the foremost advocates of the Oral Approach was Alexander Graham Bell. It was at the ill-fated (for Independent Sign Languages) Second International Congress on Education of the Deaf in Milan in 1880 and at the 1886 American Convention of Instructors of the Deaf that Bell emphatically presented the view that only speech should be taught to the deaf regardless of their degree of hearing loss (Bell, 1883). Reading and written language were not included in the ban.

Bell himself had been a teacher of deaf children in London, and within a year of his arrival in North America in 1870 he was teaching, at the age of

23, deaf children in Boston. Bell was intimately involved with deaf people and their education all of his life. His mother was deaf, his hearing father was a well-known educator of the deaf who had invented a written phonetic alphabet, *Visible Speech*, his wife was deaf, and last, but not least, he was world famous as the inventor of the telephone, which he invented in Boston in 1875, just five years after landing in America. Bell and his faction were successful: sign language was banned from most schools for the deaf and it was to take nearly a hundred years for such a restriction on the use of sign language to be overcome.

Bell versus Edward Gallaudet

Bell's anti-sign position was pitted against the leader of the pro-sign group in America. This person was the head of the Gallaudet American Asylum and was none other than the son of Thomas Gallaudet, one of the founders of ASL, Edward M. Gallaudet. The backgrounds of Bell and Edward Gallaudet were startlingly similar: both had deaf mothers and hearing fathers who were devoted to deaf education, and both men themselves were devoted to that same cause. Gallaudet scoffed at Bell's advocacy of speechreading. Yet each admired the other and they had even discussed Bell's joining the faculty of the recently established Gallaudet College in Washington, DC. It was Gallaudet College in 1880 that awarded Bell the first of his many honorary degrees. The feud that the men carried on was a friendly one.

Interestingly, Edward Gallaudet later became sympathetic to the oral method to the degree that he advocated a 'Combined Method', the forerunner of the Total Communication approach, in which both sign and speech are taught. He no longer scoffed at speechreading as he had when he first met Bell.

2.7 Public recognition of ASL and growth of deaf pride

2.7.1 ISLs out of the closet and into respectability

As recently as the 1970s some deaf educators (mainly those who opposed the use of sign language) denied that a sign language could be a genuine language. Such scholarly denial reflected the opinion of many hearing persons, as well. Some of the original bias against ASL stemmed from a poor understanding of the nature of language and the false belief that learning sign language inhibited the development of speech. There will be more on this point later in the chapter.

Until the mentalist revolution in linguistics and psychology, i.e. the bringing back of the concepts of mind and mentalism into psychology and linguistics after the downfall of the anti-mentalist Behaviourists, which was spearheaded by Chomsky in the 1960s, language was generally equated with speech in a behaviouristic type of conception. With the advent of mentalism, language began to be widely perceived as a kind of knowledge in the mind that is related to, but exists independently of, its physical manifestation in speech or sign. Such a conceptual separation was just what sign language researchers needed for pursuing their investigations into ASL. They were then able to formulate an ASL grammar for the mind, a *mental* grammar that was similar in essence to that which hearing people were believed to have. Language, and not speech, became to be regarded as the true distinguishing human characteristic. The change started slowly in the 1960s but soon gathered momentum, and by the middle of the 1970s the proponents of ASL began to succeed. Soon ASL was actively taught in a large number of schools for the deaf in the United States and Canada. Sweden and other countries also followed a similar pattern with their sign languages.

It was during this same period that, with the boost given to ASL by educators and researchers, the ASL deaf community came out of the closet, so to speak. Signers began to gain confidence and pride and to communicate such feelings to the public at large.

2.7.2 Growing recognition and interest in sign language worldwide

Nowadays it is commonplace in many countries to see various TV programmes, meetings, and special events with simultaneous interpreters present for the benefit of the deaf. Hearing people, too, see this and again the idea is planted that signing is a language. But it was not always so. Most countries were like Japan, where only in the past few years have things started to change. It was the United States and Canada and many countries of the European Community that took the lead in this respect.

2.7.3 Deaf pride in the USA

Denying deafness as an impairment

With the acceptance of ASL, the deaf community became more and more established. The deaf community, with its own language, theatre, and other activities, became a source of pride. Pride grew to an extent that a steadily increasing number of deaf people have said that they would choose *not* to be hearing. They even deny that deafness is an impairment. To them, the word 'cure' – indeed, the whole notion of deafness as an impairment – is anathema. However, if deafness is not an impairment, then government is under no obligation to help people who have this condition. This would be a significant financial loss. Most members of the deaf community are probably not in agreement with the non-impairment view.

The issue of cochlear implants and other devices

Related to the issue of whether deafness is or is not an impairment is the issue of devices that may improve the hearing of deaf people. One such device is the cochlear implant. Approved by the US Food and Drug Administration in 1985, cochlear implants are the closest thing to a 'cure' for deafness at present. A tiny chip is surgically implanted in the inner ear and connected to a magnet just under the skin, which attracts another magnet in a transmitter attached behind the ear. A wire leads from that to a 'speech processor' that can be clipped to a belt. The processor converts sound into electrical impulses and sends them to the implant, which conveys them to the brain, where they are processed as sound would be. The result is an approximation of hearing.

Supporters say implants allow some people to overcome their hearing disability, while opponents object to the very idea of trying to cure the deaf. The implants are most effective for speech-language learning when implanted in children at about the age of 2. Decisions about implanting are therefore usually made by parents, most often by hearing parents.

Cochlear implants appear to be safe and the electronic stimulation that the implant creates appears to have a positive effect on the nerve tissue that surrounds it. However, while cochlear implants can be very effective, sometimes they are not so for small children. Almost all children with implants have some 'useful' perception of sound, but the sound they receive is often too garbled for them to interpret it as language. There is a risk, too, and that is that the implant may destroy in that ear the residual hearing that a child might have.

A sensible course of action

Dr Robert Ruben, an ear-nose-and-throat specialist at Montefiore Hospital in the Bronx, has said,

> If I had a deaf child, I would implant one ear, leaving the other free in case cures develop that require an intact inner ear. I would bring up that child bilingually. Parents could phase out sign later on if they wanted, but it should not be abandoned until it becomes clear that the child can develop satisfactory oral language. The worst mistake is for parents to neglect the one most important thing – that language of any kind, no matter what kind, must somehow be got into the child soon enough.
>
> (Solomon, 1994, p. 31)

This is sensible advice. However, the activist deaf are against cochlear implants and any kind of cure that might come along. They want the deaf child for their deaf community. That may be fine for the deaf parents of deaf children but it certainly would not be fine for hearing parents who want their child for their family and their community. Since the acquisition of speech should begin as soon as possible for proper achievement, such hearing parents would want an implant for their child by the age of 2. However, they should keep in mind Dr Ruben's advice, which is that a cochlear device should be applied to *one* ear only; the other ear should be saved in the event that an inner ear can be regrown or replaced through future medical-technological development. In the meantime, it is sensible to bring the child up with sign as well as speech in case the implant fails. Whatever the decision, a written language should always be included for teaching.

2.8 The Steinberg Written Language Approach for complete communication

2.8.1 How the deaf can communicate with the hearing and succeed in the workplace

The need for literacy

Once the problem of how deaf persons are to communicate with one another has been dealt with satisfactorily (through an Independent Sign Language), the problem that remains is how deaf people are to communicate with members of the dominant hearing community. This is a different problem. Barring the very unlikely event that hearing people will learn ISL on a mass scale, the burden falls on the deaf to acquire some means of communication for use with hearing persons. In this regard two main approaches are available. One is speech (through the Oral Approach), which, as we know, benefits only those who have a moderate hearing loss. The other, little known, is the Steinberg Written Language Approach. It is this latter approach that we shall be dealing with here.

Low level of literacy leads to low-level jobs

Although Total Communication has improved the lot of the deaf in a significant way by providing sign language, in addition to speech training, one great educational problem still remains, that of literacy. On average, hearing-impaired persons, even after a Total Communication education programme, still graduate from high school with a reading level equivalent only to that of a hearing child in grade four or five of elementary school (aged 9 or 10 years in the USA) (Furth, 1971; Lane and Baker, 1974; Conrad, 1979;

Gallaudet Research Institute, 1985; Bochner and Albertini, 1988). Poor reading achievement is largely due to the use of reading methods and concepts that rely on listening and pronunciation. This is true for the USA and other developed countries and it is even lower in less developed countries.

Given the overwhelming necessity of being able to read and write in order to function well in modern society, it is not surprising that we find that most deaf people generally are able to secure only low-level jobs. With hearing illiterates having a tough time getting work, it is to be expected that non-hearing illiterates will have an even tougher time. Then, too, a reasonable level of literacy is essential if the deaf are to realize their potential, especially in this computer age. Towards this end, we believe that an additional approach that complements sign and speech can be of benefit. We call this the Written Language Bilingual Approach. Learning English or any other speech-language by the means of printed letters is what the deaf person needs for coping with modern society.

Written communication by notes

With deaf persons largely unable to have their speech understood, they can use written notes for personal communication. A note written by a deaf person will receive more attention and respect than if that person used mumbled speech. Speech by the deaf is often poorly regarded. In a study in Hiroshima where only deaf speech was used and where hearing persons were asked to make judgements regarding what they heard, the first author and his colleague found that hearing judges regarded the speech of deaf persons as having little attractiveness and as indicating lower intelligence (Kite and Steinberg, 1979). Writing, on the other hand, presents the deaf person as an *equal* in that mode of communication. When given a pad or a keyboard, it is easy for hearing persons to communicate with deaf persons.

Why teaching of reading/written language has failed thus far

Typically the teaching of reading has not been successful for the deaf. Teachers wait until a substantial knowledge of speech or sign has been acquired before they begin to teach reading (actually, written language). By this time the child is well into elementary school and reading is then taught through sign or speech. Strong (1988), for example, has advocated just this: a bilingual approach where English is taught but only after the first language, ASL, is acquired – a sequential type of bilingualism. Better still, in our view, is a simultaneous bilingual approach (see Chapter 8 on bilingualism) where parents at home or teachers in pre-school expose the child to written language in addition to sign and speech. The prime years for second-language learning are those from infancy to around 5 or 6 years of age (see Chapter 3 on early reading and Chapter 6 on second-language learning).

2.8.2 The Distinction between reading and written language

Reading

A person who knows a speech-based language and then learns to interpret the written correspondences for that speech is doing what we call reading. The typical reader therefore is a person who knows a speech-based language before learning to interpret writing. When that person can interpret writing, then we can say that the person can read. This is the way most hearing persons learn to read English or any other speech-based language. Such a person is not a bilingual but a monolingual who can read.

Written language

A person who does not know a speech-based language, such as a deaf person, can also learn to interpret writing. When that person can interpret writing, then we can say that the person is interpreting a written language. Thus, if the person knows ASL and learns written English, that person is bilingual. Written English is a complete language because, in the course of learning it, the learner acquires the same vocabulary and syntax of the English language as does a hearing person.

2.8.3 The Written Language Approach

The essential idea of this approach is that the meaningful written forms of an ordinary speech-based language, such as English or Spanish, with its words, phrases, and sentences, are to be learned initially through direct association with objects, events, and situations in the environment. Even if written language is learned with the aid of sign, the final knowledge product is a separate language.

Thus, just as hearing children learn language, initially by associating the speech sounds that they hear with environmental experiences, hearing-impaired children can learn language in a similar way, but through an association of written forms with those environmental experiences. Since most deaf children are born of hearing parents, teaching written language is something that those hearing parents can be taught to do *in a matter of hours!* Such parents do not need to spend years learning sign language before they can start to give some useful language experience to their children. This does not mean that hearing parents should not speak to their hearing-impaired child – they *should*, in order that the child may benefit from any residual hearing. Deaf parents of deaf children should teach written language in addition to signing.

By such teaching, hearing-impaired children will acquire essentially the same vocabulary and syntax of the English language as hearing children. In the writing of any language, be it English, Danish, or Chinese, virtually all of the vocabulary and syntactic structures that appear in speech also appear in writing, e.g. subject–verb relations, object–verb relations, negation, question, relative clauses, passives, etc. This is not to say that there are no differences between speech and writing. These differences are minor, however. Insofar as syntax is concerned, the differences are not great and are often more quantitative than qualitative in nature. Thus, for example, in English, passives tend to occur more in writing than in speech, and sentences end with prepositions more often in speech than in writing. Only concepts and experiences that relate to sound, such as music, noise, and sounds of nature, will be denied to the hearing-impaired, in much the same way that colour and visual shapes are denied to the blind.

Essentially, one basic grammar of a speech language such as English underlies the two forms of expression, speech and writing. Thus, because virtually any sentence or idea that can be expressed in speech can also be expressed in writing, we can say, by analogy (as we did in comparing spoken English and sign), that written language can be regarded as a complete language. Writing differs from speech concerning the physical medium of information transmission: writing involves light, while speech involves sound.

2.8.4 Advantages of the learning of written language

In teaching written language directly, six important advantages for the hearing-impaired and their education may be noted:

1. **The learning medium is appropriate**. Perception of written stimuli depends on vision, a medium in which the normal hearing-impaired are fully capable. Language can be acquired without any special obstacle on the basis of the visual medium.
2. **No new knowledge need be acquired by instructors**. Because the instructors already know how to read, they already know written language. Parents and teachers of the hearing-impaired do not have to learn the written language in order to teach it. They only have to learn the best methods and techniques to be a good instructor.
3. **Instruction can begin in infancy**. Parents of hearing-impaired children can teach their children written language at home during the children's most formative years. Children as young as 3 months of age can be exposed to written language in a natural way in the supportive comfort of their own home.
4. **All hearing-impaired children can benefit**. No effort devoted to teaching written language will be wasted. All children can benefit from it, since whatever is learned improves their level of literacy.

5. **Written language acquisition can facilitate speech**.   By learning written language, the syntax and vocabulary that underlie speech are also learned. Acquisition of written language therefore can accelerate oral instruction.

6. **Written language teaching is compatible with other approaches**. Written language can be taught in conjunction with either sign language or the oral method, without any injury to the integrity of those approaches.

2.8.5   Research on teaching written language to young children

Since the time of Alexander Graham Bell, when he taught written language to a 5-year-old deaf boy for a period of two years with some success (Bell, 1883), to the latter part of the twentieth century, there has been little interest in the teaching of written language.

This situation began to change in the latter part of the twentieth century, however, when significant research began to be conducted by a group of researchers in Japan under the leadership of Shigetada Suzuki and Masako Notoya. Studies showing that the Written Language Approach can work with profoundly deaf children have been published by the first author and his associates. These studies were done with American and Japanese children ranging in age from one to three years, and involved the learning of written English and written Japanese (Steinberg, 1980, 1982, 1984; Steinberg et al., 1982; Steinberg and Harper, 1983).

Teaching written language by means of sign

Besides teaching written language directly to young children, i.e. through direct experience as we propose, written language can be taught to hearing-impaired children through the medium of sign language. Pioneers in this type of research are Williams (1968) in teaching the reading of English, and Söderbergh (1976) in the teaching of Swedish. This has become commonplace nowadays, although, as was noted earlier, Strong still made a point of it in 1988.

2.9   A programme for teaching written languages

2.9.1   Guilding principles

For the learning and teaching of written language, two basic theoretical principles may serve as guides: (1) *words* are best acquired as conceptual wholes in a relevant context, and (2) *phrases and sentences* are best acquired in a relevant context through induction, just as hearing children learn their first language (see Chapter 1).

2.9.1.1 What to teach? The important things in the child's experience

To the extent that hearing-impaired children experience the same environment as hearing children, the hearing-impaired can acquire the same concepts relating to that environment. Their experiences of people, pets, toys, foods, etc. can then be associated with *written forms* that are provided by the parent or teacher (hereafter, the 'instructor' for whoever does the teaching). Thus, for example, written words like 'Mommy', 'Daddy', 'dog', 'car', 'banana', 'orange', 'table', and 'chair' could be written on cards and attached to the relevant objects. In time such written forms acquire a symbolic value, that is, a meaning.

2.9.1.2 Written language comprehension, not production, is primary

Again, it is useful to consider the situation for hearing persons. In acquiring language, hearing persons first learn to comprehend speech before they produce it meaningfully (Chapter 1). Now, as far as the hearing-impaired child who is learning written language is concerned, a similar primacy of comprehension over production obtains. In this case, however, comprehension consists of the interpretation of written forms, and production consists of the writing of such forms. However, an even greater lag in writing production may be expected compared with the lag that occurs in speech production. The muscle and coordination control that is needed for the use of a writing implement such as a pencil develops much more slowly than the articulators used in the production of speech. Children typically only begin to gain control of a writing implement around the age of 3 years (Steinberg and Yamada, 1980), and it takes some years before they can write numbers of sentences without tiring. This is unfortunate, for hearing-impaired children could benefit greatly through using such a communicative means of expression during their early years.

2.9.1.3 Word learning

Once a hearing-impaired child begins to acquire concepts of objects, actions, events, and situations, that child is ready to acquire the written *labels* for these concepts. Undoubtedly, the ideal way for a young hearing-impaired child to learn words in their written form is in much the same way as a young hearing child does: exposure to words in conjunction with the objects, situations, and ongoing events in the environment.

Unfortunately, although it is easy for a parent to produce spoken words while conducting the affairs of daily life, it is difficult for written words to be produced in that situation. The practical obstacles in the way of a parent writing everything that he or she would ordinarily say are formidable. Yet, even if a parent does do some writing, a significant amount of written language can be acquired. Steinberg and his associates attempted this with a 17-month-old Japanese hearing-impaired girl and her mother and the results were beneficial (Steinberg *et al.*, 1982). What the mother did was to carry around a large pad and marker and write on the pad what she would say to the child in speech. Each sheet of paper was a throwaway, just like speech disappearing into the air.

Since conditions for learning cannot be arranged so that hearing-impaired children can learn written language on their own in the ordinary course of daily events, as do hearing children, some degree of artificiality must be introduced into the learning situation. Still, the simulation of naturalness should be a goal. Language learning should be made to occur indirectly through the course of interesting activities and games and not through explicit language lessons.

2.9.1.4 Inappropriateness of direct letter learning

When hearing children experience speech words in the home, they experience them as wholes: the words dog and cat, for example, are pronounced as wholes. The child is not taught the component sounds first, for example, /d/, /o/, and /g/. Rather, parents say whole words like 'dogs', 'jumped', and 'runs' and leave it to the children to make the phoneme, syllable, and morpheme segmentation on their own. The children accomplish this through a natural analytical process of their own, which is *induction*.

Since evidence shows that the analytical and conceptualizing processes of hearing-impaired children do not differ from those of hearing children (Furth, 1971), hearing-impaired children may be expected to be able to distinguish on their own the shapes of the letters and to identify morpheme components of words in the course of learning whole written words. There is no need, therefore, to give prior (or even subsequent) training in individual letters to hearing-impaired children; such training is boring, exceedingly tedious, and sometimes may be impossible. Children are interested in meaningful units such as words, not meaningless units such as letters.

2.9.1.5 Greater use of learning meaningful written units

Although a word is longer and more complex than any of its component parts, research evidence indicates that the learning of a meaningful whole word is easier than the learning of its meaningless components. In an experiment with American pre-school children, Steinberg and Koono (1979) found that English words were learned at more than twice the rate of English letters. Similar findings have been reported for Japanese children, who learned *kanji* (complex Chinese-type characters) at least twice as quickly as meaningless syllable symbols (Steinberg and Yamada, 1978–9). Thus, children will learn written items if those items are paired with meaningful stimuli such as actual objects, events, and situations (or their pictures). So, if a written word is associated with a cookie or a picture of a dog, the hearing-impaired child can be expected to acquire the written forms that represent those objects. When the associated stimulus is not meaningful, the written item is much more difficult to learn. Only items that interest the child should be introduced for learning.

Insofar as the learning of abstract words is concerned, no special principles need be followed. The hearing-impaired child will learn to acquire such words in essentially the same way as does the hearing child, that is, on the basis of relevant environmental experience and through a process of hypothesis testing. Abstract words like 'idea', 'like', 'beautiful', 'pain', 'true', and 'thought' will naturally begin to be acquired after children come to realize the essential principle of language, which is that words can be used to express ideas. This basic principle is acquired in the process of learning concrete words. After this, the child is ready to label more abstract notions.

2.9.1.6   Phrase and sentence acquisition

Just as hearing children learn the syntax of language without direct instruction by exposure to phrases and sentences used in a relevant environmental context, hearing-impaired children learn the syntax of written language in the same way. Parents of hearing children do not teach their children syntactic rules. For example, rules about constituent order, verb inflections, and relative clause formation are learned by children on their own. Explanations would not be understood by the young child, even if the simplest language were used. Such being the case, instructors should attempt to provide the hearing-impaired child with adequate exposure to written language and environmental stimuli in as natural and interesting a way as possible, such as through story-books, magazines, pictures. Through such exposure, the children can then be expected to learn the syntax by themselves through induction and hypothesis testing.

2.9.1.7   A four-phase programme for teaching written language

A four-phase teaching programme was formulated incorporating the principles previously outlined. The four phases are (1) Word Familiarization, (2) Word Identification, (3) Phrase and Sentence identification, and (4) Paragraphs and Stories. These phases have their parallels in our recommendations for teaching reading to hearing children in Chapter 3. The programme is explained in detail in Steinberg *et al.* (2001).

2.9.1.8   Effectiveness of the teaching programme

To date, the first author has been involved in teaching written language to four deaf children on the basis of the four-phase teaching programme. Two are boys, Jerrold and Konrad, and two are girls, Jessie and Kiku. (All names are pseudonyms.) At the programme's inception, the ages of the children were: Jerrold, 3 years and 6 months; Konrad, 2 years and 5 months; Jessie,

1 year and 2 months; and Kiku, 1 year and 5 months. The first three children are Americans who learned written English in Hawaii; the fourth, Kiku, is a Japanese who learned written Japanese in Japan. In all cases, teaching was done by family members at home. All items taught were selected by them.

All of the children were profoundly deaf, having a 90 dB or higher hearing loss in their better ear. Except for Jerrold, who became deaf due to meningitis at the age of 5 months, the children had no significant hearing from birth. The main criterion for subject selection was their profound hearing loss. It was believed that a great loss would give the programme its most rigorous test, since such children would be likely to acquire only a small amount of language through residual hearing. Not surprisingly, therefore, at the beginning of the study, the linguistic knowledge of the children was at a minimum. Only the two boys had any linguistic knowledge at all. Jerrold, the oldest, could say about 15 words and understood about 40 spoken words. He could also understand about 15 word signs. The other, Konrad, knew no speech but could understand about eight words in sign language.

Some of the more important characteristics of the subjects and their families are shown in Table 2.1, as are the overall results (Steinberg and Harper, 1983; Steinberg *et al.*, 1982, for the Kiku case). It should be noted here that all of the parents of the subjects were hearing, except for Konrad's. Both of Konrad's parents were congenitally deaf and used sign language with one another. The mother, who had recently come from Japan, was still in the process of learning ASL.

Thus, it can be seen that Konrad learned the greatest number of items (648) and Jessie the least (5). Undoubtedly, factors such as the length of the instruction period and the average amount of time spent daily on instruction (parents' reported estimates) played a role in determining the number of items learned. For example, it seems that Jerrold might have learned many more items than he did had he received as much daily instruction and for as long a period of time as did Konrad. Incidentally, instruction was never given in a single block of time; it was spaced throughout the day.

Whether age is also a factor affecting the rate of learning cannot be determined from the data in the chart alone, since achievement could be due to other sources. For example, differences in teaching effectiveness on the part of the parents as well as differences in the age or innate intellectual ability of the children could have contributed to the observed results.

Konrad's results

To get a better idea of the developmental acquisition process, let us take a look at Konrad's achievement in detail. Consider the following table, Table 2.2, from Steinberg and Harper (1983). Here we see his progress on a month-by-month basis. So as to guard against the child getting an item correct by chance, Konrad was required to give a correct response to the target item on two separate occasions. He was obliged to demonstrate the meaning

Table 2.1 Background of American and Japanese subjects and number of items learned

Variable	Jerrold	Konrad	Jessie	Kiku
Written language learned	English	English	English	Japanese
Sex	Male	Male	Female	Female
Age at programme beginning	3 yr., 6 mo.	2 yr., 5 mo.	1 yr., 2 mo.	1 yr., 5 mo.
Hearing loss in better ear (dB = decibels)	Over 90 dB	Over 90 dB	Around 90 dB	Around 90 dB
Hearing loss onset	5 months	Congenital	Congenital	Congenital
Etiology	Meningitis	Unknown	Unknown	Unknown
Father's occupation	Engineer	Sewage worker	Mechanic	Engineer
Mother's occupation	Computer programmer	Homemaker	Office head	Homemaker
Father's education	University	Jr high school	University	University
Mother's education	University	Jr high school	University	University
Duration of instruction	11 mo.	15 mo.	8 mo.	20 mo.
Average daily instruction	10 min.	30 min.	30 min.	25 min.
Single words learned	180	406	5	194
Phrases, expressions, sentences learned	134	242	–	96
Total items learned	314	648	5	290

through some behaviour. While the parents recorded Konrad's successes, these results were double-checked by the main author and his assistant. As time went on, Konrad learned more and more sign language. There was then an interaction between his written language and his ASL signs.

Table 2.2 Results for Konrad: summary of words, phrases, and sentences learned

Month	Word class				Total words	Total phrases and sentences	Total all items
	Noun	Verb	Adj.	Other			
1	54	5	11	0	70	10	80
2	24	7	2	2	35	19	54
3	37	6	11	13	67	30	97
4	22	14	4	5	45	23	68
5	44	12	9	1	66	37	103
6	–	–	–	–	–	–	–
7	13	5	4	1	23	1	24
8	9	5	1	3	18	21	39
9	18	5	1	2	26	20	46
10	9	0	1	1	11	11	22
11	–	–	–	–	–	17	17
12	11	3	2	2	18	10	28
13	9	6	0	2	17	13	30
14	8	2	1	1	12	15	27
15	3	1	2	0	6	15	21
Total	261	71	49	33	414	242	656
Per cent	63.04	17.15	11.84	7.97	100.00	–	–

It might interest the reader to know that Konrad, who is 29 years old at the time of this writing (born 12 August 1976), graduated from Rochester Institute of Technology, is superior in composition and in using e-mail, and his communications to the first author demonstrate a high level of English writing ability. The first author was delighted to learn from Konrad that another of his research children, Jerrold, had also attended RIT.

2.9.1.9 Conclusion

The results show that significant written language knowledge, even of such vastly different writing systems as English and Japanese, can be acquired directly through the medium of writing by very young children who have had a profound hearing loss at or near birth. Since the Written Language teaching programme can be applied successfully by ordinary parents in the home, there is good reason to believe that it can also be successfully applied by teachers in school. Undoubtedly, young children would benefit most by being taught written language both in the home and at school.

Chapter 3

Reading principles and teaching

This chapter focuses on the nature and teaching of reading. A number of principles for the optimal learning of reading are presented, as is a reading programme based on those principles. The issue of Whole-Word vs. Phonic Teaching is included in the discussion of those principles. The issues of reading readiness and early reading are also considered.

In order to properly understand reading, an understanding of certain essentials regarding writing systems and their relationship to speech is necessary.

3.1 Writing systems and speech

Writing systems are designed to represent the *spoken words* of a language. It is through individual words that other higher units of language, such as the phrase and sentence, represented. Writing systems of the world are mainly based on one of two principles, *sound* or *meaning*. The inventory of visual symbols of writing systems is constructed on the basis of these principles.

3.1.1 Writing systems based on speech sounds: phonemes or syllables

In the sound-based system, each symbol represents a *speech sound*, either a phoneme or a syllable. There are many different sound-based writing scripts in use throughout the world today – for example, Devanagari in India, Arabic in Egypt, the Hangul syllabary in South Korea, the two Kana syllabaries in Japan, the Cyrillic alphabet in Russia and Bulgaria, and the Roman alphabet in English-speaking countries and Western Europe.

Some of these sound-based orthographies correspond highly to their spoken forms. Among these are Finnish and Spanish, which use the Roman alphabet to represent the phonemes of their spoken languages, and Korean and Japanese, which use their own native scripts, Hangul and Kana, respectively, to represent the syllables of their spoken languages. (Complexities occur with Japanese, however, because it also mixes Chinese-type characters into its writing system even though those characters (*kanji*) can be written in the syllabic forms.) The sound-based orthographies of these languages are easier to read than are sound-based orthographies where the correspondence of written symbol to sound is not high, as is the case for English.

3.1.2 The unpredicability of English orthography

Many works have been written on the inconsistencies of English spelling and the pain it has inflicted on learners. Let us present one such poem here.

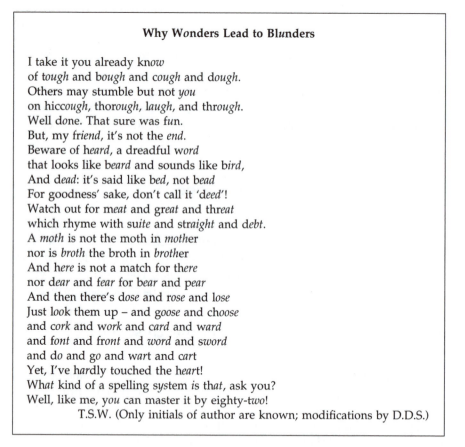

Why Wonders Lead to Blunders

I take it you already know
of *tough* and *bough* and *cough* and *dough*.
Others may stumble but not *you*
on hic*cough*, thor*ough*, l*augh*, and thr*ough*.
Well d*one*. That sure was f*un*.
But, my fr*iend*, it's not the *end*.
Beware of h*eard*, a dreadful w*ord*
that looks like b*eard* and sounds like b*ird*,
And d*ead*: it's said like b*ed*, not b*ead*
For goodness' sake, don't call it '*deed*'!
Watch out for m*eat* and gr*eat* and thr*eat*
which rhyme with s*uite* and str*aight* and d*ebt*.
A *moth* is not the moth in *mother*
nor is *broth* the broth in *brother*
And h*ere* is not a match for th*ere*
nor d*ear* and f*ear* for b*ear* and p*ear*
And then there's d*ose* and r*ose* and l*ose*
Just l*ook* them up – and g*oose* and ch*oose*
and c*ork* and w*ork* and c*ard* and w*ard*
and f*ont* and fr*ont* and *word* and s*word*
and d*o* and g*o* and w*art* and c*art*
Yet, I've h*ardly* touched the h*eart*!
Wh*at* kind of a spelling s*ystem* *is* th*at*, ask you?
Well, like me, *you* can master it by eighty-*two*!
　　　　　　T.S.W. (Only initials of author are known; modifications by D.D.S.)

What can one say? English spelling is consistently inconsistent!

Why English orthography poorly represents English phonemes

Being essentially a sound-based writing system, English letters are intended to represent the individual phonemes of the language. Because the Roman alphabet was based on the Latin language, which used fewer phonemes than English, English orthography (and those of other European lands) had to make adaptations in order to suit its language. For English, the following adaptations were made: (1) A letter could be assigned more than one sound, especially vowels. Thus, the letter a represents two phonemes, /a/ (wɑnt) and /æ/ (cɑt). (2) A combination of letters serves to represent other English sounds, e.g. th (think, that), a + C + e (/ei/ as in 'ate' as opposed to 'at') and i + C + e (/ai/ as in 'bite' as opposed to bit), where C is any consonant. While English convention also uses some morpheme symbols, e.g. 1 for the word 'one', 2 for the word 'two', + for 'plus', and & for 'and', the writing system is predominantly a sound-based one where letters represent the phonemes of the language.

Another principal reason why English letters frequently do not signal the correct sound is the failure of English spelling to reflect the changes that the spoken language has undergone. English spelling has changed relatively little over the past 600 years or so, compared to the great changes that have occurred in the spoken language.

Thus, no longer, for example, do we pronounce words like 'light', 'night' and 'right' with the sort of sound that Germans utter in words such as macht (make) and Ich (I). Such sounds have mainly disappeared from English but are still maintained in some locales (loch for lake as in the lovely Scottish song 'Loch Lomond'). The English language had such sounds because they originated with the Germanic languages that people brought with them from the Continent and from which the English language was substantially derived thousands of years ago. A very substantial French language influence on English arrived when the Norman French conquered England in 1066 AD. The result is that English pronunciation is related to its orthography in a complex and indirect way.

The origins of the English alphabet

The origins of the Roman alphabet lie with the Semitic peoples in the Middle East thousands of years ago. The Phoenicians adapted it to their needs and then carried that alphabet to Greece, from where it travelled to Rome. Both the Greeks and then the Romans made adaptations to suit their languages. The names of the letters changed as well. The letter A went from the Semitic name *aleph*, to the Greek *alpha*, to the Roman *ah* and the English *a*.

It was with the growth of the Roman Empire and later the Roman Catholic Church that the letters of the Roman writing systems spread north to various parts of Europe. Later, the Europeans, in their colonization of various countries around the world, brought with them their alphabet as well. Thus, we can find Romanized writing being used in Vietnam and Indonesia, where it was again adapted to suit the indigenous languages spoken there. (For a detailed survey of writing systems around the world, see Coulmas (1989). For a focus on Chinese, Korean, and Japanese writing systems see Taylor and Taylor (1995), and for a focus on the Japanese writing system and reading acquisition see Yamada (1997).)

3.1.3 Writing systems based on meaning: the morpheme

Chinese is essentially a system where symbols (characters) represent the morphemes of the language although symbols may be added to assist pronunciation. Japanese uses this system too (in addition to its syllabaries), having borrowed it from China more than 1300 years ago.

In the Chinese system every character represents one or more morphemes as well as a single syllable. Thus, for example, the Chinese word *kowtow* (now incorporated into the English language) consists of two morphemes, *kow* meaning 'knock' and *tow* meaning 'head'. *Kowtow* thus literally means to kneel and touch the ground with one's forehead, thereby showing submission or respect to a superior. In the Cantonese pronunciation (which was borrowed into English), both vowel sounds have a pronunciation that rhymes with English '*cow*'.

While it is true that the Chinese symbols had their origin in pictures (as have all original writing systems), probably fewer than 50 of the many thousands of characters used today retain any direct pictorial indication. The relationship between symbol and morpheme, therefore, is essentially conventional rather than pictorial, just as is the case for the English alphabet, whose letters (the capitals) are themselves rooted in ancient Semitic picture writing. We can still see the stylized outline of the head of an ox in the letter A, especially when that letter is inverted.

3.2 The Whole-Word vs. Phonics/Decoding controversy

A long-standing controversy that pervades reading theory and teaching methods concerns what the focus of learning should be. The Whole-Word proponents advocate that the focus be on meaning, with the whole word as its basic unit. The Phonics and Decoding proponents, on the other hand, advocate that the focus be on speech, particularly phonemes. Both schools share the ultimate goal of having children read fluently – it is the means that divide them.

3.2.1 The Phonics/Decoding Approach

3.2.1.1 The nature of reading according to Phonics/Decoding

The goal of directly determining meaning from written forms is not one shared by Phonics/Decoding advocates. For them, reading is conceived of as a process that converts written forms of language to speech forms and then to meaning (Ehri, 1991; Gough and Juel, 1991; Perfetti, 1991; Adams, 1994; Foorman *et al.*, 1998; National Reading Panel Report, 2000). They regard the essence of reading to be the ability to decode reading materials into speech. Once speech is obtained, they believe, meaning will follow. Thus, they propose early and systematic phonics instruction starting with the mastery of a set of letters and sounds that comprise words.

They want children first to learn the sound value of letters and letter combinations. They believe that children will then be able to read whole words by decoding them from their component phonemes. This view is concisely expressed in the Perfetti and Rieben (1991) argument: 'learning to read requires mastering the system by which print encodes the language (i.e., the orthography). This mastery, in turn, requires the child to attain understanding of how the spoken language works' (p. vii). Most of the investigators in the Perfetti and Rieben (1991) volume assume that the learning of the phonological structure of a language (speech) should precede the learning of reading.

There is also an argument elsewhere that phonological awareness precedes reading (Goswami and Bryant, 1990; Adams, 1994; Grossen, 1997; Goswami, 2002; Scarborough, 2002). Phonological awareness is considered to be the most important predictor of future reading success (National Reading Panel, 2000). Reading is primarily conceived of as the identification of words through the sound values of letters. The goal is for children to be able to decode *written* forms into their *phonemic* forms which can then be expressed by spoken words. This goal, the proponents of the method argue, cannot be achieved if the learners are taught by the whole-language method. This is untrue on two counts: (1) phonic-decoding training could be given *following* the acquisition of a stock of whole words, and (2) phoneme values for letters can be learned through the natural self-discovery process of induction. (More on this second point later.)

3.2.1.2 Supporting research evidence for Phonics/Decoding is sparse

There are studies which appear to support phonics as a more effective method than the whole-language method. For example, McGuinness *et al.* (1995) compared first-graders given a structured phonological reading (phonics) method with those given a whole-language-plus-phonics method. They found, in the phonological processing tasks given at the beginning and the end of the school year, that children given the phonics method showed significant gains in reading real and nonsense words compared to children given the whole-language-plus-phonics method. What was not tested, however, was the children's understanding of the *meaning* of items.

Eldredge and Baird (1996) compared the two instruction methods for teaching first-graders (6-year-olds) how to write. Specifically, children given the phonics method took phonemic awareness and phonics training so that they could spell words by sounds before involving them in holistic writing experiences. The analysis showed better performance for the children given the phonics than for those given the whole-language method. But, again, we must ask what the purpose of reading is. Surely it is not to facilitate writing and spelling. Of course, these skills should be taught but they should be kept separate from the teaching of reading. (See a later section on the inadvisability of linking writing to reading.)

One recent study (Wilson and Norman, 1998) reported no difference between the two teaching methods. These investigators compared Grade 2 children (7-year-olds) given either a whole-word method or a phonics-based method; subsequent reading tests showed similar results for both groups. National Reading Panel (2000) research found that successful oral reading and reading comprehension did not depend much on teaching phonics in kindergarten, and that *phonics instruction affected mostly decoding and the reading of nonsense words!* Other studies too have reported no difference between the two teaching methods. Traweek and Berninger (1997) even found that both methods produced comparable gains in word recognition. However, they observed differences in processes underlying achievement outcomes. Specifically, the first-graders (6-year-olds) given the whole-language method tended to acquire orthographic-phonological connections at the whole-word and subword levels, while those given the phonics method tended to acquire only subword connections.

Recent research reveals that phonological awareness is more a script-related skill than an early-reading prerequisite; about two in five children have some level of difficulty with phonemic awareness, and for about one in five children phonemic awareness does not develop or improve over time (data from research on reading from the National Institute of Child Health and Human Development, see Grossen, 1997). Phonological awareness only develops in a later stage of reading acquisition for German, and it proved to have little importance in reading acquisition of languages such as Greek, Portuguese, Spanish, Indian, and Japanese (Karanth, 2003). Such results clearly support the whole-word method!

3.2.1.3 Problems with the Phonics/Decoding approach

Wrongly focuses on sound rather than meaning

The principal problem with phonics and decoding approaches to reading, which focuses on the sound values of letters, is that such instruction draws the child's attention to meaningless sounds rather than to meaningful concepts. Such methods, whether they teach letter–sound correspondences in isolation or in the context of whole words (so-called 'decoding'), draw attention to the identification of sound elements which comprise words.

Learning to read in this sense is not natural, as in learning to understand and produce speech. It is *boring and too confusing* a task, particularly when the language under consideration is one such as English. Given the perversity of English orthography, it is *not* justified to focus a reading programme on the teaching of the sound values of letters and of decoding.

Decoding is a very difficult process

Then, too, the linguistic fact is that individually uttered sounds usually do *not* naturally blend to form words, as Bloomfield (1942/1961) observed more than 50 years ago. His son was having trouble learning to read at school and he decided to teach him to read at home. His solution was to write whole words that featured a sound–letter correspondence, e.g. 'bat', 'sat', 'cat', and sentences like 'The cat is on the mat'. From our point of view, Bloomfield could have done better: all of his items were presented out of context and many of them were meaningless. Unlike Dr Seuss, who rhymed words and non-words in a humorous way, Bloomfield did not present these words in any meaningful or interesting context.

Many individual letter sounds that are uttered present an added barrier to learning because their intended sound is obscured in pronunciation. For example, the individually pronounced segments in a simple word like 'picked' do not, in combination, provide the intended whole word. For 'picked', the letter p typically evokes /p^/ (the ^ represents the *u* in p*u*ppy), i evokes /i/ (l*i*t) or /î/ (t*ee*th), ck evokes /k^/, e evokes /e/, and d evokes /d^/. Altogether this provides /p^ik^ed^/ and not /pikt/. One problem here is that the consonant sounds cannot be uttered in isolation but have to be uttered in syllabic form. Another is that the child must realize that 'ed' represents the PAST morpheme and not the individual sounds /e/ and /d/. Clearly, a child could not recover words by this method if the spoken sounds of letters are directly combined.

In order to be successful, the child must devise and apply complex phonological transformations to the combination of sounds so as to derive the intended word. In the 'picked' example above, the child must *mentally delete* the /^/ from the syllables /p^/, /k^/, /d^/ in order to recover the consonants /p/, /k/, and /d/ so that they can then be assembled or combined with the vowel /i/. Then the child must deal with 'ed'. The vowel deletion process at the end of a CV syllable must be done mentally because many individual consonants cannot be uttered aloud without the inclusion of a succeeding vowel, e.g. p, t, k, b, d, g, h, w. Even the simplest of words present great problems. For example, how the letters 'a' and 'e' are to be dealt with in a simple word like 'dance' is not easy to explain to a child, or an adult!

Sounding out a new word relies on meaning

How can a child be expected to 'sound out' a new word that he or she has not heard before? How can an adult? There are three aspects to a successful interpretation: one is a meaningful context, another is knowing the probability of certain sounds for particular letters, and a third is being able to guess the word given the information provided in the two previous aspects. For example, here is a story with an unfinished word:

> The boy kept on teasing the cat. Finally the cat got so angry that it scratched the boy. He screamed, 'Ou . . .' and then ran.

Now, in all likelihood, you would interpret the vowel sound 'ou' so as to rhyme with 'foul' but not with 'colour' or 'pour' because you would guess the word to be Ouch.

Actually we can often guess what an unknown word might be simply through its consonant structure. In English, more information is given by consonant letters than by vowel letters. For example, compare sentence form A, all vowels, with sentence form B, all consonants. Each dash indicates a missing letter.

> A. --e -i--- -a- -u--e- o-- a- -e- o--o--.
> B. Th- l-ght w-s t-rn-d -ff -t t-n -cl-ck.

You might be able to get B, but it is highly unlikely that you would be able to get A. The sentence for both is: 'The light was turned off at ten o'clock.' Such a strategy, though, can only be used by a knowledgeable reader. The more words that one knows and can deal with in a meaningful context, the more likely one is able to guess correctly at new words.

3.2.2 The Whole-Word Approach

3.2.2.1 Teaching reading should focus on meaning and communication and not on speech

In the view of the Whole-Word proponents, the essential task for a reader is the *recovery of meaning* (Huey, 1908; Gates, 1928; Goodman, 1973; F. Smith, 1982, among many others). Whether a reader can say or write the words that are written is *incidental* to the reading process. Reading is a form of communication the goal of which is the reception of information through written forms. A teaching programme, consequently, should direct itself to the realization of that goal. Best suited to this aim is the whole-word approach.

There is, of course, some irony in the proposal for teaching reading through whole words, in that it advocates that English writing, which mainly has an alphabetic character, be treated for teaching purposes as though it were a morpheme writing system like Chinese.

Memory ability of children

Children have the memory capacity for learning to identify many hundreds of whole words (see a later section regarding the data gathered in the course of applying our teaching method). Young children can acquire thousands of speech vocabulary items in a relatively short time. The memorization of thousands of *written* forms poses no special problem for children either, so long as a proper teaching method is used.

3.2.2.2 Fluent readers use a whole-word strategy

Actually, all fluent English readers eventually learn to identify whole words as if they were Chinese characters; even the proponents of the Phonics/Decoding Approach admit the fact (see, for example, Byrne, 1992, or Adams, 1994). The time taken to read a page of text aloud is much longer than when the same page is read silently. Experimental evidence as far back as the last century (Cattell, 1885) shows that fluent readers use a whole-word strategy in identifying words. The work of Goodman (1973), Kolers (1970), and others reinforces this view. They find that *the prediction of meaning is the major strategy* (not the decoding of letter–sound correspondences) used in the identification of words.

Readers of this book can try to conduct a quick experiment on whole-word recognition for themselves. The following paragraph has been circulating on the Internet since 2003. Though the spelling is imperfect, the meaning can still be recovered:

Aoccdrnig to rscheearch at Cmabrigde Uinervtisy, it deosn't mttaer in waht oredr the ltteers in a wrod are, the olny iprmoetnt tihng is taht the frist and lsat ltteer be at the rghit pclae. The rset can be a total mses and you can sitll raed it wouthit porbelm. Tihs is bcuseae the huamn mnid deos not raed ervey lteter by istlef, but the wrod as a wlohe.

Since it is the case that learning to recognize whole words is basic to being a fluent reader, the learning of whole words right from the start will be easier and more effective for readers in the long run. Instilling early in children the habit of decoding every word they come upon will slow the speed of reading.

3.2.2.3 Children learn to segment their native language, morphemically, syntactically, and phonologically, by induction

All children in learning their native language have the ability to learn the vocabulary and syntactic structures of their language, not by being taught but through the process of self-analysis, i.e. induction. No one tells the child learning a first language what the individual sounds of the PLURAL, PAST, and the AUXILIARY 'be' morphemes are. (See Chapter 1 for a list of common morphemes learned by young children.)

Neither do parents teach their children the component phonemes of a word. What they do is simply utter the whole word. They say whole words like 'pushed', 'Grandma's', 'cats', and 'is playing', and leave it to the child to do the segmenting. They don't say 'pu' + 'sh^' + 'd^', or some such thing for 'pushed'. The fact that children produce words that they have never heard such as 'breaked', 'comed', 'mouses', and 'brung' through sound substitutions (see Chapter 1) demonstrates that they *do* learn sound segmentation on their own and *do* manipulate phonemes.

Clearly, in dealing with the speech they receive, children apply great analytical skill. They take whole data (words, phrases, sentences) as input, search for regularities, and then formulate rules that underlie those data. This may sound formidable but it really pales before the remarkable analytical capacity that all children display in learning the syntax and phonology of a language. None of this grammar is taught! Learning is through induction. Thus, learning the systematic letter–sound correspondences that are inherent in whole written-word data is a much less formidable task than the learning of the native language.

It is this same natural order which we wish to apply to reading: whole words first and then the sound values of letters, if necessary, later.

Learning phonological segments in first-language learning by induction

Rather than attempting to teach children to read words by requiring them to pronounce sounds aloud for letters and then blending those uttered sounds, it would be better if children learned the sound values of letters mentally by induction, i.e. self-analysis. The child would then blend those sounds mentally to form words. As was noted earlier, the sound value of letters may be introduced, but this should be done only *after* the child (1) has learned the basic principle that written forms represent meanings, and (2) has learned to read at least 50 words. If it is to be applied at all, the teaching of sound values and decoding should only be a minor aspect of the reading programme. Determining the *meaning* of written items is *primary*, while the *speech value* of letters, while important, is *secondary*. It is from this standpoint that we formulate our approach to the teaching of reading.

3.2.2.4 Research evidence in support of learning letter–sound values by induction

Research generally shows that children can learn letter–sound correspondences on their own by induction. Gates (1928) determined, on the basis of relatively long-term studies with a large number of English-speaking elementary-school children, that the sound values of letters could be learned without instruction simply through the learning of whole words. Other long-term case studies with pre-school children also support the findings of Gates. For example, Söderbergh (1971) found that her Swedish-speaking female subject learned all of the letter–sound correspondences necessary for reading without direct instruction and without any special order of materials. Similar results were found by Steinberg and Steinberg (1975) with their

English-speaking 2-year-old. Other studies by Steinberg (1980, 1981) show that the sound forms of letters are learned by induction; separate teaching of those individual components was not given. Recently Fletcher-Flinn and Thompson (2000) have also provided substantial results for the whole-word approach with a 3-year-old girl. Because particular letters do not always correspond to particular sounds, due to the nature of English orthography, correspondence rules between phonological and orthographic components were necessarily extracted by children through induction (self-analysis).

English research: words are learned faster than letters

Research evidence shows that meaningful words are easier to learn than meaningless items such as letters. For example, a study with English-speaking pre-school children who could not read showed that written words were learned twice as fast as letters (Steinberg et al., 1979). Thus, words such as 'finish' and 'dollar' were learned twice as fast as the single letters 'a' and 'n'. The words were named as they usually are and the letters were called by their phonic names.

Interestingly, in Steinberg and Koono (1981) a separate experimental group of English-speaking pre-school children was presented with the same written words and letters, i.e. 'finish', 'dollar', 'a', 'n', but this time the written words were called by phonic letter names, e.g. 'finish' was called 'a', and 'dollar' was called 'n', while, conversely, the written letters were identified by speech words, i.e. 'a' was called 'finish' and 'n' was called 'dollar'. The results decisively showed that written items (individual letters) called by speech words were learned much faster than the written items (words) called by letter names. The results were the reverse for the children (in the previous paragraph) who had written items called by their usual names. These findings show that the visual complexity of what is written plays only a minor role in learning and that what is most important is what is said together with a written form. *This indicates that meaningful spoken words lead to much greater learning* than do meaningless letter names.

Japanese research: words are learned faster than letters

In research with Japanese children in Japan, similar results were found. Pre-school children learned meaningful complex Chinese characters (*kanji*) faster than meaningless simple syllable symbols (*kana*) (Steinberg et al., 1977; Steinberg and Yamada, 1978–9). Thus, even though a word written in *kanji* was more complex in form than an individual *kana*, the children learned the *kanji* word faster. A word written in *kanji* like 'kusuri' (medicine) was learned faster than a *kana* syllable sound like 'ku' (which had no meaning for young children).

To demonstrate that it was not the shape or complexity of the written form that was determining the learning, a separate matched experimental group

		Speech form uttered	
		Word	**Syllable**
Written form shown	*kanji* 薬	'kusuri' (medicine) *fast*	'ku' (meaningless) *slow*
	kana く	*fast*	*slow*

Figure 3.1 Speed of learning *kanji* and *kana* is governed by meaningfulness of spoken word

Notes

Learning outcomes are shown as *fast* or *slow*. There are two lines of outcomes. Thus:

Line 1, left side: A *kanji* written form and an uttered word yields *fast* learning.

Line 1, right side: A *kanji* written form and an uttered syllable yields *slow* learning.

Line 2, left side: A *kana* written form and an uttered word yields *fast* learning.

Line 2, right side: A *kana* written form and an uttered syllable yields *slow* learning.

Conclusions:

Learning is *fast* when a meaningful word is uttered, regardless of whether a *kanji* or *kana* written form is shown.

Learning is *slow* when a meaningless syllable is uttered, regardless of whether a *kanji* or *kana* written form is shown.

of children were given the same items to learn (Steinberg *et al.*, 1977), but with a difference: the written *kanji* were identified by the experimenters with the syllable names of the *kana*, and the written *kana* were identified with the word names of the *kanji*. The result was that this time the *kana* were learned faster. The written *kana* 'ku' was called 'kusuri' (medicine) and was learned faster than the written *kanji* word 'kusuri' that was called 'ku'.

Thus, consider Figure 3.1. Learning is 'fast' whenever the spoken form is a word, regardless of whether the written form is a *kanji* or a *kana*. It is 'slow' whenever the spoken form is a syllable. The speed of learning the written form varies according to whether it is a word or a syllable that is spoken. Thus we see that the *kanji* written form is learned fast when it is called by the meaningful word 'kusuri' (medicine) but it is learned slowly when it is called by the meaningless 'ku'.

This demonstrates that *what was most important in the learning was the meaningfulness of what was spoken* and not the visual complexity of the written form. A spoken word such as 'kusuri' was learned faster than a spoken syllable like 'ku'. Since the difference between 'kusuri' and 'ku' is their meaningfulness (only 'kusuri' is meaningful), the controlling variable is that of meaningfulness. Counter to the expectations of some that a simple written form (the *kana*) would be learned faster than a complex written form (the *kanji*), the opposite was the case. The visual complexity of the written form had no observable effect on learning. This is not to say that the visual complexity of a written form has no effect on learning. It may, but its effect could not be detected in this experiment. At best, its effect is minuscule compared to the meaningfulness of the spoken words.

Other short-term experimental support for induction

More support for the induction of letter-sound correspondences has been obtained in some *short-term experiments*. Bishop (1964), Skailand (1971), and Steinberg (1981) found evidence of letter–sound inductions. In the Steinberg experimental study Japanese pre-school children were given whole words written in syllabic *kana* and were told what each word was. After a number of presentations, the children learned on their own the syllable sound values of the component *kana* symbols that made up each word; the ultimate test was the children's being able to read novel and meaningless words constructed of the induced *kana* sound values.

Jeffrey and Samuels (1967) and Silberman (1964), however, found little or no spontaneous induction occurring in their research. In examining these latter studies and others like them, though, it is evident that a number of important variables were often not dealt with adequately. For example, some studies did not give learners a sufficient amount of time for training and for arriving at a solution. Thus, the one short session given in the Jeffrey and Samuels experiment may well have been insufficient, as indicated by Gibson and Levin (1975, p. 291).

3.2.2.5 Learning to discriminate individual letter shapes: best in a word

In order to read different words children must become aware of the different shapes of letters. They must learn to distinguish the perceptual shape of *o* from *c* from *d*, etc. One way this could be done is to try to teach children the names of the letters, 'ey', 'bee', 'see', etc. However, after learning some of the initial letters, *a*, *b*, and *c*, there is not much to interest a child in *p*, *q*, *r*, etc. Then, too, because focusing on the names of letters detracts from their symbolic function, which is to represent *words* of the language, such teaching should only be done after a number of whole words have been learned.

There are good reasons that, if letter names are to be taught, such teaching should be in the context of a whole word. Consider that for almost every other object in our world the orientation in space of that object does not change its value. For example, whichever way a shoe is placed – with the sole facing the floor, facing the ceiling, facing to the left, etc. – it is *still* a shoe. A hat is a hat and a rose is a rose no matter which way they are held ('object constancy', in Piaget's terms).

However, consider the letters b, d, p, q. Actually, each is composed of the *same* shaped object but what distinguishes them from one another is that object's orientation in space. In one position it is a 'bee', another a 'dee', and so on. Different orientations give different values. The same is true to a lesser degree for the letters u, n, and v, for m and w, and for s and z. This gives us a total of 11 letters (out of 26) that share the same shape with one or more other letters.

It is not surprising that when first given a word on a card the child will hold it in a variety of positions. What the child has to learn is the proper orientation of letters. This is best done through learning whole words. It is the whole word that provides the necessary context for the proper identification of these letters. (The first author has found that drawing a line under the letters of the word will help the child as to orientation, and placing a dot under the first letter will give the child a clue as to the directionality of the writing – the teacher or parent takes the child's index finger, places it on the dot, and then draws the finger along the line from left to right.)

Some children have more trouble than others in identifying letters out of context; often these are left-handers and ambidextrous (either hand) persons. Sometimes such children perceive mirror or reversed images of letters. Thus, when looking at letters in isolation, they will fall into many perceptual traps. Whole words will help avoid this by providing a context of other letters.

It is better to teach whole words and let children discover for themselves how to discriminate the shapes of the individual letters. Children could, for example, be given a number of whole words, three for instance, with each word written on a card, e.g. 'doggie', 'barked', 'auntie'. A duplicate of each of these words would also be made. All six cards would then be mixed up. Then the child can be asked if any two words are the same or different. Having children inspect different words, some of which are different and some of which are the same, is a good way to get them thinking about the different shapes of the letters. This is the same process of induction that children apply in segmenting whole speech words into phonemes and syllables in the learning of their native language.

3.2.2.6 Reading should involve only meaningful words, phrases, and sentences

Only the written forms of a word, phrase, or sentence for which the child knows the meaning in speech should be selected for teaching. This will make the learning of such words easier for the child. It is easy to avoid non-meaningful items because even the average 3-year-old child can understand over a thousand words in speech. This is a large enough stock to work with.

Those who advocate beginning the teaching of reading with whole words are divided on the question of whether whole-word teaching is sufficient. Gray (1948) believed that instruction on letter–sound correspondences should be given, after a large number of whole words were learned. Gates (1928), on the other hand, believed that whole-word teaching was sufficient, i.e. no other instruction was necessary.

Try to select personal items

In selecting written words, phrases, or sentences that are to be taught, it is not enough that such items be familiar to the child. It is also important that they relate to some sort of personal context, i.e. to objects, experiences, actions, situations, or events in the child's immediate environment, e.g. car, television, hot, drinking juice, going to the store. Items from stories which the child likes and is familiar with could also be included.

It is *not* advisable to teach isolated items or prescribed vocabularies, even though the child may know the meaning of such items. For, without a personal context, such items have relatively little interest for the child and consequently are more difficult to learn and remember. At times in the past, whole-word teaching was not as successful as it might have been because so often the items taught were not meaningful or did not relate to the child's personal and immediate life experiences.

3.2.2.7 Reading should not depend on teaching new language or new concepts

A reading programme should not include the teaching of language. If language is to be taught, it should be done in a curriculum component other than that of reading. There is more than enough material that a child can be taught to read without giving the child the additional burden of learning a new language, whether it be vocabulary or syntactic structure. A 3-year-old child, for example, has already acquired thousands of vocabulary items and understands a great number of sentences composed of those items. Rather than spending time teaching new vocabulary and other aspects of language, it would be better to teach the reading of those words and structures which the child already knows.

Although some understanding of language is necessary for the teaching of reading, a complete mastery is not. Partial language knowledge is sufficient. Instead, children are presented with written items for which speech equivalents are *already* known by them. There is more than enough to deal with without giving children additional and unnecessary burdens. Since children have already acquired a wide variety of concepts before being taught to read, there is no need to explicitly teach new concepts. Reading should always try to reflect that which has already been learned in speech.

It should be noted here that the recommendation to avoid teaching new language and concepts only concerns *reading*. The recommendation does not apply where, in the natural course of events, teachers explain new ideas and stimulate children to think. Such endeavours are natural and proper.

Learning alphabet letter names and the order of letters

So long as the child is interested in the names of letters, one can go ahead with their teaching. Knowing the names of letters and their order, it should be recognized, has little to do with the reading process. Of course, such knowledge is useful in searching through a dictionary or in going through a set of files. But these are not activities that young children are likely to engage in.

There is some empirical evidence that children *can* learn to read whole words *without* having any prior knowledge of the shapes or names of individual letters. In a reading programme in which *only* whole words were taught to pre-school children (2-, 3-, and 4-year-olds) over a period of about 4 months, the first author found that 17 children learned a mean of 16 words and two phrases or sentences although they were not able to identify any letters at all by name (Steinberg, 1980). One of these was a 3-year-old who learned 31 words and two phrases and sentences. Then, too, during this same period of time, one 4-year-old learned to identify as many as 86 words and 20 phrases and sentences, although he was only able to name three lower-case letters and five upper-case (capital) ones. He had picked up the names from a children's picture dictionary that was used in class; the teacher had only mentioned the letter names in passing.

3.2.2.8 Reading should be based on speech understanding and not on speech production

It is not necessary for children learning to read to be able to speak or enunciate clearly. Reading can be learned without speaking. For example, it is often observed that persons with speech disabilities, such as cerebral palsy, learn language and learn to read. These persons acquire language by listening to others speak, and they learn to read by associating that knowledge of speech language with written forms. Thus, whether or not a child can say 'dog' or 'hippopotamus' is not essential for the child learning to read (understand the meaning of) such items.

The case of a hearing-mute Japanese girl to whom reading was taught dramatically illustrates this principle (Steinberg and Chen, 1980). The girl (Rie) was mute since birth and was able to utter only a few sounds and a couple of recognizable words, 'papa' (father), and 'mamma' (a Japanese baby word for food). Because she could hear, Rie learned to understand language.

Rie was 3 years and 9 months of age when the teaching programme began. Over a period of 11 months, this girl learned to read at least 78 words, 47 being composed of complex *kanji* (Chinese characters) and 31 of *kana* (syllable symbols). These were words that she already knew the meanings of in comprehending speech. All the items that she learned were written on cards. To verify whether she knew any item, one just needed to say, for example, 'jitensha' (bicycle) or 'enpitsu' (pencil) and she would pick out the appropriate card. Or, if the card with the word written on it was shown to her, she would point to the object to which it referred. Only about 10 minutes per day had been devoted to her instruction.

While children do not have to produce speech in order to learn to read, it is important that they be able to understand the speech that is spoken to them. For, if the child knows what is meant when someone says 'TV', 'car', 'the red truck', and 'open the door', the child will have little difficulty in learning to read the written representations of such items. The first author's first son, who was slow to speak, learned to read many words, phrases, and sentences even before he was 2 years old and could not say them (Steinberg and Steinberg, 1975). A child who is not able to understand a speech word will have greater difficulty in learning the written representation of that word than the child who already understands the word in speech. In effect, this is teaching language through the medium of the writing system, which is something we proposed for deaf children in Chapter 2. Written items selected for teaching, therefore, should only be those that the child understands in speech.

3.2.2.9 Reading should not depend on the teaching of writing

While reading is essentially a skill in which only the eyes are used, writing requires, additionally, the use of the muscles of the hand. The muscles of the fingers must be precisely trained before they have the control necessary for producing written symbols. Because appropriate physical maturation and muscular development are prerequisites for writing and because such prerequisites do not develop early, young children have difficulty in controlling a writing implement, and they fatigue easily. (According to Steinberg and Yamada, 1980, children younger than 4 years have great difficulty writing.) Such difficulties, however, are not present for reading. The visual ability of the child develops before the first year, when the child learns to identify objects, faces, etc.

Children learning to write are usually trained by copying or tracing written figures that are present as models. However, the ultimate goal of writing is to be able to write meaningful messages when no written model is present, i.e. to write from memory. This being so, it must be realized that one cannot write from memory unless one has first acquired certain knowledge through perception, i.e. one must have stored in memory the visual shapes of particular words or letters, or have learned the orthographic rules for generating written symbols from speech.

It can be fun, though, for a child to try to write words which he or she knows. However, because writing involves a motor skill that requires fine hand coordination, which young children do not have, it is advisable that writing instruction be reserved for a later time when children have become fluent readers. Even then, however, reading should never be made contingent on writing progress, because reading can be learned much faster than writing.

At this point, it may be useful to bring together the essential relations of thought, language, reading, writing, and motor control that have been discussed or implied:

1. *Reading* derives from *speech understanding* and *vision*, not from speech production.
2. *Speech understanding* derives from *thinking* and *audition*.

3.2.2.10   Learning to read should be enjoyable

Reading should be made an enjoyable activity for children. This can be done by providing instruction in the form of interesting games and activities. As a consequence, not only will children learn to read, they will want to read. Children who are interested, intellectually stimulated, and who enjoy what they are doing will learn willingly and will not mind applying some effort. No teaching activity should be included that children find boring or tedious.

3.3   A universal four-phase reading programme

3.3.1   Four phases of the teaching programme

Children may be taught to read according to the four-phase programme developed by Steinberg (1980 and 1982). The programme embodies the underlying principles that were discussed in the previous sections. These phases are: (1) Word Familiarization; (2) Word Identification; (3) Phrase and Sentence Identification; and (4) Paragraphs, Stories and Book Reading. Each phase involves meaningful language and is ordered so that a preceding phase serves as a prerequisite for the succeeding one. Prior phases may be continued concurrently with succeeding phases, however. For example, Word Identification may continue even though the child is at the stage of the Phrase and Sentence Identification.

The essential ideas of each phase, along with a few illustrative games and activities, are offered below. (For more details concerning these phases along with a teachers' manual that includes a variety of reading activities, see Steinberg, 1980.)

Phase 1: Word Familiarization

The purpose of this phase is to acquaint children with the shapes of written words and to have them become aware that different spoken words of the language have different written manifestations. Children are not taught, however, which particular spoken word is associated with which particular written word. This is reserved for the next phase, Word Identification.

For instructional purposes, one should attach word cards to objects around the room, e.g. chair, television, wall, flower, and table. The words should be ones that the child understands when spoken by the parent or teacher. Such cards are placed at the child's eye-level wherever possible. Simply the exposure of such cards in the course of the day will, even without instruction, serve to promote learning.

A number of activities may be done with the word cards around the room. Three such activities, in sequential order of difficulty, are: Room Object Pointing, Word Card Sticking, and Room Object Matching. In Room Object Pointing, the child points to the written word and the object to which it is attached. Pointing to written words brings the words to the child's attention and gives them importance. The children will come to realize that different words are associated with different objects. The child is not required to learn which particular word goes with which particular object. In Word Card Sticking, the child is given a word card and asked to place it on an object that is named. Again, the child sees that different words go with different objects. This activity sets the stage for the next activity, the important one of Room Object Matching.

In Room Object Matching, the child is given a word card and is asked to find another like it. This obliges the child to inspect written words so as to determine whether they are the same or different. By doing this, the child becomes familiar with the shapes of letters and learns to look for their differentiating features. Since the task requires only that the child compare two forms at a time, both of which are present, and make a judgement of same or different, only short-term memory is involved. Other interesting variations of the matching activity may be devised. For example, two dice with the same words on each die, e.g. 'dog', 'girl', 'apple', 'cookie', 'run', and 'catch', could be rolled with the aim of getting a match.

Phase 2: Word Identification

In this phase, the child learns which particular written words are associated with which particular spoken words or objects. The difference between this phase and the preceding one is that this one requires the use of long-term memory. Here the child must store a particular visual configuration and remember what particular spoken word it represents. For example, when seeing the written word 'apple' in isolation the child is expected to be able to point to the object 'apple' (or its picture) or to say 'apple'.

Various games and activities can be devised to teach (and test) the child to identify particular written words. For example, word cards can be removed from objects in the room and the child could be asked to place them on the correct objects. A game could be made with a pair of dice, one die with pictures and the other one with words. The dice are rolled with the aim of getting a match in terms of picture and word.

Once the child begins to learn some written words, most of which will be nouns, then other types of words, particularly verbs and adjectives, should be introduced, e.g. actions ('run', 'touch'), colours ('red', 'yellow'), and states ('happy', 'angry'). Function words such as prepositions and articles should never be included. Such words should only be introduced in context through phrases and sentences. More abstract (but familiar and meaningful) words may be introduced ('good', 'friend'), and words can be written on demand from the child.

Phase 3: Phrase and Sentence Identification

This phase is similar to that of the preceding Word Identification one, except that larger linguistic units are dealt with. Its goal is for the child to read the largest basic linguistic unit, the sentence. In teaching phrases and sentences it is not necessary that phrase teaching precede sentence teaching. Rather, whichever unit is of interest for a particular situation is what should be taught, e.g. 'a big dog', 'Diane fell'.

The written phrase and sentence should include all words without any simplification, e.g. if 'That dog is barking at the boy' is the appropriate sentence, it should not be changed to 'Dog bark boy'. The presence of the other sorts of words such as 'that', 'is', and 'at', and the suffix '-ing', provides a learning opportunity for the child. In time, such morphemes will be learned without specific training. It is not necessary that the children always know how to read every key word (noun, verb, and adjective) in a phrase or sentence, before that unit is taught. However, to avoid learning problems, the number of unknown key words should be kept to a minimum.

It is best not to create phrases and sentences for their own sake but to make them fit the events and situations that occur in the immediate environment. For example, 'Diane fell', would be of great interest if indeed it was the case that Diane (the name of the child) did fall.

Phase 4: Paragraphs, Stories and Book Reading

The paragraph involves the largest meaningful written linguistic unit. It consists of a sequence of two or more sentences that are related to one another. A sequence of paragraphs can make a story. Learning to read paragraphs and books is probably the most interesting of all reading activities for children since there is an excitement that a story can generate that the reading of isolated words, phrases, and sentences cannot. As the child progresses in reading paragraphs and books, the books may have fewer pictures and more text. Thus, over time, there will be less dependence on pictures and more dependence on the text. It is the purpose of this phase to provide children with the knowledge and skills that will enable them to read text fluently.

- *Teaching short-paragraph stories.* Activities that involve short-paragraph stories may be introduced. For example, stories with as few as two or three sentences may be composed: Story A: (1) *Sara dropped the egg.* (2) *It landed on her brother's head.* Story B: (1) *The dog was hungry.* (2) *Harry didn't know what to feed it.* (3) *He gave it some bubble gum.* Each sentence of a story is written on a card. The task for the child is to arrive at an order of sentences so that they form a story. (The child may or may not be told the story beforehand.) Such an activity will foster in the child an awareness of order and the semantic relatedness of sentences.

- *Teaching book reading.* In teaching the reading of a book, the following is one good procedure: (1) Read the book to the child, with the child looking at the pages. Point to the words in a sentence while saying them. (The child must be exposed to the written and spoken word simultaneously.) Answer any questions; discuss the plot and characters. (2) After the book has been completed in this manner, return to the beginning of the book. This time, each sentence is read aloud and pointed to, one at a time, with the child asked to imitate this by doing his or her own saying and pointing. (3) After the book has been completed in this manner, return to the beginning. This time have the child do all of the saying and pointing. Give assistance when needed.

- *Book reading should always be done.* It should be emphasized that although the child is explicitly taught to read books at this stage in the teaching sequence, this is not to imply that the introduction of books should wait until this time. On the contrary, books should be read and stories told just as soon as a child can understand what is being said. The child should be able to see the written text and to watch the pointing out of words and sentences. Such activities will make the child familiar with the nature of books and build the child's interest so that the child will be prepared when text reading is introduced.

3.3.2 Results of the reading programme in the United States, Japan, and China: in the pre-school and in the home

To date, the four-phase programme has been administered in the United States to American children learning English, in Japan to Japanese children learning Japanese, and in the People's Republic of China to Chinese children learning Chinese. In all three of these countries, research was done with both pre-school groups and with children in the home. For the pre-school groups, the regular teachers did the teaching, following the directions of the first author. For the children at home, parents did the teaching, again under the guidance of the first author. The pre-school children ranged in age from 1 to 4 years. The home-taught children were between the ages of 1 and $2^{1}/_{2}$ years.

3.3.2.1 Research with English reading

In the home (Steinberg and Steinberg, 1975)

This research involves a single subject, the first author's first son. He and his wife began introducing words to him before he was 12 months of age. Prior to this the child had been given some alphabet familiarization pointing. He was also given the task of naming letters. He was so uninterested that he refused to stay with the task. He never did learn all of the letter names until a few years later by which time he was a good reader. In all later research studies conducted by the first author, such letter activities were dropped. Children learned faster as a result.

At 12 months of age he was able to correctly identify four written words, 'car', 'baby', 'boy', and 'girl' (without being able to say any of them), while at 24 months he was able to identify 48 words, phrases, and sentences, e.g. 'blow', 'cake', 'hooray', 'come on', 'I see', and 'Peter's room', although he could say only 15 of them. By $2^{1}/_{2}$ years of age he could read 181 different items, and at $3^{1}/_{2}$ years he could read short sentences in a text fluently and with natural intonation. On average about 10 to 15 minutes daily were spent in instruction.

At 4 years 11 months of age, standardized tests placed his reading at generally beyond the third-grade (8 years) level. (These tests and all of those noted below were independently administered by the Reading Center of the University of Hawaii.) Since he had only been taught reading at home, such findings may be attributed to the effects of the reading programme. The later findings show that he was able to maintain a lead of three or more grades in reading over his grade mates. At about 8 years old, and a third-grader, his reading achievement equalled or bettered sixth-graders on vocabulary and comprehension, and eleventh-graders on speed and accuracy. And when about 12 years old and a seventh-grader, he scored higher than most tenth-graders and equalled twelfth-graders (those in their year of graduating from high school) in terms of vocabulary, comprehension, speed, and accuracy.

In a pre-school (Steinberg, 1980)

The Steinberg reading programme was introduced to 2-, 3-, and 4-year-old children in one of the most disadvantaged areas on the island of Oahu in Hawaii. It was a short-term study. The teachers did the teaching under the guidance of the first author and his Chinese research assistant. During an average of 17.2 weeks of instruction with a mere average of 10 to 12 minutes of instruction daily, the children learned to read an average of 28.7 words and 6.3 phrases and sentences. Overall, the older children learned more than the younger children.

It is worth noting that one 3-year-old child who rarely spoke learned 29 words and 12 phrases and sentences during 20.4 weeks of exposure and that the highest achiever was a boy who learned 94 words and 41 phrases and sentences during 23.6 weeks of exposure. That the children achieved what they did, coming as they did from welfare families and living in neighbourhoods where the reading level in school is low, indicates the viability of the reading programme with all children.

3.3.2.2 Research with Japanese reading

In the home (Steinberg *et al.*, 1985; Steinberg and Tanaka, 1989)

The Steinberg four-phase reading programme was administered to three Japanese children in the city of Hiroshima. The parents spent about 15 minutes per day on average in teaching the children. The children were from two upper-middle-income families, two girls (sisters) and one boy. When the programme was initiated, the sisters were 18 months and 29 months of age while the boy was 20 months of age. The girls were more linguistically advanced, being able to utter sentences. The boy could only utter a few words although he could understand many words and some phrases and sentences.

During the first five months of the programme, the boy learned a remarkable total of 311 written words (Chinese character *kanji* and syllabic *kana*) and 62 phrases and sentences, while the girls learned 189 words and 86 phrases and sentences. (The progress of the girls is identical because the mother kept the older girl to the slower pace of the younger girl.)

The boy was in the Word Familiarization phase for the first seven weeks of the programme, and it was only at the eighth week that he began to identify particular items. In that week, he learned a surprising number of 46 words, 31 of which were *kanji*. In terms of his ability to say these items, his mother noted that in the early weeks of the Word Identification phase he could pronounce only a small number of the items. It was further noted that, after just the first few weeks of identifying words, he began to remember written items after just one or two presentations.

Similar findings were noted for the girls. After just one week of Word Familiarization, the girls began to identify their first words. They began with ten words the first week, five of which were *kanji*. Their progress was much more gradual and less explosive than the boy's. Evidently, there are great individual differences in children's rate of learning. Perhaps the reason for the boy's eight-week delay in identifying words as compared to the girls was that the boy did not realize as quickly as the girls did that written words represent objects in the environment. As soon as he did make this connection, his learning exploded, with 46 words being learned in one week, whereas for all the previous seven weeks, not a single word was learned.

After about two years, all three children were given a standardized reading test. Each child scored between grades 2 and 3 (7 and 8 years) in overall achievement on sentence comprehension and vocabulary. Their ages at the time of the testing were 4 years 2 months for the boy, and 3 years 11 months and 4 years 11 months for the girls. It should be noted that this test probably underestimates the true reading ability of the children since it was designed for more socially and cognitively mature children.

With Japanese in a pre-school (Steinberg and Sakoda, 1982)

A project involving the reading programme was introduced to a class of 2-year-olds and a class of 3-year-olds in a middle-income neighbourhood in Hiroshima.

Over the eight-month period during which the programme was applied, the following results were obtained. Both the 2-year-old and 3-year-old groups proceeded from the Word Familiarization to the Word Identification phase within the first month of the reading programme. During the eight-month course of the research, on average the 2-year-olds learned 97.3 words (71.0 of which were *kanji*) and 3.0 phrases and sentences, while the 3-year-olds learned a total of 99.3 words (81.3 being *kanji*) and 1.93 phrases and sentences. While the high degree of similarity might indicate that the learning capacity of the two age groups was much the same, it is the researcher's opinion that the 3-year-olds would have done much better had the quality of instruction for the older class been as good as that for the younger class. The teachers for the 2-year-olds were more lively and enthusiastic in their teaching.

3.3.2.3   Research with Chinese reading

In the home (Steinberg and Xi, 1989)

Three children from a variety of parental educational backgrounds were taught to read by their parents in their homes in Tianjin, China. There were one girl and two boys ranging in age from 2 years 2 months to 2 years 4 months. The children learned 140 or more character words in their first 15 weeks. The programme lasted nearly two years, during which time Ke-Ke (the girl) learned 401 characters, Bei-Bei (one of the boys) learned 293 characters, and Xia-Xia (the other boy) learned 270 characters. All were able to read simple books.

In a pre-school (Steinberg and Xi, unpublished)

Thirty 2-year-olds in one class were taught reading in a pre-school in Tianjin. The programme lasted nearly 11 months. The children varied greatly in their achievement. Some progressed to reading paragraphs and simple books while others were still at a sentence level. Unfortunately, detailed data are unavailable. Nonetheless, video footage taken by the first author on a number of visits to the pre-school substantiates conclusions made here.

3.3.2.4 Implications of results

The results of the English, Japanese, and Chinese studies provide evidence in support of the effectiveness of the four-phase teaching programme. The findings strongly indicate that the guiding principles and the teaching programme itself are optimal and universally applicable.

3.3.3 When a child is ready to read

A child is ready to read when the child can understand spoken words. This is all that is necessary. While it would make things easier for certain activities if the child could say the words, such a requirement is not essential; research with children who do not have speech or have problems in speech production shows this to be the case.

A child can be taught to read the words, phrases, and sentences that the child can understand in speech. For most children, this means that they are ready to read by the age of 2. By this age, children will have developed enough understanding of speech and will have gained sufficient knowledge of life so as to be able to participate in play activities and games for the reading programme.

While reading can be taught earlier than 24 months of age, we believe that, given the wide range of differences in children, a later age is a safer choice. This would avoid any potential for frustration on the part of the teacher/parent or the child. For younger children, prior to the inception of the teaching of reading, simply placing word cards beside objects and pictures will give the child some familiarization with the visual forms of words and letters. This can be beneficial.

3.4 The adantages of early reading for pre-school age children

The research cited above on teaching reading to pre-school age children, along with the studies of Fletcher-Flinn and Thompson (2000), Söderbergh (1971), Doman (1964), Fowler (1962), and Terman (1918), demonstrates that children can learn to read at a very early age. Of course, the degree of success depends on the method that is applied. The Steinberg teaching programme outlined above is applicable to all children over the age of 2. The focus on whole meaningful words in a personal context, with such items being taught through the medium of games and other interesting activities, will inevitably bring success.

It is worth noting that none of the reported successful studies on early reading used Phonics/Decoding-type methods. All used a Whole-Word approach. That such should be the case is not coincidental, for what these studies do is exploit the natural abilities that children have for the learning of reading. As explained above, most 2-year-olds are ready to be taught to read.

Why early reading is beneficial

There are a number of important advantages of teaching reading to children in their pre-school years:

1. **Reading is a source of pleasure for the child.**   It satisfies and stimulates a child's natural curiosity and, as a source of knowledge, enriches the child. The earlier a child discovers this, the more enriched and more deeply attracted to reading the child will become.
2. **Love of reading is established.**   The warm supportive informal atmosphere of the home or the pre-school provides an excellent situation for learning. In such a situation, a positive attitude towards reading can be established without the difficulties that are often encountered in elementary school.
3. **Young children learn quickly and easily.**   They have a remarkable rote-memory learning ability and can easily acquire a multitude of written words. The older the children get and the poorer their memory (see Chapter 6 regarding memory), the more they require additional exposure and practice.
4. **The children grow up to be better learners.**   They will be able to read faster and with better comprehension than they would if they were to start reading later.

In addition to these advantages, there is another important general one. Children who learned to read early would not have to use time in elementary school learning to read. More time therefore could be devoted to the acquiring of other kinds of knowledge. This could have the effect of improving the educational level of children in all areas of knowledge. That being the case, early reading can significantly benefit the whole of society.

Chapter 4

Wild and isolated children and the critical age issue for language learning

It seems that people have always wondered about whether language is something that is as natural to humans as walking and smiling. They have also wondered whether, even without experiencing language, children are able to produce speech on their own. People are still very much interested in these and in other related questions as well, such as whether there is an age beyond which a person is unable to learn a first or a second language. Since ethical considerations today should deter scientists from conducting language deprivation experiments with children, scientists have been on the lookout for cases that occur naturally, so to speak, i.e. without their intervention, such as through peculiar circumstances or the perversity of human behaviour.

Over the past few centuries there have been a number of reported cases of children raised by wolves, dogs, pigs, sheep, and other animals. (A fascinating collection of such cases is described in Malson's 1972 book *Wolf Children*.) These children are known as wild or feral children. There are even more recent stories about children being raised by animals, such as the account of two girls raised by wolves in India (Singh and Zingg, 1942), and the recent cases of Ukrainian children who survived with dogs (discussed later in the chapter). On a different level, there are cases of children who have been kept in confinement or isolation by their parents or others, and consequently were not exposed to language. Studying such cases might provide insight into certain psycholinguistic questions.

4.1 Victor: the Wild Boy of Aveyron

Scientific investigation into the matter of wild children increased dramatically in January of the year 1800 when a boy was captured by hunters in the woods near the village of Saint-Sernin in the Aveyron district of France. (For detailed accounts of Victor see Lane, 1976, and Shattuck, 1981.)

The boy appeared to be 11 or 12 years old, was naked except for what was left of a tattered shirt, and he made no sounds other than guttural animal-like noises. He seemed to have survived on his own for years in the wild. Probably he had been abandoned originally, but at what age or by whom could not be ascertained.

4.1.1 Itard tries teaching speech but fails

Not long after, the boy's education was assigned to an eager educator, the creative and dedicated Jean-Marc-Gaspard Itard. Itard set up an ambitious programme with goals that included social as well as language training. The Wild Boy was given the name 'Victor' by Itard and his education began with intense work that involved a variety of games and activities that Itard designed to socialize Victor and make him aware of the world around him. These had a dramatic positive effect.

Speech training with Victor proved to be very frustrating for Itard. It centred around simply trying to get Victor to repeat some words and speech sounds. Victor first had to learn from where speech sounds were originating before he could associate such sounds with language. Eventually, Victor came to be able to distinguish speech sounds from other sounds in the environment and he was even able to differentiate the sounds of normal speech from the poorly pronounced speech sounds made by the deaf children in the institute for the deaf where he now resided.

Victor first learned to repeat the sound 'li', apparently his personal contraction of 'Julie', the name of the daughter of an assistant at the institute, Madame Guérin. In addition, he would repeat the phrase 'Oh Dieu!' (Oh God!), which he picked up from Madame Guérin. He also learned to say the word for milk (*lait* in French). With regard to this word, however, Itard noted that Victor would generally repeat it when given milk, but would not really use the word in a communicative sense, such as in asking for milk. On the other hand, Victor was able to comprehend speech in the form of commands for household chores, and made a specific sound each time he wanted a wheelbarrow ride. It was not clear, though, that the means of communication was actually language rather than simply the recognition of environmental context.

4.1.2 Itard tries reading and writing with success

Itard decided to abandon attempts to teach Victor language by speech imitation and moved on to another of his goals, to sharpen the boy's perceptual abilities. He embarked on a programme of having Victor learn to match colours and shapes, and then match drawings with the objects they represented.

Following an insightful idea, he then set about teaching Victor the letters of the alphabet using letters on individual cards. The boy learned the milk word *lait* again, but this time in the form of alphabetic letters. Victor was able to spell it out, at first backwards, then upside down, since that is how he had first seen it from across the table. Of his own accord, he later picked out those letters and seemed to use them to spell out a request for milk when he was taken on a visit by Itard to a friend's home. However, it is possible that Victor may have simply been showing off his new toys, the cards, to Itard's friend.

Eventually, Victor did make progress in reading. Initially, Victor took written words such as 'book' to mean a specific object, a particular book, and eventually he learned to associate the words with classes of objects, in this example, all books. (Note that although the words are written here in English, it is French spelling that is implied.)

Victor also went through some of the same problems of overgeneralization that ordinary children go through in learning language, considering, for example, a knife to be 'razor'. He learned adjectives such as 'big' and 'small', 'hot' and 'cold', and a variety of colour words. He also learned verbs such as 'eat', 'drink', 'touch', and 'throw'. Each of these words was written on a card for him. In the beginning, he communicated with others using the word cards. Later he was able to write the words himself, from memory.

In less than a year, Itard was able to issue a report stating, in effect, that Victor's senses, memory, and attention were intact, that he had the ability to compare and judge, and that he could read and write to some extent. Victor's speech did not improve, however, and it was speech that Itard was concerned with. Unfortunately, he did not follow up on teaching reading, which could have benefited Victor greatly.

4.1.3   Itard tries again at speech, fails, then gives up

Itard devoted five years to Victor. Near the end of that period, he tried once again to teach the boy to speak. These attempts failed too; soon afterwards Itard decided to end his work with Victor. He arranged for Victor to live in a house with Madame Guérin. Victor lived there for 18 years, continuing to be mute until his death in 1828 at the age of about 38.

The interested reader is urged to view the excellent movie, *The Wild Child*, (its original French title is *L'Enfant Sauvage*), made by François Truffault in 1969, which portrays the story of Itard and Victor.

4.2   Genie: raised in isolation

4.2.1   Genie is discovered at 13 years of age, brutally abused

While the case of Victor may have been that of simple child abandonment, it is quite different from enforced seclusion, where children are isolated from even the outside environment and mistreated. One such well-documented case is that of a girl whom researchers called Genie (Curtiss *et al.*, 1974; Fromkin *et al.*, 1974; Curtiss, 1977, 1981; Rymer, 1993).

Genie (a pseudonym) was discovered in the early 1970s in the Los Angeles area of California. She was 13 years old and had been locked in a small room in her house by her father for the preceding 12 years! During the day she had been kept naked except for a harness that held her to an infant's toilet seat. At night she was put into a restraining sleeping bag and placed in a covered crib that was in effect a cage. She was fed but never spoken to. Her father beat her frequently with a wooden stick and growled at her like a dog while doing so. Other than a couple of plastic raincoats, empty thread spools, an occasional magazine, and some empty containers that she was given to play with, she had nothing much to look at (the small windows in her room were covered by curtains), little to touch, little to do.

Genie's mother eventually escaped, taking the child with her. It was in this way that the case was discovered by the authorities. As for the father, he committed suicide on the day he was to be put on trial for mistreating the child.

At the time of her discovery, Genie was in a pitiful physical condition and appeared to have no language. Based on the information later provided by her mother, *the girl had started to begin to acquire language just prior to her confinement, when she was around 20 months of age*. This is about the same age that Helen Keller (discussed later in this chapter) lost her hearing and vision. However, if Genie had learned to comprehend some basic elements of speech, she would have likely lost them after 12 years of living in silence.

4.2.2 Genie is given freedom and care

Like Victor, during her first few weeks of freedom Genie was alert and curious. But, unlike Victor, she displayed some ability to understand and even imitate (although poorly) some individual words, such as 'mother', 'red', and 'bunny'. However, except for such words, she had little if any comprehension of grammatical structures (Fromkin *et al.*, 1974, p. 87). Generally, she responded only to gestures and to the intonation of words. Batteries of psychological tests indicated that her cognitive abilities were little more than those of a 2-year-old, with her language displaying many of the characteristics of 2-year-olds as they go through the initial stages of language learning.

After just a few months of care, however, Genie changed considerably. She grew, gained weight and strength, and was able to go on long walks. While her original speech production had been limited to a few utterances such as 'No-more' and 'Stoppit', by the end of a few months she had acquired the words for hundreds of objects! She had an intense curiosity about the names of things in the world around her.

4.2.3 Genie responds linguistically and socially

After about a year had passed since she was first discovered, Genie was evaluated again on her language ability (Curtiss, 1977). She was tested, for example, on a variety of syntactic structures, such as her understanding of simple negation, and could respond correctly to sentences like 'Show me the bunny that does not have a carrot' as opposed to 'Show me the bunny that has a carrot'. She was tested on her understanding of adjectives, such as 'big' and 'little' ('Point to the *big* circle'). She was required to place objects with respect to other objects, e.g. 'in', 'under', 'next to', 'behind', to see if she understood the relationships expressed by those prepositions. It was found that Genie's ability to understand speech had improved quite rapidly, although her progress in speech production was very slow and continued to be slow.

4.2.4 Genie reaches a peak in language learning

Genie's language learning was studied for about eight years, after which time she made little progress. Her language ability, both in terms of understanding and production, remained well below normal and her speech continued to be ungrammatical. Genie, like Victor, was not able to acquire a normal level of language despite receiving a great amount of care, attention, instruction, and linguistic input.

Genie was finally placed in a home for retarded adults, where she now lives (Rymer, 1993). This was the end of the scientific collection of data on Genie's linguistic or other development. (The interested reader is urged to view the fine televison programme concerning the Genie case produced by NOVA, Public Broadcasting (PBS) in the USA, available on videotape under the title, *Genie: Secrets of the Wild Child*.)

4.3 Isabelle: confinement with a mute mother

4.3.1 Isabelle's background

Mason (1942) reported a case that concerned a child, Isabelle (a pseudonym), who, because of her confinement with a mute mother, did not begin to learn language until she gained her freedom at $6^1/_2$ years of age.

The mother of Isabelle had sustained a brain injury at the age of 2, and as a result never developed speech. According to Mason, 'She was wholly uneducated. She could neither talk, nor read, nor write, but communicated with her family by means of crude gestures of her own origination' (p. 295). When she was 22, the woman had a child, Isabelle. 'During the period of her pregnancy, and for six and a half years after the child's birth, the mother and child had apparently been locked in a room behind drawn shades' (p. 295). The mother finally escaped, taking Isabelle, and it was then that Isabelle's case was brought to the attention of the authorities. This led to Isabelle's admittance to the Children's Hospital in Columbus, Ohio, in November of 1938. Mason was assistant director of the Speech Clinic of the hospital and she undertook the task of trying to help Isabelle.

4.3.2 Isabelle's progress

Isabelle's first attempt at vocalization came just one week after Mason's first visit with her. The child's first spoken sounds were approximations of 'ball' and 'car' in response to being shown a ball and a toy car and being prompted by Mason through gesture to try and say the words.

In less than three months after her entrance to the hospital, Isabelle was producing sentence utterances! We find this entry in Mason's journal:

> Feb. 8, 1939. [Isabelle] says the following sentences voluntarily: That's my baby; I love my baby; open your eyes; close your eyes; I don't know; I don't want; that's funny; top it – at's mine (when another child attempted to take one of her toys).
> (p. 301)

After just one year, 'Isabelle listens attentively while a story is read to her. She retells the story in her own limited vocabulary, bringing out the main points' (p. 302). After a year and a half, the report of a student teacher working with Isabelle noted that the child's questions now included complex structures such as, 'Why does the paste come out if one upsets the jar?' and 'What did Miss Mason say when you told her I cleaned my classroom?' (p. 303). We find represented in these sentences WH questions (why, when, etc.) with the auxiliary 'do', embedded sentences, conditional conjoining, and proper tensing!

Thus, after only 20 months, Isabelle 'has progressed from her first spoken word to full length sentences . . . [and] . . . intelligent questioning' (p. 303). Truly, this was a remarkable achievement. And so different from the outcomes with Victor and Genie. Unfortunately, no further reports on Isabelle's progress are available to our knowledge.

4.4 Chelsea: began to learn language at age 32

4.4.1 Misdiagnosed as retarded, not deaf

Another case in an entirely different context is that of a girl, Chelsea (a pseudonym), who only began to learn language at the age of 32! When she was born, Chelsea's family thought that she was deaf. Initially misdiagnosed as retarded, and because she lived in a rural area in Northern California, she did not receive any language training or instruction of any kind. Unlike Victor and Genie, Chelsea grew up in a loving family environment.

When, at the age of 32, her hearing was properly tested, it was discovered that she was not totally deaf but only partially hearing-impaired. Hearing aids were fitted to correct for the impairment and with them she was able to hear speech relatively normally.

4.4.2 Language development

Through language instruction, Chelsea has developed an extensive vocabulary. Unlike Genie, though, her syntactic profile appears to lack any word order. Curtiss (1989) provides examples of the utterances Chelsea has produced. Some of these are:

The small a the hat.	Richard eat peppers hot.
Orange Tim car in.	Banana the eat.
I Wanda be drive come.	The boat sits water on.
Breakfast eating girl.	Combing hair the boy.

The girl is come the ice cream shopping buying the man.

(pp. 119–20)

Though Chelsea has developed rapidly in vocabulary and the use of language in a wide range of speech acts (complaints, requests) and social rituals (greetings), she was unable to form grammatically correct utterances and to remain on topic. Evidently, since that time there has been improvement, since Chelsea, who is now about 50 years old, has held a job where she does some reading and writing. She interacts socially and is independent.

4.5 Helen Keller: the renowned deaf and blind girl

4.5.1 Becomes deaf and blind at 19 months then secures a teacher

Any discussion of language deprivation cannot be considered complete without the case of Helen Keller (1880–1969). Keller was born normal and then, due to illness, she became deaf and blind at the age of 19 months. Thus, before tragedy struck, she had already experienced some degree of language learning and would probably have had some degree of comprehension and production. That was the extent of her language exposure until six years later in 1887, at age 7, when Anne Sullivan Macy came to teach her language. Macy, herself partly blind and only 21 years old, was engaged by Keller's parents on the recommendation of Alexander Graham Bell.

Before becoming famous as the inventor of the telephone (and after, as well), Bell was a noted educator of the deaf, as was his Scottish father before him. Bell's mother and his own wife were deaf. Bell was, therefore, quite familiar with deafness and the problems involved in deaf education. (See Chapter 2 for more on Bell's involvement in deaf education.) Helen's case was more complex, though, since she was blind as well. On the frontispiece of this book Helen is shown communicating with Bell by hand signals while she is also communicating with Sullivan Macy by touching her lips and vocal chords with her hands.

4.5.2 Helen learns language

In spite of Keller's seemingly overwhelming sensory handicaps, Sullivan Macy's efforts to teach Helen language through the sense of touch were successful. (Sullivan Macy was trained at the Perkins' Institute for the Blind in Boston and it was there that she learned communication techniques in teaching blind–deaf persons.) Thus, Helen learned language through touch and later even learned to speak. This was accomplished by Helen's directly touching the speech articulators around the face (mouth, lips, vocal cords, throat, etc.) of Sullivan Macy and others (see frontispiece photo of Bell, Keller and Sullivan Macy).

Even though Helen was unable to hear and receive any auditory feedback of her own speech, she nevertheless was able to produce speech even though she could not receive any auditory feedback. (She may have retained some of the speech ability that she had acquired prior to her illness.) While recognizable, her speech was somewhat strange, since she spoke in a high-pitched monotone manner (similar to that of the high-pitched voice of Genie). Helen went on to learn to read and produce Braille.

Keller's (1903/1972) autobiography, *The Story of My Life*, is fascinating to read. That dramatic moment when she learned her first word is movingly described:

> [My teacher] brought me my hat, and I knew I was going out into the warm sunshine. This thought, if a wordless sensation may be called a thought, made me hop and skip with pleasure. We walked down the path to the well-house, attracted by the fragrance of the honeysuckle with which it was covered. Someone was drawing water and my teacher placed my hand under the spout. As the cool water stream gushed over one hand she spelled into the other the word w-a-t-e-r, first slowly, then rapidly. I stood still, my whole attention fixed upon the motions of her fingers. Suddenly I felt a misty consciousness as of something forgotten, a thrill of returning thought; and somehow the mystery of language was revealed to me. I knew then that w-a-t-e-r meant the wonderful cool something that was flowing over my hand. That living word awakened my soul, gave it light, hope, joy, set it free!
>
> (1972, pp. 11–12)

The essential aspect of language, that a sound, sign, or touch could represent an object, had been discovered. It is significant that although Helen had no words for the situations and events that she describes prior to her learning of her first word, she was able to think clearly about her life and then to write about it later. (This bears on the issue that is discussed in Chapter 9, which is whether language is necessary in order for persons to think.)

Keller went on to graduate from Radcliffe (the Harvard University division for women in those days) with honours and to become an acclaimed lecturer and writer in the service of handicapped people around the world.

How is it that Keller was able to attain the level of language excellence that she did? It might be argued that Keller's success in language learning was beneficially affected by the relatively short encounter she had with speech in her infancy. This may be so to some extent. However, the fact that, after the lengthy six-year period of not being exposed to language, it took as long as it did for her to learn her first word, 'water', suggests that her pre-illness exposure to language was of minimal benefit.

4.6 Oxana and Edik: raised by dogs

Abandoned children are still being found. Two cases of children being cared for by dogs have been recently reported in Ukraine.

4.6.1 Oxana

In 1991, a girl, Oxana, was discovered living in a kennel in the back garden of the family home in a town in Ukraine. She was born in 1983 and her medical history reported her to be a healthy child. However, her parents were alcoholics, and one day 3-year-old Oxana was simply left outside. Looking for shelter, she crawled into a dog house, and for the next five years a dog helped her survive, undoubtedly, by providing her with food and warmth.

When Oxana was found, she behaved and moved around on all fours like a dog. She mostly barked, could hardly speak, and did not seem to think that speaking was necessary. At the time of this writing Oxana is 19 years old, and lives in a home for the mentally ill. Her speech has improved, she can now talk in simple sentences, but she has difficulties relating to people. Like the cases of Victor and Genie, Oxana's development seems to come to a limit and progresses no further. Her doctor, Vladimir Nagorny, comments that they have been trying to find her an occupation and teach her how to live among people, but most likely she will never be considered a normal person again.

4.6.2 Edik

In 1999 in a small town in Ukraine, social workers found 4-year-old Edik in a deserted apartment. It turned out that his mother was an alcoholic, too, and though she stayed in the apartment from time to time, she hadn't cared for the boy since he was 2 years old. He had to turn to stray dogs for survival. Two years after his discovery, Edic was living in a foster home. His language skills and grammar improved, but slowly. At the age of 6, his speech was like that of a 3-year-old. James Law, Professor of Language and Communication Studies, City University, London, studied Edik and remains optimistic about his language progress; Edik's social skills, however, are likely to remain impaired, he says.

4.7 A critical age for first-language learning?

4.7.1 Why did only Isabelle and Helen fully learn language?

Why is it that Isabelle and Helen learned language to the full but Victor, Genie, and Chelsea did not? Why didn't Victor, Genie, and Chelsea learn more than they did, particularly considering their teachers' dedication to their welfare and their use of evidently sound educational ideas? One thing is certain, and that is: without exposure to language, children will not acquire language. Children need some form of exposure, be it in the form of speech, signs, writing, or touch, before language learning can occur and that exposure should be offered as early as possible in the child's life.

4.7.2 Two major factors governing language learning

In reviewing the details of the cases of Victor, Genie, Isabelle, Chelsea, and Helen, we can identify two major factors that could have operated to influence their varying success in language learning. These relate to exposure to language and the extent of non-linguistic trauma: (1) the age at which exposure to language began, and (2) the extent of any physical, psychological, and social trauma prior to exposure to language.

As far as Victor is concerned, we do not know why he had been roaming alone in the wild, nor do we know whether he had experienced any language prior to his capture. It may be that for most, or all, of the estimated 11 or so years of his life, his exposure to language and to ordinary human life had been minimal. However, he could have had some exposure to language before his abandonment. But why he was abandoned will never be known, although there is the possibility that he could have been regarded as retarded. He could not have been very retarded, for, as Malson

(1972) has argued, at least average or better intelligence is necessary for one to be able to survive in the wild.

Barring the unlikelihood of his being raised by animals, Victor must have been raised by humans, at least in infancy, for some period of time. Because we have no information regarding such crucial circumstances, there is no way we can state with any assurance why Victor was not able to attain full competence in speech or written language. Whether Victor was or was not normal at birth is something that we shall never know. Lenneberg (1967) was undoubtedly correct when he said, 'In the absence of information on such a point, virtually no generalization may be made with regard to human development' (p. 142).

4.7.3 Why did Genie not progress more than she did?

Genie, at 13 years, was about Victor's age (11 or 12 years) before she was exposed to language. Nevertheless, despite over 11 years of isolation, she was able to develop a much higher level of language than Victor; her achievement was mainly in the area of speech comprehension. Genie's accomplishment in this respect establishes that, if there is a critical age for acquiring the fundamentals of a first language, i.e. grammatical structures, grammatical rules, and vocabulary, the limiting age cannot be very young, for Genie was over 13 years old when she began to learn language.

However, there is still some controversy over Genie's accomplishments. Although Curtiss, after years of collecting data on Genie, concludes, 'She had a clear semantic ability but could not learn syntax' (Rymer, 1993, p. 156), other researchers disagree. Jones (1995) argues that inconsistencies in the presentation of the data on Genie call into question the exact extent of her progress in acquiring English syntax. Yet Genie's attained level of speech *comprehension* was significant. It is certainly beyond that which would be expected if there really were a critical age for the learning of syntax.

That Genie's speech production ability was faulty in terms of pronunciation may be related to factors that operate in the learning of second-language pronunciation by ordinary people (see Chapter 6), where it has been found that the ability to control certain muscles of the body, in particular the articulators of speech (the tongue, mouth, vocal cords, etc.), generally begins to decline around 10 to 12 years of age. The fact that Genie had not used speech from infancy until she was 13 years old probably put her at a greater disadvantage than would be the case for a typical second-language learner of the same age. At least the ordinary second-language learner would, in using his or her first language, have had the benefit of exercising the articulators of speech for over a decade. Then, too, we cannot be sure that Genie's poor speech ability was not the result of some negative psychological influence due to her long mistreatment.

4.7.4 Chelsea: insufficient evidence

Curtiss (1989) argues that Chelsea's case demonstrates that, beyond a critical age for learning, syntax cannot be learned but that other aspects of language are *not* affected, such as vocabulary and the proper use of language in context (pragmatics). This view is not substantiated. The crucial data for critical age lie in syntactic understanding and not production. Chelsea's abilities in this regard were not adequately assessed, as far as we can tell.

4.7.5 The achievements of Isabelle and Helen

The language achievements of Isabelle and Helen contrast sharply with those of Victor and Genie. Why were these two girls able to do so well? The fact that Helen had been exposed to language during her first 19 months of life is not likely to have been the deciding factor because Isabelle did quite well even though she had no exposure to language before she was discovered at 6½ years of age. One thing Helen did have that some of the other children did not is a loving family. Even during her period of language deprivation, she was a member of a family who did their utmost on her behalf so that she could enjoy life. Isabelle, too, although she was confined with her mother, could benefit from the affection that her mother had for her. So, the critical variable here may be the affection and social support which both Helen and Isabelle were able to experience. This may have allowed them to develop intellectually despite their language deprivation.

Some consideration might be given to the use of a form of communication through gesture that Isabelle and her mother used. Deaf children have been known to develop their own sign-language systems complete with rudimentary syntax even when they have no exposure to formal sign language (Goldin-Meadow and Mylander, 1998). The gesture system used between Isabelle and her mother *may* have helped Isabelle to understand and learn the relationship between object and symbol crucial for language learning.

4.7.6 Is there a critical age for first-language learning?

Most significant for the Critical Age hypothesis is the fact that Isabelle and Helen started to learn language at an *early age* following a relatively short period of deprivation: language exposure and teaching began for Isabelle at 6 years old and for Helen at 7 years. On the other hand, Victor and Genie, who were almost twice as old as these girls when discovered, did not learn as much language as Helen and Isabelle did, nor did Chelsea. This could be, as some theorists, such as Lenneberg (1967), have suggested, due to the biological maturation of the brain.

In any case, to rely only on the cases of Victor, Genie, and Chelsea to make a case for critical age is surely not warranted. There are too many unknown factors and the data, particularly for Genie and Chelsea, are not clear. Certainly, the critical age, if there is one, could not be much younger than 6 or 7 years since that would exclude Isabelle and Helen, who in fact did learn language after that age. Clearly, the ideal experimental situation for studying the problem of a critical age for first-language learning has not yet presented itself. Let us hope for the sake of some poor child that it never does.

Chapter 5

Animals and language learning

Human beings have language, but what about animals? Do apes, dolphins, or other creatures have language and use their language to communicate with one another as we do? How about household pets? If they don't have their own language, can we teach them some sort of human language? But if they cannot learn human language, would this mean that they are lacking in intelligence, or would it mean that they lack physical structures that only humans are born with?

Curiosity and fantasy are the stuff that motivates scientists. Such fantasies are reminiscent of Hugh Lofting's famous children's stories of Dr Doolittle, the doctor who could speak the languages of all the animals in the world. This, for example, is the dream of one noted animal researcher:

> I had . . . incredible fantasies about the possibilities of ape language. One of them was that I could go to some section of Africa where there are chimps in the wild and have Nim (the chimp to whom I taught sign language) serve as an interpreter for kinds of communication that are unknown to humans. That is, I would ask Nim, 'What is that chimp over there saying to the other chimp?' and Nim would explain it to me in sign language.
>
> (Terrace, 1983)

We shall begin with a review of research that attempts to teach language to apes, a Pongidae primate family that includes chimpanzees, gorillas, and orangutans and is the most highly developed form of primate life next to humans.

5.1 Teaching spoken English to apes

5.1.1 The first scientific attempt: with an orangutan

The earliest-known scientific attempt at teaching language to an ape was that of Furness (1916) in the USA, who attempted to teach an orangutan to speak. The brief four-month project ended in tragedy, when the animal died with a high fever while repeating the two words it had learned to say, 'papa' and 'cup'. Later more comprehensive scientific attempts to teach speech to animals were made with chimpanzees. These were conducted by psychologists in the 1920s through the 1940s by two separate husband-and-wife teams, the Kelloggs (1933/1968) and the Hayes (1951). Let us now consider their research.

5.1.2 Gua: the chimp raised with a human 'sibling'

Winthrop and Luella Kellogg (Kellogg and Kellogg, 1933; Kellogg, 1968) raised a female chimp named Gua along with their own son, Donald. Their idea was that by giving the chimpanzee the same input and social interaction as a human child, the chimpanzee would learn language in the same way that the human child learns its first language.

Gua, a female, and Donald, the boy, were born less than three months apart, with Gua being the younger. For nine months they were raised in the home as siblings. Initially on problem-solving tests and tests of mental ability the two scored the same, but over time the boy surpassed the chimp. The Kelloggs noted that Gua demonstrated an exceptional ability to learn by imitation but that the boy was more versatile and continuous in his learning. Gua was raised in an ordinary speech environment with no specific language training being given. The Kelloggs wanted to see if Gua could learn language as ordinary human children do, where language training is not given.

Despite the similarities of their upbringing and physical and mental skills, Gua did not learn to say any words even though words were repeated numerous times to her in context. During the same time, however, the boy had become reasonably fluent in the spoken language, even being able to produce speech with some syntactic complexity.

However, the researchers reported that by 16 months of age, and over the period of nine months that she was with the family, Gua learned to respond appropriately to 95 spoken words, phrases, and sentences.

Her speech comprehension was, therefore, substantial. She could give appropriate behavioural responses to spoken commands like 'Lie down', 'No, no', 'Shake hands', 'Don't touch', 'Give it to Donald', 'Get down', 'Kiss Donald'. Quite an impressive achievement, even in the light of later studies, although it is not clear how well the Kelloggs controlled for environmental cues that could tip off the chimp as to the correct response.

The experiment was terminated, apparently when the researchers noted that Donald was picking up too much chimpanzee-type behaviour.

5.1.3 Viki: another chimp raised in a human household

Another of the home-rearing projects was that of Cathy and Keith Hayes (Hayes, 1951), who raised a baby female chimpanzee from infancy. The chimp was named Viki. Like Gua, Viki was treated as a full member of the family; she ate her meals at the table, played games at home, and went on outings. She was lively and bright.

Unlike Gua, though, Viki was given special speech training in pronunciation. However, despite the Hayes' efforts, in which they helped Viki to make the shapes of sounds with her mouth, after three years Viki had only learned to utter four words: 'mama', 'papa', 'up', and 'cup', and these were so poorly pronounced that they were hard to understand.

As far as speech understanding is concerned, Cathy Hayes (1951, p. 227) reports, 'Are there any words which Viki comprehends without need of supplementary cues? There are a few . . . She obeys the commands: "Go to your room", "Go outside" and "Go upstairs" without error.' This result is surprising compared to the much longer list of items that Gua could understand. Yet the Hayes did seem to be aware of the need to neutralize the effect of environmental cues when testing for speech comprehension. Even so, because chimps have a great ability to mimic and to read facial expressions and body language (Fouts and Mills, 1997; Savage-Rumbaugh *et al.*, 1998), special measures have to be taken to control such variables. Perhaps it is an oversight on the part of the Hayes, but they did not include the four words that Viki could say, 'mama', 'papa', 'up', and 'cup' (the first author viewed a videotape of their home movie). Perhaps Viki could say but did not know the meaning of these words, but this does not seem likely.

There is a great discrepancy in the two studies regarding the degree of chimp learning, with Gua learning so much more than Viki. Whether this could be due to the influence of Gua's 'sibling', Donald, is not clear. One thing though is clear: in both studies speech comprehension was well in advance of speech production, a fact that coincides with that of the human child language learner. A reading of their reports indicates that the researchers paid too much attention to speech production when much more could have been gained by focusing on speech comprehension.

5.2 Teaching sign language to the chimpanzee, gorilla and orangutan

5.2.1 Washoe: the first signing chimp

In 1966, another husband-and-wife team of psychologists, Allen and Beatrice Gardner (1969, 1975), began to teach sign language to a baby chimp, a female they called Washoe (rhymes with 'show'). They reasoned that any attempt to teach chimps to speak was doomed to failure because of the simple fact that chimps do not possess the necessary vocal apparatus for human speech. Viki's failure to learn to speak could plausibly be said to be a simple physiological failure and not a mental one. Since chimps are very adept at using their hands, the Gardners conceived of the idea of teaching them a simplified form of American Sign Language (ASL).

One of Washoe's early signs was 'open', which is expressed by a throwing out of the arms. After about four years with the Gardners, Washoe learned a vocabulary of about 130 signs and, according to the Gardners, displayed two- and three-word utterances, such as, 'Go sweet', when she wanted to be taken to the raspberry bushes, and 'Open food drink', when she wanted something out of the refrigerator. The two- or three-word length of utterance seems to be similar to that produced by human children around the age of 1 to 2 years. The Gardners, unfortunately, did not focus on comprehension.

The Gardners give the impression that the language of the signing ape and that of the signing child are very similar. In one study, they go so far as to claim the ape to be superior to the child. However, as Premack (1971, 1976) and other researchers have noted, after four years Washoe's achievement never advanced beyond its very elementary level. In contrast, by the age of 4, ordinary children have learned over a thousand words and they can comprehend and produce sentences on the basis of an abstract syntax that includes negations, questions, etc. Hearing-impaired children who have learned ASL from infancy also acquire a similarly high level of language knowledge.

Yet, despite the many years of training and exposure to sign language that Washoe experienced, she could not advance beyond an elementary level of human achievement. But even the claims for this elementary level have been questioned. Many of the gestures that the Gardners recorded as signs seem to have already been part of the chimpanzees' natural gesture system, such as shaking the hand at the wrist for 'hurry'. These gestures were among the most frequent of the signs used by Washoe and were often included in her two- and three-word utterances. Concerning such word combinations, it is not clear whether they were actual reliable syntactic combinations rather than single signs formed in close proximity to each other.

5.2.2 Loulis, son of Washoe, and a community of signing chimps

After a number of years, Washoe was moved to a facility in the state of Washington and became part of the research conducted by Roger and Debby Fouts (Fouts, 1973; Fouts et al., 1989), another research couple, who were working with a number of chimps. The Fouts regard their chimp subjects fondly and have established a primate reserve where chimps are taught some of the rudiments of human culture, such as using tools, for example, with the aim that they start their own community.

The Fouts' primary interest is in looking at how language may or may not develop in the social context of such a community. Thus, their emphasis is placed on creating the best environment for chimpanzees to develop conversations and not on teaching them syntax (Fouts, 1983a). One particular interest of theirs was Washoe's 'adopted' son, Loulis, who, they say, learned signs from Washoe (Fouts *et al.*, 1989).

However, Washoe's signs seem not to have been picked up by chimps other than Loulis, who unfortunately died when still very young. As yet, this line of research has not provided strong evidence for the creation and learning of signs from chimpanzee to chimpanzee.

5.2.3 Nim Chimpsky and the Chimpskyan revolution

The optimism of animal language researchers in the 1960s turned sour in the 1970s when Terrace (Terrace, 1979a, 1979b; Terrace *et al.*, 1979), a psychologist who was an early enthusiast of chimps being able to learn sign language, worked with a chimp that he named Nim Chimpsky. By giving the chimp this name, Terrace evidently set out to make a monkey out of Noam Chomsky by proving that animals *can* learn language. (It is a quote from Terrace that we used to start this chapter.) Chomsky has argued that only humans have language. Just who was made a monkey's uncle is the question we will now consider.

Like the Gardners, Terrace used a modified form of American Sign Language for teaching language to Nim. Initially he reported positive findings: 'I felt that I had the best evidence of anyone that in a very primitive sentence a chimpanzee could combine two or more signs according to a particular grammatical rule very much as a young child might' (Terrace, 1983). Examples of Nim's two-, three-, and four-sign sequences are 'more drink', 'tickle Nim', 'banana Nim eat', 'banana eat Nim', 'eat drink eat drink', and 'banana me eat banana'.

However, by the time the project ended, Terrace had radically changed his mind about Nim's grammatical abilities. After studying the research video tapes, Terrace concluded that Nim, knowing that he had to make signs in order to get what he wanted, would take some of what the teacher signed and give the appearance of producing structured two- or three-word utterances, without producing a consistent subject-verb or verb-subject word order. When Nim made longer utterances, Terrace says that all he was doing was mainly imitating what the teacher signed and adding words almost at random until he got what he wanted. (Terrace's examples in the previous paragraph seem to bear this out.) Terrace thus came to the conclusion that chimpanzees were capable of learning only a few of the most elementary aspects of language.

The most important clue as to why a chimpanzee does not advance to producing long utterances, in Terrace's view, is that its demands can adequately be taken care of with single words. This may not be true, though. For, as child language learning research shows, even though many of the demands of a small child can also adequately be taken care of by single words, they do advance beyond that single-word stage quite quickly. There must be more to the process of language learning than the simple satisfying of demands. The child seems to want to express ideas more clearly and unambiguously and for this it needs more than single-word utterances. Why wouldn't the chimp have such a motivation? It may, but it may be lacking in the intellectual ability to create longer utterances.

Some critics of Terrace's conclusions, such as the Fouts, say that the negative results of his experiments are not due to the limitations of the chimpanzees but rather are due to inadequacies in Terrace's experimental procedures. Nim was kept in a small room with a one-way mirror and drilled intensively for three to five hours a day by hundreds of different tutors at the expense of normal social and spontaneous interaction with caregivers. The confinement of Nim within a small room for the language learning sessions was meant to remove the effects of extraneous variables, variables which were not controlled for in other studies. Such an approach, the Fouts say, fails to get at the spontaneity of a good relationship between a researcher and an animal. According to Roger Fouts (1983b), 'We talk to people we like – and people we like don't ask us the same dumb questions 50 times in a row. We converse about things.'

However, here we may note that even in the cases of human children who are badly treated, but, spoken to, by their parents, such children, if they are not born with physical and mental defects, generally learn language. Nim, on the contrary, was treated with affection by his tutors. Thus, it seems likely to us that, even given the restricted language-learning situation in which Nim was placed, a human child would have mastered most or all of what was presented during the training sessions.

5.2.4 Teaching sign language to Koko, the gorilla

Francine Patterson (1978a, 1978b, 1980) reports remarkable results with the gorilla Koko, born in 1971, whom she has trained in American Sign Language and speech since 1972. Unlike Washoe, Koko received speech input from her trainers as well as sign. Teaching has consisted of ten hours per day of sign and speech exposure, with help in moulding the hands for sign making.

One interesting fact Patterson discovered was that Koko was productive in her sign language. Koko could make new words to describe new objects by combining previously known ones. Koko, for example, created 'eye-hat' for mask, 'white-tiger' for a toy zebra, 'finger-bracelet' for ring, and 'bottle-match' for a lighter. Human languages, of course, include similar devices for word-making, e.g. 'blackbird' in English and 'white bird' for swan in Japanese.

After four and a half years of instruction Koko had learned 132 sign words. After ten more years that total came to 500 or more. This is impressive compared to the achievements of the chimpanzees; it is below the level, though, of that of a 3-year-old human child, whose vocabulary is in the thousands. Interestingly, despite her large vocabulary, Koko's syntax has not progressed beyond the same elemental level as that of the chimpanzees who were taught language, i.e. two- or three-word utterances.

As far as speech is concerned, it is claimed that Koko is able to comprehend in speech whatever she can understand in sign (Patterson and Linden, 1981). As far as speech production is concerned, this was virtually zero. This is to be expected, given the gorilla's physiological limitations for speech articulation.

Koko is friendly and apparently tries to start up sign-language conversations with strangers. Sometimes she signs to herself when she is alone. For example, on a videotape of Koko that we have seen, Koko spontaneously made the sign for smoking while browsing through a magazine and coming across an advertisement for cigarettes. On the same tape, Koko also used signs to tell Patterson that someone was hiding behind a tree.

Such events contradict Terrace's claim that apes will sign only when they want something. Another of Terrace's claims, that apes will not attempt to give names to objects on their own, is also contradicted by Patterson's data, since Koko did create words such as 'eye-hat' and 'white-tiger' to describe newly encountered objects. On the other hand, we are sure Terrace would point out that while the extent of Koko's vocabulary is substantial, her syntax, like that of the chimpanzees, is quite rudimentary. Further testing, however, could show that Koko's syntax for *comprehension* might be more advanced.

5.2.5 Teaching sign language to Chantek, the orangutan

In the late 1970s, Miles (1983, 1990) started to teach American Sign Language to a male orangutan named Chantek, which in Malaysian means 'beautiful'. An orangutan was chosen for this research because they 'generally score higher on cognitive tests than do gorillas or chimpanzees' (Miles, 1983, p. 47). Miles's project differed from others that have focused on language; she was more concerned with the cognitive and communicative processes that might underlie language development. Chantek was not just trained to use signs but was immersed in a human cultural environment to learn the appropriate ways for behaviour and interaction. No attempt, though, was made to raise Chantek like a human child. Rather, his natural arboreal habitat was maintained to the extent possible at the research centre.

After seven years of interaction with his caregivers, Chantek learned to use a vocabulary of 140 signs that signify objects, actions, proper names, attributes, locatives, and pronouns. Miles (1990) states that in the second month of training Chantek began to combine signs into sequences spontaneously. An interesting observation that she noted concerned Chantek's use of the verb 'give' (and only this verb): Chantek was more likely to name a physical object first ('Object + give') if the object was present. But, he would produce a reverse order ('give + Object') if the object was not present. This word-order regularity appeared despite the absence of models provided by his caregivers. However, this reversal phenomenon was not found for any other verb or combination of words.

By 8 years and 3 months of age Chantek was inventing different signs, including 'no + teeth' to indicate that he would not use his teeth during rough play, and 'eye + drink' for the contact lens solution used by his caregivers (Miles, 1990). Overall, Chantek acquired vocabulary items but, like the other apes, little syntax. Chantek's general achievement was lower than that of Koko and was more like that of Washoe.

5.3 Teaching artificial languages to chimpanzees

5.3.1 Lana: the computer chimp

The Rumbaughs (Rumbaugh, 1977; Savage-Rumbaugh and Rumbaugh, 1978) (another husband and wife team!) taught the chimp Lana a simple artificial language called Yerkish (after the Yerkes' Primate Center). Lana was named after the research programme, which was called the LANguage Analogue project. Lana was just over 2 years old when the project began.

The language consisted of seven colours and nine geometrical shapes, which represented mainly objects and actions. These items were displayed on a large keyboard and the keyboard was connected to a computer in another room. Lana had to press certain keys in the right sequence to make requests and consequently receive desired items, e.g. 'Please machine give milk' or 'Please Tim give ball'. Lana learned hundreds of sentences in this fashion. She had names for people, food, objects, and even a special phrase 'that-which-is' to name things she did not know the name of. Once she even asked the trainer to leave the room after he had purposely mixed up one of her sentences to test her reaction!

However, Lana did not create sentences according to rule but learned them by rote, in a way similar to memorizing important whole sentences in a foreign language such as 'Where is the toilet?' More learning would be necessary for Lana to be able to create novel sentences.

Sue Savage-Rumbaugh herself believes that apes have but a limited ability for language acquisition. She says it is not likely that chimps might be able to talk about their dreams or tell us about how it feels to be a chimp. However, still the optimist, she goes on to say that while it is not yet possible to state what chimps might or might not be able to do, the possibility that they might be able to communicate new ideas remains. Her hope lies in improving teaching techniques. However, the fact that human children learn language without being taught, simply through being exposed to meaningful speech in conjunction with objects, situations, and events in the environment, suggests to us that the search for better teaching techniques is not likely to yield much better results.

5.3.2 Sarah: the magnetic plastic token chimp

An ingenious piece of research was one conceived by David Premack of the University of Pennsylvania involving a chimp by the name of Sarah.

Rather than using sign language or electronic keyboards, Premack (1970, 1971, 1976) gave Sarah 130 plastic tokens with magnets so that they could be manipulated easily by her and others. These included tokens for the names of colours such as 'red' and 'blue', for different fruits such as 'banana' and 'peach', and for actions such as 'wash', 'cut', and 'take', and some functions such as 'QUESTION'. A typical question that might be posed to Sarah was 'QUESTION banana red' (Is the banana red?), to which she would correctly answer 'no' by means of a token. The tokens would adhere to a metallic board.

Premack's research with Sarah makes it very clear that chimps are intelligent creatures. For example, Sarah had little trouble dealing with a feature once thought to be characteristic only of human language: displacement, i.e. the ability to talk about things that are not present. She was easily able to use her plastic tokens to request items that were not present, such as asking for fruit, e.g. 'Give banana'. When told 'brown colour of chocolate' (Brown is the colour of chocolate), she was able to learn the new word 'brown', thereby demonstrating that she could learn new vocabulary items by instruction through language! (She had already acquired the meaning of the abstract word 'colour', which is, in itself, a notable achievement.)

Other apes in Premack's research were also able to distinguish between strings of words differing only in word order, such as 'red on green' and 'green on red'. This clearly demonstrates that some syntax has been acquired, although this syntax is obviously of an elementary nature, since it involves only the order of nouns (in a locative relationship). Premack himself has taken the view that little more syntax than this can be learned by apes.

5.3.3 Kanzi: a pygmy chimp produces synthesized speech

A pygmy chimpanzee, or bonobo, is said by the principal researcher, Sue Savage-Rumbaugh (of Lana fame – see above), to be more similar to humans than to other apes in terms of evolution and with respect to communicative behaviours such as eye contact, gestures, and vocalizations

(Savage-Rumbaugh *et al.*, 1986). Such being the case, she and others believed the bonobo to be a better candidate for language research than the other apes that researchers had used. Thus it was that the bonobo male chimp, Kanzi, and his younger sister, Mulika, were selected for study.

In their training the researchers would point to a keyboard and speak in English in reference to objects, actions, locations that were of interest to the chimps. The lexigrams (visual word symbols) on the keyboard were made up of arbitrary geometrical symbols, each matching an object, action, or location. When touched, the lexigrams on the computer keyboard would produce synthesized English speech sounds for a particular word. Gestures and some sign-language signs were not taught but allowed to develop spontaneously. No attempt was made to teach language. Rather, in the way that children learn language, the bonobos were exposed to language during normal interaction.

Greenfield and Savage-Rumbaugh (1990) say that tiny Kanzi, when around 5 years old, learned over a period of five months to use grammar equivalent to that of a 2-year-old human child and had a vocabulary of about 250 words. It is also said that Kanzi has acquired grammatical rules that allow him to produce an infinite number of sentences (an extravagent claim, we must say) and even invent his own symbols and use them consistently. The researchers state that 'Kanzi showed an incipient ability to use difference in symbol order to signal difference in meaning' (Greenfield and Savage-Rumbaugh, 1990, p. 567). The word 'incipient' properly weakens the claim because symbol order may not have been acquired; strict scientific controls, particularly regarding knowledge of the world, were not employed.

It seems, therefore, that Savage-Rumbaugh's comparison of Kanzi's comprehension level to that of a human $2^{1}/_{2}$ years old (Savage-Rumbaugh *et al.*, 1998) is unwarranted until stricter testing is done. It cannot be concluded that Kanzi has demonstrated any greater acquisition of language than the apes in other language studies. Why Kanzi's younger sister Mulika has yet to achieve results equal to those of Kanzi is not explained.

5.4 Teaching language to dolphins

5.4.1 Elvar: the whistling dolphin

There is much anecdotal lore about the intelligence of dolphins and whales. Until the 1960s, though, no scientific attempt had been made to determine their communicative abilities. In one of the first studies, Lilly (1962, 1965) tried to teach a dolphin to force air through its blow-hole in such a way that it would allow the dolphin to imitate human speech sounds. A young male dolphin named Elvar produced approximations of the word 'squirt', which Lilly had been trying to teach him to pronounce. Lilly also claimed that

Elvar interchanged human sounds with dolphin sounds as if he were attempting to translate, but Lilly provided no scientific substantiation in this regard. In fact, pronunciation difficulties were so great that Lilly was obliged to discontinue the study. He then moved on to investigate the means by which dolphins communicate with one another.

Notwithstanding Lilly's extravagant claims to the contrary (including claims that dolphins have an intelligence and a religion(!) that is superior to those of humans), research has yet to show that these animals use anything as complex as what we could call language.

5.4.2   Akeakamai and Phoenix: learning artificial languages through sight and sound

A radically different and more scientific approach to the teaching of language to dolphins was later initiated by Louis Herman at the Dolphin Institute, University of Hawaii. In an early study, rather than have dolphins mimic human sounds, Herman and his associates (Herman and Wolz, 1984) trained a bottlenosed dolphin to mimic computer-generated sounds.

The dolphin not only demonstrated that it could learn to make new whistles but also that it could apply these whistles to the naming of objects such as 'ball', 'hoop', and 'frisbee'. This is similar to the apes' abilities to name objects through sign language or computer symbols. From this production-oriented research, Herman then turned his attention to the primary process of language comprehension. In his investigation of the dolphin's language comprehension, Herman and his associates (Herman *et al.*, 1984) conducted experiments using two different types of artificial languages, one involving sounds, the other involving visual gestures, i.e. signs. He wanted to see if, or how well, dolphins could learn to comprehend language. This was done not only to see if the animal could learn a human-created language system, but also to discover more about the cognitive abilities of dolphins.

In 1979, a teaching programme was begun with two dolphins, Phoenix and Akeakamai (the latter's name meaning 'lover of wisdom' in the Hawaiian language). Each dolphin learned one of the two artificial languages. Akea was taught the gesture-based language, while Phoenix was taught the sound-based language. Each was taught a vocabulary of about 30 words, mainly names of objects, agents, actions, and modifiers. The sound-based language had its sounds projected underwater into the dolphin tank. These sounds were controlled by Herman and his assistants from their underwater laboratory, which had a window view into the tank.

The visual language of gestures, invented by Herman and his colleagues, involved the use of the trainer's arms and hands. The trainer stood by the side of the tank out of the water where he or she could be seen by the dolphin. The trainer would place and move his or her arms in different positions as in a sort of semaphore signal system. To avoid the unconscious giving of helpful cues to the dolphins, the trainers wore opaque goggles so that the dolphins could not see their eyes. The two dolphins learned to carry out correctly a number of commands in the water. The commands consisted of two-, three-, four-, and even five-word sequences, with each command constructed on the basis of object and action words. Thus, 'window tail touch' is to be interpreted as 'Touch a window with your tail'. The basic sentence structure was of the Subject–Object–Verb variety.

Of special interest are Herman's results, which show that generally the dolphins correctly responded to what are often called 'semantically revers- ible sentences', i.e. sentences for which the subjects and objects cannot be interpreted by meaning alone but where the use of syntactic knowledge is required. For example, the English sentences 'Jack pushed Tom' and 'Tom pushed Jack' describe two different events, one in which Jack is doing the pushing and another in which Tom is doing the pushing. Given our lack of knowledge about Jack and Tom, we can only judge that either event is equally likely to occur.

Such equal reversibility would not be the case, however, with sentences like 'The cat chased the mouse' and 'The mouse chased the cat' since, based on our knowledge of the world, we would generally expect the cat rather than the mouse to be doing the chasing. Our expectations for certain events or situations can influence the interpretation we give to words. Similarly, an animal such as the dolphin might be able to respond appropriately to a string of words, not on the basis of their structural word order but on the dolphin's life experience. A proper test for grammatical knowledge must take this phenomenon into account.

Herman was aware of this problem, so, as part of his research, he pre- sented the dolphins with commands involving semantically reversible structures. He gave them, for example, both 'pipe hoop fetch' (Take the hoop to the pipe) and 'hoop pipe fetch' (Take the pipe to the hoop). Since the dolphins generally responded appropriately to both commands, Herman was able to conclude with some certainty that the dolphins had acquired a syntactic structure that involved relational and prepositional functions. Because word order in these commands indicates different semantic or mean- ing relationships, it is reasonable to claim that the dolphins had acquired such syntactic relational notions as direct object and indirect object.

The dolphins, Herman emphasizes, can also respond to novel sentences on the basis of understanding words and their relations in a command structure. Once the structure and relations are learned, then all new sentences with those characteristics should be understood, providing, of course, that the meaning of component words is already known. Thus, after acquiring the notions of direct and indirect object, Akea responded correctly on her first exposure to the sentence 'person left frisbee fetch' (Take the left frisbee to the person). Herman is therefore able to deflect any criticism that the dolphins are merely carrying out the same sort of fixed stimulus–response type of shaped behaviour that dolphins and whales in marine parks are trained to do. He correctly points out that it could not be simple stimulus–response shaped behaviour because the dolphins respond appropriately to specific commands that they have never received before.

In later research, Herman introduced the dolphins to various notions such as Question (Herman and Forestell, 1985; Herman *et al.*, 1993; Holder *et al.*, 1993). A key aspect of this research is the dolphin's ability to report on the absence of objects. In the wild, animals typically signal the presence of food or danger but probably seldom deal with topics relating to absence. Akea correctly responded to question forms such as 'hoop Question' ('Is there a hoop?') and 'frisbee Question' ('Is there a frisbee?') after searching the tank for these items. Moreover, when the question form was contrasted with the imperative (command) form, the dolphin would give the correct answer. Thus, given the question 'hoop Question', Akea would correctly press the 'yes' or 'no' paddles in the tank.

Herman's research is one of the most scientific and methodologically reliable on the learning of language by animals. It remains for further research to demonstrate whether dolphins would be able to express in production what they have already learned in terms of language comprehension. Devising such an appropriate means of production, however, is not easy. Perhaps Herman should return to his earlier work where he trained a dolphin to mimic computer-generated sounds.

5.5 Teaching spoken English to an African Grey parrot

We all know that parrots and certain other birds can be taught to mimic human speech. But can they learn language? Prior to Irene Pepperberg's research, most of us thought not. Pepperberg's fascinating research has proven us wrong (particularly the first author in previous writings!).

Pepperberg (Pepperberg, 1987, 1993; Pepperberg and Kozak, 1986) has worked with a male African Grey parrot she calls Alex. She used the speech mode because of the parrot's excellent vocal and hearing abilities. Alex is now able to understand and answer questions on the colour, shape, and material of more than 100 objects. He can correctly name a host of items such as key, chain, tray, toy truck, block, cup, and box. Furthermore, he can identify them on the basis of seven colours (green, red, blue, yellow, grey, purple, and orange; although grey and green are sometimes indistinguishable because of Alex's pronunciation of green as 'gree'), and of a number of shapes, up to those with six corners, including triangles, squares, pentagons, and hexagons. He can even tell you what an object is made of, such as cork, wood, paper, or wool. Alex is not only adept at identifying items but he can request them, refuse them, and answer questions pertaining to the abstract categories of shape, colour, material, and quantity. He has shown clear knowledge of these abstract categories by using them to refer to new objects that were not in his training.

Thus, in a test of Alex's cognitive abilities involving a variety of questions, '"What color is object-X", "What shape is object-Y?", "What object is color-A?", or "What object is shape-B?"' (Pepperberg, 1993, p. 235), Alex performed correctly on more than 80 per cent of the questions. Alex's few errors are even more interesting than his correct performances. He initially produced 'box' as 'bock' and then replied to a question on colour with the answer 'rock' instead of the correct 'block'. Then, when asked which object was blue, he confounded 'box' and 'rock' on two questions. Alex's errors demonstrate that he behaves in much the same way as humans in making phonological errors.

Alex's accomplishments are admirable and in some ways, especially with his recognition of abstract categories, he has surpassed aspects of language knowledge that the apes and even the dolphins have demonstrated. He has not yet, though, reached the level of syntax that the dolphins have mastered. However, given that this research with Alex is ongoing and given that parrots are noted for their longevity, there is still a chance that Alex might acquire more syntax.

Why Pepperberg has been successful with her parrot while others over the centuries have not is a puzzling question. It has been over 15 years since Pepperberg's first investigation was published (Pepperberg, 1987), yet no other parrot study has appeared to our knowledge. (For more information about Pepperberg's research, the reader can check her website, the address of which is given at the end of the chapter.)

5.6   Teaching Rico the dog to understand spoken English words

The recent appearance of a language study with a dog has led us to wonder why household pets have not been brought to the university for language instruction more often. Rico is a $9^{1}/_{2}$-year-old border collie who has learned to understand more than 200 words for different objects, such as toys and balls, that have been said to him (Kaminski *et al.*, 2004). He can learn a new word after being shown an unfamiliar object just once (an achievement that is the envy of these authors). No syntax, but still, Rico's large vocabulary is greater than a lot of the animals who have been given language instruction. It is not likely, however, that any syntax would ever be learned. After all, household pets have been living together with humans for many thousands of years under the close scrutiny of their owners and nothing has ever been reported of dogs or cats learning more than single words, mainly commands for action.

5.7 Conclusion

The research with animals clearly shows that animals have only a rudimentary language ability. What is puzzling and requires explanation is why their language ability is so low when their overall intellectual ability is so much higher. Apes exhibit, for example, intelligent complex behaviour regarding social organization, food acquisition, and problem solving. And documented studies with apes going as far back as the First World War (the research of the renowned psychologist Wolfgang Köhler) demonstrate that they are creative and inventive in solving other types of problems. Why, then, are they not able to learn more of the language that is taught to them? After all, human children learn language (speech or sign) in all of its complexity. And why couldn't the apes at least have learned to comprehend human speech, given that they have a hearing acuity that is as good as or better than human hearing? After all, there are human beings who are born with a deficit in speech production – the cases of Nolan, McDonald, and Rie in Chapter 1, for example – yet they can learn to comprehend language in all of its complexity.

Contemporary theorists basically offer two types of explanations on the issue of animals vs. humans in the acquisition of language. Pro-intelligence theorists like Piaget, Putnam, and others, including ourselves, hold that animals lack certain aspects of intelligence that are needed for the learning of such a complex ability as language. Innatists like Chomsky, on the other hand, argue that the effect is due to animals being born without a special language ability, an ability that is little related to intelligence.

Chomsky has offered a very telling argument against researchers who teach language to animals. If apes really had the ability to use a grammar, they surely would have developed it on their own by now; especially with language being so advantageous for survival. It would be rather odd to think that an animal would have developed, through evolution, the highly complex capacity for language but would not have used that capacity until humans from universities came along to show them how.

Whether animals lack intelligence as the Empiricists say, or lack a special language ability as the Rationalists say, it seems evident that animals do *not* have much of a capacity for a grammar-based language.

5.8 Websites for more information

A number of websites regarding the research discussed in this chapter and other research are available to the interested reader.

Fouts Research and Washoe:
http://www.cwu.edu/~cwuchci

Herman and Dolphin Research:
http://www.dolphin-institute.org
http://www.dolphins.org/Learn/lmm-dcmm.htm

Patterson and Koko Gorilla Research:
http://www.gorilla.org

Pepperberg and Parrot Research:
http://www.alexfoundation.org
http://wildcat.arizona.edu/papers/93/139/01_5_m.html
http://csbi.mit.edu/faculty/Members/IrenePepperberg

Savage-Rumbaugh Research:
http://www.littletree.com.au/koko.htm

Language and Apes Research:
http://www.cs.uwaterloo.ca/~dmswitze/apelang.html
http://whyfiles.org/058language/ape_talk.html

Second-language learning

Chapter 6

Children vs. adults in second-language learning

6.1 Children are better: a common belief

Most people believe that children are better than adults in learning a second language. This seems to be backed up by the common observation that young second-language learners seem to pick up another language quickly, just by exposure and without teaching. Whether this is truly the case is the focus of this chapter.

Factors involved in second-language acquisition can be divided into two categories: (1) psychological, and (2) social.

1. **Psychological**.   In this section, we shall consider: *intellectual processing*, which is involved in an individual's analytical determination of grammatical structures and rules; *memory*, which is essential if language learning is to occur and remain; and *motor skills*, which concern the pronunciation of the sounds involved in the second language, i.e. the use of the articulators of speech (tongue, lips, mouth, vocal cords, etc.). We shall further consider the role of *motivation* and *attitude* regarding the learning of a second language. In Chapter 8, we will consider how the similarity between a first language and the target second language can affect learning, also known as transfer problem.
2. **Social**.   The types of situations, settings, and interactions which an individual experiences can affect the learning of a second language. Thus, we will be concerned with where and with whom exposure to the second language occurs. In particular, the *natural* situation (family, play, workplace) in contrast to the *classroom* situation will be focused on. In addition we will consider whether the second language is learned in a foreign community (the EFL situation), or in the community of the first language (the ESL situation).

6.2 Basic psychological factors affecting second-language learning

6.2.1 Intellectual processing: explication and induction

Essentially, there are only two processes by which one can learn the syntax of a second language: someone can explain rules to you, *explication*, or you can figure them out for yourself, *induction*.

6.2.1.1 Explication

The nature of explication

Explication is the process whereby the rules and structures of a second language are explained to a learner. This explanation is given in the first language of the learner. The learner is then expected to understand, learn, and apply the rule in the second language.

Why a language cannot be learned completely by explication

While parts of a second language can be learned by explication, it is impossible for it to be learned entirely by explication. This is because not all of the rules of any one language have been discovered and written down. Even for a language such as English, the most researched of all languages, one still finds linguistic journals discussing the concepts involved in such commonplace features of English as tense and the article.

Explication is rarely applicable to young children

Explaining is rarely done by parents or others when children acquire a native language, yet children by the age of 4 or 5 can understand and speak most of their native language quite well. They have learned language by self-analysis, induction. You do not hear a parent saying: 'Now, Mary, to make the plural of "dog" you add a "z" sound to the end of the word, while with "duck" you add an "s" sound. You do this, Mary, because the last sound of "dog" has a voiced consonant and the last sound of "duck" has an unvoiced one.' Similarly, parents do not tell their children that, in order to negate a sentence like 'John wanted some chocolate ice cream', the negative marker, 'not', must occur before the verb, 'do' must appear before the NEG, the tense on the verb must be shifted on to the 'do', so that do + PAST becomes 'did', and 'some' must change to 'any' for agreement, so that the sentence 'John did not want any chocolate ice cream' will be the result. Even college students taking linguistics courses can find such explanations daunting!

Teaching simple and complex rules

However, rules that are simple can be learned by explication without much difficulty. An example of teaching a simple rule would be a case in which a mature Korean speaker studying English would be told that there is a Subject + Verb + Object order of constituents (Korean has S–O–V). On the basis of such a description, a learner can learn relevant usable rules, though they may need practice before the rules can be applied with any speed or reliability. In such cases, explication may even be a faster means of learning than induction, since induction requires that a learner be repeatedly exposed to words, phrases, and sentences along with relevant situations that give some indication as to their meaning. Robinson (1996), for example, found that explication improved the learning of simple Subject–Verb rules.

6.2.1.2 Induction

Learning rules by self-discovery is the essence of the process of induction. The child who is exposed to second-language speech and remembers what he or she has heard will be able to analyze and discover the generalization or rule that underlies that speech. Actually, not only must the learner devise the rule based on the speech that has been heard, but he or she must also figure out how those rules are to be applied in other cases. For example, given the sentences 'John danced then John sang' and 'John danced and then he sang', spoken in relevant situations, the learner can determine that the two sentences are related, with 'he' being a replacement for 'John'. The learner must also figure out that while 'he' can replace 'John' in the second of the conjoined sentences, it cannot do so in the first sentence (as in 'He danced then John sang') since in that case the pronoun 'he' must refer to someone other than John. With such a rule, the learner is on the way to being able to use and understand increasingly complicated structures involving pronominalization. Such phenomena as pronominalization, negation, and the plural are learned by induction and become part of a young native speaker's language knowledge quite early, long before the child enters school.

The second-language learner is always trying to figure out language by induction. This is simply the natural thing to do. So long as the structures involved are not far beyond the learner's level of syntactic understanding, there is a good chance that the learner can discover the rules by self-analysis.

6.2.2 Memory

Vocabulary learning and rote memory

Memory is crucial to learning. It is inconceivable that a person with a severe memory impairment could ever learn his or her native language, much less a second language. The learning of the simplest word requires memory. A person learning the word 'dog', for example, must retain a connection between the hearing of 'dog' and the experience of seeing, touching or smelling a dog. Such a connection between the sound and the object is arbitrary. There is no logical relationship between the sound 'dog' and its meaning. Usually more than one occurrence of the sound and meaning is necessary for learning.

The greater the number of related occurrences needed for learning, the poorer a person's memory. Second-language learners and teachers are forever talking of practice and review. The reason that practice and review is necessary at all is because of some lack in memory ability.

Syntax learning and episodic memory

Memory is similarly crucial for the learning of grammatical structures and rules. For example, in order to determine the type of questions that require 'do' (as in 'Do you want some candy?' but not in 'Is the dog barking?'), how to negate sentences, how to use politeness structures ('Please close the door', 'Would you please close the door?', 'Would you be so kind as to close the door?'), etc., memory is essential.

It is only through memory that a learner can accumulate the vast amount of speech and *relevant situational data* that serves as the basis for analyzing structures and formulating rules. It is not enough to remember whole phrases and sentences, the learner must also remember the situations in which these sentences were uttered in order to derive the meaning of those phrases and sentences and their syntax. The type of memory that involves situations is what Tulving (1983) and others refer to as 'episodic memory'. Thus, for example, outside the classroom, the degree of politeness of an utterance must be determined from the situation in which it occurs. The learner must note who is talking to whom and what their status is. This information must be remembered and associated with the different expressions, e.g. 'Please close the door', 'Would you please close the door?', 'Would you please be so kind as to close the door?'

Children's memory ability

Children under 7 years display a phenomenal ability at rote memorization. Older children, however, do not, with some decline beginning around 8 years of age and with more of a decline from about 12 years of age. Harley and Doug (1997) investigated students who were in an immersion language education programme (the teaching of subject matter through a second language). Older children began to apply their cognitive abilities in analyzing the syntactic rules of the second language while younger children relied more heavily on their use of rote memory for language learning. One could interpret these data as indicating perhaps that the older children jumped to syntactic analysis sooner because they realized that they had difficulty in remembering all of the sentences that they heard. In this regard, it seems that children's ages can be usefully divided into at least two categories, under 7 years and 7 to 12 years. This is the rough categorization that we shall use.

6.2.3 Motor skills

Articulators of speech

Good pronunciation is clearly an important part of learning a foreign language. The better our pronunciation, the better we can communicate with others. The creation of speech sounds is related to the ability to control the muscles that manipulate the organs of speech. Motor Skills is a term that psychologists use to describe the use of muscles in performing certain skills, from general ones like walking to fine ones like writing and speech. The Motor Skills that are involved in speech utilize what linguists call the articulators of speech. These include the mouth, lips, tongue, vocal cords, etc., all of which are controlled by muscles that are under the general control of the brain. The articulators of speech have to do the right thing at the right time (open the mouth in a certain way, position the lips and tongue in a certain way, etc.), if one is to utter sounds accurately.

Decline in general motor skills

We all recognize that to be able to attain a high level of proficiency in a motor skill, e.g., gymnastics, skating or piano playing, one should start young. But why? Because somewhere around the age of 12 years, the ability to acquire new motor skills begins to decline. The reason for this decline in the fine control of the muscles of the body is as yet unknown, although, since the decline is of such a general nature, involving many muscle groups, it seems likely to be due to some change in central functioning in the brain. Hormonal changes prior to puberty may have something to do with this but this is only speculation on our part.

Decline in ability for new articulations

As we age and as our ability to acquire new motor skills declines, our ability to command our articulators of speech is negatively affected. Consequently, we can expect that children will do much better in the pronunciation of a second language than adults because children have the flexibility in motor skills that adults generally have lost.

A number of studies have demonstrated that the earlier the age at which acquisition of the second language begins, the more native-like the accent will be (Asher and Garcia, 1969; Oyama, 1976; Tahta *et al.*, 1981). The Oyama study of Italian immigrants, for example, showed that the younger the children, the more native-like would be their pronunciation. The subjects were 60 Italian-born male immigrants who lived in the greater New York metropolitan area. The subjects were categorized according to 'age at arrival in the United States' (6 to 20 years) and 'number of years in the United States' (5 to 20 years). It was found that the younger arrivals performed with near-native English pronunciation while those who arrived after about the age of 12 years had substantial **accents**.[1] Length of stay had little effect.

6.2.4 Summary of three important psychological factors affecting second-language learning

Let us now summarize the effects on second-language learning of the various psychological variables. In Table 6.1, three basic psychological categories are represented: Intellectual, which is subdivided into Inductive and Explicative; Memory; and Motor Skills. Along the left margin of the table, persons are divided into three age groups: Children under 7, Children 7 to 12, and Adults over 12.

- **Induction.** We can see that insofar as Induction is concerned, this ability remains at a relatively high level with age, except with certain individuals in old age. Such an ability allows us to make new discoveries in our

Table 6.1 Important psychological and social factors affecting second-language learning for children and adults

	Psychological factors				Social factors	
	Intellectual				Situation	
	Inductive	Explicative	Memory	Motor Skills	Natural	Classroom
Children under 7	High	Low	High	High	High	Low
7–12	High	Medium	Med/High	Med/High	Medium	Medium
Adults over 12	High	High	Medium	Low	Low	High

[1] The authors observed the same phenomenon in their own families. The first author's father and his brothers came from Russia to Canada before the Communist revolution; however, only the youngest brother, who was 10 to 11 years old, picked up perfect Canadian English. All of the brothers, including the first author's father, who was 17 years old when he came, always spoke English with a heavy Russian accent (as did all of the other brothers, who were older than he was). As a child, the first author was amazed that the brothers could be of the same family.

The second author started to learn English as a Foreign Language in her native Russia at the age of 7 in a classroom environment before moving to the United States at the age of 33. At present, while her writing skills are good, she still speaks English with a Russian accent. However, her son, who was only 9 years old when they came, took only a year to pick up accentless English!

everyday life, even to the extent of being able to analyze the syntactic structures of a second language. Thus the assignment of High for each age category.

- **Explication**.   We see that this ability increases with age. Young children would have great difficulty in understanding abstract and complex explanations about a second language. We thus see a rise from Low to High on this variable.
- **Memory**.   This is an ability in which very young children are High. Such an ability, though, declines with age and so we have assigned a Medium/ High value for ages 7 to 12 and a Medium value for Adults. One might want to assign a lower value to adults because of the great age range involved. For simplicity's sake, we made only one category of adults. Certainly we would expect a difference in the memory ability of teenagers (13 to 19 years) as compared to persons in their thirties or forties.
- **Motor Skills**.   The table indicates a general decline from a *High* for young children to *Low* for adults. These data reflect what research (discussed in a later section) indicates about pronunciation proficiency. It is difficult for most adults to achieve native-speaker pronunciation. While adults may greatly improve their bowling, golf, or their billiards (these are *perceptual*-motor skills – a combination of perception and motor skills), most of these people will not be able to improve their pronunciation (a *pure* motor skill).

6.2.5   Two other important psychologial variables: motivation and attitude

6.2.5.1   Motivation

A number of factors that affect second-language learning operate only in certain types of situations. The question of motivation for learning a second language, for instance, is not likely to arise in a natural type of setting such as with a young child. A 1- or 2-year-old needs no motivation to learn a second language; given language input, the young child will automatically learn – with learning even occurring in negative circumstances. An older child of 4 or 5 years, however, may need motivation in order to learn a second language since by that age the child may be aware of whether a language is positively or negatively regarded by others, or the child may prefer other activities.

The planned learning situation such as the classroom, however, presents a very different problem. There is an element of choice involved in attend-ing class, listening to the teacher, participating in activities, and in doing assignments. The amount of exposure that one receives and the amount of attention and effort that one devotes to learning may be affected by one's motivation. Dislike of a teacher, for example, could seriously affect language learning unless it is balanced by a high degree of motivation that enables one to persist.

There is no reason to suppose that some sort of special motivation or purpose is necessary for second-language learning. In general, there are a large number of variables involved in second-language learning, such as intergroup attitudes and climate, social situation, personality and self-confidence, desire to communicate with a particular person, to name just a few (MacIntyre *et al.*, 1998). In an actual classroom situation any one of them could affect motivation. Teachers are generally well aware of this possibility and often devise ways to increase positive motivation and attitudes (Crookes and Schmidt, 1991).

6.2.5.2   Attitude

A negative attitude towards the target language or its speakers, or the other members of the class, may also affect one's determination and persistence to be involved in the classroom and its activities (Gardner and Lambert, 1972; Oller *et al.*, 1977, 1978; Chihara and Oller, 1978; Gardner, 1985). This same negative attitude could impair memory functioning and detract from focusing on the target language. In the same way, any of a host of personality and sociocultural variables could have deleterious effects (Brown, 1987). Many variables, such as status and cultural background, become more potent with the age of the learner and are important considerations in the classroom learning situation.

This is not to say that attitude may not play a role in the natural situation as well. By 4 years of age children have developed attitudes towards language. They know how people react to different languages. For example, children may not wish to use their native, but foreign for this country, language outside of the home. They may prefer to conform to their peers and other members of the dominant language community.

6.3   Social situations affecting second-language learning

There are many social situations in which a second language is learned. Basically, we can cover the most important of them according to three categories, the natural, the classroom and community context. The natural situation in which a second language is learned is one that is similar to that in which the first language is learned. It can involve social situations such as those involving family, play, or the workplace. The classroom situation involves the social situation of the school classroom. Each of these types of social situations has its own advantages and disadvantages. The community context allows students to have access to a natural situation outside of the class and thereby supplement their classroom learning.

6.3.1 The natural situation

Characteristics of the natural situation

A natural situation for second-language learning is one where the second language is experienced in a situation that is similar to that in which the native language is learned. That is, language is experienced in conjunction with the objects, situations, and events of everyday life. The paradigm case would be that of a young child going to live in another country and learning that country's language, not by any explicit teaching, but by interacting with playmates. For example, an English-speaking 5-year-old girl from New York goes to Tokyo with her parents. Through playing with Japanese children, she soon learns Japanese. In fact, she learns the language in less than a year, which is not uncommon for children this age, and her speech is indistinguishable from that of native speakers. *A child can learn a second language faster than the first language*!

With age, language is more essential for social interaction

It is important to note that for adults, social interaction mainly occurs through the medium of language. Few native-speaker adults are willing to devote time to interacting with someone who does not speak the language, with the result that the adult foreigner will have little opportunity to engage in meaningful and extended language exchanges. Adult second-language learners will typically have significantly fewer good language-learning opportunities in a new language community than will children. If the adults mainly stay at home, they will not be able to meet and talk much to native speakers. Going shopping, going to the bank, and other such chores, while beneficial, are very limited in time and scope. Second-language interactions in the workplace could also be very limiting, for, because of their lack of second-language ability, adult learners would not be hired to do work that required native speakers to linguistically interact with them in any depth.

In contrast, the young child is often readily accepted by other children, and even adults. For young children, language is not as essential to social interaction. So-called 'parallel play', for example, is common among young children. They can be content just to sit in each other's company speaking only occasionally and playing on their own.

Older children can have problems

Sometimes older children may not want to identify with a new community and will consequently resist learning the new language. Preston (1989) suggests that because children have not yet developed their own identities, they may be more accepting of the social norms of a new community. Thus, while younger children will be more likely to accept learning a new language and the culture it involves, older children may strive to maintain their own identity and cultural beliefs by avoiding situations that would expose them to using a language and culture that might challenge their view of themselves.

Conscious willingness to communicate is also considered critical for acquiring and improving a foreign language. In a series of studies conducted with Japanese high school students who came to the United States to study English and experience a different culture, participants pointed out that 'taking initiative to communicate with American classmates or host families' helped them gain confidence and improve their language skills (Yashima *et al.*, 2004). Other studies (e.g. MacIntyre *et al.*, 2002, among many others) confirm the view.

Conclusion

The opportunities to experience language in a natural situation decline with age. This is indicated in Table 6.1, where young children are assigned a *High* value but adults are assigned a *Low* value.

6.3.2   The classroom situation

The classroom is isolated from other social life

The classroom for second-language learning is a planned situation. As we all know, physically, there is a room that is isolated from the rest of social life. In the room there is a teacher and a number of students. The teacher is the one who knows the second language and the students are there to learn the language. In the enclosed space of the classroom, nothing happens (linguistically) unless the teacher makes it happen. Students do not act on their own but follow the directions of the teacher. All other aspects of life are suspended or subordinated to language learning. This, of course, is very different from the home or community where a lucky second-language learner would eat at a table with others, walk around doing things, work in the garden, go for a drive, etc., all the while hearing and using the second language in conjunction with these activities.

Learning language as part of a group and not as an individual

There are other characteristics of the planned classroom situation that distinguish it from the natural situation. These include social adjustment to group process (individuals must subordinate their behaviour and follow classroom procedures for the benefit of all), the need to attend class in order to learn, the need for long periods of concentration, and, when required, having to do home study.

As far as language is concerned, the explicit teaching of grammatical structures and rules may be involved, depending on the method used (see Chapter 7 on second-language teaching methods). Using books and taking notes are often expected of the student. Students have to get used to learning language as an academic subject. Thus, when considering overall the demands of the classroom situation, it is clear that the older one is, the better one is able to adjust and function within that situation. Young children often will not do as well as older children and adults.

Conclusion

Generally, the ability to learn in a classroom setting improves with age because older children and adults can adapt better to the classroom regimen and are more receptive to materials taught through explication. Thus, a *High* is assigned to adults in Table 6.1. A *Low*, though, is assigned to young children. To the extent that the children's second language experience in the classroom can be one of learning through play, this value can be raised – even to *High*, in the proper setting with the right teacher.

6.3.3 Who is better? Children or adults?

6.3.3.1 In a natural situation

Predicting from the values in the table

In the natural situation, *younger children will do best*. Looking along the line, we have a *High* on Natural Situation and a *High* on Inductive. (The *Low* on Explicative is not relevant here because in the Natural Situation learning is through induction not explication.) There are *Highs* on both Memory and Motor Skills.

Adults have a *Low* on Natural Situation and *Highs* on both Inductive and Explicative intellectual learning. Unfortunately, the *High* on Induction does not help much in learning syntax because the adult learner does not get enough relevant language and non-language data for analysis through the Natural Situation. Explication is not relevant to the Natural Situation because rarely will people be able to explain grammatical points in the learner's native language (in the rare event that they would want to). Given these facts in addition to the *Medium* on Memory and the *Low* on Motor Skills, the adult would be expected to do quite poorly.

Older children would do better than adults because they are *Medium* on Natural Situation and *Medium/High* on both Memory and Motor Skills.

The natural situation is more favourable to children because adults generally undergo a marked decline in the quality and quantity of the social interaction conducive to good language learning. Psychologically, while both children and adults have optimal powers of induction, and are able to induce the grammar of a second language more or less equally well, nonetheless, it will be easier for children to learn syntax than it will be for adults.

Conclusion

In the natural situation of second-language learning, young children will do better than adults, with older children doing better than adults too.

6.3.3.2 In the classroom situation

In the classroom situation, *adults will do better than young children*, because not only are they better in explicative processing but, simply put, they know how to be students. They have sufficient maturity to meet the rigours of a formal learning environment, where concentration, attention, and even the ability to sit still for a long time all play a role in learning. Older learners have cognitive experience lacking in small chilren, and, thus, can be better learners (Edwards, 2004). Matsui (2000) found out that experience with the native language helps adults even to achieve near-native level of pronunciation if given explicit instruction. In a classroom-based study comparing junior high school students with elementary school students (Politzer and Weiss, 1969), the older students scored higher on all tests.

Because the older child's memory and motor skills are better than the adult's, the advantage in explicative processing enjoyed by the adult may not be sufficient to overcome the disadvantages experienced in these areas. Thus, *the older child will probably do better than the adult* in the classroom situation. Research from as long ago as 60 years (Thorndike, 1928; Cheydleur, 1932) has yielded the same result. The best age to learn a second language in the typical explication classroom situation is probably that age where the individual retains much of the memory and motor skills of the very young, but where the individual has begun to reason and understand like an adult. That age would probably be somewhere around 10 years.

Conclusion

In the classroom situation, older children will do best. Adults will do better than young children to the extent that the young children's classroom is not a simulation of the natural situation.

6.3.4 ESL or EFL community context

Language community context: English as a Second Language (ESL) or English as a Foreign Language (EFL)

Whether the classroom is in a school that is in a community where the second language is spoken is a matter of some importance, for this will allow students to benefit from both a natural situation outside the class and their classroom learning. Thus, for example, Pakistanis learning English in a classroom in London will have beneficial language experiences outside the classroom that Pakistanis learning English in a classroom in Karachi will not. The former (learning English in London) is an English as a Second Language (ESL) context while the latter (learning English in Karachi) is an English as a Foreign Language (EFL) context. Because the ESL context provides more language-learning opportunities for the second-language learner through exposure to natural situations outside the classroom, such learners, unsurprisingly, will generally progress more rapidly than learners living in an EFL context (Fathman, 1978).

Furthermore, in comparing children and adults, we may say that, given that the natural situation benefits children more than adults, the ESL context will benefit children more than it will adults. Of course, the ESL context will benefit adults too, but to a lesser degree. Conversely, adults can do better in the EFL context where they can apply their superior cognitive skills for learning in the classroom situation.

6.4   Is there a critical age for second-language learning?

In Chapter 4, on wild and isolated children, the concept of a critical age for first-language learning was raised. Recall, if you will, that although solid evidence was lacking, some theorists hypothesized that there was an age (puberty, for example) beyond which it would be impossible to acquire a first language. Brain changes were suggested as a possible explanation for such a psychological barrier.

Adults *can* learn a second language

It is reasonable to ask the same question about the acquisition of a second language. Is there any barrier to the learning of a second language and, if so, at what age does this barrier become operational? As far as adult second-language learning is concerned, we have the common observation that a very great number of adults do, in fact, learn the syntax of other languages perfectly. There are those who speak second languages so well that, on the basis of the grammar alone (not the pronunciation, which we shall deal with shortly), they would be judged native speakers.

No demonstrated critical age for learning syntax

There are, however, studies which demonstrate a differential effect for the age at which acquisition of syntax began. Patkowski (1980) had native speakers of English rate the syntax of transcripts of spontaneous speech from immigrants to the USA who had entered before or after the age of 15. Transcripts were used to remove any possible influence of accent on the raters. The scores showed two very distinguishable groups: those who arrived before 15 years of age scored very high, while those arriving after scored lower. Johnson and Newport (1989) found the same effect when they had native speakers of Korean and Chinese rate the grammaticality of English sentences. The earlier the age of arrival, the better the subjects were at determining the ungrammaticality of English sentences. A similar result was reported by Mayberry and Lock (2003): early exposure to language, no matter wheter spoken or signed, contributed the most to later success in learning a second language.

On the other hand, research exists providing data to refute the claim of a critical period for the acquisition of grammar. The same Mayberry and Lock (2003) study still shows that adult learners can achieve a near-native competence of second-language grammar. In another study using a grammaticality judgement test in which native speakers of French were compared with high-level learners of French, no differences were detected between the two groups on their test scores or in the process of how they judged the syntax (Birdsong, 1992). Further research (van Wuijtswinkel, 1994; White and Genesee, 1996, Birdsong and Molis, 2001) shows that even learners who begin to acquire a language after puberty can reach native-speaker levels. It is safe to affirm the view that there is no critical age in terms of acquiring the syntax of a second language.

Critical age for pronunciation

This brings us to pronunciation. Is it possible to learn a second language so well that one truly sounds like a native speaker? Mack (1986) and Perani *et al.* (2003) argue that even if highly competent second-language speakers *seem* to perform on a native level, experimental tasks will reveal the difference both in grammar and in pronunciation. Sebastián-Gallés and Bosch (2001) suppose that even pre-school age is already too late for aquiring near-native phonology. One psycholinguist, Thomas Scovel, has claimed that *no adult* can ever be successful in that regard. 'The critical period for accentless speech simply means that adults will never learn to pass themselves off as native speakers phonologically . . . ' (Scovel, 1988, p. 65). He describes this as the 'Joseph Conrad phenomenon', after the famous novelist and master of English prose, who, a native speaker of Polish, did not even begin to study English until he was 20. Scovel has in mind a certain category of adult second-language speakers: those who have mastered the grammatical and communicative complexities of another language but still speak with an accent.

We could add to this class two European-born US Secretaries of State, Henry Kissinger (under President Nixon) and Zbigniew Brzezinski (under President Carter). Both of these men speak English that is heavily accented with their native languages, German and Polish, respectively. In other respects, they excel in the English language. Kissinger came to the USA when he was 15 and Brzezinski came when he was 10 years old. While Kissinger was beyond our posited motor-skill critical age of 13 years, discussed earlier in this chapter, Brzezinski was not, but still he spoke with an accent. A more recent example of a foreign-born United States official is Arnold Schwarzenegger, who became governor of California in 2003. Born in Austria, he moved to the United States when he was 21. At present he appears to speak English with near-native speaker syntax, although his strong German accent may often obscure that fact!

However, there is a growing body of research that challenges any strong criterion of a critical period for accentless acquisition of a language such as the one that Scovel proposes. Some adults *do appear* to pick up accentless speech. Neufeld (1978) trained adult learners in the pronunciation of Chinese and Japanese. Judged by native speakers, half of them were able to pass as native. Furthermore, in two recent studies on this question, Bongaerts and associates (Bongaerts *et al.*, 1995, 1997) argue that there were flaws in studies by researchers who claimed that late learners could not acquire correct pronunciation. The flaw was that in subject selection advanced learners were not included. Correcting for this error by including highly successful learners, Bongaerts and associates found that they could indeed pass for native speakers on a number of criteria. They suggest that 'a very high motivation . . . continued access to target language input . . . [and] intensive instruction in the perception and in the production of the speech sounds' (pp. 462–3) were instrumental for these late language learners' acquisition of native-like pronunciation.

Matsui (2000) refers to a number of most recent studies proving that some adults can pick up near-native foreign language pronunciation even without explicit instruction. Current neurological research of blind people suggests that the human brain retains its flexibility throughout life, and changes to adapt language challenges even for older people. Special brain exercises are even reported to help people regain language functions despite various deficits (Ariniello, 2000). Perception training, for example, resulted in long-term improvements in Japanese adults' perception and production of English words with 'r' and 'l' sounds (Akahane-Yamada *et al.*, 1996), and in Korean adults' perception and production of English vowels (Yeon, 2003).

Thus, while we would agree with Scovel that in second-language acquisition there is no critical age for syntax, we cannot agree that there is an absolute critical age for pronunciation. Native-speaker pronunciation may well be achieved by some adults.

Chapter 7

Second-language teaching methods

7.1 Characterizing the essentials of methods

Second-language teaching is a field that provides an excellent meeting ground for the many theoretical and practical aspects of psycholinguistics to come together. It is here that we have a chance to see how ideas of human language and learning interconnect.

In our view, language-teaching methods may be conveniently characterized according to three principal dimensions (Steinberg, 1993): (1) Language Focus: Speech Communication vs. Literature; (2) Meaning Learning: Direct Experience vs. Translation; and (3) Grammar Learning: Induction vs. Explication. These dimensions involve theories which have been realized in principal second-language teaching methods. A brief description of each of these dimensions, some aspects of which are also considered elsewhere in this book, follows.

7.1.1 Language Focus: Speech Communication vs. Literature

Methods can be divided into two categories of focus, those that teach language through the speech of the target language (the 'target language' being the language to be learned) and those that approach the target language through reading and writing. Except for Grammar–Translation, which focuses on reading, writing, and the translation of written words, most other methods focus on speech and the use of speech in communication. A principal aim of Grammar–Translation is often to get students to be able to read, and, ultimately, to read literary works and documents. Other proponents of the method see literacy as a foundation and a means for approaching speech communication. The problem with starting out with literacy when the goal is speech is that students may never get to the speech stage unless they go to a school where they may come into contact with fluent instructors. Even at a university, though, the focus may remain on literacy, as is the case in Japan and Russia, for example.

Generally, the proponents of speech-based methods regard Grammar–Translation (GT) as their ultimate enemy, since they consider communication through speech to be primary in the learning of language. Speech-based methods attempt to provide a speech environment in which students may learn the target language. Reading and writing may be used, but only to reinforce what is initially learned in speech.

7.1.2 Meaning Learning: Direct Experience vs. Translation

In providing the meaning of target language items, translation may be used, as is commonly the case with the GT method. For example, English-speaking students studying Italian may be told that 'libro' means 'book', or that '¿Come sta?' means 'How are you?' Thus the native language (in this case, English) is used to provide the meaning for the target language (Italian). The meanings of single vocabulary items and entire phrases and sentences may be learned in this way. This is very different, though, from acquiring meaning by being exposed to actual objects, events, or situations in which the target language is used. For example, the learner can be shown a book and hear the teacher say 'libro', or see two persons meet, with one saying to the other '¿Come sta?' The meaning here is to be learned through direct experience and not by the use of the native language to provide translation.

7.1.3 Grammar Learning: Induction vs. Explication

Explication involves explanation, in the native language, of the grammatical rules and structures of the second language. For example, a teacher can explain to Japanese students in the Japanese language that English has a Subject + Verb + Object ordering of basic sentence constituents. (Japanese has a Subject + Object + Verb ordering.)

In learning the same by induction, however, students would have to discover the order of constituents on their own. It would be necessary for them to hear sentences of the sort, 'Mary caught the ball', while experiencing a situation in which such an action (or a picture of the action) occurs. In this way they would discover for themselves, through self-analysis, i.e. induction, that English has a Subject + Verb + Object ordering.

7.2 Traditional methods: Grammar–Translation, Natural, Direct, Audiolingual

With the above three dimensions in mind, let us now examine some other major second-language teaching methods. For a more in-depth treatment of the three oldest methods, Grammar–Translation, the Natural Method, and the Direct Method, the reader should refer to the works of Kelly (1969), Titone (1968), and Darian (1972). For consideration of the historical movement between the old and new methods see Howatt (1984), and for an overview of most current methods see Richards and Rodgers (2001). Since the 1980s little that is new has happened in teaching methods. Some theorists, such as H. Douglas Brown, even contend that the age of methods has passed.

Under the heading of Traditional Methods, we shall consider the following: (1) the Grammar–Translation Method, (2) the Natural Method, (3) the Direct Method, and (4) the Audiolingual Method.

7.2.1 The Grammar–Translation Method

Features of GT

Grammar–Translation (GT) essentially involves two components: (1) the explicit explanation of grammatical rules using the native language, and (2) the use of translation, in the native language, to explain the meaning of vocabulary and structures. Translation is the oldest of the components and is probably the oldest of all formal teaching methods, having been used in ancient Greece and Rome and elsewhere in the ancient world. The grammar aspect of GT was rather limited in those times since grammatical knowledge itself was limited. It was later in Europe, particularly in the seventeenth century, that intensive and detailed studies of various languages were conducted. With this spirit of the Renaissance came an interest, too, in the understanding and teaching of ordinary vernacular (non-Classical) languages.

The teaching of grammar went hand in hand with translation for the teaching of a second language, with both relying on the use of the native language to impart knowledge. With the growth of grammatical knowledge, however, the grammatical component played a greater role in teaching, eventually dominating the translation aspect. By the end of the eighteenth century in Europe it had become a full partner in the method. The growth of the grammatical component continues to the present day. Rules are explained by the teacher, then memorized, recited, and applied by the student. Typically, textbooks using GT have lessons that include a reading passage in the target language, a list of vocabulary items and their translations, and an explanation in the native language of important points of grammar exemplified in the text. The lesson often ends with a series of exercises, ranging from straight translation to questions on points of grammar. Translation is typically done from the target language into the native language, with reverse translation (from the native language into the target language) seldom being done. The teacher will spend most of the class time explaining the grammar points, while occasionally questioning students about a particular translation or having students read aloud and explain the meaning of what they have read.

Advantages of GT

Despite the method's indifference to speech and oral communication, and despite its being disparaged by leading language educators for such an indifference, the GT method has enjoyed and continues to enjoy acceptance in many countries around the world. This may seem a mystery, until one looks at the important advantages of GT:

1. **Non-fluent teachers can teach large classes.** The method can be applied by teachers (1) who lack verbal fluency in the target language, both in terms of understanding and producing speech, and by teachers (2) who have an incomplete knowledge of the language. This situation is common in many countries, typically underdeveloped ones, where knowledgeable teachers are scarce. It is not uncommon in such countries for teachers to be placed in a class with 40, 50, and more students. In effect, language learning is treated as a mass lecture course where, typically, students only meet once a week.
2. **Self-study is possible.** The method also lends itself well to self-study. By using books, students can study on their own outside the classroom. There is much that they can learn from studying and reading on their own. Of importance, too, is the fact that the method is appropriate for all levels of learners. From the introductory to the very advanced, there is an abundance of materials available for classroom use.
3. **Adapts to changing linguistic and psychological theories.** One of GT's strongest points is its capacity to adapt to ever-changing linguistic and psychological theories. The distinguishing feature of the method, the explication of grammar, can easily be adapted to new ideas and theories. Grammatical explanations can be couched in the linguistic theory of the day. Whether a grammatical point is to be explained according to Chomsky's or Bloomfield's theory of grammar is of no concern to the method – GT is neutral with respect to any specific grammar. Whatever grammar it is fed, that is the grammar it will explain. Similarly GT is neutral about whether a Behaviourist or a Mentalist psychological theory is applied.

In this way, GT need never become obsolete from a linguistic or psychological point of view. The fact that it thrived under Structural linguistics and Behaviouristic psychology did not prevent it from thriving under Mentalism and Mentalistic linguistics.

Success and failure

Almost everyone who has theorized second-language teaching methods has criticized GT. They believe that there has to be a better way to teach language. Yet, despite sustaining centuries of attack by opposing methods GT survives. Although we, too, are members of the opposition we do recognize that GT is not a failure. It could not be a failure and last for hundreds of years. It is a fact that many students can learn an important part of a second language through GT.

Where GT fails, however, relates to its secondary treatment of communicative oral skills. Students who pass through many years of strict GT training often come out unable to comprehend or utter sentences at a level that allows them to engage in even simple conversations. Then, too, GT cannot be used with young children: young children cannot read or write and are unable to understand grammatical explanations. Perhaps this is a blessing in disguise for countries that are predisposed to GT, such as Japan. Since Japanese children in the early grades are often taught English and other languages, and since this cannot be done through GT, more natural speech-communication-based techniques are going to have to be used.

7.2.2 The Natural Method

The Natural Method as a product of the Enlightenment

The Natural Method (NM) developed as a reaction to Grammar–Translation and was the outgrowth of scientific thought on the nature of language and language learning. Such knowledge flowered in Europe with inspiration from the work of Comenius (1568), Rousseau (1780), and other theorists such as Pestalozzi (1801). The philosophy of the Enlightenment during the eighteenth century was particularly concerned with the natural state of human beings. Questions about the natural development of humans and their language became of great interest.

NM began to be formed early in the nineteenth century and by the latter part of that century the method had become firmly established through the writings of such as Sauveur (1878) and Gouin (1880). Gouin observed children learning language and noticed that this occurred within the context of meaning-related situations (see Chapter 1). This observation of children's language learning was then applied to second-language teaching methods for children and adults.

Natural order of language learning

The approach to language learning, where 'natural is best', so to speak, led to a method of teaching that stressed the value of introducing a second language to a learner exactly as the native language had been experienced. The model for the Natural Method of second-language learning was the child learning its native language. This meant adherence to the natural sequence of the child's acquiring its first language, i.e. (1) speech comprehension, (2) speech production, and, much later, (3) reading and (4) writing. Grammar was not taught directly. Rather, grammatical rules and structures were to be learned through induction (self-analysis) by experiencing speech in a situational context. Meaning was to be gained through experience and exposure to objects, situations, and events; translation was to be avoided.

Typically, teachers would not use prepared situations or material. Learning was through 'spontaneous' conversation and demonstration, all of which was done in the target language and supported with gestures and actions. The teacher used language appropriate to the students' level of understanding, much in the way parents would with a child. The method was totally oriented towards the acquisition of oral skills. Student participation in situational activities was the essence of this kind of second-language learning.

Advantages and disadvantages

The great advantage of NM was that by exposure to natural language in a natural context, learners could acquire a speech capability both in understanding and production. However, one problem for this method is that it requires the teacher to create interesting situations so that students may be naturally exposed to language. This, and the reliance on spontaneous speech, places an extremely heavy burden on even the best of teachers. Besides possessing an undue amount of ingenuity teachers must, of course, be fluent in the target language. Such a demand cannot always be met, particularly if mass education is involved.

Class size, too, could be a problem, since the number of students must be quite small, usually less than 15. Actually, the problems mentioned here are not unique to NM. Indeed, all speech-based methods have similar problems, given their emphasis on exposure to natural speech and student participation in a variety of communicative situations.

7.2.3   The Direct Method

The Direct Method develops from the Natural Method

The Direct Method (DM), appearing in the late nineteenth and early twentieth centuries, developed from the Natural Method. Like the Natural Method, it emphasized the learning of speech, acquiring meaning in environmental context, and learning grammar through induction.

The advocates of DM, while approving of the Natural Method, sought to improve upon it by providing systematic procedures based on scientific knowledge of linguistics and psychology. For example, in psychology, Franke in the 1880s argued for the exclusive use of the second language in the classroom and discussed the importance of the direct connection between meaning and form in the second language. The native language was not to be used as an intermediary in any way. The name, Direct Method, incidentally, refers to this direct connection between the second language and meaning.

DM theorists believed that by applying scientific knowledge from psychology and linguistics, language learning could be made more efficient, with the result that students would learn faster than they would under the spontaneous and unplanned lessons of the Natural Method. Harold Palmer (1922) was perhaps its most articulate and eminent advocate.

DM advocates natural learning but with graded materials

Like the Natural Method, DM is mentalistically oriented since it presumes that the learner is a thinking being who can learn abstract language ideas. Also, like the Natural Method, DM relies on learning the language by induction. However, unlike the Natural Method, language materials for teaching in DM are explicitly preselected and graded on the basis of linguistic complexity. Simple sentences, for example, precede those with relative clauses or in the passive construction. All of this is done for the purpose of making the acquisition task easier for the learner. While there is still much spontaneous use of speech by the teacher, it is considerably less than is the case for the Natural Method.

Dialogue and action materials

Lessons in DM are mainly devoted to oral communication and follow (as with NM) the acquisition order of the first language. Thus speech understanding precedes speech production, which is then followed by reading and then by writing.

Elementary social dialogues are introduced almost immediately: 'How are you?', 'Fine, thanks', as are questions: 'Where is . . . ?', 'When is . . . ?', 'Who is . . . ?', and commands for action: 'Stand up', 'Sit down', and 'Give the book to Mary'. (The similarity here to the fundamentals of the Total Physical Response Method, which was proposed some 50 years later, is important to note and will be discussed later.)

Sometimes oral pattern drills and memorization of dialogues were also included in DM lessons. Such techniques were devised and applied for the purpose of giving practice in speech production. Interestingly, these same techniques later came to be used (perhaps more accurately overused) by proponents of the Audiolingual Method.

Sometimes, too, translations might be given verbally, as might grammatical explanations. However, these were used sparingly. For the most part, DM is typified by its reliance on natural speech in context and on the students' mental powers of induction.

Teacher fluency and class size

The structured nature of the Direct Method is such that, in the hands of a good teacher, it can be used in relatively large classes of 30 or even 40 students, with teachers getting students to speak in chorus. Still, like the Natural Method, DM requires a teacher with some inventiveness and high fluency in the second language.

Demise of DM

With the advent of the Audiolingual Method, DM was crushed. However, after a few decades, DM was reincarnated in the form of some current methods such as Total Physical Response and the Natural Approach. These methods reflect many of the essential ideas of DM.

7.2.4 The Audiolingual Method

Popularity of American linguistics and psychology and the rise of ALM

The phenomenal rise of the Audiolingual Method (ALM) was due to the popularity of the new American linguistic and psychological theories which it incorporated into its foundations. The great popularity and influence of America itself in the world, following the end of the Second World War, is a factor here. The language analyses provided by American Structural linguists, particularly Charles Fries and the stimulus and response learning psychology provided by American Behaviourists endowed ALM with great credibility. The Direct Method, which implied a Mentalist psychology, went out of fashion, except in Continental Europe (see Chapter 10 for a detailed discussion of Behaviourism and Mentalism).

ALM incorporates Structural Linguistics

Structural linguists such as Fries regarded sentences as sequences of grammatical word classes or phrases. New sentences would be created by substituting words within a word class. For example, a sequence such as Article + Adjective + Noun + Verb + Article + Noun could yield a large number of sentences such as 'The rich boy bought a car' and 'The friendly girl kissed the boy', by substituting members of the same grammatical class. Because Behaviourist psychologists, too, regarded sentences as the simple association of key words (Skinner) or word classes (Staats), it was not much of a step for ALM to adopt sentence patterns as the learning fundamentals for language.

Unfortunately for the theory, substitution cannot prevent the creation of sequences like 'The happy dust memorized the table', or 'A poor mountain elapsed the wine', which also fit the pattern for the sentence 'The rich boy bought a car'. There were other more serious problems with the theory, which Chomsky (1957, 1959) pointed out.

ALM incorporates Behaviourist psychology

ALM incorporated Behaviourist psychology (Watson, 1924; Thorndike, 1932; Skinner 1957), which was the dominant school of psychology in America for most of the first half of the twentieth century. Behaviourist psychology regarded mind and thinking to be irrelevant for the understanding and production of speech. Language learning was regarded as no different from other types of learning in which a stimulus and response paradigm was operating. Repetition and mechanical drills involving words as stimuli and responses were considered to be the essence of learning.

The defects of such a view concerning language and psychology were demonstrated by Chomsky during the 1950s and served as the basis for the subsequent collapse of Structural linguistics in the 1960s, the downfall of Behaviourism, and a rise of Mentalism as the principal explanation for linguistic behaviour in the 1970s.

Features of ALM

The Audiolingual Method incorporated into its methodology many of the same features that the Direct Method had developed, namely, planned situations, graded materials, and such techniques as pattern drills and dialogue memorization (Brooks, 1964). In contrast with DM, the Audiolingual Method almost entirely dropped the use of natural situations and spontaneous speech. There was even a tendency for some ALM advocates, such as Moulton, to reduce the meaningfulness of the speech that was taught – a practice that was frowned on by Fries, one of the founders of ALM.

Demise of ALM

In its time ALM generated an enormous amount of enthusiasm. Teachers everywhere lined up to teach second languages according to principles that reflected the latest scientific word on how humans learn language. However, the fact is that ALM failed to produce the fluent communicating speakers it had promised. All that remains of ALM today is the occasional use of Pattern Practice drills as an auxiliary exercise.

7.3   Offbeat methods appear then disappear: Cognitive Code, Community Language Learning, Silent Way, Suggestopedia

Since the downfall of the Audiolingual Method in the 1960s, a number of new methods have arisen. However, only a small number have managed to survive, and fewer still have managed to thrive. Four that have not survived are Cognitive Code, Community Language Learning, Silent Way, and Suggestopedia. Some adherents are sprinkled about, just as there are some Audiolingualists around, but the methods are disappearing with the passing of their proponents.

7.4 Contemporary methods: Total Physical Response, Communicative Language Teaching, Natural Approach, Content-Based Instruction, Task-Based Language Teaching, Computer-Assisted Language Learning

7.4.1 Total Physical Response

Rationale of the method

Total Physical Response, frequently referred to as TPR, is very much a 'natural'-type method: speech understanding precedes speech production, which, in turn, precedes reading and writing. Only the target language is used in the classroom and meaning is derived from actual objects and situations. Students are encouraged to induce rules on their own and speak when they are ready. Again, as with other natural-type methods, things go best with a small number of students.

James Asher, the founder of TPR in the 1970s, considers its unique characteristic to be the learners' performance of physical actions in response to the teacher's commands in the target language (Asher, 1966, 1969, 1977; Asher *et al.*, 1974). His idea is that memory will be enhanced by motor activity with the result that language will be more easily remembered and accessed. Interestingly, this idea and the other major ideas comprising TPR are to be found in the Direct Method, particularly with Herald Palmer in the book, *English Through Actions* (Palmer and Palmer, 1925). Asher, though, has emphasized physical activity much more than did Palmer. In any case, there is no doubt that TPR is a very useful method and one that deserves attention.

Classroom materials and activities

Initially, in a classroom of beginners in English for example, commands are given such as 'Stand up', 'Sit down', 'Open the door', 'Walk to the table', 'Point to the table', 'Point to the door', 'Where is the table?', 'Where is the book?', etc. Soon after, sometimes even within the same class hour, statements or questions are paired with commands: 'This is a book. Give the book to Susie', 'The book is on the table. Put the book on the chair', 'Who has the book? You? All right. Give the book to Anne', 'Where is the ball? On the table? All right. Tony, bring me the ball.' After the proper groundwork has been laid, students are presented with more complex sentences, like 'Give the book to Bob and give the pen to Jean', 'Walk to the table and then turn around', 'Take the yellow card and place it under the book', 'If you have a blue card then raise your hand', 'If you have the big card then place it under the small card'.

From the beginning the student is introduced to whole sentences in context. The teacher demonstrates the meaning of the words and sentences by pointing to the objects and by acting on the commands for all to see. It is claimed that with this method a student can easily learn around 25 new lexical items in an hour, along with a variety of structures. Based on our experience, we believe this to be true. In fact, with regard to vocabulary, the number could be much higher.

A demonstration project: Japanese students learn German

Japanese students in a psycholinguistics class in Japan, which was taught by the first author of this book, were given a TPR demonstration lesson in German by a colleague, Rudolf Schulte-Pelkum. The students, who had not learned German before, in just a little over an hour, learned to understand more than 50 different words as well as a variety of imperative sentences ('Stand up', 'Turn around', 'Open the door', 'Close the door', 'Give the ball to Karen and give the book to Emil'). (The students were given German names.) While hesitant in their action at first, the students soon gained in confidence, performing their tasks swiftly and with assurance. Such behaviour is a direct measure of their progress in speech comprehension.

Interestingly, when a videotape of this TPR German lesson was shown to Japanese students in other classes, they learned about the same number of items. They did not perform any actions but simply observed what was happening on the tape. *Observation was sufficient for learning!* Whether the students who performed the actions retained more over time than the students who simply observed the actions was not measured, unfortunately. TPR would predict that doing the action would solidify memory.

Advancing with TPR

After the teacher has determined that the students are firm in understanding what they have learned, they are then encouraged to speak. They are asked to give commands to their classmates with their classmates performing the actions. Games can be devised to encourage speaking.

TPR has essentially the same advantages and limitations as the Direct Method. Students do learn to communicate in speech in a natural way and also relatively quickly. In order for this to happen, however, they must have fluent and creative teachers. Nowadays, though, perhaps the teacher need not be especially creative since a great deal of curriculum material has been developed and published for TPR instruction.

TPR is best used for the early phases of second-language learning. With more advanced language knowledge, actions become less useful and relevant to communication. Then, too, there is the problem of homework. Once out of the classroom, there is little a student can do to review or gain knowledge unless recordings are made. In this regard, adopting the Grammar–Translation method along with TPR might be one good solution.

Children vs. adults

One problem with adults with TPR relates to its special reliance on action ('Physical Response'). For social reasons, many adults, more so than children, may feel embarrassed marching around a room doing things. While the required action could be modified to lessen this problem, there is not much else a teacher can do to remedy this situation. Adults may become more accepting in time, though, especially after they see their teacher doing the same things that they are obliged to do.

TPR works especially well with children, but with adults it may be best utilized in combination with other methods. Thus, TPR should not be viewed as a self-contained method that is applicable to all language-teaching contexts. Nevertheless, with such flexibility, it may well be considered the best of the speech-based teaching methods.

7.4.2 Communicative Language Teaching

In the early 1970s, Wilkins (1972) proposed a system of dividing communicative speech into two aspects: *functions* and *notions*. *Functions* (called Speech Acts in linguistics) involve requests, denials, complaints, excuses, etc. and are expressed through whole sentences. Essentially the learner is provided with a means for performing a given function. For example, learners may be told that there are various ways to make a request: they may be told 'Shut the window', 'Please shut the window', 'Would you shut the window?', 'Would you mind shutting the window?', 'Will you be so kind as to shut the window?', etc. (Wilkins, 1976, p. 51).

Notions are expressions of frequency, quantity, location, etc. These are typically words or phrases within a sentence. For example, students may learn 'I often go to the movies', 'I have a lot of friends', and 'He's standing by the window'.

Communicative Language Teaching (CLT) presumes that students want to communicate and it helps them to do just that. Lessons often start with the GT-like exercise. This may be the simultaneous reading and listening to a dialogue based on a real-life everyday situation, such as greeting a friend or buying something in a shop. Initially, there is no translation and no explanation of the structures involved, although the method does not exclude native language aids if that is what the students feel they need for a particular point. There is total reliance on situations and the students' desire to communicate within those situations.

This kind of teaching stresses communication and allows anything into the classroom so long as it will further the communicative ability of the student. This can include GT-type translations and grammatical explanations in the native language. Or, if a teacher feels that an Audiolingual technique such as drilling a phrase a number of times might help a student, then the teacher does it, so long as the practised phrase or sentence is later used in a meaningful situation.

Often, there are phrases or sentences which a student starts to create, but has trouble with. For example, if a student would like to say in English something like 'I wish I could have gone' but can get out only 'I wish . . .', the teacher might model the whole sentence a few times, let the student repeat it a few times, and then return to the situation in which the student was trying to use it and let him or her use it. (This technique seems to be taken from the Community Language Learning counselling method used by Curran and LaForge in the 1970s.)

Later, there might even be an explanation of the grammar involved, or even a structure drill, such as letting the student substitute other past participles in a sentence: 'I wish I could have eaten it', 'I wish I could have done it', 'I wish I could have seen it'. However, such techniques are only employed in the interest of assisting the students to communicate their ideas.

In comparing Communicative Language Teaching with strictly speech-oriented methods such as the Direct Method, Total Physical Response, and the Natural Approach (to follow), we can see that there are marked differences. CLT permits reading and writing almost immediately, as long as it serves the cause of communication. It also permits grammatical explanations, not relying totally on the student learning by induction. Furthermore, it permits translation.

Given the above, it would appear that CLT is not so much a particular method as an eclectic method that borrows, as it does, aspects of other methods, such as Grammar–Translation, Audiolingual, Community Language Learning, and TPR. The concern of CLT's advocates is to get people to communicate by any means possible. It is probably because of its eclecticism that CLT has become one of the most widespread of teaching methods in use today. This is especially so in the United Kingdom where so many of its originators and developers have been active (Wilkins, 1976; Alexander, 1978; Widdowson, 1978; Brumfit and Johnson, 1979; Yalden, 1983).

7.4.3 The Natural Approach

Speech understanding to precede production

The Natural Approach (NA) is the name given by Terrell (1977, 1982) and Krashen (Krashen and Terrell, 1983) to their 'new philosophy of language teaching' developed in the early 1980s. It is to be distinguished from the nineteenth-century Natural Method, although NA has a number of similarities with that and with other natural speech-based methods such as the Direct Method and TPR. (Really, not so 'new' after all.) Yet, perhaps the Natural Approach is more of an attempt to provide a theoretical description of the processes involved in second-language acquisition than it is a body of innovative techniques for teaching.

In accord with the Natural Method, Direct Method, and TPR, the importance of listening comprehension and delayed speech production is stressed in the Natural Approach. Production is delayed until the student is believed to be ready. The idea that you can only effectively produce speech that you already understand is in keeping with the understanding-precedes-production aspect of native-language acquisition.

Graded materials and syntax by induction

As for grammatical structures and rules, these are seldom explained and are expected to be acquired by receiving appropriate language input. In this respect, sentences are presented in a simple-to-complex grading and at a level that may be slightly higher than students can understand. This is very similar to the Direct Method and TPR.

NA defines itself as a method for developing basic personal communicative skills, oral and written. Goals of the method would include the ability to engage in simple conversational exchanges, to understand announcements in public places, to read newspapers, write personal letters, etc. Like most other speech-based methods, teachers of the Natural Approach make ample use of pictures, objects, charts, and situations in the classroom as the source of language input.

The Affective Filter

Such personal learning factors as motivation, self-confidence, and anxiety are given special consideration in NA. These constitute what Krashen calls the learner's 'Affective Filter' and play a significant role in gaining a language. A 'low' condition of the Affective Filter is said to be most desirable, for in such a case students would be highly motivated, very confident, and under little stress. Such desirable conditions can be fostered if, for example, students are allowed to communicate in situations without having to worry about any grammatical mistakes they may make. On the other hand, a 'high' condition of the Affective Filter would have the opposite effect, blocking any learning through too much anxiety and low motivation.

However, there are other views that hold that Affective Filter factors such as anxiety can actually be useful for language learning. Scovel (1978) contends that a student may have 'facilitating' anxiety, which pushes them to greater efforts, rather than 'debilitating' anxiety which is the type of anxiety that the 'Affective Filter' is most concerned with. Then, too, according to Skehan (1989), high motivation may be a result of language learning under conditions of little stress as well as a cause of that learning as in the premise of the Affective Filter. For example, a learner with high motivation who succeeds in learning would, as a result, probably have their motivation increase even more. The opposite would be true for a learner with initial low motivation: the low motivation would lead to failure in learning, decreasing motivation for further learning. It is thus not clear to what extent motivation is a cause (as Krashen and Terrell posit) or an effect of language-learning success. While it is probably the case that students learn better when they are motivated, not over-anxious, and when they feel relaxed and receive encouragement for their efforts, to label this an 'Affective Filter' is rather pretentious, but harmless, academic jargon.

It is odd though that Terrell and Krashen, who are such advocates of simulating a child's natural language acquisition, should posit an Affective Filter at all, since even children who are raised in anxiety-ridden homes do learn their native language.

The Monitor Hypothesis and the acquisition-learning distinction

The Natural Approach differentiates between acquiring and learning a second language (Krashen, 1982). Acquisition is said to involve a kind of inductive process similar to that which occurs in the acquisition of the native language. Such a process is claimed to be automatic and unconscious. Learning, on the other hand, is said to involve a formal process by which one consciously learns rules such as those taught by a teacher. According to Krashen, language knowledge that is 'learned' never becomes unconscious or automatic as does knowledge that is 'acquired'. (We would like the reader to note that we make no such distinction, and we use the terms 'learning' and 'acquisition' interchangeably throughout this book.)

The distinction is based on Krashen's so-called Monitor Hypothesis. According to the hypothesis, 'learned' rules are always monitored, i.e. consciously applied in the production of sentences. No such 'monitoring' of speech production, however, is said to occur with a grammar that has been 'acquired'. It is because of the monitoring process that Krashen claims that once students 'learn' grammar (instead of 'acquiring' it) they will be unable to use it unconsciously, and thus effortlessly, in production.

The 'learned' system can only be applied under certain conditions adequate for 'monitoring'. Only when learners have adequate time, are focused on grammatical form, and know the rule of the grammar can they produce speech using what they have 'learned'. For example, the 'learned' system might be used during a language test or during writing. The consequence of the limited application of the 'learned' system is that the teaching of grammar rules by explication is frowned on by advocates of the Natural Approach.

Criticism of the Monitor Hypothesis

The Monitor Hypothesis has been subjected to severe criticism by many theorists, such as McLaughlin (1978), Bialystok (1979, 1981), Gregg (1984) and Steinberg (1993). Krashen has not really answered his critics, nor has he provided convincing evidence in support of his claim that knowledge gained from the presentation of rules and their explanations cannot become unconscious and automatic (Krashen and Pon, 1975; Krashen and Scarcella, 1978). The validity of the Monitor Hypothesis, therefore, is very much in doubt.

The distinction is counterintuitive

An alternative to the Monitor Hypothesis is provided by a model of learning proposed by Bialystok (1979, 1981) in which consciously learned language can become automatic and unconscious through practice. Certainly, Krashen's claim is counterintuitive to what many people experience when they produce sentences in a second language. For example, according to Krashen, English speakers who are told in their first Japanese lesson that Japanese has a Subject + Object + Verb ordering would continue to consciously monitor this ordering even after six weeks or more. This was certainly not the experience of the first author of this book who had lived in Japan. Initial awareness disappears rather quickly. Of course, there are times when second-language learners do become aware of applying certain grammatical rules in the construction of sentences. However, this typically occurs only in the early stages when the learner has not yet integrated that knowledge well enough.

Monitoring awareness also occurs with 'acquisition'

Actually, monitoring awareness may occur even when rules are acquired by induction. Language problems are forever occurring to the second-language learner and such problems will often be considered consciously. For example, an English learner of Japanese could have figured out on his or her own what a certain verb ending in Japanese means and then properly use that ending. This might prompt the learner to consciously think more about other verb endings and how they relate to one another. Such 'monitoring' will aid, not hinder, acquisition.

Arithmetic and the acquisition-learning distinction

Let us approach the adequacy of Krashen's acquisition-learning distinction from another point of view, one which includes an area of knowledge different from but still quite relevant to language, that is, arithmetic. Suppose we ask you now to divide 954 by 6, and to do it as quickly as possible. (You can do it on paper or in your head.) Do you have the answer?

Now, were you conscious of every step of the process whereby you came up with this answer? Let us ask you, if, according to one common method of division that we shall use, you were aware that your first step was to begin by considering the single leftmost (not rightmost) digit of 954, the number to be divided? That is, 9.

Then, were you aware of deciding that, since 6 is less than 9, you must subtract 6 and so have 3 remaining? Were you aware that because the remainder was less than 6 you would write a 1 for the beginning of your answer? What did you then do with that 3? Were you conscious of having to place it in front of the next leftmost single digit of 954, which is 5, and then treat the two digits of 3 and 5 as 35?

Next you divided 35 by 6 and got an answer of 5. But how did you do that? Were you conscious of dipping into the multiplication table ($1 \times 1 = 1$, $1 \times 2 = 2$, $1 \times 3 = 3 \ldots 6 \times 4 = 24$, $6 \times 5 = 30$, $6 \times 6 = 36$, etc.), which you had memorized years ago in elementary school?

You needed that knowledge to determine that the product of 30, which is produced by 6×5, will bring you closest to 35 without exceeding it; 24 would not be as close as 30, and 36 would exceed that number, and therefore you selected 5 as an answer and you then placed that 5 to the rightmost of your answer of 1. You would then have 15 and be on your way to completing the answer.

Were you aware of all the steps that would bring you to the answer of 159? Not likely! Yet, all of these steps were taught to you *explicitly* in the classroom, and, through your teachers' explanation of the process, you 'learned' the process. Now, certainly, while the initial learning was formal and presented through explication, nevertheless, through time and practice, the rules of the process became largely unconscious and automatic.

Krashen's claim, therefore, that learning never becomes unconscious and automatic is one that cannot be upheld with regard to arithmetic knowledge. This being so, there is no reason to believe that a special case should be made for one particular kind of knowledge, language knowledge. Clearly, much of the learning that is gained in a formal situation can become unconscious and automatic. Since Krashen's acquisition-learning distinction is not a valid one, there is no good reason to suppose that teaching grammar by explication in a second-language situation cannot, at times, be beneficial. Such grammar knowledge may later become unconscious and automatically used.

Rules can be taught

Since there is no sound reason to ban the formal teaching of all rules in the classroom, simple rules can be taught directly. The learner can internalize them so that they can be used later in an automatic and unconscious manner. Of course, if a teacher spends too much time on explaining rules, the results might be as Terrell and Krashen predict.

Then, too, there are some very good ways to teach more complex rules than by traditional statement and example. The student can be presented with data and given a chance to discover the rule on his or her own. These are what Ellis (1994) refers to as 'consciousness raising' tasks. After the students have had an opportunity to figure out the rule for themselves, the teacher can then make certain that everyone understands the rule under consideration. The sensible teacher will strike a balance with direct speech experience, consciousness-raising tasks, and rule explication.

7.4.4 Content-Based Instruction

Content in language teaching is most frequently defined as the substance or subject matter that we learn or communicate through language (Richards and Rodgers, 2001, p. 204). Content-Based Instruction (CBI) is based on the same principles and on the same psychological and linguistic orientation as Communicative Language Teaching; therefore, it might be better to say that CBI is an approach to language instruction, rather than a separate method.

CBI differs from CLT in its focus on instructional input: CBI organizes language teaching around the subject that students need to master, rather than around a linguistic syllabus, and uses the target language as a means to present the subject matter. The core principles and techniques of CBI are outlined in Mohan (1986), Brinton *et al.* (1989), Stryker and Leaver (1993), Stoller (1997), and Richards and Rodgers (2001).

Language features

CBI is built upon three main features. First, language is focused on as a means for getting information. Information is constructed and delivered in texts and discourse. Thus, *language instruction is based on texts and discourse,* and not only on sentences, clauses and phrases. Second, because real world language skills such as comprehension and production, and reading and writing, are intertwined, so too should language instruction involve mastering several skills together. Third, it is assumed that language is purposeful. People learn a second language more successfully when they use this language to get information, which is interesting, useful, and leads to a desired goal. Thus, it becomes essential for the learners to realize the purpose of the language samples they are studying, and link it to their own goals.

CBI understands speech communication on the one hand, and literacy on the other hand, as two aspects of the same goal to achieve. No separate grammatical instruction becomes necessary, because grammar is seen as a component in the operaion of other skills. Then, too, grammar is more often explained than presented for learning by induction. The teacher is responsible for finding relevant grammatical material to fit into the topic or theme to be learned. Quite often this material needs to be modified by the teacher to be accessible for the students. This may involve simplification (e.g. use of shorter units and clauses), well formedness (e.g. using few deviations from standard usage), explicitness (e.g. speaking with non-reduced pronunciation), regularization (e.g. use of canonical word order), and redundancy (e.g. highlighting important material through simultaneous use of several linguistic mechanisms) (Stryker and Leaver, 1993).

Teaching procedures

In most CBI courses, the syllabus is organized around specific topics and subtopics, which are chosen in accordance with language learning goals. Richards and Rodgers (2001) refer to the organization of the Intensive Language Course at the Free University of Berlin, which consists of a sequence of modules spread over the academic year. The topical themes of the modules are Drugs, Religious Persuasion, Advertising, Britain and the Race Question, Native Americans, Modern Architecture, Microchip Technology, and the like. A typical ESP course for the Department of Economy in Ulyanovsk State University, Russia, where the second author used to teach, consists of units on Fundamentals of Management, Distribution, Money and Banking, Securities, etc.

In a CBI class students might read a text, make notes, listen to a tape recording, and respond orally or in a written form; they might study letters, reports, book chapters, or they might be involved in meetings and discussions; every type of activity being included into a subject topic.

Teaching materials and activities are selected according to the extent to which they match the type of programme. The materials must be authentic, of the type that is typically used with the subject matter of the content course in native-language instruction.

Advantages and disadvantages of CBI

The teacher is required to play a very active role in the process of learning: they must match student's specific interests with appropriate language material which they might need to pursue academic goals. Students are supposed to 'understand their own learning process and ... take charge of their own learning from the very start' (Stryker and Leaver, 1993, p. 286). Most CBI courses expect students to support each other, sometimes becoming sources of content themselves, sharing their experience of the subject.

However, the quantity of new material might be overwhelming for some students, who now have to master both a new subject matter and new language skills. Some students in CBI courses have been reported to prefer more structured, traditional classrooms (Richards and Rodgers, 2001, p. 213). As for teachers, who mostly have been trained to teach language skills rather than a certain subject, they have to cope with a double workload, spending large amounts of time and energy to prepare for classes. Given such burdens for the students and teacher, the teacher might simply take the easy way out and run a Grammar–Translation class!

7.4.5 Task-Based Language Teaching

Task-Based Language Teaching (TBLT) is yet another offspring of Communicative Language Teaching. Unlike other approaches, TBLT focuses more directly on the instructional factor, stressing the importance of specially designed instructional tasks as the basis of learning. The main idea is that learners learn the target language by interacting communicatively and purposefully while engaged in the activities (Feez, 1998). Task definitions vary, however (see Nunan, 1989; Pica, 1994; Skehan, 1998). Most often a task is defined as an activity or goal that is carried out using language, such as finding a solution to a puzzle, reading a map and giving directions, making a telephone call, writing a letter, or reading a set of instructions and assembling a toy. The task should also involve a communicative act on its own, that is, the task should provide a sense of completeness.

Theory of language

TBLT relies upon a theory of learning rather than a theory of language. The core concepts are given in Feez (1998). They boil down to the following three assumptions. First, learners are considered to learn the target language better when they are engaged in a meaningful activity. Second, a task is exactly what stimulates communication and regulates information input and output. Third, tasks will serve to improve learner motivation and promote learning because they typically use authentic materials.

Advantages and disadvantages of TBLT

The use of tasks and puzzles as a unit in curriculum has always been a good idea, and, in fact, such tasks are widely used in language instruction nowadays. However, TBLT's reliance on tasks as the main vehicle of instruction opens the approach for criticism. TBLT-based language teaching programmes did not enjoy much success. The basic claim of TBLT as a more effective basis for teaching than other language teaching approaches is still far from being a fact, is the conclusion of Richards and Rodgers (2001, pp. 223–41).

7.4.6 Computer-Assisted Language Learning

Work in Computer-Assisted Language Learning (CALL) began as early as the 1960s when the idea of using a computer for language instruction developed. Still, by 1980, in a survey of 1810 foreign language departments in America published in Modern Language Journal, of the 602 who responded, only 62 made use of CALL systems: CALL was evaluated as prospective, but hardly useful for mass instruction purposes because of cost (Olsen, 1980).

With the introduction of microchip technology, and then the invention of the Internet, things have changed dramatically. Computers became cheaper, smaller, and more powerful, and as a result, their role in education has grown immensely. By the beginning of the 1990s, a survey conducted in elementary through university educational institutions in the United States indicated that almost every student had access to a computer (Ely, 1995). Another study reported that a majority of colleges and universities across Canada were using CALL (Kidd, 1997), while in the USA, more than 40 states provide educators with some sort of Internet access, with at least 20 per cent of public school teachers reporting using computers for teaching or curriculum design (Harris, 1998).

Advantages and disadvantages of CALL

The greatest benefit of CALL is the fact that it is largely oriented to the individual learner: a computer program delivers exactly the material a learner needs and the process of learning can go at the learner's pace. If necessary, a computer program can be used for mere drilling to get language skills automated by providing a variety of structured exercises on any grammatical or lexical problem. A computer program can be used at home, and a student can spend as much time as he or she needs to master a language skill. In a classroom setting, CALL can significantly enlarge the class capacity without increasing teaching staff.

CALL is still far from being used widely due to a number of problems, particularly with regard to different computer operational systems, such as lack of good software and incompatibility of a Mac program with Windows or Linux. At present, CALL is only a helpful auxiliary technique in learning the target language.

7.5 Goals must be considered in the selection of a teaching method

It is safe to say that students will learn something from any method. No method is a total failure because, in all methods, students are exposed to the data of a second language and are given the opportunity to learn. Thus, to the disappointment of all, there is no magic method. No method has yet been devised that will permit people over the age of 12 or so to learn a second language as effortlessly as they did their native language. Still, teachers can do much to make the experience for a learner rewarding and enjoyable, whatever method is employed.

In judging the relative merits of teaching methods, one must consider goals. Just what is the purpose of having people learn a second language? If the ability to speak and understand a second language is the primary goal, then a speech-based method would be best for them. If, on the other hand, the ability to read and write is the primary goal, then perhaps Grammar–Translation could be the method of choice.

The goals of a nation are important in determining second-language teaching programmes in the school system. One country may wish to promote the study of reading and translation of scientific material from a second language, and would, therefore, wish to stress the knowledge that is gained through reading. In such a case, the Grammar–Translation Method may well be appropriate. Other countries, however, may regard communication through speech as the highest priority. As such, speech-based methods may be preferred, providing, of course, that adequate finances are available for the specialized training of teachers in such methods and that the school system can afford teaching classes with small numbers of students. When large numbers of students are to be taught and few teachers are available, Grammar–Translation might well be chosen by default, since, practically speaking, no other choice is viable.

A teacher who can afford the luxury of selecting a method for the classroom might well consider putting together a personal method of second-language teaching. For example, with both speech and literacy as objectives, one could use Communicative Language Teaching and then supplement it with physical activities (from Total Physical Response), pattern practice drills (from the Audiolingual Method), and explication and translation (from the Grammar–Translation method). Most methods will have some feature that can benefit the language learner.

Chapter 8

Bilingualism, intelligence, transfer, and learning strategies

Is it a good idea to become bilingual? Just what is a bilingual? Will learning a second language affect one's intelligence? Should a young child learn a second language? If so, when should that be? How might learning a second language be affected by the first? In this chapter, we shall attempt to provide answers to some often-asked questions, and others as well.

8.1 Varieties of bilingualism

Any two languages: speech, sign, or written

To begin with, it would be useful to consider just what the term 'bilingualism' includes. Most of us, without a second thought, would think of a bilingual as a person who is able to speak and understand two languages (languages like English and Russian, or Chinese and Arabic) and, for the most part, we would be right. Beyond this, though, there might be varieties of bilinguals that would strike many of us as odd at first. On second thought we would realize that there are people who, besides an ordinary speech-type language, also know a *sign* language, such as British Sign Language or Swedish Sign Language, which are true languages (see Chapter 2). Many deaf persons are such bilinguals. Moreover, there are people who can read a second language fluently, even write it well, but who cannot speak or understand its spoken form to any significant degree – many Sanskrit bilinguals would fall into this category. These people have not learned reading but they have learned a language in the *written* mode (see Chapter 3).

Because language in all its complexity can be acquired through a variety of modalities – sound (speech), sight (writing), and visual motion (signs) – an adequate concept of a bilingual should allow for any of these realizations. Thus, we may say that a person is bilingual if he or she knows: (1) two languages in the *same modality*, for example, two speech-based languages such as spoken English and spoken German, or, two sign-based languages such as American Sign Language and Japanese Sign Language, or (2) two languages based on *different modalities*, e.g. spoken German and American Sign Language, or, spoken French and written Sanskrit.

8.2 Is bilingualism beneficial or detrimental?

Most of us consider bilingualism as something good, an advantage. For one thing, knowledge of another language enables people to communicate with members of other cultures in their own language. This, in turn, provides a means for furthering cooperation and understanding among nations and peoples. Knowing another language is also important within countries where there is more than one prevalent or official language, as in Switzerland, which has four official languages: German, French, Italian, Romansh. Or Canada, with its two official languages, English and French. At a personal level, the pleasure and cultural benefits of bilingualism, too, are obvious. Who would not like to be able to travel around the world, to Paris, Moscow, Helsinki, Shanghai, or Tokyo, and be able to talk with the people there in their own language? What lovers of movies and theatre would *not* like to understand performances in the original language? This being the case, where then is the controversy?

First, it must be said that the arguments offered against bilingualism are typically restricted to young children learning a second language. Some people believe that if a second language is learned at an early age, it can be harmful in two main respects: (1) the learning of the second language would retard or negatively influence the learning of the native language, or (2) it would intellectually retard the development of thinking and of such cognitive capacities as mathematics and reading. Many states in the USA after the First World War banned the teaching of a foreign language because the knowledge of that language was regarded as potentially detrimental to young children's cultural values (see the Meyer case in Chapter 9).

Secondly, it must be said that the criticism that has been levelled against early bilingualism is primarily of another era, the early half of the twentieth century. That was a time when conceptions and experimental methodology involving language and intelligence were at a rather naive level and when the mood in America (where most of the research was done) was one of isolationism and a wariness of foreign influences. With the advent of the ethnic pride movements in the 1960s, both in America and Europe, along with the increased wealth that allowed ordinary people to travel to foreign lands, attitudes towards foreign languages changed significantly to the positive. Still, the questions must be answered scientifically.

8.3 Effects of early bilingualism on first-language development and intelligence

8.3.1 Effects on first-language development

Can learning a second language at an early age, while the child is still in the process of learning the native or first language, have a negative effect on the learning of the native language? There is the concern that bilingualism might somehow retard first- or even second-language development with the result that, for example, a child raised with two languages might never really learn either language as well as would monolingual speakers of those languages. This is an empirical question and one to which researchers have addressed themselves.

Negative reports

One well-known and influential piece of research for its time was that of Smith, back in the 1930s. Smith (1939) gathered comparative data on the language of pre-school children in Iowa, where she did her graduate work, and on children in Hawaii, where she went to teach. The Iowa children were essentially white and monolingually English while the Hawaii children were ethnically diverse, of Chinese, Filipino, Hawaiian, Japanese, Korean, and Portuguese parentage, and bilingual, with English as one of their languages. Smith recorded sentences uttered by the children and evaluated the sentences in terms of standard English usage. The principal finding was that the bilingual children from Hawaii had many more errors in their English speech than did their Iowa counterparts. This led Smith to conclude that bilingualism caused retardation in language development.

However, by defining English errors the way she did, Smith could not help but come up with the results that she did. Because the children in Hawaii in general spoke a dialect of English that was prevalent there, so-called 'pidgeon', and was not the standard English spoken by the children from Iowa, the Hawaiian children were penalized. Smith's bias is reminiscent of the later work of researchers such as Bereiter and Engelman (1966) and Basil Bernstein (1960, 1961) in the 1960s, who claimed that non-standard speakers of English – in particular, inner-city African-Americans in the USA and working-class whites in Britain – had poor language knowledge compared to standard English speakers.

The brilliant work of Labov (1970) and other linguistic researchers in the 1960s and 1970s, however, conclusively demonstrated that non-standard dialects of English are every bit as complex as standard dialects (as typified by Midwest speech in America, for example) and are linguistically comparable.

Positive reports

More sophisticated investigations comparing the linguistic skills of monolinguals and bilinguals have been made by Lambert and his associates in Canada. One long-term study by Bruck *et al.* (1976) with native English-speaking children in a French immersion programme found that, by the fourth or fifth grade, the second-language French skills, including reading and writing, were almost as good as those of native French-speaking children. Importantly, all of this was achieved at no loss to their English native language development (as compared to a control group of English monolingual children). In addition, the immersion group did better than the English monolingual group on creativity tests. In many cases, their mathematics and science scores were also higher.

However, other research demonstrates that in some aspects these students do not achieve native levels in productive skills such as speaking and writing (Lapkin *et al.*, 1990). This may be because they were only exposed to classroom language. Without a great degree of interaction with native speakers over a long period of time, native-speaker proficiency is not easily achievable (Tarone and Swain, 1995; Yeoman, 1996).

Positive effects with very different languages

The studies reviewed above discuss bilingualism in terms of two similar languages, English and French. What about the effects of bilingualism in terms of two languages that are quite different? For example, English and Japanese not only have completely different syntactic structures but they also have completely different writing systems. Regarding syntax, for example, Japanese uses a Subject–Object–Verb ordering and uses a system of *post*position particles (as opposed to *pre*positions as in English) that follow nouns and noun phrases. It also differs from English in that English is a right-branching language where relative clauses follow the noun they modify, e.g. 'the dog *which Mary bought* was a happy dog', while Japanese is a left-branching language where modifying clauses precede the noun. Regarding the writing systems, while English uses a relatively simple Roman type of alphabet, Japanese writing is complex, using Chinese characters along with two different syllabaries (a syllabary being a system in which each sign represents a syllable).

In a study of the first English immersion programme in Japan, Bostwick (1999) compared two groups of Japanese students in the same elementary school. One group consisted of children learning the elementary school curriculum through the medium of English; this was the experimental immersion group. The other group, the control group, consisted of children learning through the regular medium of Japanese. The results revealed no negative effects on first-language acquisition. Furthermore, both groups performed equally well on tests of academic achievement. The results showed that, the immersion students scored better on tests of English. Thus the Japanese–English immersion students equalled their Japanese monolingual peers in first-language learning and academic achievement, while at the same time they learned a foreign language.

8.3.2 Effects on intelligence

Does learning a second language at an early age, while the child is still in the process of acquiring some aspects of the native or first language, have a positive or negative effect on a child's intelligence, thinking ability, creativity, or cognitive functions such as mathematics? As was the case in considering effects on the development of language, most early research tended to find a negative effect. The possibility that learning a second language could in some way have a *positive* effect on intelligence was not something that was considered tenable until relatively recently.

Negative reports

Perhaps the earliest study on bilingualism and intelligence was done in America. Goddard (1917) gave the English-language version of the Binet intelligence test to 30 recently arrived adult immigrants at Ellis Island. On the word-fluency portion of the test, it was found that less than half of the adult immigrants could provide 60 words, a figure much below the 200 words that 11-year-old American children could provide. Based on these results, Goddard classified 25 of the 30 people as 'feeble-minded'.

Similar results were found in comparisons of monolinguals and bilinguals in Wales (Saer, 1922, 1923). Saer tested the intelligence of 1400 children between the ages of 7 and 14. Based on the higher scores for monolinguals on IQ tests, he concluded that bilinguals' thinking processes were confused by the use of two languages.

What is wrong with these and other similar studies is the fact that knowledge of the target language itself plays a great role in determining the outcome of scores on the intelligence test. Since language is crucial in order to comprehend questions and to understand the multiple-choice answers, a low level of language knowledge will result in a low score and hence a low level of intelligence. The failure of the test makers and givers of intelligence tests to take into account the role of language in influencing scores greatly biased the tests. Not surprisingly, immigrants and non-standard English speakers fared especially badly.

Positive reports

It was only in the 1950s that psychologists seriously began to realize that test items that required knowing language was not a fair measure of intelligence and that the content of items in many widely used intelligence tests was culturally biased. Once these methodological errors began to be taken into account, research studies found no disadvantage for bilinguals. More than that, there was good evidence of a positive effect!

One of the first studies to find positive effects on intelligence for bilingualism was that of Peal and Lambert (1962). They concluded that bilingualism results in greater mental flexibility and abstract thought. Furthermore, they suggested that rather than the two languages causing 'confused thinking', bilingualism improved thinking. This idea is supported by an impressive amount of recent studies (see Bialystok, 2004, for a review): if children have more than one language to analyze, they pay more attention to structural patterns and functions of words, which, in turn, has a crucial effect on further reading and academic success.

To date, one of the most impressive studies in the field has been that of Bain and Yu (1980). They compared monolingual and bilingual young children in different parts of the world (Alberta, Canada; Alsace, France; and Hong Kong). The tests that Bain and Yu used involved puzzles and having to carry out verbal instructions. Some of the instructions were quite linguistically complex for a 4-year-old; for example, the child was told, 'When the red light goes on, say "squeeze", and squeeze the ball'. By the time the children were around 4 years old, the results of some cognitive performance tests showed the bilinguals to be superior to the monolinguals, in addition to their having acquired two different languages.

Positive results were also found recently by Ellen Bialystok of York University in Toronto. She tested the 'fluid intelligence' of 154 bilingual and monolingual English and Tamil adult speakers. The participants were given the Simon Test where they were required to focus and respond to rapidly changing tasks. The older bilinguals (ages 60 to 88) did far better than their monolingual counterparts of the same age. In fact, their results were about the same as of younger monolinguals (ages 30 to 59) (Picard, 2004).

8.3.3 Conclusion regarding the effects of early bilingualism on language and intelligence

It is unlikely that learning a second language negatively affects intelligence in a permanent or important way. In fact, some research suggests there may even be beneficial effects. Given the advantages of knowing another language and of young children's propensity for speedy language acquisition, there is good reason to favour early bilingualism.

8.4 Sequential and simultaneous learning situations

There are essentially two conditions according to which a person may become bilingual: (1) the two languages can be acquired *sequentially*, such as the second language being learned later at school, or (2) *simultaneously*, such as where the young child is exposed to two different languages in the home at the same time. Simultaneous learning, by its very nature, is thus for children only. On the other hand, sequential learning can occur with both children and adults; the second language can be learned during lower-level schooling, e.g. elementary school, or it can be learned after the person has become an adult, e.g. at university or in another country.

8.4.1 Sequential learning of two languages

Consider, for example, an immigrant couple who have come to America from China with their 4-year-old daughter. They send their daughter to an English-speaking pre-school but they continue to speak only Chinese at home. By the time the child is 5 years old, she is speaking fluent English with her playmates and teachers while continuing to speak Chinese at home with her parents. Her English is as good as the English of her friends. The child has thus learned two languages, Chinese and English, sequentially; with the second language being introduced after a great deal of the first language had been learned. Although the child begins learning English, Chinese continues to be learned from her parents at home. From this point on, the advanced learning of the two languages will be occurring simultaneously. What is sequential is the different starting time, with a four-year gap before the introduction of the second language.

In sequential bilingualism young children are said to pass through four common stages (Tabors and Snow, 1994): (1) Children attempt to use the language learned at home with other children in the wider community where a different language is used. As they come to understand that others do not understand their home language, they give up trying to communicate in the home language outside of the home. They are *silent*. (2) They abandon their home language in favour of communication through *gesture*. Children at this point are beginning to comprehend some of the second language. (3) The children begin to use the second language in ways similar to children learning a first language. They *produce abbreviated utterances* without function words as in the telegraphic speech of first-language learners. (4) Finally, they begin to *produce grammatical utterances* in appropriate situations.

8.4.2 Simultaneous learning

One person speaks one language only, or, one person speaks two languages

There are two basic situations in which a child may learn two (or more) languages at the same time: (1) Each person speaks one language only to the child: *One Person–One Language*, or (2) Each person speaks two different languages to the child: *One Person–Two Languages*.

Typical of the first case is when the mother speaks one language while the father speaks another. Or it can be a frequent babysitter or other family member who speaks the other language. Each person uses one language exclusively. For example, the mother might speak to the child only in Spanish while the father speaks to the child only in English. This is the one-person-uses-one-language-only situation: 1P–1L, for short. The other learning case is when the same person uses two different languages when speaking to the child. For example, the mother uses both Spanish and English, and the father does the same. The two languages are mixed by each parent. Thus, each person uses two languages: the 1P–2L situation, for short.

The 1P–1L situation is better

It seems that children are so flexible that they can become fluent in both languages by the age of 3 or 4 years, regardless of the language situation (1P–1L or 1P–2L). Although direct evidence bearing on this issue is not available, it seems more likely to be the case that the child in the 1P–1L situation will learn the two languages faster than the child in the 1P–2L situation and attain a higher level of proficiency. This would be due to consistency. In the 1P–1L situation, the child on hearing speech would not have to puzzle over which of the two sets of language knowledge is being referred to. The child would know that the mother will speak one language while the father will speak another.

A simultaneous trilingual case (1P–1L) × 3

One interesting and actual (1P–1L) × 3 example is that of friends of the first author who lived in an English-speaking community in Honolulu. In the family, from the time of the birth of each of their two sons, who are about three years apart in age, the mother spoke only Japanese and the father spoke only English. To add to the situation, there was a live-in grand-mother who spoke only Russian to the children. The result? By the age of three, each of the boys, in turn, became trilingual in English, Japanese, and Russian! These languages were maintained by the children into adulthood.

Developmental stages in bilingual language learning

Children learning two first languages simultaneously follow the same route as other children learning their first language (Lyon, 1996). The 1990s bilingual infant research demonstrated that bilingual infants, even those raised in an environment where similar languages are spoken (like English and French, for example), separate the two languages in the first months of their lives. They acquire phonological properties of their native languages at the same rate as monolinguals, but gradually they start to prefer one language, which becomes their dominant (Sebastián-Gallés and Bosch, 2001). Other than that, bilinguals move through the same stages of one-word utterances, two- and three-word utterances, then increasing complexity with morpheme acquisition and complex sentences (see Chapter 1). In the two- and three-word stages some mixing might occur between the two languages, especially for 1P–2L learners.

In the past, theorists postulated that the two different languages were functioning as one language for the child. That is, the child was somehow mixing the vocabulary and syntax of the two languages to form one language system. However, the current view is that the child is simply switching between the two languages in the way that adult language learners do. An adult or a child who cannot think of a word in one language might then use a word or phrase while speaking the second language. This is called 'codeswitching'. Simultaneous bilingual children, it seems, tend not to do this as much.

8.4.3 First-language and second-language relations affect learnability: the transfer effect

8.4.3.1 First language similar to second language

What one's first language is will affect one's learning of the second language. Thus, not every second language will be learned at the same rate. The nature of the similarity relationship between the first and second languages will determine the rate of learning. For example, after having learned English as a first language, learning French would not be as difficult as would learning Japanese. There are differences between English and French syntax but these differences are small in comparison to the monumental differences between the syntax of English and Japanese.

To the extent that two languages have similarities, such as the position of the article (as in English and French), gender (designation of nouns as masculine or feminine, as in French and Italian), obligatory marking of nouns for plurality, and similar syntactic structures (as in English and French), there will be a greater facilitation. There is that much less for the second-language learner to learn. The higher the similarity the faster the learning.

There can be significant similarities in terms of vocabulary, as well. Just looking over the past few sentences we can note shared vocabulary between English and French such as: vocabulary/vocabularie; similarity/similarité; difference/différence; monumental/monumentale; and comparison/comparison. A learner would not be starting at zero as he or she would if learning Japanese. (Although Japanese has many borrowed words from English, the nature of Japanese pronunciation and writing tends to obscure them.) It works the other way as well; the Japanese speaker learning English is placed in a comparable position to the English speaker learning Japanese. Yet, if the Japanese speaker were to learn Korean, the Japanese person would find it relatively easy because the syntax of these two languages is very similar. Pronunciation would be a major learning problem, though, because the sound systems of those two languages are quite different.

Studies in Finland provide evidence that it is easier to learn a second language that is similar to the first (Ringbom, 1978; Sjoholm, 1979). About 7 per cent of Finns speak Swedish as their first language. Research findings demonstrate that Finns who speak Swedish as a first language learn English at a faster rate than those who speak Finnish as a first language, i.e. Swedish-to-English is faster than Finnish-to-English. Undoubtedly this is because Swedish is closer to English, with which it shares a Germanic and Indo-European origin, than Finnish, which belongs to an entirely different language family, the Uralic.

Thus, we may conclude that the greater the similarity between two languages in terms of their syntax, vocabulary, and sound system, the more rapid the rate of acquisition in the two languages. If we had to scale the importance of these variables, we would give syntax and then vocabulary the greater weight. Good pronunciation cannot compensate for poor syntax or vocabulary. Good syntax with good vocabulary is a winning combination for second-language success. (California governor, Arnold Schwarzenegger, is a good example.)

8.4.3.2 Facilitation occurs even between very different languages

It is clear that the knowledge of a prior language will help the learning of a second language even when the two languages are quite different with respect to vocabulary, syntax and pronunciation. The fact that a 5-year-old child in a foreign environment (a New York child moving to Tokyo) can often learn a second language in less than a year, which is much faster than the child's learning of its first language, strongly suggests that there is some sort of commonality among languages that is separate from the usual similarity measures that are used in comparing languages. Such commonalities, which *all* languages share, would consist of such principles as: words have a morpheme structure and a phoneme structure, words combine into phrases and into sentences and clauses, basic constituents must be ordered in some way, and such operations as substitution, deletion, and addition are involved. The knowledge that words and sentences represent objects, ideas, situations, and events, for example, is something that the first-language learner brings to the second-language situation and does not have to struggle to relearn.

8.5 Strategies for second-language production

8.5.1 The First-Language Strategy and the Second-Language Strategy

Because errors are easy to observe and are good indicators of a person's level of second-language knowledge, there have been many good studies done on errors (see Corder, 1981, for a review). There is some confusion, though, when it comes to interpreting just what the cause of errors might be. In our opinion, only a minority of errors can be attributed to interference, where the first language intrudes on the second. Rather, most errors are systematic, being the result of the application of what we shall call the 'First-Language Strategy' and the 'Second-Language Strategy'. These strategies are applied when relevant second-language knowledge is not yet available or is incomplete.

Consider the following errors made by the first author's Japanese university students while writing English answers to an examination question (* indicates ungrammaticality).

1. *Now Tom happy is.

This sentence follows Japanese constituent order with the verb placed at the end.

2. *Afterwards they ate the dinner.

The article is improperly inserted before the mass noun 'dinner'. There was no previous reference to a specific 'dinner'.

For the sake of fairness, let us now consider an error commonly made by English speakers who are learning Japanese. The English speaker might well produce the following order of constituents in 3a while translating from English to Japanese:

3a. *John Mary met theatre at yesterday. (Spoken in Japanese by an English speaker)

Here the Japanese Subject + Object + Verb constituent order is correct but the adverbials, 'theatre + at' and 'yesterday,' are improperly placed. They must be at the beginning of the sentence, not at the end. The preposition 'at' correctly follows the noun it is associated with (in English prepositions precede the noun), thus, 'theatre + at' is a type of Prepositional Phrase. No article appears with 'theatre' because Japanese does not have the article. Thus,

3b. Yesterday theatre at John Mary met.

is the proper order in Japanese (Adverbials + Subject + Object + Verb).

Let us now discuss these sentences and the cause of the problems that they raise:

1. Error caused by *Interference*:

*Now Tom happy is. (Written in English by a Japanese speaker)

For the Japanese student who has had years of English and knows English word order well, it is likely that this is a case of interference. In the process of constructing the sentence, perhaps because of haste, the Japanese order of constituents intruded on the process so as to cause the error.

2. Error caused by *Second-Language Strategy*:

> *Afterwards they ate the dinner. (Written in English by a Japanese speaker)

The student has to some extent learned the article rule and its application to types of nouns but perhaps mistakenly thought that 'dinner' here is a countable noun that requires the article. Another possibility is that because the student was unsure of the status of 'dinner', she employed what could be called an Article Insertion Strategy. That is, when in doubt, insert the article, because nouns taking the article are more frequent in the second language. Thus, this error is the result of applying general knowledge of the second language to production of the second language.

3. Error caused by *First-Language Strategy*:

> *John Mary met theatre at yesterday. (In Japanese, by an English speaker)

Supposing that the English-speaking person did not know the Japanese rule, then this could well be an instance, not of interference, but of the result of using the First-Language Strategy, that is, applying first-language knowledge to the second language. When second-language knowledge is lacking, this strategy is very useful. It is one that, we believe, all second-language learners automatically use and rely on, especially in conversation. Usually it is better to say something, even if wrong, than to say nothing. This strategy will allow for something to be said, even though it is based on knowledge of the first language.

8.5.2 Strategies for sentence production and communication

Strategies that are used for the purpose of keeping the conversation going involve 'communication' strategies (Faerch and Kasper, 1983; Kasper and Kellerman, 1997). Communication strategies may have an effect on learning since the more the learner speaks the greater linguistic input the learner will receive. The greater the input, the more the opportunity for language learning. This type of strategy includes overgeneralization, in which a rule of the second language is applied in inappropriate contexts such as the definite article being used with 'dinner' in the example above.

Communication strategies may also involve using words or phrases from the first language when they are unknown in the second language (codeswitching), or coining new words such as 'airball' for 'balloon' (Varadi, 1983).

8.5.3 Strategies for becoming a better second-language learner

Learning strategies which will assist in the acquisition of a second language is a different topic from the one just discussed. The topic previously under discussion mainly concerned using strategies for improving and maintaining communication and conversations. What strategies a person might develop so as to improve the learning of a second language is another topic. Researchers such as Rubin (1981), Wenden and Rubin (1987), Cohen (1998), O'Malley and Chamot (1990) and Oxford (1990, 1996) are involved in such issues.

Thus, for example, according to Rubin (1981) the strategies used by successful language learners include: (1) verification: checking to see if their hypotheses about the language are correct, (2) inductive processing: creating hypotheses about the second language based on one's second- or first-language knowledge, (3) deductive reasoning: using general logic in problem solving, (4) practice: such as repetition, rehearsal, and imitation, (5) memorization: including mnemonic strategies and repetitions for the purpose of storage and retrieval, and (6) monitoring: being alert to the making of errors and paying attention to how one's message is received by the listener. While one could argue that these are strategies that any language learner *naturally* uses, research indicates that the *explicit* teaching of such strategies will improve the capacity of the learner. (See Cohen (1998) for a review of this phenomenon.)

8.6 Teaching reading in a bilingual situation at home

8.6.1 How to teach the reading of two languages

Suppose that parents are raising their child bilingually with, say, English and Chinese. Suppose too that the parents wish to teach the child to read both languages.

First, the parents should be using the One Person–One Language (1P–1L) approach, which was discussed earlier in this chapter. In this approach, each parent speaks one language only to the child, e.g. the mother speaks Chinese and the father speaks English, and the child learns both languages (as speech) simultaneously.

As for teaching reading, however, we recommend that the teaching be done sequentially, with the second language following the first after a year or two. Suppose that the parents start teaching the child to read English. At least one parent must be involved, the one who speaks English to the child. (It would be beneficial if the other parent joined in too, but just for reading and not for language teaching.) After about a year or so, by which time English reading is established in the child, then the teaching of Chinese would be started. The lead teacher should be the parent who speaks Chinese to the child.

In our view, the simultaneous teaching of reading is not advisable, not just because of the risk of the child confusing the two writing systems, but because the parents would be greatly burdened. They would have to keep and use two sets of reading materials and vie for time for teaching. Since many of the reading activities involve placing cards on objects, the clutter with two cards, each in a different language on each object, might be excessive, and inconvenient to the child.

8.6.2 Which language should be read first?

We would recommend that the language to be learned first is the one that is most important for the child's welfare. Basically, it should be the language that is used in the community and in school. By learning to read the language of the community, the child will be able to read the signs that are everywhere outside the home. This will reinforce the child's learning at home and motivate the child to read more. Attaining a high level of reading before the child begins school, where such reading is the norm, will assist the child in being able to deal with whatever is offered in school in terms of reading, and give the child a head start.

The second language will not be hard to teach to read after the first, because once the child can read the first language, he or she will have learned the basic principles of reading. These principles will make the learning of second-language reading easier.

Language, mind and brain

Chapter 9

Language, thought and culture

9.1 A relationship at the heart of psycholinguistics

The relationship of language, thought, and culture is a topic that is central to psycholinguistics. People throughout the ages have wondered whether speech or language is necessary for thought. Can we think without language? Does language influence culture? Does language affect our perception of nature? Does language affect our view of society and the world?

We shall deal directly with these questions. However, before doing so, we would like to begin in an indirect way – by recounting a court case, one that exemplifies the issues that we will consider. The case and the fate of Robert Meyer is true and it happened in the United States about 85 years ago.

9.1.1 The arrest of the Sunday School teacher

In May of 1920, in Hamilton County, which is a rural area in the state of Nebraska, Robert Meyer was arrested for violating a certain state law. This Nebraska law forbade the teaching of a foreign language, that is, a language other than English, to children under the age of 13 years. Meyer had been teaching Bible stories in German at Zion Parochial school to a 10-year-old boy. Since German was a foreign language for the boy, Meyer was in violation of the law. According to Nebraska's 1919 Siman Act,

> No person shall teach any subject to any person in any language other than the English language. Languages other than English may be taught only after a pupil shall have . . . passed the eighth grade. . . . Any person who violates any of the provisions of this act shall be deemed guilty of a misdemeanor and, upon conviction, shall be subject to a fine of not less than twenty-five dollars ($25), nor more than one hundred dollars ($100) or be confined in the county jail for any period not exceeding thirty days for each offense.
> (US Supreme Court Reports, 1922, pp. 392–403)

Actually not only Nebraska but 21 other states prohibited the teaching of foreign languages. Only so-called 'dead' languages such as Latin and

Greek could be taught. The states had passed these laws essentially with the German language as the target. America had just finished a war with Germany and generally there was a hatred of Germany and things German, particularly its military and authoritarian values, ideals, and political institutions. The language law reflected the widespread American belief that the German language itself embodied all that was wrong in German culture and so to teach such a language to young Americans would be immoral and corrupting.

It is here that the psycholinguistic question arises. Is it the case that a particular language such as German embodies the culture, values, and ideals of a particular people such as the German people? Let us put aside this question for the moment and return to the fate of Robert Meyer.

Meyer appeals to the Nebraska Supreme Court

Meyer was in fact found guilty. However, he decided to appeal his lower-court case to the Supreme Court of the state of Nebraska. (Each state in the United States has its own Supreme Court.) Ironically, lawyers for the state of Nebraska made essentially the same claim that the famous German philosopher, Wilhelm von Humboldt, made for the German language in 1836 (von Humboldt, 1971). That is, a language *by its very nature* represents the spirit and national character of a people. Never could von Humboldt have dreamed that the German national character and spirit (of which he was so proud), along with the German language, would be held in such disrepute by other countries as to result in their demanding the banning of anything German! The state of Nebraska argued that by teaching children the grammar, structure, and vocabulary of the German language, Meyer could harm American children by instilling in them the wicked German values that were embedded in the German language.

The US Supreme Court takes a position on language, thought, and culture

The Nebraska Supreme Court denied Meyer's appeal, but Meyer was not content with that ruling. He took his case to the highest court in the country, the United States Supreme Court. There he won his case, with the court overturning his Nebraska convictions. The court declared as unconstitutional all laws in the United States that forbade the teaching of a foreign language. In its 1922 ruling, the court stated as one basis (there were others on constitutional grounds) for its decision that 'Mere knowledge of the German language cannot reasonably be regarded as harmful' (p. 400). It maintained that knowing a foreign language would not in itself provide the values and culture of the country from which that language is derived. Was the court correct? It is up to us, in effect, to assess the validity of the court's psycholinguistic conclusion.

9.1.2   Can we distinguish a 'safe' from a 'harmful' second language?

In the present case, the question is clear: if teaching a second language to children is antithetical to the morals and values of the society in which they live, then clearly children should *not* be taught a second language. Perhaps, though, a second language could be taught if that language is a 'good' language, i.e. does not conflict with the first language. But, if so, how are we to decide which are the good languages and which are the bad ones?

Is it safe to teach American children the Italian and Russian languages since Fascists and Communists are no longer in control in Italy and Russia? On the other hand, is it dangerous to teach British children Chinese and Vietnamese because Communists control China and Vietnam? But then, what about teaching Korean, for there is Communism in North Korea but democracy in South Korea? And how about the teaching of Spanish – after all, there is Communism in Cuba but democracy in Spain? Just what are the safe or dangerous second languages, if any? These are among the problems with which we will deal in this chapter.

9.2   Four theories regarding the dependence of thought and culture on language

It seems that most people take it for granted that thought is somehow dependent on language. However, there are a number of formulations that idea can take. Four principal formulations (some overlapping) concerning the relationship of language, thought, and culture that have been expressed over the centuries are as follows:

- **Theory 1: Speech is essential for thought**.   We must learn how to speak aloud, otherwise we cannot develop thinking.
- **Theory 2: Language is essential for thought**.   We must learn language, how to produce or understand speech, otherwise we cannot develop thinking.
- **Theory 3: Language determines or shapes our perception of nature**.   The learning of language will determine or influence the way we perceive the physical world, visually, auditorily, etc.
- **Theory 4: Language determines or shapes our world view**.   The learning of language will determine or influence the way we understand our culture and the world.

Let us now discuss the adequacy of these four theories so that we may determine if further theorizing is necessary.

9.3 Theory 1: Speech is essential for thought

9.3.1 Proponents of the theory

Proponents of this view hold that thought is a kind of behaviour that originates from speech production. Typically, such theories are held by Behaviourists who wish to get rid of mind and Mentalism in psychology, linguistics, and philosophy and to replace the notion of thought or cognition with something that is *physically* observable or potentially observable. The psychologists Watson, Skinner, and Staats, the linguists Bloomfield and Liberman, and the philosophers Ryle and Quine are but a few of the many who advocated such a conception. They define thought as *subvocal speech or behaviour* and not something mental, as in the traditional view of psychology.

The following quotations characterize the theory that thought originates from uttered speech:

> The simplest and most satisfactory view is that thought is simply behavior – verbal or nonverbal, covert or overt. It is not some mysterious process responsible for behavior but the very behavior itself in all the complexity of its controlling relations, with respect to both man the behaver and the environment in which he lives.
>
> (B. F. Skinner, 1957, p. 449)

> The fully literate person has succeeded in reducing these speech movements to the point where they are not even visible. That is, he has developed a system of internal substitute movements which serve him for private purpose, such as thinking and silent reading, in place of audible speech sounds.
>
> (Leonard Bloomfield, 1961, p. 31, from a 1942 paper)

> Articulatory movements and their sensory effects mediate between the acoustic stimulus and the event we call perception.
>
> (Alvin Liberman, 1957, p. 122)

Liberman proposed the Motor Theory of Speech Perception, according to which, before we can understand speech, we must first repeat subvocally or internally what another person has said. Only by this prior motor act can we understand speech.

9.3.2 Inadequacies of the theory

We would like to raise objections with regard to the adequacy of this theory. Sometimes, given the abstract and intangible nature of the subject matter, not all objections can be expected to be definitive. Our principal aim, however, is to provide a number of objections whose combined effect is to raise reasonable doubts about the theory in question. We shall raise six objections to this theory. They are: (1) Children having no speech production can comprehend speech and think; (2) Speech comprehension, which implies thought, develops before speech production in normal children; (3) Simultaneously speaking aloud while thinking about something different commonly occurs in everyday life; (4) Telling a lie; (5) Meaning and thought occur without behaviour; and (6) Interpreting between languages can be done. Each of these objections will now be discussed in turn.

9.3.2.1 Children having no speech production can comprehend speech and think

While the ability to utter speech in appropriate situations is a good indicator of language knowledge, the absence of the ability to produce speech may not indicate a lack of language knowledge. There are many hearing persons who are born mute. People such as these may be born with cerebral palsy or some other abnormality that prohibits them from articulating speech. In Chapter 1, we described among others the cases of Nolan, the noted Irish writer, and Rie, the 3-year-old Japanese child who learned to read words, with understanding, that she could not say. None of these persons could speak.

Were these people able to think? Let us answer this question by implication, since a direct answer would require a lengthy and contentious thesis on the nature of thought. If a person can comprehend the meaning of speech, that person *must* have the ability to think. It would be ludicrous to have to argue that persons exist who understand the meaning of speech but are unable to think. Surely the ability to answer items on an intelligence test presupposes the existence of thought in the person taking the test.

It must therefore be concluded that persons without the ability to speak *can think*. The notion that speech production is necessary in order to think is clearly false.

9.3.2.2 Speech comprehension, which implies thought, develops before speech production in normal children

As was discussed in Chapter 1, the developmental process is that speech comprehension precedes speech production. It is the pattern that continues throughout the acquisition process (Ingram, 1989), whether it be for first words (Clark and Barron, 1988), elaborate syntax such as passives (Golinkoff and Hirsch-Pasek, 1995), or the later acquisition of idioms and figurative speech (Levorato and Cacciari, 1995).

The comprehension and production processes develop in a parallel mode with production always trying to keep up with comprehension. As the child acquires an aspect of language in comprehension, the child can then try to figure out how to use it in production. The child attempts to co-ordinate production with respect to the system that has been developed for understanding (Clark and Hecht, 1983).

Thus, Huttenlocher (1974), who studied four young children aged 10 to 13 months over a six-month period, found that they were able to comprehend speech at a level *beyond* that to which they had progressed in production.

Similarly, Sachs and Truswell (1978) found that children who could only produce single-word utterances (they were at the one-word stage of speech production) nevertheless could understand syntactic structures composed of *more than one word*. The outcome was the same for the child in the Steinberg and Steinberg (1975) research, where a 2-year-old boy learned to read (understand the meaning of) many written words, phrases, and sentences *before* he was able to say them.

That children would *not* be able to utter words or sentences *for the purpose of communication* (not simple imitation), without gaining a prior understanding of speech, is surely to be expected. One could not use speech meaningfully unless one knew what meaning such speech had.

Thus, it must be concluded that for normal children as well as for mute-hearing children, *speech comprehension is the basis for speech production* in the mind. Since the ability to comprehend speech implies the existence of thought, it therefore must be concluded that speech production is not necessary for thought.

9.3.2.3 Telling a lie

Neither would telling a lie be possible if thought is a kind of speech. The very essence of a lie is *saying* one thing while *thinking* something quite different. Behaviourists wish to use one process of sentence creation for both processes (saying and thinking) simply by distinguishing the overt (speaking aloud) sentence from the covert (speaking to oneself or subvocally) sentence. However, because there is only one sentence-making apparatus, an overt pronunciation of one sentence and the covert pronunciation of an entirely different sentence (the covert sentence being the Behaviourist's idea of thought) cannot occur simultaneously. Clearly, a valid psycholinguistic theory must allow *two* distinct processes with different content to occur at the same time. The issue of lying demonstrates that the Behaviourist cannot define thought out of existence!

9.3.2.4 Meaning and thought occur without behaviour

Behaviourists: behaviour of the body is essential for thought

In his theory of the origin of thought, Skinner suggested that behavioural responses could be the basis of thought in addition to speech utterances. Such behavioural responses could be muscular or glandular in nature. It seems that Skinner was influenced by the work of some Behaviourist psychologists who were his contemporaries around the 1950s. Experiments showed, to the delight of Behaviourist psychologists, that changes in electrical potential occurred in certain parts of the bodies of subjects when the subjects were instructed to think of certain motor activities. For example, changes in electrical potential in the musculature of the right arm occurred in response to instructions to think about lifting that arm. They concluded that thinking was nothing more than a reflection of physical events in the body. Many psychologists then believed that they had begun to localize meaning and thought in the body so that once and for all mind could be banished from psychology.

It was not long, however, before the inadequacies of such a formulation became apparent. The major problem with this theory is that it incorrectly predicts that a loss of thought or meaning will occur with damage or removal of body parts. In fact, people do not lose the meaning of words nor are they unable to think when a limb is lost or their larynx is removed. (See Osgood, 1953, p. 648, for a critical review of such research attempts prior to 1950.) One is reminded of the debilitating losses of muscle control that occurred in the bodies of the physicist/astronomer Stephen Hawking and of the late actor Christopher Reeve (of Superman fame). Hawking lost the ability to speak but still has some bodily controls while Reeve retained the ability to speak but lost control of most of his body. The result? These intrepid souls responded with an even greater mental output! Clearly, neither control of the vocal apparatus nor of most of the voluntary musculature of the body is relevant to thought.

A daredevil researcher's body is paralyzed by a drug

About 50 or so years ago, a group of researchers (Smith *et al.*, 1947) wondered what would happen to the thinking of a person if that person's body were almost completely paralyzed. Their wondering led to the researcher Smith having himself injected with a curare-like drug that temporarily induced complete paralysis of the voluntary muscles of the body. Since only smooth muscle systems such as the heart and digestive system continue to function under the drug, Smith needed the assistance of an artificial respirator in order to breathe.

When the effects of the drug wore off, Smith reported that he had been able to think quite clearly; also he could solve the series of problems given to him by the other researchers. At the risk of his life, Smith had made a scientific point. Since while paralyzed he could in no way speak and could make only minimal bodily responses, it is clear that thought was *not* dependent on body movement or movements of the organs of speech, because no movements occurred, not even subliminal ones.

9.4 Theory 2: Language is essential for thought

9.4.1 Proponents of the theory

Theorists such as Sapir, Whorf, and Vygotsky hold that the language system, with its rules of vocabulary, is necessary for thought. This theory is broader than the prior theory, which held that thought was derived from speech production, since it encompasses all of language, both speech production and speech understanding.

Let us consider some choice quotations to get some idea of the scope of this theory. For example:

> The writer, for one, is strongly of the opinion that the feeling entertained by so many that they can think, or even reason, without language is an illusion.
>
> (Edward Sapir, 1921, p. 15)

> Thought is not merely expressed in words; it comes into existence through them ... The relation between thought and word is a living process: *thought is born through words.*
>
> (Vygotsky, 1934, pp. 125, 153; emphasis ours)

> The background linguistic system (in other words, the grammar) of each language ... is itself the shaper of ideas, the program and guide for the individual's mental activity, for his analysis of impressions, for his synthesis of his mental stock in trade. Formulation of ideas is not an independent process, strictly rational in the old sense, but is part of a particular grammar, and differs, from slightly to greatly between different grammars. We dissect nature along lines laid down by our native language.
>
> (Benjamin Whorf, from his 1940 paper (Carroll, 1956, pp. 212–13))

9.4.2 Inadequacies of the theory

We have two objections to raise regarding this theory. They are: (1) Deaf persons without language can think; (2) Multilinguals are whole persons.

9.4.2.1 Deaf persons without language can think

There are many deaf children who do not begin to acquire language until quite a late age, often after 3 years, when they begin to attend special schools. These are typically children who have a congenital hearing loss of over 90 decibels and are unable to receive speech, and whose parents (usually hearing) do not know sign language. These children, when at play and when participating in activities around the home, behave just as intelligently and rationally with respect to their environment as do hearing children. If one holds that language is the basis for thought, one would have to argue that these children do not think; that they were automatons, mere robots.

Furthermore, if one holds that grammar determines how we 'dissect' nature, then it must be argued that either the non-language deaf children cannot dissect nature or, if they do, they do so differently from children who do have grammars. No such difference has ever been noted, nor has it ever been observed that deaf children who acquire language late undergo a radical change of perception. Rather, research evidence points to the opposite conclusion. Furth (1966, 1971), for example, provides research data that shows no difference in intelligence between normal and deaf persons, even though the language knowledge of the deaf persons is generally far below that of hearing persons.

The case of Helen Keller, whose language knowledge was minimal until she was 7 years old, is also relevant to this issue. Keller reports in her book, *The Story of My Life*, many memories of the period in which she was without language (Keller, 1903/1996). For example, in one pre-language incident she remembers getting angry when her teacher tried to teach her the words 'doll' and 'mug'. She got so angry that she threw the doll down on the floor. It would be insupportable to maintain that Keller could not think or sensibly perceive the world prior to the age of 8, when she had little or no language.

A more recent case is that of a 27-year-old deaf man (Schaler, 1991) who demonstrated that he understood objects, situations, and events even though he had no language for them. Furthermore, when he later acquired sign language, he was able to describe experiences in his life that had occurred before the acquisition of sign language. The man was a thinking human being even before he had acquired language. Such a fact cannnot be explained by the theory that thought comes to existence through language.

9.4.2.2 Multilinguals are whole persons

Consider persons who are proficient in more than one language, where two or more languages had been learned in childhood. If the language system forms thought, and if different languages form different thought systems, then such persons would have formed more than one system of thought. (It would not have been possible under the theory to form a single system because, according to the theory under consideration, opposing concepts derived from the different languages would be involved.)

If multilingual persons have more than one thought process (one for each language), such persons would not be able to think coherently or would have separate thought intelligences or personalities. Different guiding ideas would be involved with the different languages. Then, too, such persons would have difficulty in using the knowledge gained through one language when operating in the other language(s), since thought is supposed to be language-specific and not universal, according to this theory. However, no evidence of such malfunctioning or any other sort of problems for multilingual persons has ever been observed.

Cases of persons who live in only one environment but have learned a number of languages simultaneously in that environment provide perhaps the best test of the theory in question. The environment is constant except for language. In this regard, the first author would like to offer the case of a family he knows well since they are his friends. The two sons grew up in that family speaking English, Japanese, and Russian. They were trilingual by the age of 3 years! This occurred because the father spoke English to the children, the mother spoke Japanese, and the grandmother, who lived with them, spoke Russian. The two boys, four years apart in age, each learned all of these languages simultaneously from birth.

The children appeared no different from monolingual English-speaking children of their age in terms of beliefs, values, personality, and their perceptions of the world and nature. One would not expect such an outcome from a theory that predicts that significant mental differences will result from the effects of learning such disparate languages as English, Japanese, and Russian.

9.5 Theory 3: Language determines or shapes our perception of nature

9.5.1 Proponents of the theory

Whorf, Sapir, Korzybski, and others are of the view that one's knowledge of vocabulary or syntax influences one's perception and understanding of nature.

> Newtonian space, time, and matter are not intuitions. They are recepts from culture and language. That is where Newton got them.
>
> (Benjamin Whorf, from Carroll, 1956, p. 153)

> Einstein's relativity of time is a reform in semantics, not in metaphysics.
>
> (Philipp Frank, 1953, p. 218)

9.5.2 Inadequacies of the theory

We will raise a number of objections to the theory. These will be under the headings of: (1) Perception, interest, and need determine vocabulary; (2) Colour and snow vocabulary; (3) Hopi 'time' and Chinese 'counterfactuals'; (4) Lack of vocabulary does not indicate lack of concept; (5) Knowledge overrides literal word meanings; and (6) Multilinguals' view of nature.

9.5.2.1 Perception, interest, and need determine vocabulary

Psychologists have tried experimentally to determine what effects, if any, knowledge of the vocabulary of language has on perception or behaviour. (See Niyekawa-Howard, 1972, for an older but interesting survey of such research.) Rather than vocabulary determining our interest and need, researchers have found the contrary to be true. It is our interest and need that determines our coinage of vocabulary and its use. Nowadays people know little of the vocabulary surrounding horses and horse-driven transportation. We know a lot, though, about automobiles and their parts and functions. Vocabulary is selected for use. Once it fails to serve a need, it falls out of use.

Regarding interest and need as the prime motivators for the acquisition of vocabulary, we find that American children, like children in many other countries, are enchanted by dinosaurs. They can often name 25 or more! It is not the case, however, that they perceive the types of dinosaurs because of their language. Rather, it was through perception that they developed their interest in dinosaurs so that they seek the names of these objects. Pronouncing the names for such creatures is not an easy task, as many a parent will testify!

9.5.2.2 Colour and snow vocabulary

Colour words

Some languages have only a small number of colour words. The Dani language of New Guinea has only two colour words, one for light colours and one for dark colours. If language were the basis of thought and of the perception of nature, as Whorf and the others contend, then one would expect speakers of this language, with such a limited repertoire of colour terms, to have perceptual difficulty in distinguishing colours they have no terms for. Research has generally shown that this is not the case, although some conflicting results have been obtained.

Kay and McDaniel (1978) in a large cross-cultural investigation found no difference in perception of colours for different language speakers. Heider (1972) found similar results in testing the Dani people, who have only two colour terms in their language. Thus, speakers of languages that have only two, three, or four colour terms are as capable of distinguishing among the many colour bands of the visible spectrum as those whose languages have more than eight basic colour terms. People can see the differences but will not give them a name unless there is a good reason to do so. Kay and McDaniel (1978) conclude that 'rather than language determining perception, it is perception that determines language' (p. 610).

A recent investigation, Robertson (1999), however, contends that the perception of colour is determined by the colour words of a language. The researchers studied the Berinmo, a people who live in Papua New Guinea close to the Dani and who have five colour words in their language. They report that in a matching task, the Berinmo were more apt to match colour tokens together according to their language; just as English speakers were more apt to put colour tokens together according to their language. Now, supposing that these results are valid, what is one to conclude?

In a *New York Times* report Robertson (1999) states that 'Berinmo color vision is the same as ours. If they are asked to identify a single color from a group of colors, they would do it in the same way as you or I. But say that you have three colors, and call two of them blue and one green. We would see them as being more similar because we call them by the same name. *Our linguistic categories affect the way we perceive the world*' (emphasis ours).

But, is this conclusion justified? Clearly not, because Robertson's conclusion contradicts what she had said before, that Berinmo colour vision is the same as ours and they can identify a single colour from a group of colours.

It is clear from this statement that the colour terms of the Berinmo language did *not* affect the Berinmo's basic perception of colours. If the Berinmo are able to identify colours as English speakers can, it follows that the Berinmo's *perception* of colour has *not* been affected by their language.

Snow words

There are dramatic vocabulary differences from language to language. The Inuit (previously called Eskimos), for example, have a large number of words involving snow. In Hawaii, there is only one, the English word 'snow'. The Inuit, though, have single words for snow-on-the-ground, hard-snow-on-the-ground, block-of-snow, and others. Incidentally, the superficiality of the linguistic analyses of the Inuit language has been documented by a number of theorists. (For an excellent summary and discussion on the snow example see Martin, 1986.)

There is no reason to suppose, though, that Inuits learn to perceive varieties of snow because of their language rather than through their life experience and needs. It is because of the importance of snow in their lives that they have created more words for snow than have Hawaiians. Then, too, English-speaking skiers in cold countries do distinguish a variety of types of snow despite the lack of vocabulary in English. What they do to describe in language the physical condition of snow is create phrases, e.g. 'powder snow', 'wet snow', etc. It is this language device of creating phrases that every language has that makes up for any vocabulary deficiency.

9.5.2.3 Hopi 'time' and Chinese 'counterfactuals'

Hopi people and time

Whorf's research in the 1930s with the Hopi, Native American people, convinced him that their language forced them to see the world in a completely different way from speakers of European languages. He believed that the Hopi language had few words relating to time, and that this gave them radically different concepts of space and time.

More recently, however, other researchers have found that Whorf was wrong in claiming that the Hopi language is a 'timeless' one. Gipper (1979), for example, who lived with a Hopi family for a period of time and studied their language, found that while Hopi does not have a formal tense, it nevertheless contains a whole series of expressions for time. Many of these expressions appear as adverbs or prepositions. According to Malotki (1985), another researcher who spent many years living with the Hopi, Hopis actually *do* use a variety of time referents such as periods relating to harvest, the moon, the sun, and other significant events. We do much the same in English ('Let's go when *it gets dark*', or 'I'll fix it when *the weather gets warm*'). Malotki very neatly concludes, 'People are not different because of their languages, but because of their experience. Deep down, we're all the same. It couldn't be otherwise.'

The Chinese language and 'counterfactuals'

Reminiscent of the Whorf claim for Hopi and its later debunking by Gipper and Malotki is the claim by Bloom (1981) about Chinese. After a superficial analysis of Chinese, Bloom claimed that Chinese were not as able as English speakers to think hypothetically about what is not true (to think 'counterfactually') because of certain grammatical features of the Chinese language. Again, someone who really knew the language, in this case Au (1983), found that the results obtained were due to faulty translations, and that once proper translations were made, there was no basis for claiming a difference in thinking.

9.5.2.4 Number vocabulary in the Amazon

Interestingly, two studies on Amazonian languages were published in 2004, both of which concerned with speakers' numerical understanding. Pica *et al.* (2004) investigated the Munduruku language, while Gordon (2004) investigated the Piraha language. Both of these languages have a rather small set of number words. Munduruku has words only up to the number 5, while Piraha has only words for 1, 2, and many (more than 2).

After applying some tests, in both cases the authors of the studies concluded that the speakers of these two languages were conceptually affected negatively because of the small size of their number vocabulary. The reaction to this conclusion was quick and pointed. The critics demonstrated problems in the reasoning of the researchers, particularly Premack and Premack (2005) for Pica *et al.*'s Piraha study, and Casasanto (2005) for Gordon's Munduruku study. In the latter case, the criticism was so telling that Gordon (2005) reversed his earlier position. The dominant view emerging is that, given the proper settings, speakers of these Amazonian languages would not show a cognitive defect because of their language. Premack and Premack (2005) argue that these limited numerical systems are convenient and suitable for the needs of these Amazonian speakers, who are hunter-gatherers. They say, 'Although hunter-gatherers had little need for exact numbers, one can imaging that no owner of stored goods would wish to receive three casks of oil when he had stored four' (Premack and Premack, 2005, p. 673).

9.5.2.5 Lack of vocabulary does not indicate lack of concept

Simple vocabulary is *not* a good measure of the concepts that speakers of a language may hold. It is a fallacy to believe that the vocabulary of a language represents the sum total of the concepts that a person or culture may have. Experience does not always lead us to coin vocabulary items; sometimes we choose to create phrases. For example, English speakers are quite aware of their hand, yet although we have a vocabulary item for the underside, 'palm', we have no word for the topside. Instead we use a phrase, 'back of the hand'. Lack of a vocabulary item is not indicative of a lack of a concept.

Many theorists do not realize that a lack of vocabulary does not imply the lack of a concept. Thus we find an educator like Tadao Suzuki saying that 'We recognize the fragments of the universe as objects or properties only through words . . . without words we could not even distinguish dogs from cats' (Suzuki, 1984, p. 35). However, if dogs and cats can distinguish one from the other without language, it would be absurd to think that humans could not do the same thing. New animals, plants, and other things in nature are continually being discovered. The discoverer notes the difference, then offers a name. Not the other way around! There would be no discoveries if we first had to know the name of what it is we would discover!

9.5.2.6 Knowledge overrides literal word meanings

Consider such items as: 'the sun rises', 'sunset', 'red hair', 'time flies', and 'white wine'. The theories under consideration imply that, as the result of our hearing and using such items, we would come to believe that the sun actually rises or sets on its own, that a person's hair is actually red, and that white is the colour of white wine.

The fact of the matter is that we can believe something quite different from what the language literally specifies and that the continual use of a language form may not change an underlying thought. We know that the sun does not rise or set no matter how many times we hear people say it or we say it ourselves. English speakers have simply stuck with the original coinings even though it came to be known that it was the earth and not the sun that was doing the moving.

Such a fact, where one thing is said but another is understood (similar to lying, except that everyone knows that what is said is not true) runs counter to the implications of the theory being assessed here.

9.5.2.7 Multilinguals' view of nature

If the language system forms or guides thought in the way we perceive nature, then multilinguals must be said to have a variety of ways of viewing the physical world. The multilingual would have as many different conceptual–perceptual systems of the physical world as he or she has languages. If it is true that different languages have distinctive and important effects on the way we view nature, then the multilingual must similarly have distinctive and important ways of viewing nature. As was noted in a section on multilinguals earlier in this chapter, no such differences have ever been noted. The multilingual person is a whole and integrated person who perceives nature as other humans do.

9.5.3   Conclusion

There is no foundation to the claim that vocabulary affects our view of nature. In fact, the evidence shows the reverse to be true. One would think that on such an important issue, the proponents of the theory would offer sound evidence in support of their view. The fact is that Sapir, Whorf, and the others offer little beyond mere assertion in favour of their claims.

9.6   Theory 4: Language determines or shapes our cultural world view

9.6.1   Proponents of the theory

Some theorists believe that even if language is somewhat distinct from thought, nevertheless, knowing a language will itself condition and influence one's cultural, social beliefs or views of the world. For example, in the early part of the nineteenth century, Wilhelm von Humboldt held that language embodies the spirit and national character of a people. The views of the following theorists are of a more recent vintage, and would include Whorf (quoted in the previous section) and others.

> Language is a guide to 'social reality.' Though language is not ordinarily thought of as of essential interest to the students of social science, it powerfully conditions all our thinking about social problems and processes. Human beings do not live in the objective world alone, nor alone in the world of social activity as ordinarily understood, but are very much *at the mercy of the particular language which has become the medium of expression for society . . . No two languages are sufficiently similar to be considered as representing the same social reality*. The worlds in which different societies live are distinct worlds, not merely the same world with different labels attached . . .
>
> (Edward Sapir, 1929, p. 209; emphasis ours)

> . . . a language, any language, has at its bottom certain metaphysics which ascribe, consciously or unconsciously, some sort of structure to this world.
>
> (Alfred Korzybski, 1933, p. 89)

> . . . the aristotelian type of education (through language and its subject-predicate form of representation) leads to the humanly harmful, gross, macroscopic, brutalizing, biological, animalistic types of orientations which are shown today to be humanly inadequate. These breed such 'führers' as different Hitlers, Mussolinis, Stalins, etc., whether in political, financial, industrial, scientific, medical, educational, or even publishing, etc., fields, fancying that they represent 'all' of the human world.
>
> (Alfred Korzybski, 1933, p. xxi)

Exactly how we are 'at the mercy of the particular language which has become the medium of expression for society' Sapir doesn't tell us. In any case

Sapir, Whorf, Korzybski, and others clearly claim that the language system *does* provide a view of culture and society and an outlook on the world.

9.6.2 Inadequacy of the theory

If these theorists are correct, we would expect to find differences and similarities in such essentials as philosophy, religion, politics, or societal structure to be a function of language. In this regard, we would like to provide objections to these contentions. These are: (1) Same language yet different world views; (2) Different languages yet similar world views; (3) Same language but world view changes over time; (4) Multilinguals have a unitary world view.

9.6.2.1 Same language yet different world views

Consider, for example, the United States, where we can find native speakers of the same English language who vary greatly in terms of their philosophical, religious, and political ideology. Variation may be observed among speakers in the same neighbourhood and even in the same family. Consider, for example, a monolingual English-speaking family where the mother is an atheist, the father a Christian, the daughter a Moslem, and the son a Zen Buddhist. If it is true that language influences or determines one's world view, then we should expect uniformity of religious outlook since only one language system is involved, English. This is obviously false.

The theory predicts that we should not expect differences in politics, social organization, or metaphysical thinking among speakers of the same language because their views must somehow be conditioned by their language. Not only the existence of various religions but of various political parties (from Fascism to democracy to Communism) and cult doctrines shows that monolingual speakers of English are not at all restricted by their 'subject-predicate' grammar.

9.6.2.2 Different languages yet similar world views

Consider that many countries having widely different languages may share similar political, social, religious, scientific, and philosophical views. If a language system influences or determines world view, then we would expect that people with different languages would hold different world views. Such is not the case.

Christian doctrine, for example, is shared by speakers of various languages around the world. The same can be said for Communist doctrine. In China, North Korea, Vietnam, and Cuba, Communism is shared by speakers of widely different languages. Obviously it was not the language but other cultural and historical events that brought those countries to adopt Communism. It should be remembered that the origin of Communist doctrine came from the writings of a German speaker, Karl Marx. As far as differences go, the grammars of Chinese, Korean, and Vietnamese are as remote from the German language as any language can be.

Then, too, if it were really believed by the Chinese Communists that knowledge of a foreign grammar, like English, would itself be a danger to the government, the country would not allow its teaching. However, the Chinese government *does* promote the teaching of English. The government is not afraid of the grammar of English. They simply have students learn English grammar with sentences having the content that they consider appropriate.

For example, the wife of the first author, who was born and raised in Beijing, was a Red Guard and then a member of the Communist Youth League at the time that she began studying English as a second language in high school. It is interesting to note some of the sentences included in her lessons: 'Long live Chairman Mao!' 'Keep fit, study hard, work well!' (Mao's instruction to children), 'We love our Motherland; we love the Communist Party; we love the people', 'We study Marxism, Leninism and Mao Zedong thoughts', 'We love our great Socialist country', 'We learn from the People's Liberation Army'. Change 'Mao' to 'Lenin', and you will get the same sentences that were learned by the second author in Russia at school English lessons.

The same can be said for the Roman Catholic Church in the advocacy of its doctrines. The Catholic Church is not wary of languages but it is wary of books in those languages that can spread ideas that are opposed to the teaching of the Church. The Church bans books but it does not ban languages! The grammar of a language is not a threat – the potential threat lies in the sentences that the speaker of a language may produce with that grammar.

Thus, we may conclude, along with the Chinese and former Russian Communist Government, and the Catholic Church, that it is the use of the grammar of the language that is important and that *the characteristics of the grammar itself are not relevant.*

9.6.2.3 Same language but world view changes over time

We may observe that a society may change its social structure and world view even though its language remains relatively unchanged. For example, in about 100 years, China has changed from feudalism under the Qing (Manchu) dynasty, to capitalism (under Chiang Kai Shek) to versions of Communism (under Mao and subsequent leaders). Yet the Chinese language has changed relatively little over that period in terms of its basic grammar. Similar changes may be noted in the history of many countries, such as Russia. These facts are something that the theory under discussion cannot explain. If the grammar does not change, then the culture and world view should not change either.

9.6.2.4 Multilinguals' world view

If a person is multilingual, the theory predicts that such a person will have as many distinct world views as language systems. Thus, a multilingual would have to hold competing views as being true, which would surely confuse a person's functioning. For example, would a Chinese–English bilingual think like a Communist (assuming, for the sake of argument only, that the Chinese language has Communist doctrine inherent in it) when speaking Chinese but think like a capitalist exploiter (assuming, for the sake of argument only, that the English language has capitalist doctrine inherent in it) when speaking English? If so, the bilingual person would be deemed schizophrenically insane. But that is not true. Since the implications of the theory are absurd, the theory must be regarded as false.

9.7 Erroneous beliefs underlying the four theories

What led the theorists whose theories we have discounted to advocate the theories they did? Discarding the anti-Mentalist position of some of the Behaviourist theorists who would treat thought as some sort of speech or behaviour, there are certain erroneous beliefs which might have been held by the other non-Behaviourist theorists that led them to invalid conclusions. We will consider three such mistaken beliefs: (1) Their analysis of language is adequate; (2) The meaning of words is linguistic in origin; and (3) There are primitive languages and primitive human intelligence.

9.7.1 Erroneous belief 1: Their analysis of language is adequate

The most serious deficiency in the theorizing of Whorf, Sapir, Korzybski, Skinner, von Humboldt, and others concerns the assumption that the directly observable words or the structure of a sentence represent all of the semantic or thought elements of that sentence. These theorists drew conclusions largely based on what linguists today would consider a superficial surface structure analysis. Whorf (Carroll, 1956), for example, states that 'Our Indian languages show that with a suitable grammar we may have intelligent sentences that cannot be broken into subjects and predicates' (p. 242), and that 'the Hopi language contains no reference to "time" either explicit or implicit' (p. 58). Such statements (disavowed by subsequent linguists) are made essentially because it is assumed that surface structure directly signifies all of the meaning of a sentence. These linguists thus had a tendency to focus on the *differences* between languages. The idea that grammatical differences made thought differences was not long in coming. It seems that most of the linguists simply played with the idea, because they offered little or no evidence for their assertions. They had other concerns. Except for Whorf, they did not bother to seek out hard evidence to support their contentions.

It was only when Chomsky came along and postulated underlying structures that it was realized that languages had a lot of *similarities*. It is not surprising, therefore, that only after Chomsky did the search for *language universals* begin in earnest, although the linguist Joseph Greenberg was an earlier initiator.

9.7.2 Erroneous belief 2: The meaning of words is linguistic in origin

Except for the minor case of onomatopoeia (speech sounds imitating environmental sounds), the relationship between a word and its meaning is conventional. That is, there is no necessary relationship between the sound of a word and its meaning. There is no inherent reason for a dog to be called 'dog' and not 'pen'. Thus, when one hears a word for the first time, e.g. the obscure English word 'tantivy', its meaning is not understood, unless it is composed of known morphemes. The meaning that is to be associated with a particular sound sequence must be learned. It is not possible to know from the sound sequence alone (especially if not in a phrase or sentence) that the meaning of 'tantivy' is related to horses and indicates 'a gallop or rapid movement'.

Meaning for words is acquired in four main ways: (1) a sound form is associated with an object, situation, or event in the world, e.g. the sound 'dog' with the object 'dog'; (2) a sound form is associated with an idea or experience in the mind, e.g. 'pain' with the feeling of 'pain'; (3) an inference may be made in a linguistic context, an idea may be suggested, e.g. in reading a paragraph one word may not be known but because everything else is understood, its meaning may be guessed at by inference; and (4) an analysis of known component morphemes may suggest a meaning for the sound form, e.g. the meaning of 'unprimitive' can be gained through knowledge of the morphemes 'un' and 'primitive'.

In considering these four ways of acquiring word meaning, we may note that the first two involve non-linguistic sources. In (1) the experiencing of objects, situations, and events in the world provides a basis for meaning, and in (2) experiences in the mind itself provide the basis. These are the experiences that attach to empty sound forms and thus form a meaningful word. While (3) and (4) do provide meaning through the medium of language, it must be recognized that such mediums themselves are composed of language that was derived from non-linguistic origins, i.e. through the experience of items in the world (1) or through experience of items in the mind (2). Thus, the ultimate source of all meaning is based on non-linguistic experiences of the world or mind.

The mistake of Whorf and others is to assume that the mere hearing of the sound form of a word (an unknown one) itself provides some sort of meaning. They do not allow for a prior mental experience because that would imply that thought precedes language. A language sound form itself, however, does not provide meaning.

9.7.3 Erroneous belief 3: There are primitive languages and primitive human intelligence

One often hears observers of other cultures say that such and such a people are not logical or rational or that they are somehow deficient in intellect. Such supposed deficiencies are frequently attributed to their having a primitive language. Yet modern linguistic research has never found a single language that could be called 'primitive'. Thus it is that Chomsky (1967a) can with some assurance assert that all languages are of similar complexity, with each having similar basic forms and operations. And, while other linguists may disagree with Chomsky on what the basic form and operations might be, they do not disagree that all languages are constructed and operate with essentially the same principles.

It appears to us that Sapir, Whorf, and the others assumed that there was such a thing as a primitive people and that those people had a primitive grammar. Since they supposed that the primitive grammar of these people reflected their thought, they concluded that their thought was primitive too. How else could Whorf have concluded that the Hopi people had no concept of time, even with the faulty linguistic data that he gathered from those people? Such notions about primitive peoples and primitive languages were virtually taken for granted in the first half of the twentieth century when Sapir and Whorf were doing their theorizing, when the world still had undiscovered peoples and lands. Those days seemed long gone.

Then, too, there is a case of non-standard speakers of such dialects as Black English, whom many naive people regard as irrational. Labov (1970), however, clearly demonstrated that logic *does* underlie the utterances of those speakers. Once one learns the premises that a people hold, their behaviour and statements that were previously thought to be strange or illogical immediately become rational.

9.8 The best theory: Thought is independent of language

9.8.1 Thought is independent of language

The relationship between language and thought that will be proposed here is essentially the one that was advocated by the philosopher John Locke some three centuries ago. It is that thought is independent of language, that language is dependent on thought, and that the function of language is to provide a means for the expression and communication of thought.

The thought system in the mind of the child develops over time as input stimuli of the world, such as visual, auditory, and tactile stimuli representing objects, events, and situations in the environment, are experienced by the child. Until thought is sufficiently developed (ideas of objects, relations of objects, states and actions of objects), words uttered in the presence of the child are not meaningfully processed. When that happens and when language input is experienced in coordination with objects, events, and situations, then language can begin to be learned. Over a period of time, the language system, with its vocabulary and grammatical rules, is formed.

Part of the language system is actually part of the thought system, for the meaning and semantics of the language system are those ideas that are part of the content of thought. There is not one idea for 'dog' in language and another in thought. Such a view would be unparsimonious in the extreme. Rather, the thought and language systems are joined through meaning and ideas.

9.8.2 The development of thought precedes the development of language

As thought develops, the child seeks to express those thoughts to others. Through speech understanding the child develops a grammar and finds a means through speech production to provide meaningful speech (see Chapter 1). The grammar develops as the result of prior thought. Thus, the sequence is as follows:

Thought → Speech understanding → Speech production

It is with this sequencing of thought, speech understanding, and speech production that we can explain all of the problems that were raised in objection to the four previously described theories. None of the other theories can do this.

9.8.3 The notion of 'thinking in language' is a fallacy

It is often observed that sound forms of words come to one's awareness while one is thinking. It is a mistake, however, to conclude from this that the sound forms themselves are thought. Such word forms are merely reflections of some underlying ideas. *It is thought that determines the selection of word forms.* As children, we learn to encode thoughts into language and then into acoustic speech. Because we discover that in order to interact effectively with people, we must be instantly ready to express our thoughts into speech, we consequently develop a habit of converting thoughts into speech at a mental level. It is this mental sound form that we sometimes become aware of when we think. The connections from particular thought to mental language and then physical speech are mainly automatic and it is only with conscious effort (our normal condition) that we do not say every-thing that we think. When a child first learns to speak, it seems that the child does not have suppression control and that much of what he or she thinks is articulated into speech. What the child must and soon does learn is that while it is all right to automatically convert all thoughts to sentences in the mind, it is not all right to convert all of those sentences to overt speech. Socially unpleasant consequences result for those who do.

9.8.4 John Locke said it best

Concerning the relation of language and thought, in our view John Locke said it best:

> The Comfort and Advantage of Society, not being to be had without Commun-ication of Thoughts, it was necessary, that Man should find out some external visible Signs, whereof those invisible Ideas, which his Thoughts are made up of, might be made known to others.
>
> (Locke, 1690: Book III, ch. ii, sect. 1)

Chapter 10

Where does language knowledge come from? Intelligence, innate language ideas, behaviour?

10.1 How do we acquire knowledge?

10.1.1 Perfect circles, God and language

You say the world is not flat. How do you know that this is true? You say you know what a perfect circle is. Did someone tell you? How do you know that what they told you is true? Can your measurement be perfect? You say God exists or does not exist. How do you know this? Do ideas exist? Do we have minds and are there ideas in our minds? We have knowledge but what is it and where did it come from?

The study of the nature and origin of knowledge is a branch of philosophy called 'epistemology'. In psycholinguistics, we too are interested in epistemology since we are concerned with how a certain kind of knowledge, language knowledge, is acquired. Back in Chapter 1, we discussed how children learn language, but what we did not discuss is how the human infant got started in analyzing and learning a language. Does the human infant use *intelligence* or *innate language ideas*, or both? If it is the use of intelligence, are infants then born with this intelligence or do they have to develop it? And if it is the use of innate language ideas, what are those ideas and how are they activated so as to enable the infant to learn language? Or, is it the case that neither are relevant and a study of behaviour conditioning or functions can provide the explanation?

The various philosophical *isms* that we shall be concerned with in this chapter, Empiricism, Rationalism, Behaviourism, and to a lesser extent Philosophical Functionalism (to be distinguished from Linguistic Functionalism), are types of explanations that have been given in response to the question of how it is possible for language to develop in the child and to be used by mature speakers. We shall be assessing the different explanations offered by these 'isms'; at the same time we hope to be able to provide you with a critical framework from which you may draw your own conclusions.

10.2 Mentalism vs. Materialism

10.2.1 The essence of Materialism

The psychologist John B. Watson, the founder of Behaviourism, regarded mind and consciousness as religious superstitions that were irrelevant to the study of psychology. For him, there was only one kind of stuff in the universe, the material or matter and the study of physiology *is* the study of psychology.

Such a philosophy has its origins in the ancient Greeks (Epicurus, the Stoics) and with La Mettrie in eighteenth-century France. Some recent philosophical Functionalists follow in this tradition but take this view a step further and grant mental characteristics, including consciousness, to any inanimate device so long as there is identity of function with that of humans (Chalmers, 1996).

Other Behaviourists, like Skinner (1971) and Osgood (1971), might allow that mind exists but they would give it no power and certainly would not study it. The philosophical Behaviourist theories of Ryle (1949, p. 199) and Quine (1960, pp. 34–5) take a similar view, i.e. that the object of psychological study should not be mind but bodily dispositions for behaving: mind and mental processes can be reduced to the physiological functioning of the body.

Despite the diversity of these anti-Mentalist theorists, they hold one principle in common: they argue for the study of the physical body (including the brain) where they can relate bodily processes and functioning of the body to situations and events in the physical environment.

10.2.2 The essence of Mentalism

In opposition to the materialistically inclined theorists noted above, the Mentalist holds that mind is of a different nature from matter. Thus, there are qualitatively *two* kinds of substances in the universe, the material and the mental. Such a doctrine goes back to the ancient Greeks, such as Aristotle, through Locke and Descartes, up to the present day, including such theorists as Chomsky and Searle and the authors of this book.

For the latter theorists, the understanding of mind and consciousness is essential to the understanding of the intellectuality of human beings, particularly language. Most modern-day psycholinguists and linguists are Mentalists, placing their emphasis as they do on the study of mind and the interaction of body and mind in order to understand the processes of language and its learning by children.

Two basic mind and body relationships with respect to environmental stimuli and behavioural responses in the world are: the *Interactionist* and the *Idealist*. We characterize these two views as follows.

10.2.2.1 Interactionism

Body and mind are seen as interacting with one another such that one may cause or control events in the other. An example of body affecting mind would be the activation of a pain receptor in the body after being stuck with a pin, resulting in a feeling of pain being experienced in the mind. An example of mind affecting body would be when a person doing trimming in the garden decides, in the mind, to cut down a certain plant, and then does so. According to this interactionist view, which is similar to the one proposed by Descartes (1641, Meditation VI), persons behave the way they do as the result of either the body acting alone (as in breathing, and the circulation of the blood) or the body interacting with mind (as when one intentionally holds one's breath or lifts one's hand).

Incidentally, the Interactionist would argue that it is because of the two basic types of 'stuff' in the universe, the material and the mental, that sentences such as 'The idea of square is purple' and 'Happiness weighs 3 grams' are meaningless if taken literally. For in these sentences physical attributes (weight and colour) of the material world are attributed to non-physical mental entities (idea and mental state) of the separate mental world.

10.2.2.2 Idealism

Certain Mentalists, such as Plato, Berkeley in the early eighteenth century, and Hegel in the nineteenth century, took the radical position that *mind is the only stuff* of the universe. According to this radical Mentalist view, *Idealism*, the body and the rest of the physical world are mere constructions of the mind. The world exists only in the mind of conscious individuals, with the only true substance being the mental. For Plato eternal ideas were the only reality. For Berkeley all minds were part of the mind of God. In a sense, subjective Idealism is at the other extreme from radical Materialism. While for the Materialist only matter exists, for the Idealist, only the mental exists.

Nowadays, there is little interest in Idealism. Rather, Interactionism is the principal notion of Mentalism being advocated (Searle, 1997). It is this notion of Mentalism that we are concerned with, especially as it is realized in the competing doctrines of Empiricism and Rationalism.

10.2.3 Why the Mentalist–Materialist controversy?

Why all the controversy and all the *isms*? Why can't everyone agree on body and mind? The age-old dilemma, to paraphrase Crane (1995), is this:

- If we believe that the *mental* is qualitatively different from the *physical*, then how can the two interact? Here the Mentalist is stuck for an answer.
- If the *mental* is not qualitatively different from the *physical*, then how can we make sense of the phenomenon of consciousness? Here the Materialist is hard put for an answer.

10.3 Behaviourist wars: Materialism vs. Epiphenomenalism vs. Reductionism

10.3.1 Materialism

In this view, only the physical body exists. Mind is a fiction and thus only body should be studied. Quotations from the works of the original behaviourist psycologist Watson (1924) give a clear idea of what this philosophy is all about. For example:

> Belief in the existence of consciousness goes back to the ancient days of superstition and magic . . . Magic lives forever . . . These concepts – these heritages of a timid savage past – have made the emergence and growth of scientific psychology extremely difficult . . . No one has ever touched a soul [or a mind] or seen one in a test tube, or has in any way come into relationship with it as he has with other objects of his daily existence.

> (pp. 2, 3)

Thus, psychology was regarded as indistinguishable from physiology.

10.3.2 Epiphenomenalism

The essence of this view is that although both body and mind exist, the mind simply reflects what is happening in the body. Since the mind has no causative powers, the proper study of psychology is still, as Watson held, the body. Supporters of this view, for example, are Skinner and other psychologists, and the language philosophers Ryle (1949, p. 199) and Quine (1960, pp. 34–5). Quine posited bodily dispositions and tendencies to behave. (A potential to behave in a certain way would indicate a certain meaning.) He scoffed at such Mentalistic notions as 'meanings' of words and said they should be relegated to museums.

According to Skinner, 'The fact of privacy (non-objective subjective events) cannot of course, be questioned' (1964, p. 2). However, while he allows mind to exist, which Watson did not, he gives mind no power over behaviour. Thus, Skinner (1971) said, 'It [Behaviourism] rejects explanations of human behavior in terms of feelings, states of mind, and mental processes, and seeks alternatives in genetic and environmental histories' (p. 35). Psychology is thus the study of the physical.

The epiphenomenal Behaviourist philosopher Ryle (1949) similarly scoffed at what he terms Descartes' 'ghost in the machine' concept, where Ryle uses 'ghost' pejoratively to signify mind and mental events and 'machine' to signify body. He and other epiphenomenal theorists would rather have us think that it is more reasonable to believe that machines can produce 'ghosts' but that these 'ghosts' can have no effect on our behaviour!

10.3.3 Reductionism

While mind, as well as body, is said to exist, proponents of reductionism also believe that mind can be reduced to the physical, i.e. body. For many of these theorists, body and mind are two aspects of a single reality, as the seventeenth-century Dutch philosopher Spinoza argued. (Spinoza's view contrasts with the epiphenomenal view which holds that body is the primary reality.) Since, by taking this dual-aspect position, one can learn all there is to know about mind by doing a thorough study of body, there is no need to study mind (Feigl, 1958; Smart, 1959; Armstrong, 1968). Thus, mind is reduced to body. Such being the case, mind can be studied entirely through body in relative metaphysical comfort.

Psychological proponents of this view such as Osgood (1980), Mowrer (1960), and Staats (1968, 1971) have posited that stimuli and responses occur in the body and brain and thus mediate between an overt stimulus and an overt response, where 'overt' represents events outside of the body. Overt stimuli could, for example, be a flash of light or someone asking a question while overt responses could be the blinking of the eyelid or the uttering of speech in answer to a question.

10.3.4 Objections to Behaviourism

Chomsky (1959) raised absolutely telling arguments against Behaviourism, arguments that brought him to a Mentalistic conception of the relationship of language and mind. A further three arguments in favour of Mentalism by the first author are presented in the following section.

10.4 Philosophical Functionalism and our objections to it

10.4.1 Philosophical Functionalism

In more recent years, along with the development of artificial intelligence, computer languages, and cognitive science, a new theory of philosophy/psychology, called Functionalism, has been proposed. The philosophers Putnam and Fodor were prominent in the founding of this movement but it now seems as though both may have given it up. Dennett and particularly Chalmers are its most vocal advocates today.

Like Behaviourism, Functionalism is a Materialism. Even when Functionalists do allow for mind and consciousness, as does Chalmers, for example, they consider mind and consciousness in physical terms. With their focus on behaviour and brain, and on inanimate machine functions (this is what is new), the Functionalists are the natural successors to the Behaviourists. Thus, when we hear Chalmers (1996) say, 'The very fact that [conscious] experience can be coherently subtracted from any causal account implies that [conscious] experience is superfluous in the *explanation* of behaviour' (Chalmers, 1996, pp. 158–9), we know we have not come far from Skinner's quintessential assertion, noted a few sections before.

Functionalism is foundational for those cognitive sciences that would abstract from details of physical implementation in order to seek principles common to all intelligent processing devices (Dennett, 1978; Fodor, 1980; Dretske, 1981). So long as the function of a calculator is identical to the function of a human being doing arithmetic, in that they have the same input and output relations, the Functionalist has a basis for asserting that the calculator can have similar mental states and experiences as does the human. It is in identity of functions, same input (16×3) and same output (48), that the state of the calculator can be regarded as equivalent to the mental state of a human, with both providing the same output in response to the same input. Because of this functional equality, a Functionalist like Chalmers is willing to grant the attributes of 'mental' and 'mind' to the calculator.

The language philosopher Searle (1997) sharply criticized this position of Chalmers, after which Chalmers modified his assertion about inanimate objects having experiences. He now says that he is not firmly committed to that position and that 'I merely explore it and remain agnostic' (Chalmers, 1997, p. 165). But how can anyone seriously consider that inanimate objects have conscious experiences? To admit to being 'agnostic' on such an issue is like being agnostic on the notion that dogs can design computers. Sure, it is possible, but how probable?

10.4.2 Objections to Philosophical Functionalism

Without mind and consciousness, the Functionalists cannot deal with certain problems (Shoemaker, 1975; Block, 1978; Lewis, 1980). The same sort of objections that can be raised with regard to Functionalism can also be applied to Behaviourism (Steinberg *et al.*, 2001).

1. **Insincerity and Lying.** How do we explain what it means to be insincere or lie without resorting to a *conscious intention* in the mind of the speaker who made the promise? Because Functionalist theory has only one level

of analysis, the physical, there can be no such thing as 'insincerity' or 'lying'. We cannot even meaningfully ask if a person is lying. With everything physical and functional there is no place for morality or ethics. Responsibility for actions is meaningless to contemplate. Any system of law, and the judicial system, is rendered virtually meaningless. Certainly it makes no sense to accuse a computer of lying!

2. **Dreams and Speech**.   How, *based on a subjective experience such as a dream*, can a person say and do things related to that dream? How can a Functionalist theory explain this? Again two levels, physical and mental, are necessary for an adequate explanation. How can a computer have dreams?

3. **Toothache and Dentist**.   Why does a person who *experiences the pain* of a toothache speak about pain and then go to the dentist's surgery for treatment. How believable is it that a computing device can experience anything?

This is precisely the point that Maloney (1987) raises. (See Antony, 1994, for other objections.) As Maloney puts it, the whole theory of Functionalism is based on the premise that it is *possible* for the mind to be realized in something outside of the brain. This premise is dramatized by supposing, for example, that it is possible that carbon-free Martians have minds but lack brains. But what justifies the crucial assumption of the real possibility of brainless, silicone Martian minds? It is no answer to reply that anything imaginable is possible. For in that case, one can easily imagine the opposite, i.e. that it is necessary that minds be associated with brains. Maloney argues that until the Functionalist can 'certify' (bring evidence to bear on) the possibility of a mind without a brain, the Functionalist philosophy itself can only be regarded as a mere possibility. Until then, Functionalism must remain in the realm of science fiction.

10.5   Mentalist wars: Empiricism's Intelligence vs. Rationalism's Innate Ideas

10.5.1   Mentalisms: Empiricism and Rationalism

10.5.1.1   Empiricism

According to the conception of most Mentalists, a person is regarded as having a mind. This mind is related to body but is not synonymous with it, since a mind has consciousness and consciousness can use mind to control behaviour. In order to understand a person's behaviour, including speech, it is necessary to study what controls that behaviour, that is, mind. Thus, *Mentalism is characterized by a belief in mind, ideas, consciousness and the role of consciousness in behaviour.*

Empiricist view no. 1: Intelligence is derived from experience

While all Mentalists will agree on the existence of mind and that in their minds humans have ideas, i.e. knowledge ('ideas' are often synonymous with 'knowledge' in the tradition of philosophy), what Mentalists basically do not agree on is *how* those ideas got there. The Empiricist view is that ideas are derived entirely through experience (*empeir* is Greek for 'experience'). Empiricists will then argue with one another as to whether something more, such as intelligence, is innate. Intelligence, thus, is not considered as knowledge but as a means for acquiring knowledge. In Locke's radical view, the mind at birth is blank; experience then imprints ideas on it and develops intelligence from those ideas.

Empiricist view no. 2: Intelligence or its basis is innate

But, how can something (intelligence) come from nothing (the blank mind)? The contemporary philosopher Putnam (1967) has held that humans are born with intelligence, an innate intelligence that has developed through evolution. Such an intelligence would incorporate 'General Multi-Purpose Learning Strategies', he says. Presumably such strategies would seek similarities in sensory data and derive ideas based on an inductive analysis. Beyond this, Putnam offers little that is specific as to the nature of innate intelligence.

Piaget took a middle position between Locke and Putnam. He did not argue, as did Locke, that there was nothing in the mind at birth. Nor did he argue, as has Putnam, that basic intelligence was already in the mind at birth – rather Piaget posited innate 'indifferentiated schemas' out of which intelligence would develop. Just what these schemas consisted of Piaget did not say. In any case, Piaget preferred to derive intelligence from action and experience (Piaget, 1968; Piaget and Inhelder, 1969).

Our own view is that children are born with the essence of propositions and the entities that they involve, as well as the essence of the analytical operations of inductive and deductive logic. It is through the operations of these analytical logical procedures on the data that they experience that children acquire their knowledge of the world and then the language with which they may deal with the world and the people in it.

Confusion in terminology for 'Empiricism' and 'Empiricist'

Before continuing, there is an important matter concerning terminology which is confusing and must be cleared up. The word 'Empiricist' (and 'Empiricism') has developed two distinct meanings. One, the more philosophical-traditional, concerns the mentalistic philosophical school, of which Aristotle (fourth century BC) and John Locke (1690) were proponents.

The other meaning is that of placing a high value on facts and subordinating theory and speculation in accord with those facts. All of us often use the word 'empirical' to indicate this meaning. However, in this interpretation nothing is implied about Mentalism. This sense is the one that Behaviourist theorists, in particular, imply whenever they use the words 'Empiricist' and 'Empiricism'. 'Empiricalism', perhaps, would be a better term to label their outlook.

10.5.1.2 Rationalism

The Rationalist view, as typified by Descartes (1641) in the early seventeenth century, is that basic ideas (God, triangle, etc.) are already in the mind at birth. To activate these ideas, one uses reason (*ratio* meaning reason in Greek) in conjunction with experience.

Today Chomsky is the theorist who epitomizes Rationalist philosophy. (He virtually single-handedly brought down Behaviourism, beginning in the middle of the twentieth century with his notion of a generative rule-governed grammar (Chomsky, 1957) and a devastating (and well-justified) review of Skinner's 1957 book, *Verbal Behavior* (Chomsky, 1959).) He has greatly modified Descartes' original conception, however. For while, like Descartes, Chomsky takes the view that many basic ideas are already in the mind at birth, he further claims that there are ideas of a distinct *language* nature. He calls this set of innate language ideas 'Universal Grammar'. (Formerly he used the name LAD, for Language Acquisition Device.) Furthermore, Chomsky claims that a particular grammar develops through certain distinctive innate language processes of Universal Grammar. Such processes are said to be *independent of reason*, logic, or intelligence (Chomsky, 1967a). This is a radical departure from the classical Rationalism of Plato in the fourth century BC, or of Descartes and Leibnitz in the seventeenth and eighteenth centuries, who all hypothesized that, along with experience, the operation of *reason* was necessary to make innate knowledge functional.

Other modern Rationalists, like Bever (1970), however, did not separate language from other types of ideas. Rather, Bever argued that innate ideas are of a general nature. Such general and basic ideas in this view serve to yield language as well as other types of knowledge such as mathematics. This is a tenable point of view.

Despite these divergences, all Rationalists agree on the essential principle that some knowledge is innate in humans. Different Rationalists, for example, have posited that concepts such as 'justice', 'infinity', 'God', 'perfection', and 'triangle' are innate. They argue that such ideas cannot be intelligibly derived from the experience of an individual human. For example, how can the idea of 'infinity' or 'God' be derived from finite experience? A difficult problem indeed for the Empiricists. But, on the other hand, the Rationalists have the problem of explaining how any such ideas became innate in humans in the first place. Would not innate ideas somehow have had to be gained, originally, through finite experience? For Descartes (1641), the answer was simple, it was God who placed ideas in the minds of human beings. Taking a god-neutral point of view, however, as science does nowadays, dumps a very heavy explanatory burden on evolutionary theory.[1]

10.6 Chomskyan arguments for innate language ideas and the inadequacy of those arguments

10.6.1 Chomsky's faculties of the mind and Universal Grammar

According to Chomsky, humans are born with minds that contain innate knowledge concerning a number of different areas. One such area or faculty of the mind concerns language. The set of innate language ideas that comprises the language faculty is called 'Universal Grammar', UG for short. This UG is universal because every human being is born with it; it is further universal because with it any particular language of the world can be acquired. Thus, UG is not a grammar of any particular language but it contains the essentials with which any particular grammar can be acquired. This contention is one basis for Chomsky's oft-repeated assertion that language acquisition is independent of intelligence and logic and that animals do not have language because they are not born with UG (Hauser, Chomsky and Fitch, 2002).

The role of experience

It is important to note that Universal Grammar does not become functional or operational unless a person receives certain speech input from the environment. Thus, for example, given English sentences as input, UG will construct a grammar of English in the child's mind. The acquisition of a particular grammar therefore involves the *interaction* of UG with experiences of the world. The role of language experience is to activate UG so that it can develop the grammatical essentials of a particular grammar. These essentials involve certain principles and parameters which are universal. (They are discussed more fully in the next section.)

Such a view differs from the view of Empiricists who place a greater role on experience, which is the provider of ideas. Yet modern Empiricists like Putnam and Piaget also postulate some sort of processor in dealing with

[1] See Pinker and Bloom (1990, pp. 707–84) for an attempt to show that Universal Grammar could have been developed by a neo-Darwinian process. Others too debate this question in the same issue of Behavioural and Brain Sciences. We think that all of this is a nice exercise. But why speculate on the evolutionary origins of the Universal Grammar when there is no convincing evidence for its very existence!

raw experience, i.e. *intelligence*. The abstract operations involved in the creation of a negative sentence in English, for example, cannot be explained by the simple experience of raw speech. According to the Empiricist, abstract rules are created on the basis of speech data (strings of physical sounds appearing in the environment through the operation of intelligence). It is intelligence that enables the child to process and construct *all* kinds of ideas, be they for language, mathematics, or playing games.

Some aspects of Chomsky's Universal Grammar

For Chomsky, Universal Grammar is defined as the core grammar containing the principles and parameters that apply to all languages. The other aspects of the grammar of any particular language are referred to as 'peripheral grammar' and a 'mental lexicon'. These must be learned separately from UG because the peripheral grammar and the lexicon are not universal but are specific to particular languages. Thus, presumably the example of 'do Support' for negation in English would not be handled by UG but by the peripheral grammar of English. Whether intelligence is to account for the learning of such an aspect of grammar is something that, in our reading, Chomsky does not consider worth theorizing about. Instead he is focused on the matter of setting the switches of parameters that 'can be fixed by quite simple evidence' (Chomsky, 1986, p. 146). 'The environment determines the way the parameters of universal grammar are set, yielding different languages' (Chomsky, 1988, pp. 133–4).

Thus, according to Chomsky (1986, p. 150), what children know innately are ideas concerning (1) the principles of the various subsystems of Universal Grammar, (2) the manner of their interactions, and (3) the parameters associated with these principles. The precise content of these various UG categories is not provided by Chomsky.

10.6.2 Chomsky's arguments for Universal Grammar

Let us now consider some of the major arguments that Chomsky presents in support of his UG theory. The arguments and the emphasis he places on each have changed as he has revised his theory of grammar over the years. We will present objections to his four main continuing arguments plus adding a new objection to the dispute. Objections to other of his arguments may be found in Steinberg (1982, 1993) and in Steinberg *et al.* (2001).

Chomsky's four main arguments for the necessity of UG are: (1) Degenerate, meagre, and minute language input; (2) Ease and speed of child language acquisition; and (3) The irrelevance of intelligence in language learning. Our additional objection to UG will be (4) Simultaneous multilinguals and the problem of multiple settings on a single parameter.

10.6.2.1 Chomsky argument no. 1: Degenerate, meagre, and minute language input

Chomsky argues that children's acquisition of a well-formed grammar of the language, despite their being exposed to inadequate language data, is evidence of the assistance of innate language ideas. The language data, Chomsky (1967a, p. 6) insists, consist, 'in large measure, of sentences that deviate in form from the idealized structures defined by the grammar that he [the child] develops'. These data are a 'minute sample of the linguistic material that has been thoroughly mastered'. Such inadequate data would necessarily result in an inadequate grammar, if one accepted the Empiricist point of view. As Chomsky (1986, p. 12) puts it, 'It seems there is little hope in accounting for our knowledge [of language] in terms of such [Empiricist] ideas as analogy, induction, association, reliable procedures, good reasons, and justification in any generally useful sense, or in terms of "generalized learning mechanisms" (if such exist).' This latter reference, the reader might recognize, is a dig at Putnam and his Empiricist theory of General Multi-Purpose Learning Strategies.

Objections to Chomsky argument no. 1: Degenerate, meagre, and minute language input

Degenerate input   Empirical research by Labov, Newport, and others has convincingly demonstrated that the preponderance of sentences are grammatical and not degenerate and ungrammatical as Chomsky has argued. As Labov (1970, p. 42) neatly phrases it, 'The ungrammaticality of every-day speech appears to be a myth with no basis in actual fact. In the various empirical studies which we have conducted . . . the proportion of truly ungrammatical and ill-formed sentences falls to less than two percent.' Similarly, Newport (1975), in a long-term study with 15 mothers, reports an incidence of only one ungrammatical utterance out of 1500. (See Cromer, 1980, for a review of such studies.)

Instead of invoking Chomsky's complex theory of Universal Grammar to try to deal with the mere 2 per cent of ungrammatical sentences (which might be due to a speaker being interrupted in mid-sentence, a change of thought, etc.), would it not be much simpler to suppose that the child simply disregards those sentences he or she cannot analyze? A 2-year-old child is not likely to spend much time puzzling about the complexities of passive sentences that he or she hears, even when such sentences are grammatical. (Passive sentences are typically understood years later.) The child takes in what it can understand and simply discards what it cannot process.

Meagre and minute language data as input   As to Chomsky's claim that only a 'meagre' and 'minute sample' of language is experienced by the child, we are aware of no empirical evidence which he presents to support that claim. Rather the opposite seems to be the case. The sentences that the child experiences (finite though their number may be) do contain in them an adequate representation of the syntactic structures that the child must learn. The multitude of child language studies that have been conducted by Chomskyan supporters seem to bear this out. Researchers do not report instances of children having learned of syntactic structures without ever having been exposed to sentences embodying those structures.

10.6.2.2 Chomsky argument no. 2: Ease and speed of child language acquisition

According to Chomsky (1962, p. 529), 'A young child is able to gain perfect mastery of a language with incomparably greater ease and without any explicit instruction. Mere exposure to the language, for a remarkably short period, seems to be all that the normal child requires to develop the competence of the native speaker.' Since, according to Chomsky, the child's remarkable accomplishment in acquiring the grammar could not have been through an accumulation of language learning that the child would have had to experience if one were postulating an Empiricist-based acquisition process, this phenomenon could only have occurred with the assistance of the Universal Grammar. It is through the help of innate language ideas that the acquisition of language is made so easy and rapid. Chomsky's claim is, thus, that the Empiricist cannot account for such ease and speed of acquisition.

Objections to Chomsky argument no. 2: Ease and speed of child language acquisition

Actually, since Chomsky has not provided any data on this issue, what he says is less an argument than a straight assertion. Apparently he believes that the reader will readily assent to his assertion.

However, Putnam (1967) has countered Chomsky's argument by comparing the number of hours spent by a child in learning language with that of an adult learning a language. He contends that a child of 4 or 5 years who has learned the essentials of the language has spent much more time in the process than would an adult in learning a second language!

To elaborate on Putnam's argument, let us create our own example. First let us estimate the number of hours of exposure to language that an ordinary 4-year-old child gets. We could assume that the number of hours per day that the child is exposed to language is about 10 hours. Of course, when the child was younger, the child would have slept more, been awake less, etc., but let us take 10 hours as a round figure. (A few hours here or there won't make much difference, as you will see.) Now, since there are 365 days in a year, that gives us 3650 hours per year. Over a period of four years, that is 14 600 hours (3650×4). Is 14 600 hours a large number of hours? But wait!

Perhaps it is not fair to attribute a full four years of language input to a 4-year-old: in the first half-year of life, the child is just getting going with regard to language and much of the input is wasted. So, let us say that the 4-year-old child has a solid three years of language experience. For three years, that is $3650 \times 3 = 10\,950$ hours. *Is 10 950 hours a short time?*

Well, let us compare it with the number of hours that, say, a student is exposed to in one language course at high school over the period of a semester (term). If the student has five class hours per week and does two hours of study after each class hour (5 days $\times$ 2 hours = 10 hours per week), all of this (class plus after-class study) comes to 15 hours per week. (Too idealistic? Let's give Chomsky the benefit of the doubt, since the more hours per week, the faster the student will complete his or her learning.) If one semester lasts 18 weeks, then that would be a total of $15 \times 18 = 270$ hours for the semester. Let us say the student studies all the year round by taking three semesters of the language; that would make $270 \times 3 = 810$ hours per year.

Now, if the student is to have as many exposure hours as the child, then the student would have to study a language continuously at school (three semesters per year) for the equivalent of (10 950 $\div$ 810) 13.5 years! Is 13 years long enough for a student at school to learn the grammar of a language commensurate with that of a 4-year-old? Putnam thinks so, and so do we. And so would almost every language teacher! In fact, the student would probably be able to learn the requisite amount of grammar in significantly less than 13 years. That being the case the student would then be an even faster learner than the child!

Therefore, considering the number of hours that a child spends in learning its native language, when compared to that of a student learning a second language, the speed of the child is not fast at all! The relatively long length of time implies, as well, that the language could not have been so easy to learn! As far as speed is concerned, there is plenty of time for the child to learn language along Empiricist lines. There is thus no justification here for Chomsky's positing the existence of an innate Universal Grammar.

Does UG weaken or die with age?

Another problem which we would like to pose concerns an implied premise for Chomsky's argument for speed and ease of child language acquisition: that children learn faster than adults, and that this superior speed is the result of the *child* having Universal Grammar to help out. The implication here is that *adults do not have the benefit of Universal Grammar!*

Why should this be so? If adults are denied the benefit of Universal Grammar, then Chomsky would have to argue that Universal Grammar either weakens or dries up altogether with age. The result of such an argument? Adults would never learn a second grammar. Yet this is not so because adults are able to learn a second language. If Chomsky wishes to argue here that adults would, with the weakening or loss of Universal Grammar, have to learn language in some Empiricist way (rather than by the flash of Universal Grammar), then he would have to argue, contrary to fact, that adults would fail in such learning. Otherwise Chomsky would be contradicting one of his other major arguments for the existence of Universal Grammar: the argument that every language has certain essential principles or functions that could not possibly be acquired through experience. Yet it is a fact that, given enough time and proper language and environmental input, adult language learners can learn a foreign grammar, sometimes very well – pronunciation problems aside.

10.6.2.3 Chomsky argument no. 3: The irrelevance of intelligence in language learning

In his conception of faculties of the mind, Chomsky has contended that language learning is essentially independent of intelligence. In support of this thesis, he argues that because grammar has a peculiar form (his own formulation of a grammar!) and it is not a logical form, hence, it is not a direct function of a rational operating intelligence, but must be a function of innate language knowledge. Thus, concerning humans he has asserted, 'vast differences in intelligence have only a small effect on resulting competence [knowledge of a particular grammar]' (Chomsky, 1967a, p. 3). By this he implies that if intelligence is relevant to language acquisition, then more intelligent people should acquire greater language knowledge and in less time.

But, he claims, more intelligent persons do not acquire a greater competence than do less intelligent persons. That being the case, Chomsky then concludes that different degrees of intelligence do not affect language acquisition, and hence intelligence itself is irrelevant to the acquisition of language. But how then to explain the uniformity (Chomsky's claim) of language knowledge for speakers of a language? If it is not due to intelligence, it must be due to something else. That something else must be Universal Grammar, claims Chomsky.

Objections to Chomsky argument no. 3: The irrelevance of intelligence in language learning

Grammar of humans with high or low intelligence   Chomsky claims (without evidence) that persons with high or low intelligence acquire the same grammar. This, he asserts, is due to Universal Grammar because the Empiricist would predict that the more intelligent the person, the better would be the grammar.

There is a serious problem with Chomsky's claim. It is the assumption that a low level of intelligence is insufficient for the acquisition of a grammar. For, it could well be that *low intelligence is sufficient* for the acquisition of a grammar! After all, people of both high and low intelligence (unless defective) learn to drive cars, play cards, and do many other things. Thus, it may well be that although intelligence is relevant for those tasks, and for language too, only a low degree of intelligence is necessary for their mastery; a high degree is superfluous. Along our line of thinking, therefore, it is possible that the acquisition of language is only affected if the level of intelligence is too low.

There is some evidence that supports the hypothesis that too low a level of intelligence will result in language deficits. There are persons with Down's syndrome. Their IQs vary, but they are usually around 50 (a score of 100 is average), and often they too are greatly impaired in lexical and grammatical abilities (Bellugi *et al.*, 1994; Fowler *et al.*, 1994). A very low level of intelligence, therefore, can be expected to affect the level of language acquisition. The recently discussed case of Laura (Yamada, 1990) would seem to be one of this kind.

Mathematics and intelligence   In 1975 Putnam provided a particularly strong argument against Chomsky on the issue of intelligence. This was at a conference in France where he, Chomsky, Piaget, and other notable thinkers were present (Piattelli-Palmarini, 1980).

Putnam challenged Chomsky with the following argument. The concepts of mathematics could not have developed genetically through evolution because humans have been using such concepts for only several thousands of years. The use of mathematics did not come into existence 'until after the evolution of the race was complete (some 100 000-odd years ago)', said Putnam (1980, pp. 296–7). Since such a complex system of thought as mathematics could not be the result of genetic inheritance, because human evolution was completed long before the existence of mathematics, mathematics therefore must be an 'invention' of the intelligence of the mind. And, if such an intelligence can invent mathematics, it surely should have no trouble inventing grammar as well. Thus, Putnam concludes, there is no need to postulate the existence of innate language ideas.

Chomsky (1980a) in response asserted that, considering 'fairly deep properties of the number system, I suppose that this ability is genetically determined for humans. . . . [and that] These skills may well have risen as a concomitant of structural properties of the brain that developed for other reasons' (p. 321). In other words, Chomsky asserted that the particular essentials of mathematics are genetically determined as part of other skills.

Such an argument in response to Putnam's challenge must have struck even Chomsky himself as weak, for what we find in Chomsky's later writings is the formulation that mathematics is *not* independent of language but is one of the outcomes of Universal Grammar. (A complete reversal of his *independent* faculties-of-the-mind hypothesis!) We find Chomsky (1988) saying that, 'At this point we can only speculate, but it is possible that the number faculty developed as a by-product of the language faculty' (p. 169).

Chomsky further speculates that our language ability and our number ability have certain features in common, most notably the notion of 'discrete infinity' (to be distinguished from an innumerable mass). Language, too, has the property of discrete infinity in that while any particular sentence has a finite number of words, in principle the sentence can be expanded in length to infinity (theoretically) by the addition of modifying and conjoined clauses, and the like.

Thus, according to Chomsky's latest formulation, mathematics is a product of Universal Grammar. However, one cannot but wonder whether by expanding the scope of Universal Grammar in order to take in problem areas (areas that could challenge the very existence of UG) like mathematics, UG has become too powerful a theory, one that could potentially encompass any complex abstract field of human endeavour. (This situation is reminiscent of the 'too powerful nature of transformations' that forced Chomsky to abandon them in the 1970s.)

It well may be that humans do have some innate capacity for numerosity. But this capacity could very well be independent of language. If so, unless Chomsky is able to specify in more detail the contents of UG, UG will simply serve as a filing cabinet for unsolvable problems, filed away for later consideration and then forgotten.

10.6.2.4 Objection no. 4: Simultaneous multilinguals and the problem of multiple settings on a single parameter

According to Chomsky's grammar, with respect to Noun Phrases, English is a head-first language while Japanese is a head-last language. Now, each parameter can be set either head first or head last. Suppose, then, we have a child being raised in an English–Japanese bilingual household where the child receives both English and Japanese language input simultaneously from birth. Let us say the mother speaks Japanese and the father speaks English. It is commonly observed that in such a situation the child learns these two different languages without any special difficulty and is fluently bilingual by the age of 4 or 5 years.

How can Universal Grammar allow for two different settings on the *same* parameter? Is there more than one Universal Grammar in the child's mind? Or, does the mind duplicate another Universal Grammar for each of the other languages that are to be learned? As noted in Chapter 8, a good friend of the first author raised his two sons in a trilingual household where they simultaneously learned English, Japanese, and Russian.

Did the children have three different Universal Grammars by making two duplicates out of the one original? This solution goes against the grain of UG having evolved through evolution. If UG did evolve through evolution, it is highly implausible that it would have developed a process whereby it could duplicate itself. By Chomsky's definition, UG is universal and can itself account for the acquisition of all languages. And, if it were postulated that there was a dominating *intelligence* that governed what UG should do, by making duplicates, that intelligence would have to be more powerful than UG itself. That being so, there would be no need for UG in the first place! (Flynn and Martohardjono (1994) have earlier dealt with the problem of the bilingual child and conclude that Chomsky's theory cannot account for the phenomenon.)

10.6.3 Conclusion regarding Chomsky's arguments for Universal Grammar

If Universal Grammar exists, as Chomsky claims, as yet there is no credible evidence that supports it. All of Chomsky's arguments for Universal Grammar have been shown to be inadequate.

10.7 It is time for Emergentism to re-emerge?

An Empiricism which was popular in the early part of the twentieth century and has returned in a reformulated version is one called Emergentism (Sperry, 1969; Beckermann *et al.*, 1992; McLaughlin, 1992). It is a form of the Mind–Body Interactionism view that was discussed earlier in this chapter. Essentially, Emergentism is based on the view that certain higher-level properties, in particular consciousness and intentionality, are emergent in the sense that although they appear only when certain physical conditions occur, such properties are neither explainable nor predictable in terms of their underlying physical properties. The properties of mind are genuinely novel and bring into the world their own causal powers. Thus, mind may have some control over behaviour, which is in accord with the most commonplace of human observations.

It is thus highly likely that we are born with a brain that has inherent in it physical properties that allow for the development of intellectual processing powers. Such powers would be able to process environmental input from the physical world and yield all manner of intellectual objects including language and mathematics. This commonsense kind of philosophy/psychology is one that we favour and would like to see more fully developed along more contemporary lines in the coming years.

Chapter 11

Natural Grammar, mind and speaker performance

11.1 Psychological criteria for assessing grammars

Linguists have long argued over what the main goal of linguistics should be. Should a grammar *describe language in formal terms*, where such terms need not refer to psychological entities, or should a grammar describe *what speakers know about a language, where all terms refer to* psychological entities? We shall provide a brief history of that controversy, and then, given the desirability of the latter goal for psychology, we shall assess the psychological adequacy of grammars. Towards this end we shall also take into account the nature of child language acquisition, particularly the relation of speech comprehension and speech production. The psychological adequacy of current grammars will be assessed and the outline of a new unique psychological conception, Natural Grammar, will be offered.

11.1.1 Psychological criterion no. 1: A 'God's Truth' grammar

Linguistics as a branch of psychology

In the first half of the twentieth century, linguists were divided on the psychology issue. Some linguists, like Bloomfield (1942/1961), argued for the psychological validity of the language descriptions that they were writing. (Bloomfield was an advocate of Behaviourism and, as such, was anti-Mentalistic.) Linguists like Bloomfield held that what they wrote was not only a description of language but a description of what people had learned, as well.

Others, however, such as Twaddell (1935), rejected a psychological goal for linguistics. They considered the description of a language to be the goal of linguistics, where entities like noun and verb were regarded simply as convenient fictions, i.e. formalisms, which were useful for *notational* purposes only.

The linguist Householder (1952) neatly formulated the basic differences between linguists as a 'God's Truth vs. Hocus-Pocus' bifurcation. The God's Truth approach is where the linguist attempts to describe psychological language entities. This contrasts with the Hocus-Pocus or 'mathematical games' approach where the linguist attempts to describe language in any systematic way by the use of convenient formalisms; whether or not the descriptions corresponded to psychological entities was irrelevant to the enterprise. Householder, by the way, chided Chomsky's mentor, Zelig Harris, for vacillating between the two approaches. As we shall see, the same could be said of Harris's illustrious student, Chomsky, as well.

Nowadays most linguists have adopted the God's Truth goal for a grammar. They agree that we have a grammar in our minds and that grammar in some way is used in the psycholinguistic processes of producing and understanding sentences. Interestingly, this now-dominant God's Truth trend was started by Chomsky, who, strange to say, had originally been an advocate of the opposing Hocus-Pocus school.

11.1.2 The illustrative case of Chomsky: his shift from Hocus-Pocus to God's Truth

The case of Chomsky is a good one with which to illustrate the two main opposing views of the goal of linguistics, for here is a linguist who, at different periods of his theoretical development, had advocated each of these points of view. He was for Hocus-Pocus in the 1950s but shifted to God's Truth in the 1960s.

During his Hocus-Pocus period, the study of meaning, semantics and Mentalism were derided by Chomsky as involving 'mysticism' and 'ghosts'. He shared Bloomfield's anti-Mentalist stance, although he diverged from Bloomfield's psychological approach to grammar, preferring a non-psychological formalistic approach (Chomsky, 1955, pp. 158–9).

It was in the next decade that Chomsky came down heavily on the side of a Mentalistic linguistics, going so far as to define linguistics as a branch of cognitive psychology: 'Hence, in the technical sense, linguistic theory is mentalistic, since it is concerned with discovering a mental reality underlying actual behavior' (Chomsky, 1965, p. 4). 'The linguist's grammar is a scientific theory, correct insofar as it corresponds to the internally represented grammar' (Chomsky, 1980b, p. 220). Not only did he advocate Mentalism but he even went so far as to posit *innate* psychological entities in the tradition of Descartes and Leibnitz (Chomsky, 1966).

Chomsky's 1950s Hocus-Pocus period

In his original theorizing, Chomsky fiercely attacked Mentalism and argued against the inclusion of meaning/semantics in a grammar. These views are most emphatically presented in his doctoral dissertation, 'The logical structure of linguistic theory' (Chomsky, 1955). They are not much dealt with in his book, *Syntactic Structures* (Chomsky, 1957), which is essentially an excerpt of that dissertation and focuses mainly on grammatical rather than on psychological or philosophical issues. This being so, our focus will be on his dissertation.

Using Chomsky's own words we will demonstrate the essentials of his thinking during his Hocus-Pocus period. (We have numbered the quotations for convenience sake.) All quotations are from his dissertation (Chomsky, 1955) unless noted otherwise, and emphases are ours unless otherwise indicated.

1. The fact that a certain general criterion of significance has been abandoned does not mean that the bars are down and that 'ideas' and 'meanings' become proper terms for linguistics, any more than it means that ghosts are proper concepts for physics. If this rejection of an old criterion is not followed by construction of a new one, then it simply has no bearing on the selection of the legitimate terms for a scientific theory. Where it is followed by some new sense of 'significance,' then if this new sense is at all adequate, it seems to me that it will rule out mentalism for what were essentially Bloomfield's reasons, i.e. its obscurity and generally uselessness in linguistic theory.

(pp. I 19–20)

2. Whatever the situation may be in other sciences, I think that there is hope of developing that aspect of linguistic theory being studied here on the basis of a small number of operation primitives, and *introduction of dispositions (or mentalistic terms) is either irrelevant, or trivializes the theory.*

(pp. I 20–1)

Again Chomsky rejects Mentalism and Mentalistic terms (ideas and meanings) as being irrelevant or trivial in the construction of a linguistic theory!

3. The danger in the *'God's truth' approach* [as opposed to the 'Mathematical Games' or 'Hocus-Pocus approach'] is that as it has been formulated, it sometimes *verges on mysticism.*

(pp. I 58–9)

Chomsky criticizes linguists who take a 'God's Truth', i.e. psychological approach, to linguistics. He characterizes such a view as bordering on mysticism! Rather, Chomsky favours the formalistic non-psychological approach, i.e. the Hocus-Pocus view, one that involves sets of rules that are *non-psychological* in nature.

4. The fundamental aim in the linguistic analysis of a language L is to separate the *grammatical* sequences which are the sentences of L from the ungrammatical sequences which are not sentences in L and to study the structure of the grammatical sequences.

(*Syntactic Structures* (Chomsky, 1957), p. 13; Chomsky's emphasis)

For Chomsky, the primary goal of linguistic analysis was *not* to represent the knowledge of speakers. It was to provide *a formalistic mechanism* (a generative grammar) which would be able to *distinguish grammatical from ungrammatical sequences*. The function of a grammar was to yield grammatical strings. It certainly was *not* intended to describe the actual behaviour, knowledge, or thought of a speaker.

A successful grammar is one that duplicates what a speaker can do, i.e. provide an indefinite number of grammatical sentences as output. Only the *output* of the grammar, i.e. a string of phonemic symbols, *not* the mechanism (rules, etc.) of the grammar itself, corresponds to speaker behaviour. Thus, other than for output, no psychological correspondence is claimed. In fact, at no time in the 1950s does Chomsky make any claim for the psychological reality of his generative mechanism, the various sets of rules of his grammar. It is only in the 1960s that Chomsky begins to make psychological claims. Such claims lead to an acceptance of mentalism because, given his denunciation of Behaviourism in his critical review of Skinner's book *Verbal Behaviour*, where else could abstract rules be stored except in the mind?

Chomsky's *Syntactic Structures* (Chomsky, 1957) clearly reflects the ideas in the quotations cited above. The grammar is composed of various sets of rules. What is strange about this grammar is that there is no component for dealing with the meaning of sentences. The essence of Chomsky's Syntactic Structures grammar is simply:

> *Syntactic Structures grammar (1957)*
> Syntax → Sound

Chomsky's embrace of God's Truth Mentalism

Chomsky's formulation of a generative system of rules was of special interest to these theorists. Many psychologists were quick to attribute generative systems to the minds of speakers and quick to abandon what had become a stagnant Behaviourism. Soon Chomsky himself was to assign generative grammars to the minds of speakers. We find Chomsky now saying, 'Obviously[!] every speaker of a language has mastered and internalized a generative grammar that expresses his knowledge of his language' (Chomsky, 1965, p. 8). His assertion that linguistics is a branch of cognitive psychology is one that Chomsky continues to hold. This view was so persuasively advocated that it became widely accepted by most linguists. Even most of Chomsky's staunchest critics today are in accord with him on the goal of linguistics, as a description of the language knowledge that people have and use language. Chomsky's original theorizing had taken a complete about-face. He renounced Hocus-Pocus and went all out for God's Truth, declaring linguistics to be a branch of cognitive psychology. Soon he was reinforcing his views with books like *Cartesian Linguistics* in 1966 and *Language and Mind* in

1968 in which he promoted and defended mental grammar and his unique doctrine of innate language ideas, Universal Grammar.

Unfortunately for Chomsky this basic change in thinking was not accompanied by any basic change in his conception of the organization of grammar. Chomsky has continued to maintain one fundamental principle in how his grammars are organized: *the syntax of the grammar is primary* while meaning and sound are secondary, with the meaning and sound forms of a sentence essentially being derived as a function of syntax. This crucial oversight has resulted in Chomsky's grammatical theorizing over the past 40 years being psychologically contradictory and invalid, as we will see further in this chapter.

11.2 The explanatory inadequacy of Chomsky's syntax-based grammar

Bearing in mind the psychological criterion for a sound theory of grammar, let us now consider the psychological adequacy of current illustrative grammars. First we shall look at Chomsky's syntax-based grammar in the light of types of performance models. Later, after considering a further criterion of the adequacy of a grammar – one that is based on the essentials of child language acquisition – we shall judge the adequacy of meaning-based grammars such as those of the Functionalists (Dik, Bates, and MacWhinney) and those of the Conceptualists (Langacker) and Cognitivists (Lakoff).

11.2.1 Chomsky's Competence–Performance Theory

The term 'grammar', for Chomsky, is synonymous with 'competence', which is the grammatical knowledge people have concerning their language (Chomsky, 1965). The goal of linguistics is to describe this competence. While Chomsky's specification of grammar has changed over the years, his view of grammar as representing competence has not: grammar purports to be the mental knowledge that people have of their language.

For Chomsky, the activities involved in producing and comprehending sentences involve competence, a single mental grammar that serves both of these two crucial *performance* processes. It is for a theory of performance (1) to explain sentence production, i.e. how speakers take ideas and render them into speech sounds, and (2) to explain sentence comprehension, i.e. how speakers, on receiving speech sounds, recover ideas from those sounds. Grammar functions as a resource for the knowledge that each performance process requires.

The relationship of competence to performance for Chomsky is that of part to whole, with competence being a part or component of the whole, which is performance. Competence is the knowledge that persons have of their grammar while performance involves knowledge of an operational sort (heuristics, strategies) for using that competence so that the processes of sentence production and sentence comprehension can be realized.

Now, if the specification of competence is the primary goal of *linguistics*, what then should the goal of *psycholinguistics* be? In Chomsky's view, psycholinguistics has two major goals: (1) to specify how people use competence so that they are able to produce and comprehend sentences (a theory of performance); and (2) to specify how children acquire competence. Based on a division of labour that he himself established (Chomsky, 1965), Chomsky states that it is for the linguist to describe grammar while it is for the psycholinguist to describe how that grammar is acquired and used in performance. Psycholinguists have generally ignored this dictum.

11.2.2 Why Chomsky's grammar itself cannot be a performance model

Because of the organization of Chomsky's grammar, with syntax being primary, it is clear that his grammar does not conform to either of the performance processes of speech comprehension or speech production. A true comprehension process must begin with sound as input and meaning as its output. (A person hears speech sounds and assigns a meaning to them.) The schema for the comprehension process would be:

Speech comprehension process
Sound → X → Meaning

Conversely, a true production process begins with meaning as input and sound as output. (A person has ideas according to which he or she provides speech sounds so as to convey their meaning.) The schema for such a process would be:

Speech production process
Meaning → X → Sound

In these two schemas the X represents intervening modules, one such being a Chomskyan grammar, plus other modules (heuristics, strategies) that enable a person to provide a particular output given a particular input.

Given how meaning, sound, and syntax are related in Chomsky's conception of grammar (shown earlier), it is clear that his grammar could not possibly, by itself, be a model of speaker performance either for the comprehension or for the production of sentences. For Chomsky's point of origin in his grammar is neither with the meaning of the sentence nor with its sound; rather it is with the syntax of the sentence. In his view, syntax functions independently, 'autonomously', of meaning and sound.

Thus, in effect, Chomsky posits a type of performance model where his grammar serves as a knowledge resource for the processes of speech

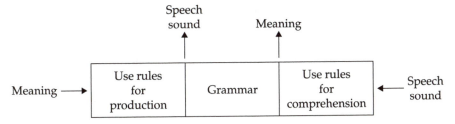

Figure 11.1 Chomsky's resource grammar performance model

comprehension and production. An outline of this model is shown in Figure 11.1.

11.2.3 The psychological contradiction in Chomsky's theorizing

Despite the attempts of many brilliant Chomsky supporters such as Bever, Fodor, and Garrett, and despite the fact that they and others have been at it for more than 30 years, no one has been successful in devising a model of performance using his grammar. We maintain, along with many others, that it is the very nature of Chomsky's grammar that is at fault. Moreover, we maintain that there is a *psychological contradiction* in Chomsky's theorizing.

The essence of our argument lies in the fact that *Chomsky's grammar generates linguistic derivations that have no psychological existence.* As Chomsky (1967b, p. 435) himself has said: 'It would be tempting but quite absurd, to regard it [the grammar] as a model of performance as well' (p. 435).

Chomsky has fallen into a trap here. Since, as he himself notes, a speaker would not directly use the rules, principles, etc. of his derivations in actual performance, what reason is there to believe that they would ever be used? There is none, since the rules, principles, etc. in a derivation are *not* designed with a view to speaker performance but with a view to assisting the linguist in the task of connecting the components of his grammar in accord with the order that Chomsky has asserted. Since the specification of rules, principles, and parameters, etc. is entirely dependent on what Chomsky conceives to be the relationship of syntax, meaning, and sound, i.e. syntax being primary and generative with meaning and sound being secondary, and since the directionality of such a relationship is not one that would be used in speaker performance, one can only conclude that such rules etc. are for the most part simply *formalistic artefacts* and, as such, *psychologically superfluous.* Chomsky therefore is in violation of the very criterion for a grammar that he himself adamantly advocates, its psychological reality. (A cynic might even offer that Chomsky's competence–performance distinction is merely a brilliant attempt to salvage the psychological validity of his peculiar grammar.)

While in the 1950s it was fine for Chomsky to construct derivations according to the syntax-primary principle (and without meaning) within his formalistic 'mathematical games' approach to linguistics, his continuing to champion this syntax-primary principle *after* adopting a Mentalistic approach has led to internal contradiction. The derivations which his grammars entail are necessarily psychological fictions. Little wonder that no workable model of performance using Chomsky's grammar has been formulated. (For more details concerning the origination of the argument and its history, see Steinberg, 1976, 1999, and Steinberg *et al.*, 2001)

It is worth noting that Chomsky has not weakened in his resolve to hold on to the essential aspects of his original 1950s thinking. Relatively recently, Chomsky (1991) has said, 'The language . . . "strongly" generates a set of structural descriptions [including derivations]; we may take this to be the structure of the language. This is essentially the point of view developed in my unpublished manuscript, *The Logical Structure of Linguistic Theory* of 1955, differing only in terminology' (p. 8).

11.2.4 An empirical problem with Chomsky's notion of an idealized speaker-hearer

When Chomsky asserts that his generative grammar concerns the knowledge of language possessed by every normal speaker, he adds a peculiar twist to that assertion. He contends that 'Linguistic theory is concerned primarily with an *ideal speaker-listener* . . . who knows its language perfectly and is un-affected . . . in applying his knowledge of the language in actual performance' (Chomsky, 1965, p. 3, emphasis ours). Whether actual, non-pathological (Chomsky's wording) speakers, rather than idealized speakers, really have essentially the same knowledge of language is an important question, and whether performance affects grammatical judgements are issues which require psycholinguistic research. Professor Hiroshi Nagata is one psycholinguistic researcher whose experimental studies address just these problems.

There are two aspects in Chomsky's alleged final steady state of knowledge of language. One concerns the final state that is described as being 'relatively stable' (Chomsky, 1986, p. 25) and the other concerns the final state that embodies the generative grammar consisting of a variety of syntactic principles and conditions. One group of Nagata's studies deals with the former aspect, while another group deals with the latter. It must be mentioned, however, that Chomsky has neither specified what he means by 'relatively' and 'stable' nor has he listed which principles or conditions are known and used by a speaker of a language.

11.2.4.1 Stable state of language knowledge is tested

In one study, Nagata (1988) exposed Japanese speakers to a repetition treatment where Japanese sentences either were or were not placed with another sentence. Judgements changed when sentences were presented singly but not when presented with another sentence. In another study, Nagata (1989a) required speakers to adopt either a differentiation or an enrichment strategy during the repetition phase. The former strategy involved differentiation by syntactically analyzing the sentences, while the latter involved enrichment by supplying situational contexts for the sentences. Again, the differing strategies produced different judgements of grammaticality. The judgements of grammaticality of sentences are also influenced by the cognitive style of speakers such as field-dependence or field-independence. Nagata (1989b) showed that field-independent speakers tended to adopt a more stringent criterion on judgements after than before repetition, whereas no change in criterion was obtained for field-dependent speakers.

Furthermore, Nagata (1992) showed an anchoring effect in the judgements of the grammaticality of sentences. In this experiment, all the three groups of speakers judged the target sentences with an intermediate level of judged grammaticality. However, the first group of speakers judged these sentences paired with the sentences involving high grammaticality (high anchor); the second group judged them when paired with the sentences involving low grammaticality (low anchor); the third group judged them without being given anchor sentences. A clear contrast effect was found such that the speakers given low-anchor sentences judged the target sentences as more grammatical, while those given high-anchor sentences tended to judge them as less grammatical. An anchoring effect was found also for sentences violating a syntactic constraint (Nagata, 1997a, 1997b).

The above studies, which involve a variety of experimental manipulations, suggest that the criterion speakers use when judging the grammaticality of sentences is not as stable as Chomsky assumes but changes quite easily and in conformity with the predictions of psychological theories. Manipulations result in an unexpected fluidness in notions which actual speakers have concerning grammaticality.

11.2.4.2 Speaker conformity to grammatical knowledge is tested

In the second group of studies, Nagata (1995a, 1995b) shows that speakers do not always behave in conformity with the particular syntactic principles or conditions that they supposedly know. Using sentences that clearly violate one or another type of syntactic principle or condition, in judging the grammaticality of these sentences, speakers did not behave consistently in accord with Chomsky's theory. Reflexive-antecedent associations were not differentiated in either on-line and off-line reflexive resolution tasks. Similarly, Japanese speakers did not exclude sentences involving an uninterpretable superfluous propositional argument as completely ungrammatical in conformity with Chomsky's principle of Full Interpretation that is supposed to operate in an all-or-none fashion (Nagata, 2003a, 2003b). Instead, these sentences were assigned a moderate level of judged grammaticality. Furthermore, merely adding a punctuation mark (Nagata, 2004) or emphasis (Nagata, 2005) increased the judged grammaticality of the sentences violating this principle. These findings seem to be incompatible with Chomsky's claim that his generative grammar reflects ideal knowledge of language that provides the basis for actual use of language by a speaker-hearer.

11.2.4.3 Conclusion

Chomsky's theory has been put forward on the basis of considerations that, when empirically tested, may not substantiate his theorizing. There seems to be an inconsistency between his notion of an idealized speaker-hearer possessing the full knowledge of language and the results obtained in actual speaker performance.

11.3 Performance-related grammars

Many thoughtful linguists and psycholinguists have puzzled over the peculiar nature of Chomsky's grammar where syntax is held to be primary, that is to say, independent of meaning and sound. As a result many rejected Chomsky's conception of a grammar and generally created grammatical conceptions that assigned a *primary role to meaning* and a secondary role to syntax and sound. The original opposition grammarians included the Generative Semanticists (Lakoff, Ross, and McCawley), in the late 1960s and into the 1970s, and their successors up to the present, including the Cognitivists (Lakoff, Langacker) and the Functionalists (Dik, Bates, and MacWhinney). All of these grammars assign a primary role to meaning and an interpretive role to syntax and sound. From the 1970s and the 1980s onward, most opposition theorists have striven to formulate psychologically valid ('God's Truth') grammars, grammars that themselves comprise a performance process. They reject Chomsky's compartmentalization of grammar where a 'competence' grammar is formulated independently of whether or not a means for using it in performance can be described. Rather, these theorists only postulate rules, principles, or functions that they can directly assign as being part of a performance process. Let us look at some ideas that these theorists have proposed.

11.3.1 Cognitive grammar

The notable language theorists George Lakoff and Ronald Langacker have proposed ideas that consider grammar as a component of what a person knows and does with regard to language.

According to Langacker (1991),

Language is neither self contained [like Chomsky's competence approach] nor describable without essential reference to cognitive processing [performance functions]. *Grammatical structures do not constitute an autonomous formal system . . . it is ultimately pointless to analyze grammatical units without reference to their semantic value.*

(p. 275, our emphasis)

Linguistic semantics must therefore attempt the analysis and explicit description of conceptual structures; since these reside in cognitive processing, our ultimate objective must be to characterize the types of cognitive events whose occurrence constitutes a given mental experience.

(p. 278)

This is also a view that Lakoff (1987) has endorsed since the 1970s. The aim of the Cognitive theorists thus goes well beyond what is generally considered to be the bounds of Chomsky's grammar. They are concerned, like the Functionalists, about the nature of language and how it relates to thought. For all of these theorists, the organizational directionality of the components of their grammar may be expressed as follows:

Directionality of grammar process for Functionalists and Cognitivists
Meaning → Production process grammar → Sound

Such a grammar directly serves the performance process of speech *production*. It transforms meaning to syntactic and lexical structures which can be expressed in sound. Unfortunately, these grammars do not recognize the primacy of speech comprehension over that of speech production.

11.3.2 Functional grammars

Dik follows somewhat along the lines of the earlier Generative Semantics movement but with more semantic articulation and development geared to the process of production. He begins with abstract predicate frames and a lexicon from which syntactic and pragmatic representations are formed and then realized, by means of syntax, as speech forms. According to Dik (1991), the language system is not considered as an autonomous set of rules and principles (as in Chomsky's grammar): '[r]ather, it is assumed that the rules and principles composing the language system can only be adequately understood when they are analyzed in terms of the *conditions of use*' (p. 247, our emphasis).

11.4 Primacy of speech comprehension

A principal foundation of a psychologically valid grammar must lie with the process whereby children acquire language. Basic to this understanding is the relationship of speech comprehension and speech production.

In order to more easily grasp this relationship, we shall begin with a consideration of children who are mute but who do have hearing. We shall then consider the case of normal children. Since these issues were discussed in detail in Chapter 1, they will only be briefly reviewed here.

11.4.1   Children with no speech production can comprehend speech

There are many hearing persons who are born mute. People such as these may be born with cerebral palsy or some other abnormality that prohibits them from articulating speech. In Chapter 1, we presented the cases of Nolan, the noted Irish writer, McDonald, the art lover and writer, and Rie, the 3-year-old Japanese child who learned to read words, with understanding, that she could not say. None of these persons could speak. Other documented cases are similarly described in that section. These persons were able to comprehend speech despite having no speech capability.

Conclusion: grammar can develop in the absence of speech production

Persons who are mute but hearing *can* develop the ability to comprehend speech *without* their being able to produce speech. Since that is the case, *how* are such people able to comprehend the sentences that they do? It must be that these mute persons developed a grammar, a *mental grammar based on speech comprehension*. Such a grammar enabled them to comprehend the speech to which they were exposed. Consequently, the sentences that they can comprehend reflect the essential characteristics of language, i.e. the comprehension of and unlimited number of grammatical and novel sentences, recognition of synonymy and ambiguity, etc.

11.4.2   Speech comprehension develops prior to speech production in normal children

As was detailed in Chapter 1, the developmental process is that speech comprehension precedes speech production. It is the pattern that continues throughout the acquisition process (Ingram, 1989), whether it be for first words (Clark and Barron, 1988), elaborate syntax such as passives (Golinkoff and Hirsch-Pasek, 1995), or the later acquisition of idioms and figurative speech (Levorato and Cacciari, 1995).

The comprehension and production processes develop in a parallel mode with production always trying to keep up with comprehension. As the child acquires an aspect of language in comprehension, the child can then try to figure out how to use it in production. Thus, the child attempts to coordinate production with respect to the system that has been developed for understanding (Clark and Hecht, 1983).

As was shown in Chapter 1, Huttenlocher (1974), who studied four young children, aged 10 to 13 months, over a six-month period, found that they were able to comprehend speech at a level *beyond* that to which they had progressed in production. Similarly, Sachs and Truswell (1978) found that children who could only produce single-word utterances (they were at the one-word stage of speech production) nevertheless could understand syntactic structures composed of *more than one word*. Obviously the children's level of speech comprehension was well in advance of their level of speech production.

The same was the outcome in the Steinberg and Steinberg (1975) research, where their 2-year-old son learned to read (understand the meaning of) many written words, phrases, and sentences even *before* he was able to say them in speech.

That children are *not* able to utter words or sentences for the purpose of communication, without gaining an understanding of speech first, could not be otherwise. It is unimaginable for a person to have the ability to produce meaningful speech without having the ability to comprehend speech. One cannot use speech meaningfully unless one knows what meaning such speech indicates.

Incidentally, cross-modality language systems are not exceptions in this regard since there, too, comprehension precedes production. For example, Helen Keller, as we saw in Chapter 4, *did* learn to utter meaningful speech, but not before she had learned its equivalent in terms of a language system based on touch and through the use of hands.

Thus, it must be concluded that for normal children, as well as mute-hearing children, *speech comprehension is the basis for the construction of a grammar in the mind*. This is not to say that speech production is not an important process. It obviously is. However, production is a secondary process and as such it is most probably derived from the grammar based on the primary process of speech comprehension.

In a God's Truth Comprehension Grammar, which is part of what the first author calls *Natural Grammar*, speech comprehension performance would look like this schematically:

> *The performance process of speech comprehension in a Natural Grammar*
> Sound → Comprehension Grammar → Meaning

11.5 Inadequacy of Functionalist and Cognitive grammars

We have seen how Cognitive and Functional theorists have posited grammars that conform to a performance process, that of speech *production*. The ordering of components and processes in their grammars is such that they begin with meaning, proceed through the syntax and lexicon, and then end in sound. That is: Meaning → Grammar → Sound. However, the facts show that, for both normal and speech-handicapped children, it is the speech comprehension process that is primary for language acquisition.

That being the case, grammars such as the Functional, Cognitive, etc., which are formulated to conform to the process of speech production, a process that they consider primary, must be judged as *psychologically inadequate*.

11.6 How the child learns a Natural Grammar

11.6.1 The mind of the child and how it becomes prepared for language learning

11.6.1.1 Children strive to comprehend the world they are born into

The newborn infant finds itself in both an external physical world and an internal world, each of which it seeks to understand. The baby experiences the physical world through its senses and apprehends a number of basic entities: objects, events, and situations. Through psychological operations the baby assigns attributes and evaluations to such entities. Familiar entities and psychological assignments are apprehended by the baby in seeking to understand its own mental experiences concerning hunger, taste, pain, formulating motives, etc. It is the proposition, with its predicates, arguments, and quantifiers, and their interrelations with other propositions, that is the essence of a system of thought that in turn can be modified by other thoughts. Such a propositional structure is universal to all human beings, as are the operations for identifying and developing the elements that fill those structures. It is only after babies have perceived some of the basics of the myriad aspects of the world before them that they begin to learn language. The child then begins to realize, through listening to speech in conjunction with objects, situations, and events in the environment, that such speech may relate to propositional structures or their parts in a child's mind. This, in turn, motivates the child to postulate lexical and grammatical structures so as to better comprehend the meaning of what people say.

Whether the various entities, propositions, and analytical operations which function in the mind of the child are in some way innate is an issue which will not be discussed here since the principal purpose is to present the outlines of a comprehension-primary grammar. Readers are free to render the nature of thought into a Piagetian (Bates, 1979), Fodorian (Fodor, 1976), or other framework of their choosing. Our own view is that children are born with the essence of propositions and the entities that they involve, as well as the essence of the analytical operations of inductive and deductive logic. It is through the operations of these analytical logical procedures on the data that they experience that children acquire their knowledge of the world and then the language with which they may deal with the world and the people in it. While we do not share the view of the Chomskyans that specific *language* ideas are innate, we might admit (along with Bever, 1970) that certain general entities and predicates are innate. After all, the innate analytical operations must operate on something, and that something must be the essence of entities that are necessary for human survival and development. The entity logically is the 'Argument' which, in conjunction with the 'Predicate' forms the basic 'Proposition'.

11.6.1.2 Basic mental entities derived from the physical world

To begin with, let us consider some basic mental entities that relate to the physical world and which babies soon acquire. We shall provide some examples of each using the convention of enclosing, in single quotes, the items that represent the idea. (1) *Objects*: 'mother', 'nipple', 'father', 'hand', 'dog', 'blanket', 'ball', 'banana'. (2) *Attributes and modifiers of objects*: 'big', 'small', 'black', 'soft', 'good-to-eat', 'smells-bad'. (3) *Events*: where objects are involved in an action or movement: 'mother is walking', 'father is shaking my hand', 'the dog is barking', 'the ball is rolling'. (4) *Situations*: where objects are involved in a stative (non-active) relation: 'the banana is on the table', 'the dog is behind the chair', 'mother is standing by the door'. (5) *Attributes, modifiers and evaluations of events and situations*: just as objects can be assigned attributes or evaluations, so too various attributes, modifications, and evaluations such as 'good-for-me' and 'bad-for-me' can be assigned to events and situations. A basic proposition can become modified by another predication, which in turn create more complex propositions, e.g. 'That cute dog which Dad brought home is friendly'. Thus ideas of objects and the propositions involving those objects and states as arguments develop in the child along with predications that relate to the child's attitude, evaluation, etc. of those propositions and form a comprehensive knowledge network.

11.6.1.3 Children become aware of their own mental world and strive to understand it

At the same time that children are striving for an understanding of their external world, they are also striving to understand and organize their own inner subjective world of mental experiences and thoughts. They learn to differentiate particular ideas concerning mental experiences involving their own physical bodies and certain experiences such as hot, cold, itch, pain, tasty, pleasure. They also formulate *thoughts* in propositional form (not to be confused with sentences, which are the reflections of thoughts), using these ideas or others that they may have picked up from their experiencing of the world. One such thought might be 'That stove is hot, it hurt my finger'.

11.6.1.4 Children accumulate and organize knowledge from physical and mental worlds

As time goes by and the child experiences more and more, the child accumulates more knowledge about its physical and subjective worlds. The child learns to identify various objects, their attributes, and how such objects figure in events and situations. These ideas and thoughts are integrated to further the child's understanding. Like animals, the child can learn much about its environment and the beings that inhabit it *even with the absence of language*. However, as time goes on, one unique feature of the child's environment continues to attract the child – and that is speech. Children notice that along with the objects, events, and situations in the environment there is a generous peppering of sounds that others around them make. Like everything else in their environment, children take on the challenge of making sense of these speech sounds.

11.6.2 The Development of *Natural Grammar*, a grammar based on speech comprehension

11.6.2.1 Establishment of a mental lexicon

In observing their environment, children naturally wonder why people make the speech sounds that they do and they seek to make sense of this phenomenon. They search for uniformities and eventually they come to notice that certain speech sounds occur in close association with certain environmental objects, events, or situations with which they are familiar. The simplest task is first to identify objects. Thus, for example, children may notice that the sound 'banana' is uttered by someone when a banana is given to them, that the sound 'mama' is made when a certain woman comes into the room, and that the sound 'dog' is made when a dog runs by. In time the child realizes that sounds signify objects; language learning, in the form of speech comprehension, begins. The ideas and thoughts that children have already acquired in their first year or so provide them with plenty of targets when they begin to comprehend speech. The child typically learns words for which the meaning is already in the child's mind, as, for example, the concept of 'cat'. The child can also learn words when a new object such as an elephant toy is experienced with the speech sound 'elephant'.

Young children who do not have the idea of 'cat' or other ideas cannot be expected to acquire the meaning of the speech sound 'cat' no matter how many times it is said to them without the object (cat), or some representation of it, being present. There are no special qualities to the sounds of words (outside of a small number of onomatopoeic ones) that give a clue as to meaning. Even for ideas that the child does have, such as 'cat', simply repeating the speech sounds of that word, 'cat', does not give any clue as to what idea the sounds may signify. The child needs to associated the observed speech sound to some object before the child can begin to connect a meaning to the sound.

When children learn to comprehend the meanings of spoken *words* such as 'dog', 'cat', 'run', and 'jump', they store this language knowledge in a mental lexicon, which includes not only words but recurrent phrases and sentences, such as 'bread and butter', 'good boy', 'Don't touch!' and 'Come here'. (Seasoned linguists may have stored such items as 'Colorless ideas sleep furiously' (Chomsky) and 'It's turtles all the way' (Ross).) For the sake of brevity, we shall limit ourselves to touching on the learning of single words and some aspects of morphology.

As far as memory storage in the mental lexicon is concerned, there is a *directionality* regarding the connection of the speech sound and the meaning of the word. In the beginning stages of language learning, before the advent of production, the mind is primed for comprehension, that is, to connect speech sounds to thoughts in the mind. The child hears others utter speech sounds. Certain of those speech sounds will elicit in the child a meaning insofar as a connection between the two has previously been established.

Initially, the child is a wholly passive receiver of speech sounds, e.g. the sound 'cat' elicits the meaning 'cat'. Since the child is not producing speech sounds, the directionality is one way, from sound to concept. Thus, in the lexicon in the child's mind entries are essentially of the form:

Lexical entry: Speech sound → Concept

Consequently, when the child hears a familiar acoustic signal in the physical world, the child is able to recover its concept by means of the representation of the speech sounds that it has stored in its mind. By the frequent recurrence of certain speech sounds that others create, the mind of the child is primed to receive acoustic signals of speech sounds and can recover their meaning directly. In this way, not only the meaning of words but of entire phrases and sentences can be recovered directly without the processing of a grammar. For less familiar and novel items a more complex process, grammatical analysis, is necessary.

11.6.2.2 Development of syntax

In their minds children have thoughts and perceptions of the environment and themselves. The child is forever thinking about its world and the actions of objects and living beings in it. Arguments and predicates are what make up the fundamentals of propositions that lie at the essence of thoughts and their reflection in sentences. Such propositions – say, those for the actions 'run' (requires one argument, e.g. '*John* ran'), 'hit' (requires two arguments, e.g. '*John* hit *Tom*'), and 'give' (requires three arguments, e.g. '*John* gave *Tom the ball*') – are already known to the child. The task of the child in learning language is to identify particular speech sequences which represent the particular predicates and arguments so that propositions may be formed: it is through this process that they can make hypotheses regarding the syntactic structure of sentences. Therefore, what the child must do in learning to comprehend syntactic structures from speech is: (1) Identify the predicates – the verbs, adjectives, and relational terms such as prepositions and conjunctions; (2) Identify the arguments – the nouns and noun phrases (NPs) and their semantic roles, (1 and 2 may be in any order) and (3) Identify, through hypothesizing, the syntax whereby these elements of a sentence are expressed. The comprehension process thus moves from speech sounds, initially identified as vocabulary items or phrase chunks so that a proposition (complete thought) can be hypothesized. Further syntactic analysis may be necessary to achieve this. All of this is done by identifying the conceptual entities and predicates so that the components of propositions (arguments and predicates) can be completed in the mind. Conceptually, an argument is composed of an entity (object, state, situation or event) along with a meaning relation role (agent, instrument, receiver, etc.) with respect to the predicate, while a predicate is an action, state or relation. Often in language, entities get realized as noun and noun phrases while predicates get realized as verbs and adjectives.

Predicates will include the main propositional ones such as actions ('The cat *ran*'), and states ('I *want* chocolate'). As for adjectives, for example, in 'The dog is *black*', black is a physical attribute, while in 'Bobby is *hungry*', hungry is an internal state. Prepositions will signal the role that the argument, as a noun or NP, plays with respect to the predicate, for example, in 'at school', 'at' indicates that the argument 'school' is a location with respect to some proposition, while in 'the banana is *on* the table', 'on' indicates the nature of a particular locative relationship concerning two objects, the arguments of 'the banana' and 'the table', where the position in the sentence of the first NP followed by the copula indicates that this is the object that is on top of the other.

The child's prior knowledge concerning the situation or event that it is currently perceiving in the environment or in its own body or mind helps the child to guess at the nature of the role of an NP and at the type of predicate in the speech that it hears. A child could guess what relationship a preposition like 'on' might signal when hearing 'the banana on the table' in an environmental context where a banana is on a table, and where the child knows the meaning of the words 'banana' and 'table'. In such a case, the prior knowledge of the meaning of the nouns is crucial since without that knowledge the child would have little chance at guessing which relational predicate is being expressed by the prepositions of speech.

11.6.2.3 Nouns, word order, prepositions as indicators of NP roles and arguments

As a language, English generally relies on the meanings of nouns (or sentential clauses) to signal an argument and on word order and prepositions to signal the particular nature of the argument. For example, in the sentence

'Mary gave the candy to the monkey', 'Mary', 'the candy', and 'the monkey' are all nouns or NPs with meanings that indicate argument status. Each NP serves a different role with respect to the predicate verb of 'give'. The structure signals to the child that the first NP before the verb, 'Mary', is an agent argument, the NP directly following the verb and without a preposition, 'the candy', is an object argument, while the NP following the verb and with the preposition 'to', 'the monkey', is the patient (receiver) argument.

At the beginning, though, the child is only able to interpret some of the syntactic signals and primarily relies on the meanings of the nouns and the verb. Thus, with the common sentential structure of NP + Verb + (NP), e.g. 'The dog jumped', 'The dog chased the cat', the child, on the basis of the frequency of occurrence of such structures, is set to interpret the first NP as an agent argument on hearing the word 'dog', and 'jump' as a one-place predicate that does not semantically require a completion, although 'chase' would be a two-place predicate that would semantically require a completion, which would be satisfied when the child in linear order hears 'cat'. Thus, in linear order 'dog' elicits an agent argument, 'chase' elicits an action predicate, and 'cat' elicits an object argument. Items like articles and tense suffixes may be overlooked or given secondary attention by the child at this stage.

Soon the child will learn that the same semantic roles may be realized syntactically in a number of different word orders, e.g. (1) 'Mary gave the monkey candy', (2) 'Mary gave candy to the monkey', and, later in the child's learning, (3) 'The monkey was given candy by Mary' and (4) 'Candy was given to the monkey by Mary'. In these sentences meaning roles for the arguments underlying the NPs of 'Mary', 'monkey', and 'candy' are constant. (*Mary* is doing the giving, *the monkey* is doing the receiving, and *candy* is what is being given.) What differs, and what the child must realize, is that *the basic syntactic relations of the sentence* (subject, direct object, indirect object) *may vary greatly*. What differs in sentences 1 (and 2), 3, and 4 is that a different NP occurs as the subject in the initial NP. Yet, the essential underlying argument structure is *the same in all*! Placing a NP in the initial subject position gives that NP greater psychological prominence. Also, for proper argument identification, the meaning of prepositions as well as NP ordering must be learned.

11.6.2.4 Development of complex structures

Children learn to comprehend the complexities underlying *negative* sentences, *question* sentences, sentences with *relative clauses*, *passives*, etc. again by the process of guessing the meanings of the unknown speech constructions; only then can the child take note of how such meanings are expressed in speech. It is the co-occurence of such constructions with respect to relevant objects, events, and situations in the environment that gives the child clues as to meaning. For example, the child hears 'no' or 'don't' in situations where the child is denied something, prohibited, etc. and quite readily understands the meaning of such words.

In time the child's hypothesizing about the principles and rules that underlie the speech occurrences bears fruit. It is in this way that knowledge of complex syntactic structures is formed into a grammar in the mind of the child. Such a grammar, it must be noted, is geared to comprehension – there is a directionality where speech is provided as input to the grammar so that meanings in terms of propositional frames can be provided as output.

The elements of a propositional thought are not linear in the mind like the elements of a sentence are in speech. Because languages of the world express various preferred orders for the elements of their sentences (Subject-Verb-Object for English, Subject-Object-Verb for Korean, Verb-Subject-Object for Hawaiian and literary Arabic, etc., although OSV and VOS languages are less common[1]), unless one is a linguistic imperialist, there is no basis for choosing one order and claiming that that particular order reflects the order of the elements in thought. Such language data indicate instead that propositions in the mind may be even circular or multidimensional, with the elements in no linear order. If it were natural for propositions to occur linearly in the mind (whatever that may mean!), we would expect that mental linear order to be reflected in all languages of the world. Interestingly, the first author's mentor, the psychologist Charles E. Osgood firmly believed that Subject-Verb-Object was the cognitive order (as a neo-Behaviourist he shied away from using the term 'mental' and preferred the more vague 'cognitive') which underlies every language. He stated, '. . . regardless of the basic adult surface ordering of sentence constituents (VSO, SVO, or SOV), the prelinguistically based natural ordering of components in cognizing will universally be "SVO".'[2] His own research on this matter later proved him wrong. A respecter of empirical data, the gentleman was obliged to accept the outcome.

While children can easily form a thought with a particular negative function, *and* while they can recover such a thought when hearing others use negative words and constructions based on the situations in which others use negative speech, it is *not* so easy to express that thought in speech. As Klima and Bellugi (1966) noted, English-speaking children first use 'no' in front of any utterance in order to make a negation: 'No money', 'No the sun shining', or just plain 'no' (see Chapter 1). Although these utterances are of a telegraphic nature, nevertheless, the full propositional meaning underlying these utterances is clearly known by the children, just as it is in the case of an adult in a foreign language situation who has only a similar knowledge of the language at his or her disposal.

It is only later, after the child comprehends more of the fine features of the negative, that such features will begin to appear in production. As the child improves in the syntactic knowledge of comprehension, so too this

---

[1] Personal correspondence. We are indebted to Prof. Anatole Lyovin, University of Hawaii for this correspondence.

[2] Personal correspondence. We are indebted to Prof. Hiroshi Nagata, Kawasaki University of Medical Welfare, Japan, for this information.

improvement will be reflected in the quality of its negative utterances. Again, the essence of the sentence comprehension process is as follows:

> *The performance process of speech comprehension in a Natural Grammar*
> Sound → Natural Grammar → Meaning

11.6.3 How speech production derives from speech comprehension

11.6.3.1 The lexicon

Irreversibility of lexicon entries

As was noted earlier, for comprehension, a lexicon would list entries beginning in speech and ending in meaning, i.e. Speech → Meaning. The lexicon must be organized on the basis of speech sounds for the purpose of perceiving speech. Sequences of sounds that are similar or different from one another would be differentiated and catalogued on such a basis. To comprehend even speech that is uttered at a normal rate, which is exceptionally fast, a person must have ready access to chunks of sounds, for without them the associated meaning would be nearly impossible to find.

On the other hand, a lexicon that is organized for the purpose of production would have to provide a meaning-based organization. A person who wants to utter a sentence will select a lexical item according to its meaning so that the proper speech equivalent can be sought for production. Let us simply deal here with single words and leave aside the more vexing question of searching for subtle and distinctive meanings that would require the use of adjectival phrases and relative clauses.

The nature of the lexicon

For the purposes of production we would wish to access a lexicon using our propositional frame as our guide. We know what thought we wish to express but we have to find a way to utter it in sound. We would want our lexicon to catalogue entries on the basis of meaning, i.e. Meaning → Sound. In effect, our lexicon is a kind of mental thesaurus.

We could simply say that lexical entries are associations of sound and meaning, Sound → Meaning, and that no directionality is implied. That flies in the face of the facts: (1) Comprehension develops prior to production and so sound-based lexical entries would naturally develop first, and people *do* comprehend speech at an astonishing speed; (2) People also produce speech at an astonishing speed, therefore production requires meaning-based lexical entries. Yet there seems to be an imbalance: comprehension is faster.

Typically, given a meaning we have more difficulty in searching for the speech form of a word (a crossword-puzzle type of situation) than we do in searching for a meaning given a speech sound (more of a Scrabble kind of situation). The fact that we hear more speech in our lives than we produce would further reinforce the sound-to-meaning connections.

11.6.3.2 Development of speech articulation and the development of linear sequences of speech

There is great variability as to when children begin to utter their first words. One child might say its first word at 5 months while another might not say its first until around 2 years. Such facts by no means indicate that the delayed child necessarily has less of a conceptual organization of the world or comprehends commensurately fewer words, for despite such differences in the onset of speech, by around 3 years of age most differences in the ability to speak have largely disappeared. Undoubtedly some of the variability has to do with physical development with respect to both the articulators of speech and the connections that must be formed in the brain (Bates *et al.*, 1992). It is not easy to make particular speech sounds. The child's brain must form connections for selecting strings of words and for articulating them in a linear sequence. The comprehension of speech is not as difficult since the sequence itself is given as input.

It is not surprising, therefore, that at the beginning children should try to make single-word utterances do the work of full sentences, holophrases, which are a reflection of full thoughts (see Chapter 1). The child has a thought that it wishes to express, and even though it has many words in its lexicon and even though it can comprehend two-, three-, or more word phrases and sentences that mature speakers say, there is typically a barrier, probably of a neurological nature, that allows the child to pass from the one-word stage to the multi-word stage. A child stuck at the one-word stage will do its best at production even if it is only to utter a single word or a number of separate single words (Bloom, 1973; Scollon, 1976).

11.6.3.3 Production from comprehension: the development of an Auxiliary Production Module

Having a ready syntax based on comprehension to dip into so as to enable the process of speech production is essential for the child in producing multi-word sentences. With respect to the production of sentences, it is not simply a matter of reversing the functions, operations, and rules of the syntax of comprehension in order to formulate sentences. While the syntactic basis of speech production will involve most of the same features of speech comprehension syntactic operations, a simple reversal of these rules (functions/operations/principles) will not provide the desired result. Contextual restrictions will prohibit simple reversibility, for, if a grammar is successful in comprehension (where sound is the input and meaning is the output), it will not be successful in production by simple reversal. In effect, production strategies must be developed by the child, ones that utilize the syntactic characteristics that comprise the Comprehension Grammar, which is part of

Natural Grammar. Such a module would be comprised of strategies and specific functions for interacting with the Comprehension Grammar.

It is the application of the Production Module to the Comprehension Grammar and their interaction that allows the child to produce syntactically sound sentences. As the linguistic knowledge of the child in the Comprehension Grammar increases, and the child attempts using that knowledge in production, the contents of the Production Module will be correspondingly adjusted. Schematically, the process would appear as shown in Figure 11.2.

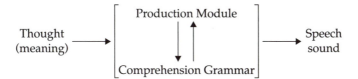

Figure 11.2 The performance process of sentence production in a Natural Grammar

11.7 Towards a theory of Natural Grammar in relation to thought and its functioning in the comprehension and production of sentences

11.7.1 Thought as a process that is non-linguistic in nature and includes ideas indicated by speech

It is our view that, aside from the Natural Grammar itself, there is a *central thought processor* that has as input thoughts as well as *emotions* and *feelings* that it experiences (from the body) and *values* and *goals* that inhere in the mind and guide the processing of thought. Situations and events, linguistic and non-linguistic, that are experienced from the external environment are provided with access to the body and mind. It is with such a variety of input, both external to the body and internal to the mind, that the Natural Grammar attempts to comprehend the speech input.

In this model, the 'central thought' is conceived of as a primary pre-linguistic entity with propositional formats, arguments and predicate forms, as well as innate analyzing processes including logical analysis from which knowledge and language can be derived from experience. The conception proposed, therefore, is partly one of an Empiricist cast in the mode of Putnam (1967, 1980) and Steinberg (1993) with their postulation of learning strategies and deductive logic. But it is partly one of a semi-Rationalist cast since it also consists of the essence of ideas (general but non-linguistic) which are innate in the mind. As Jerry Fodor convincingly argues in his theory of thought (Fodor, 1976), before an analysis of operations can begin to function, it must be able to identify entities to which the operations can apply; without the essence of objects and predicates, nothing can be learned. Such innate essences of ideas were suggested by Bever (1970) some 30 or more years ago to be independent of language but used in deriving language. Given what has been learned in recent years about genetics and how genes manifest themselves in the specific behaviour and perception of a wide variety of living creatures, there is little reason to doubt the probability of certain inheritances in human beings that relate to the world that they are born into.

It is doubtful, though, that specific language ideas in a certain organization (Universal Grammar) are inherited. Chomsky's own arguments for his Universal Grammar are hardly convincing (Steinberg, 1982, 1993, and Chapter 10). A central thought processor, which is already able to construct in our minds a representation of the world around us, and with which we can construct mathematical and scientific theories as well as infer the personalities and potentialities of other human beings, certainly should be capable of constructing grammars without the need to resort to innate ideas of a linguistic nature.

11.7.2 Outline of a complete Natural Grammar

Both the processes of speech comprehension and speech production are accounted for by Natural Grammar. In the comprehension process, speech sound is the input that is processed by the Comprehension Grammar so as to provide meaning as output. In the production process, meaning serves as input to the Auxiliary Production Module whose strategies interact with the Comprehension Grammar so as to provide sound as output. These processes are incorporated in Natural Grammar and are related to Central Thought as outlined in Figure 11.3. Except for sound, which is an occurrence in the physical world, all other aspects of the model are aspects of mind. Thus, the Comprehension Grammar and the production strategies are stored as *mental knowledge and processes* that can be activated by the input of physical sound or by mental meaning. Central Thought integrates meanings (of sentences) into its network of knowledge and likewise generates meanings that it intends to be expressed in speech.

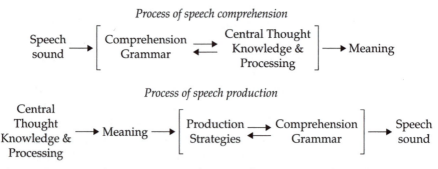

Process of speech comprehension

Process of speech production

Figure 11.3 Natural Grammar: speech comprehension, speech production, and thought

11.7.2.1 Chomsky, Pinker and others on recursion

Recently, Chomsky along with other colleagues (Hauser *et al.*, 2002) have asserted that there is only one aspect of language that is uniquely human and linguistic, i.e. syntactic recursion, where linguistic structures are enlarged through internal means, and not just added at the end, for example. Thus, a sentence like 'The dog barked at the cat' can be expanded internally when a sentence like 'The man disliked the dog' is introduced, and as a result the sentence 'The dog the man disliked barked at the cat' obtains. In this case the sentence 'The man disliked the dog' is embedded in the main sentence between 'The dog' and 'barked at the cat' (with the modification that the object of disliked, the dog, does not occur). Pinker and Jackendoff (2005) object to the HCF claim that the only aspect of language that is unique to humans is syntactic recursion. They argue that many other aspects of grammar are also unique to humans, e.g. phonology and morphology. They state that 'The recursion-only claim, we suggest, is motivated by Chomsky's recent approach to syntax, The Minimalist Program, which deemphasizes the same aspects of language' (p. 201).

Pinker and Jackendoff may be correct about phonology and morphology but they, along with Hauser *et al.*, may be entirely incorrect in regarding syntactic recursion as unique to human language. In response, Fitch, Hauser and Chomsky (2005) claim that most of Pinker and Jackendoff's arguments and examples are irrelevant and that more empirical research needs to be done. Recursion, it should be recognized, is primarily an aspect of thought and concept formation. Humans, and animals, create complex thoughts in their minds by joining other thoughts together in what may be called thought-process recursion – propositions are combined in thought creation. Only humans thought have the means of expressing these recursive thoughts in language but animals do not. Now, when humans express these recursive thoughts must they necessarily use syntactical recursive rules? Perhaps yes, but the answer may be no. Given the framework of Natural Grammar, in the performance process of producing a sentence syntactic recursion rules may not be necessary; rather, the phonological representations of phrases and lexical items are more direct reflections of the recursive thought. In this view, syntactic recursion is but an artefact of propositional recursion.

11.7.3 From pessimism to hope

Some language theorists are quite pessimistic in dealing with the problems of language performance. Concerning a model of comprehension, Jerry Fodor (1976) has said, 'if we started now and worked very hard, we might be able to build one in five hundred years or so' (p. 167). With all due respect to this renowned thinker, Fodor's error was in presupposing that a Chomskyan grammar was essential to such an enterprise!

Chapter 12

Language and the brain

12.1 General brain structure and function

12.1.1 Why do we have body preferences?

Imagine that you are at the beach and there is a little beachball at your feet. Someone calls out, 'Kick it!' Imagine now kicking it really hard. Good! Now suppose the ball is at your feet again and someone calls out, 'Pick it up and throw it to me!' Imagine now throwing that ball. Good! Now, one last thing. You are sitting in the doctor's office facing the door into the doctor's room. You hear some people talking in the room but you can't make out what they are saying. So you strain to hear. You turn your head slightly towards the door. Now, you can make out what is being said!

Now, which foot did you use? Which hand did you use? And, which side of your head did you turn? Most people would have used their right foot to kick, their right hand to throw, and they would have turned the right side of their head towards the sound. A minority of people, mainly male, would have used the opposite sides for these tasks. Try now to imagine kicking the ball, throwing the ball, and listening with the opposite side of your preference. How does it feel? Not so satisfying, is it?

Why do we have these preferences? We have them from childhood and throughout our lives. Why? The answer lies in the brain, its structure and function. We will begin with a discussion of the brain and in doing so we will explain why it is that we have the preferences that we do.

12.1.2 The hemispheres of the brain

The general structure of the brain is that of a whole which is divided into vertical halves that seem to be mirror images of one another. It looks much like a walnut with the two parts joined around the middle, except that there is little space between the two halves in the real brain. Each half of the brain is called a hemisphere. There is a *left hemisphere* and a *right hemisphere*. The hemispheres come out of the brain stem, which connects to the spinal cord.

The hemispheres maintain connection with one another through a bundle of fibres called the *corpus callosum*. The brain, together with the spinal cord, is referred to as the central nervous system of the human body. There is a covering on each hemisphere, called the *cortex*, which is a furrowed outer layer of cell matter. It is the cortex that is concerned with higher brain functions in both humans and animals.

The cerebral cortex developed last in the course of evolution. While in fish, for example, the cerebral cortex is barely visible, and is one of the smallest parts of the brain, in humans it has increased in size and complexity to become the largest part of the brain. In time, due to the growth in the number and complexity of brain cells in the life of the human, the cerebral cortex becomes more dense and takes on a greyer and less pink appearance.

Each cerebral hemisphere is divided into four parts or *lobes*: from front to back there are the *frontal*, *temporal*, *parietal* (located above the temporal), and the *occipital*. This division of the brain into lobes is loosely based on physical features and not on actual separations.

General functions such as cognition (to some degree) occur in the frontal lobe, hearing occurs in the temporal lobe, general somaesthetic sensing (feeling in the arms, legs, face, etc.) in the parietal lobe, and vision in the occipital lobe. Each hemisphere has these lobes with these functions. As we shall see later, there are other hemispheric-specific functions that are also located in some of these areas. For example, the left hemisphere typically involves language.

The *corpus callosum* not only serves to connect the hemispheres but is itself a principal integrator and coordinator of the mental processes carried out in the two hemispheres. See Figure 12.1 for an overhead view of the hemispheres and a side view of a typical right hemisphere. The locations of the lobes are noted in both views.

Language areas:

The areas that have been proposed for the processing of speaking, listening, reading, writing, and singing are mainly located at or around the Sylvian and Rolando fissures. Several specific areas have been identified:

- The front part of the parietal lobe, along the fissure of Rolando, is primarily involved in the processing of sensation, and may be connected with the speech and auditory areas at a deeper level.
- The area in front of the fissure of Rolando is mainly involved in motor functioning, and is thus relevant to the study of speaking and writing.
- An area in the upper back part of the temporal lobe, extending upwards into the parietal lobe, plays a major part in the comprehension of speech. This is 'Wernicke's area'.
- In the upper part of the temporal lobe is the main area involved in auditory reception, known as 'Heschl's gyri', after the Austrian pathologist R. L. Heschl (1824–81).
- The lower back part of the frontal lobe is primarily involved in the encoding of speech. This is 'Broca's area'.

Overhead view

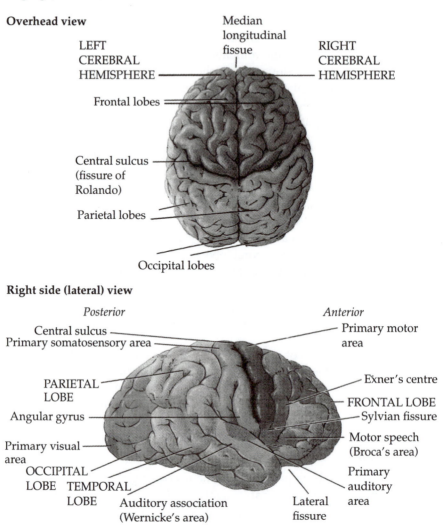

Figure 12.1 The brain: overhead and side views

- Another area towards the back of the frontal lobe, 'Exner's centre', may be involved in the motor control of writing.
- Part of the left parietal region, close to Wernicke's area, is involved with the control of manual signing.
- The area at the back of the occipital lobe is used mainly for the processing of visual stimulae.

Some of the neural pathways that are considered to be involved in the processing of spoken language:

1. **Speech production.** The basic structure of the utterance is thought to be generated in Wernicke's area and is sent to Broca's area for encoding.

The motor programme is then passed on to the adjacent motor area, which governs the articulatory organs.

2. **Reading aloud.** The written form is first received by the visual cortex, then transmitted via the angular gyrus to Wernicke's area, where it is believed to be associated with the auditory representation. The utterance structure is then sent on to Broca's area, as in (1).

3. **Speech comprehension.** The signals arrive in the auditory cortex from the ear, and are transferred to the adjacent Wernicke's area, where they are interpreted.

12.2 Hemispheric structure and function

12.2.1 Left and right hemispheres control opposite sides of the body

The brain controls the body by a division of labour, so to speak. The left hemisphere controls the right side of the body, including the right hand, the right arm, and the right side of the face, while the right hemisphere controls the left side of the body. Those who have suffered a cerebral haemorrhage, commonly called a 'stroke', provide clear examples of how this kind of cross-over control operates. A stroke in the right hemisphere of the brain will affect victims on the left side of the body. Thus, they can lose control over the muscles in the left hand, left leg, and the left side of the face (including that side of the tongue and mouth). A stroke to the left part of the brain will similarly affect the right side of the body.

12.2.2 Hemispheric dominance

Typically, the left hemisphere dominates the right

Now, even though the hemispheres of the brain divide the labours of the body, they do not do so evenly. In a sense, we might say that the body cannot serve two masters: one side must take charge. For a human to have the two hemispheres competing over which hand or foot should be used first to fight off an attacker or to jump at an animal in a hunt would not be advantageous for the survival of the species. This phenomenon, where one hemisphere is the controlling one, is called *dominance*.

Generally, animals, including chimps, have not been thought to have a genetic hand/foot preference. Rather, individual animals were thought to develop a personal preference over their lives. However, some recent research seems to indicate there may be left and right hemispheric differences in chimps and that such differences might result in preferences (Freeman *et al.*, 2004). Clearly, though, such differences are not as striking as in humans.

Hand and foot preference

Most persons prefer their right hand and their right foot. This generally indicates that the left hemisphere dominates the right hemisphere. The result of such dominance is that such people (left-hemisphere dominant) would tend to prefer the right side of their bodies.

Incidentally, regarding the questions asked at the beginning of this chapter about the beachball, you can now understand why it was that you imagined that you kicked and threw the ball with the particular foot and particular hand that you did. A left-hemisphere-dominant person would tend to use the right hand and the right foot while a person who is right-hemisphere dominant would tend to use the left hand and left foot.

Left-handers

About 90 per cent of the population worldwide are left-handed but, counter to expectations, only about 30 per cent of left-handers have right-hemisphere dominance (Klar, 1999). The majority of left-handers are left-hemisphere dominant but their dominance tends to be much less marked than in natural right-handed persons. The lack of strong dominance for left-handers is believed to be a factor contributing to speech disorders and to various reading and writing dysfunctions, such as stuttering and dyslexia, which includes the reversal or mirror-imaging of letters and words when reading or writing. Lamm and Epstein (1999), for example, report that left-handed native Hebrew speakers perform less well than right-handers in the study of English, particularly reading. Such dysfunctions seem to be caused by the two hemispheres vying with one another for dominance. Some even argue that left-handers die younger (Halpern and Coren, 1991), although this has been challenged by others (Salive *et al.*, 1993).

Worldwide there is a higher proportion of males who are natural left-handers than females. In the USA estimates indicate that more than twice as many males as females are likely to be left-handed. The effect of sexual hormones released in the brain during the development of the fetus may be related to this phenomenon.

Because dominance is a congenital condition, the practice of forcing children who are naturally left-handers to use their right hand for writing, etc., will not remedy such problems but may serve to worsen them and create others. Many countries still force natural left-handers to be right-handers.

Sound preferences

Speech sounds are differentiated from other types of sounds including music, animal sounds, and noises. The two hemispheres specialize in processing these two types of sounds (speech and non-speech). For true right-handers, speech sounds are mainly processed in the left hemisphere while music, noises, and animals sounds are mainly processed in the right hemisphere. The opposite will be the case for some left-handers. Because of the nature of the arrangement of large and small bundles of fibres, right-handed persons with lateralization for language in the left hemisphere will perceive speech sounds more readily through the right ear than the left.

This phenomenon was artfully demonstrated in an ingenious experiment by Kimura (1961). What this researcher did was to present subjects with a different speech syllable in each ear by means of earphones. The speech sounds were presented simultaneously to both ears (a 'dichotic listening' experiment). Thus, for example, a person was simultaneously presented with 'ba' in the left ear and with 'da' in the right ear. The result? The 'da' was perceived more strongly or dominantly. The 'ba' was barely heard, if at all. To understand this phenomenon, it is necessary to bear in mind the following:

1. From each ear, a big bundle of fibres will cross over to the other hemisphere while a small bundle of fibres will go directly to the nearby hemisphere. Thus, from the right ear a big bundle of fibres will cross over to the left hemisphere, and a small bundle of fibres will go directly to the right hemisphere. Similarly, from the left ear a big bundle of fibres will cross over to the right hemisphere, and a small bundle of fibres will go directly to the left hemisphere.
2. The left hemisphere is the main language hemisphere for true right-handers. The opposite will be the case for some left-handers but for simplicity's sake we will consider only the case of the right-hander.

Because the right ear hearing 'da' has a big bundle of fibres to carry the sound impulse to the left hemisphere, the sound passes to the speech-processing centres in the left hemisphere. On the other hand, the 'ba' speech sound coming in the left ear has only a small number of fibres with which to carry the sound directly to the speech-processing centres in the left hemisphere for language processing. Therefore, the small impulse of 'ba' will reach the speech centre first while the big impulse of 'da' follows. The big impulse of 'ba' will follow much later since it has to travel from the left ear to the right hemisphere, where it is rerouted back to the left hemisphere. The effect is for the big impulse of 'da' to dominate, for it is the 'da' that subjects typically report perceiving.

Listening behind a closed door

Now we can answer the last of the questions posed at the beginning of this chapter, which concerned imagining straining to hear what people are saying behind a door. The answer, if you are a right-hander, is: 'Right ear forward'. This is because (1) speech sounds are processed in the left hemisphere, (2) the first big impulse of speech sound will be transmitted to the left hemisphere from the right ear, and (3) the first big impulse will precede and dominate any other big impulse. If you are a true left-hander, you probably would have imagined turning your left ear forward.

12.2.3 Lateralized hemispheric functioning

Lateralization

Besides their general functioning, the hemispheres have some very specialized structures and functions. Some functions occur in one hemisphere while other functions occur in the other hemisphere. This separation of functions is called *lateralization*. Incoming experiences are directed to the left or right hemisphere depending on the nature of those experiences, be they speech, faces, or sensations of touch. We will see that speech production and speech understanding are mainly located in the left hemisphere.

Left-hemisphere specializations

Research has clearly shown that language centres predominate in one hemisphere or the other. The main language centres are *Broca's area*, in the front part of the brain, *Wernicke's area*, towards the back, and the *angular gyrus*,

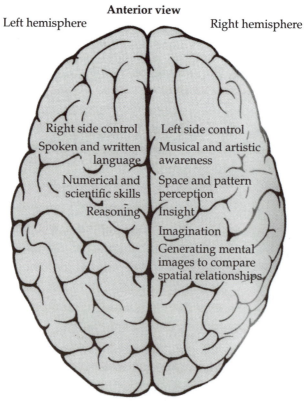

Figure 12.2 Lateralized hemispheric functioning

which is even further back. Broca's area and Wernicke's area are connected by tissue – the *arcuate fasciculus*. (See Figure 12.1.)

For most people, language is in the left hemisphere: for roughly 99 per cent of right-handers and about two-thirds of left-handers (Damasio and Damasio, 1992). Language is located in the right hemisphere in less than 5 per cent of the US population. For these persons, in addition to language, all other specific left- and right-hemispheric functions are also reversed. For convenience sake, we shall use the majority case (left hemisphere for language, etc.) for the purpose of discussion.

In addition to language, the left hemisphere is concerned with logical and analytical operations, and higher mathematics.

Right-hemisphere specializations

The right hemisphere is involved in recognizing emotions, recognizing faces, and perceiving the structures of things globally without analysis. Unilateral right-hemisphere stroke can lead to problems with both immediate and delayed memory, when patients have trouble learning and remembering individual words (Halper and Cherney, 2004). If the area of the brain that deals with faces, for example, is damaged, the person will not be able to recognize the faces of people, even close family, and even that person's own face when looking into a mirror! Needless to say, such a situation is devastating to the life of the person.

The right hemisphere also deals with music and non-linguistic sounds, such as noises and animal sounds. Interestingly, patients with right-hemisphere damage seem to have difficulties in processing pitch as a prosodic syntactic distinction. When presented with a sentence 'The queen said the knight was singing' (a man is singing) as opposed to 'The queen, [pause] said the knight, [pause] was singing' (a woman singing), a patient with the right-hemisphere damage was reported to have difficulty apprehending this syntactic distinction (Hoyte *et al.*, 2004).

As we shall see later, new research shows that the right hemisphere has some language functions and can take over the complete language functioning of the left hemisphere when that hemisphere has been surgically removed or damaged.

Split-brain effects

Certain aspects of lateralization have been dramatically confirmed by the work of Sperry (1982), who separated the two hemispheres of the brain by severing the connecting tissue, the corpus callosum, of a number of patients. Such a drastic operation was believed necessary to save the patients, who were suffering from extreme cases of epilepsy.

After surgery with the corpus callosum no longer intact, information no longer flowed from hemisphere to hemisphere as it does in normal persons.

The functions of the complete brain were no longer integrated. Such being the case, it was possible for Sperry and his group of researchers to test some of the abilities of the separate hemispheres.

It was found that 'split-brain' persons could still use speech and writing in the disconnected left hemisphere but that their right hemisphere had little such capacity. In normal persons, the right hemisphere has more capability.

When tactile (touch) information passed to the left hemisphere, split-brain patients were completely capable of verbally describing objects and talking about things they had just touched. If, however, the touching experience of patients passed only to the right hemisphere, they could not talk about the experience at all; the information could not be passed through the corpus callosum to the left hemisphere for expression in speech because the corpus callosum had been severed.

The right hemisphere, in general, was also incapable of imagining the sound of a word, even a familiar one, and patients failed simple rhyming tests, such as determining by reading which word, 'pie' or 'key', rhymes with 'bee'. The right hemisphere was found to be good at spatial tasks such as matching things from their appearance, such as being able to correctly reassemble halves of photographs.

In August 2000, BBC News reported an interesting case of a man, who suffered from epilepsy and had to go through surgery, which separated the left and right hemispheres of his brain. Now the left brain performs well at language skills, while the right brain does best with shape puzzles (*The Man With Two Brains*, 2000).

12.3 Language areas and their functioning

12.3.1 Broca's area, the motor area, and speech production

Pierre Paul Broca was a French pathologist and neurosurgeon (1824–80) who made the first great discovery regarding brain and language. He discovered a certain area of the cortex that is involved with the production of speech; that part of the cortex bears his name, Broca's area.

Broca further noted that the speech area is adjacent to the region of the *motor* cortex that controls the movement of the muscles of the articulators of speech: the tongue, lips, jaw, soft palate, vocal cords, etc. He posited that speech is formulated in Broca's area and then articulated via the motor area (see Figure 12.1).

Subsequent research substantiated Broca's theory. The link between Broca's area and the motor area was later shown to be the nerve fibres of the arcuate fasciculus. The speech-production process would begin in Broca's area, pass on through the arcuate fasciculus to the motor area and from there to the articulators of speech for vocalization.

12.3.2 Wernicke's area, the auditory area, and speech understanding

Speech comprehension

Carl Wernicke, a German neurologist (1848–1905), in considering that Broca's speech area was near the part of the brain that involves areas that control the articulators of speech, investigated whether two other areas of the brain are involved in the process of speech *comprehension*. In his research he discovered, near the part of the cortex in the temporal lobe that receives *auditory* stimuli, an area that was involved in the understanding of speech. Wernicke hypothesized that this area, later named Wernicke's area, must in some way be connected to the auditory area. Later research showed that these areas are indeed connected, by fibres of the arcuate fasciculus.

The model that Wernicke posited over a century ago is still largely the model which most researchers use today in describing how we understand speech. According to Wernicke, on hearing a word, the sound of a word goes from the ear to the auditory area and then to Wernicke's area. It is from Broca's area that the vocalization of speech would then be activated (see Figure 12.1).

Reading

When a word is read, according to Wernicke, the information goes from the eyes to the visual area of the cortex in the occipital lobe, from there to the *angular gyrus*, then to Wernicke's area and then to Broca's area, which causes the auditory form of the word to be activated. Wernicke had the mistaken belief that all written words *had* somehow to be speech activated (said aloud).

Recent research in brain-scan imaging actually shows that the latter part of the reading process, where Wernicke thought that Broca's area would be activated, does *not* occur in many instances. In other words, one can directly recover the meaning of written words without having to access their sound. This must be the case, for example, in rapid reading where speed precludes any such distinctive activation.

Language in other areas and the other hemisphere

Although most language processes occur in Broca's area, Wernicke's area, and the angular gyrus, some language functioning occurs elsewhere in the left hemisphere, as well, and some even occurs in the right hemisphere. (Right-hemisphere language functions are a relatively recent discovery and these are considered in the next section.) The ability to understand the meaning of intonation, such as the rising tone of a question, the ability to interpret emotional intentions, such as anger or sarcasm, from inflections in the voice, and the ability to appreciate social meanings from something such as whispering, may very well be located outside of what have been traditionally regarded as the main language areas of the brain. Say, the cerebellum and basal ganglia used to be considered as subcortical nuclear systems dedicated to the regulation of motor function, the cerebellum being in charge of the real-time fine-tuning of movement, and the basal ganglia, the selection or inhibition of action commands. However, contemporary neuroimaging studies have revealed that the cerebellum is actively involved in search strategies for verbal responses, and the basal ganglia appear to participate in the selection of specific lexical items (Murdoch *et al.*, 2004). However, the exact way in which these processes regulate linguistic function remains largely undetermined.

12.4 Right-hemisphere language abilities

12.4.1 Typical language functions

While the left hemisphere is involved in most language tasks, recent evidence indicates that the right hemisphere too is involved in language processing (see Beeman and Chiarello, 1998, for a good review). More precisely, 'both hemispheres receive similar input and both attempt to process input, for every language process . . . the hemispheres compute information differently at each level of processing (e.g. semantic processing), so that each hemisphere is most adept at handling particular inputs and producing particular outputs' (Chiarello and Beeman, 1998, p. x).

Understanding discourse and other minds

There is increasing evidence that the right hemisphere is critical for understanding discourse (Hough, 1990; Kaplan *et al.*, 1990; Beeman, 1993, 1998; Brownell and Martino, 1998; Stemmer and Joanette, 1998; Paradis, 2003). Thus, patients with right-hemisphere damage have impairments concerning narrative script, interpretation, integration of information or conceptualization of the unit as a whole, construction of new conceptual models, and inferences about another person's beliefs and intentions (Stemmer and Joannett, 1998).

The right hemisphere has an ability to use 'knowledge of the world', involved in scripting, where a number of sentences are related to a topic. Patients who have damage in their right hemisphere show structuring problems in story recall (Moya *et al.*, 1986), and their speech is disrupted, particularly at the level of discourse, jumping from one topic to another incoherently (Brownell and Martino, 1998).

12.4.2 The right hemisphere can take over left-hemisphere functions

It is important to remember that the brain operates as a whole. Any task is represented by a network of areas. For the brain's overall performance the amount of removed tissue matters more than its location (Posner, 2001). Therefore, the brain is able to readjust its circuits to process language in case normal processing cannot occur. For example, brain scans revealed that blind persons receive verbal communication help from the brain areas that normally process visual and touch information in sighted people (Ariniello, 2000). Researchers at the University of Marburg in Germany compared language processing time in blind and sighted subjects who were asked to decide if the last word made sense in sentences like 'we sleep in a tent when we go camping' as opposed to 'tomorrow Bobby will be ten years hill'. They found out that blind persons were twice as fast on the task. This difference in timing can lead to the idea that the part of the brain normally associated with vision is redirected to process language by blind people (Jones, 2000).

Brain plasticity accounts for the growing evidence that damage to language areas in the left hemisphere of young children is compensated for, with the right hemisphere taking over the reacquisition of language. This sometimes happens with adults, as well. Recently, MRI scans (see Section 12.8.2) of stroke patients revealed that about six months after the stroke, the area on the right side of the brain corresponding to the inferior frontal gyrus was heavily used to restore language skills. It suggests that the brain develops previously underused areas and transfers language processing to those areas to help compensate the damage (Rosen *et al.*, 2000). While the extent of functional plasticity is not yet established, it is clear that the right hemisphere *is capable* of taking over left-hemisphere functions.

Case studies

Smith and Sugar (1975) report on a boy, BL, aged $5^{1}/_{2}$ years, who had his entire left hemisphere removed (hemispherectomy) because he suffered right-sided seizures. Before surgery, BL's speech was reportedly characterized by poor intelligibility. However, four months after the surgery, at the age of 6, BL's speech improved to normal. When tested 21 years later, he showed normal language and intellectual capacities. BL attended regular elementary and high school and graduated from college with a bachelor's degree with a double major in business and sociology. At present, BL's performance appears to be normal in pronunciation, grammar, semantics, and usage, also with some deficits in production of phonemically complex words and in comprehension of linguistic contrasts in prosody (Vanlancker-Sidtis, 2004). The right hemisphere and other intact residual structures must therefore have compensated for the loss of the hemisphere.

Another boy, Alex, also had a left hemispherectomy, at the age of 8½ years (Vargha-Khadem *et al.*, 1997). Although his language abilities were only equivalent to a 3- or 4-year-old before the surgery, he suddenly began to acquire language when he was 9 years old, attaining with the right hemisphere alone a level of language abilities equivalent to an 8- or 10-year-old after about five years. Again the right hemisphere served in the learning of language. Such findings indicate that Krashen's (1973) notion that the right hemisphere will not be able to take over a damaged left hemisphere after the age of 5 years is in error.

Both monolingual and bilingual children and adults, too, can have language skills restored after massive damage to the left hemisphere. There are reports of a significant recovery of language skills in three patients ten years after a stroke (Shankweiler *et al.*, 2004), and in some bilingual and multilingual patients (*The Boy With Half a Brain*, 2000; *Half Brain Girl 'Fluent in Two Languages'*, 2002; Paradis, 2004).

Conclusion

The right hemisphere is often capable of taking over typical left-hemisphere functions, even after the entire left hemisphere has been removed.

12.5 The bilingual brain

Recent neurolinguistic research has shown growing interest in how bilinguals represent different languages in the brain. Two central issues have been the focus of research: whether different languages are represented in the different hemispheres of the brain, and if the age at which a second language is learned is related to lateralization. As we shall see, results are not consistent on either question.

Studies showing right-hemisphere involvement

Albert and Obler (1978), Karanth and Rangmani (1988), and Wuillemin *et al.* (1994) report greater involvement of the right hemisphere in bilinguals than in monolinguals. Albert and Obler (1978) argue that 'the right hemisphere plays a major role in the learning of a second language, even in adulthood' (p. 243). Their position is based partly on the finding that aphasia (language dysfunction) is more likely to be found following right-hemisphere lesions in bilinguals (10 per cent) than in monolinguals (1–2 per cent). If the right hemisphere is damaged, and aphasia results, then they argue that the location of the second language must be in the right hemisphere. Indeed, there is evidence of different degrees of recovery after a stroke for each language (Paradis, 1977, 2004; Junque *et al.*, 1995). Extreme cases have shown impairment for one language postoperatively, with spontaneous recovery after eight months (Paradis and Goldblum, 1989). A more recent case has been used to suggest that there is a clear neuroanatomical dissociation between the languages (Gomez-Tortosa *et al.*, 1995).

Studies finding no dominance

A number of studies, on the other hand, have reported no difference in lateral dominance for the first and the second language. For example, Soares (1982, 1984), Walters and Zatorre (1978), and Zatorre (1989) found no difference between bilinguals and monolinguals. Galloway and Scarcella (1982), in a Spanish–English dichotic-listening study, found no evidence for the right hemisphere being involved more in the initial stages of informal, adult, second-language acquisition.

Conclusion

While findings are not consistent, the fact that right-hemisphere difficulties are involved in so many studies suggests the distinct possibility that a second language sometimes locates in the right hemisphere and sometimes not. There may be variables that determine hemispheric location but these have not been identified as yet. One such factor may be the age at which the second language was learned.

12.6 Sign language

Left-hemisphere damage affects signing

Right-handed deaf signers, like hearing persons, exhibit aphasia when critical left-hemisphere areas are damaged (Poizner *et al.*, 1989). Approximately one dozen case studies provide sufficient detail to implicate left-hemisphere structures in sign-language disturbances. A subset of cases provide neuro-radiological or autopsy reports to confirm left-hemisphere involvement, and provide compelling language assessment to implicate aphasic language disturbance.

In addition, there are five cases of signers with right-hemisphere pathology. Since their sign-language skills were relatively intact, this would indicate that the left hemisphere is the primary location of sign language.

Disruptions in sign-language ability following left-hemisphere damage are similar to those patterns found in hearing users of spoken languages. For example, execution of speech-articulation movements in hearing persons involves the cortical zone encompassing the lower posterior portion of the left frontal lobe (Goodglass, 1993), which is the same region implicated in sign-language production (Poizner *et al.*, 1987).

Language impairments following strokes in deaf signers exhibit the characteristic pattern of left frontal damage leading to non-fluent output with spared comprehension, while left posterior lesions yield fluent output with impaired language comprehension. These impairments are local in nature, and do not reflect general problems in symbolic conceptualization or motor behaviour.

Conclusion

The left hemisphere appears to be centrally involved in sign language, as it is with non-signers. The right hemisphere also is intricately involved with signers but in ways different from that of non-signers.

12.7 Language disorders: aphasias

12.7.1 Two basic groups: Broca's aphasias and Wernicke's aphasias

Language disorders, known as aphasias, are presumed to have as their cause some form of damage to some specific site in the hemisphere where language is located. Such damage causes characteristic problems in speech, as well as in reading and writing. An extensive study using radio-isotope scanning by Benson and Patten (1967) served to support the traditional distinction that aphasias are generally classifiable into two groups, Broca's aphasias and Wernicke's aphasias. In addition to these two basic groups, other aphasic sites were also found.

12.7.2 Broca's aphasia

It was in 1861 that Broca published the first in a series of studies on language and brain. This was the beginning of the true scientific study of cases of aphasia, a term that covers a very broad range of language disorders that are commonly caused by tissue damage or destruction in the brain. War injuries, strokes, and car accidents are frequent causes of such injuries. Broca was one of the first researchers to discover that damage to certain portions of the brain, but not to others, results in speech disorders.

One particular condition, now called Broca's aphasia, is characterized by meaningful but shortened speech and also occurs in writing. In the condition, grammatical inflections are often lacking, such as the third-person present tense '-s' ('Mary want candy' for 'Mary wants candy'), and the auxiliary 'be' ('Joe coming' for 'Joe is coming'), as are articles, prepositions, and other so-called function words. In a way, the speech is similar to that of children at the telegraphic stage of speech production (Chapter 1).

Although the most noted feature of Broca's aphasia is the fragmentary nature of speech production, it has recently been discovered that speech comprehension is also affected. In one experiment with a patient with Broca's aphasia, when presented with the spoken sentence, 'The apple that the boy is eating is red', the patient was able to understand the sentence, particularly with regard to who was doing the eating (the boy). However, when presented with the sentence, 'The girl that the boy is looking at is tall', the same patient could not figure out who was doing the looking (the boy). In the previous sentence, the patient could guess the meaning simply from knowing the vocabulary items 'apple', 'boy', and 'eat', and from knowing what usually happens in the world ('boys eat apples' and not vice versa). But the patient could not guess the meaning of the second sentence simply from the vocabulary, because boys look at girls and girls look at boys. To understand such a sentence, one must be able to analyze its syntactic relations. This the patient could not do.

Thus, there is a loss of syntactic knowledge in both speech production and understanding for those with Broca's aphasia. Interestingly, people with Broca's aphasia can often sing very well, even using words and structures they are unable to utter in conversation. This shows that Broca's aphasia is not simply a breakdown in the muscular control of speech movements, since those with this disorder *can* pronounce words. The loss, therefore, must be due to something of a deeper nature.

12.7.3 Wernicke's aphasia

Nonsense double-talk

This condition is characterized by speech that often resembles what is called nonsense speech or double-talk. It sounds right and is grammatical but it is meaningless. It can seem so normal that the listener thinks that he or she has somehow misheard what was said, as is often the case in ordinary conversation.

A patient with Wernicke's aphasia may say, 'Before I was in the one here, I was over in the other one. My sister had the department in the other one', 'My wires don't hire right', or 'I'm supposed to take everything from the top so that we do four flashes of four volumes before we get down low'.

Word substitution

Patients with Wernicke's aphasia commonly provide substitute words for the proper ones on the basis of similar sounds, associations, or other features. The word 'chair', for example, elicited the following in some patients: 'shair' (similar sound), 'table' (association), 'throne' (related meaning), 'wheelbase' (?) and 'You sit on it. It's a . . .' (word loss). As with Broca's aphasia, Wernicke's aphasia can also cause a severe loss of speech understanding, although the hearing of non-verbal sounds and music may be unimpaired.

12.7.4 Reading and writing aphasias: dyslexias

One type of aphasia that involves disorders in reading and writing is called dyslexia. There are many sorts of dyslexia, one category of which is due to damage to the brain, *after* reading and writing have been acquired. With children, however, dyslexias may be observed while they are in the process of acquiring reading and writing skills. Problems of hemispheric dominance or defects in visual perception, for example, may play some role in causing difficulties in reading and writing. Some children may only be able to write backwards (*deer* as *reed*) or upside down, or in reading they may confuse letters (*b* with *d*, *p* with *q*, *u* with *n*, *m* with *w*) and engage in other anomalies. As was noted earlier in Chapter 3 on reading, the orientation of letters is a general exception to the way we observe other objects. For example, pick up a pencil and no matter which way we hold it, we still identify it as a pencil. To help remedy such problems as those with letters, it is best not to present the letters to the child in isolation but in a context with other letters. Thus, b and d should be shown in words, e.g. tu*b*, *d*og. In this way, the child can see the proper orientation of the letter and the word in which it appears.

Dyslexia may be subdivided into two basic categories: *alexia*, which involves disorders in reading, and *agraphia*, which involves disorders in writing. One may be afflicted by both conditions at the same time, in which case the person is unable to either read or write properly. In *pure agraphia* there is a total loss of the ability to write, even though the hand can be used skilfully for other purposes. Thus, for example, a person who has had a left-hemisphere stroke may be able to read the simple sentence 'How are you?', and yet be unable to write it.

Japanese writing aphasias

Studies involving languages with special writing systems provide interesting findings. Japanese aphasics display quite unusual characteristics due to the nature of their complex writing system, which involves both a syllabic system (in which symbols represent syllables) called *kana*, and a Chinese-character type (in which symbols represent morphemes) called *kanji*. In Japanese, anything that is written in *kanji* can be written in *kana* (but not vice versa). Imura (1940) studied a patient with Broca's aphasia who was able to write the correct *kanji* for dictated words but was unable to write the same words in the syllabic writing system, *kana*, something that any normal Japanese can do, especially since *kana* is considered the easier of the two systems.

Then there was a patient with Wernicke's aphasia who was able to write characters quite fluently but what was written was nonsensical: the *kanji* were malformed or made up of invented sets of strokes.

Besides writing problems, reading by Japanese can also be affected in strange ways. The noted researcher Sasanuma (1994) has found that while some patients may have their reading of *kana* words impaired, their reading of *kanji* words may not be much impaired, or vice versa, even when the *kana* and *kanji* words are familiar. These are right-handers who have had damage, due to strokes or automobile accidents, in the temporal or parietal regions of their left hemisphere. The loss may be due to damage of storage areas in the brain for *kana* and *kanji* words, or there may be damage to some processing or retrieval areas in the brain.

Incidentally, it might be worth pointing out here a common fallacy concerning Chinese-type characters, i.e. *kanji*. These are *not* located in the right hemisphere (in ordinary right-handed persons) as in the visual aspect of objects, even though these symbols are historically derived from pictures (as is the case for origination of all natural writing systems). *Kanji* are largely abstract figures and they are stored in the left hemisphere, as are all writing systems.

12.7.4 Sign-language aphasia

There is a striking parallel between speech and sign language that is especially interesting since it confirms what research has found about language and the hemispheres of the brain. Readers will recall that the right hemisphere has been shown to be superior at spatial tasks such as facial recognition and visuo-constructive tasks such as copying designs and patterns.

Following this broad division of the hemispheres as 'left for language' and 'right for spatial', it might seem that the right hemisphere would be the one to be more involved with the production and comprehension of sign language, since signing is a visual space-related phenomenon. Strong evidence, however, from the study of sign-language aphasics shows that this is not the case. Signs and the signing system are located in the left hemisphere.

Broca's aphasia with signers

Native signers of American Sign Language who have suffered trauma such as a stroke to the left hemisphere will produce sign language equivalents of Broca's aphasia or Wernicke's aphasia. The signed language of a Broca's aphasic consists largely of uninflected forms with little ability to use the signing space as a grammatical framework to mark verb inflections, person, aspect, or morphological changes. It is as awkward and as halting as is Broca's aphasia in spoken language. Patients may be accurate in making a single sign in response to a request to name an object or they may make a sign successfully when it has a simple uninflected meaning but be unable to produce a correct movement to indicate grammatical function such as the direct object. One patient was able to make the proper path movement towards the body to sign 'accept', but not a similar movement for 'blame me'. The implication is that the inability to produce correct signs is not due to a motor dysfunction but rather a defect in the ability to access the grammar properly.

Wernicke's aphasia with signers

A signer with Wernicke's aphasia will produce fluent but nonsensical strings of signs, particularly for morphology, aspect, pronoun reference, etc. There are frequent errors with substitutions made in terms of the three elements of signs (configuration, location, and movement). The result is the production of many meaningless individual signs or of signs that have meaning but are nonsensical in sentences. And, just as in Wernicke's aphasia for speech, much substitution occurs within the same lexical category: nouns for nouns, verbs for verbs, etc. Furthermore, substitution occurs, too, along semantically related lines, such as 'daughter' for 'son' or 'bed' for 'chair', producing similarly bizarre results. One signing patient displayed Wernicke's aphasia symptoms in his writing as well as sign language, leading researchers to conclude that there is a general linguistic dysfunction at work and not just a motor dysfunction impairing the ability to sign.

Signers who have suffered damage to the right hemisphere generally do not display aphasia symptoms in the production of signs. Their sign production seems to remain grammatical and unimpeded. However, these same persons are likely to suffer some impairment in their comprehension of signs. Why it should be the case that their ability to understand signs is disturbed but their ability to produce signs is untouched, as yet remains unexplained.

In any case, the same general patterns of aphasia emerge in sign as with speech. Patients with left-hemisphere damage suffer the same aphasias whether their language is a spoken one or a signed one. Thus, even though the right hemisphere is disposed to process spatial tasks, when the task involved is a linguistic one and spatial syntax is involved, the left hemisphere asserts dominance. Clearly this shows that it is the left hemisphere that is specially equipped to handle language, whether the modality of the language is speech or sign.

12.7.5 Localism and holism

Much of the discussion in this chapter has been aimed at showing in a very broad way how the production and comprehension of language is related to certain areas of the brain and their interconnections. This particular model of looking at the structure and function of language by relating specific aspects of language to certain localized areas of the brain is called the *localist* model. Although it is true that certain areas of the brain are involved in language, it is also necessary to take into account *holistic* or global brain phenomena in order to understand what is happening.

The effect on language of broader psychological factors, such as attention span, motivation, alertness, the rate at which auditory and visual memory traces dissipate, etc., must be considered. A holistic type of model does just this. For example, you start to say something and suddenly you are distracted and break off, or you forget what you wanted to say. It would be foolish to conclude that you suffered a momentary breakdown in speech production due to damage to your Broca's area. Or, when a friend says something but you do not catch the words and respond with 'What?', this is not an indication of damage to your Wernicke's area. Some sort of holistic multi-dimensional explanation is required here.

The localist model has been successful in explaining roughly 85 per cent of aphasias, but the other 15 per cent are anomalous and baffling. They represent people who have language disorders but do not have damage in the expected language areas, or, conversely, certain damage has not resulted in the predicted symptoms. This cannot but make us reflect on the more global possibilities of language functioning in the brain.

While there is an impressive accumulation of scientific knowledge on the brain to date, it is well to keep in mind the fact that even linguistic concepts as simple as that of the noun or the verb have yet to be localized. Science has yet to provide the detailed knowledge of the correspondence between language and the brain's structure and function.

12.8 Methods of investigating brain and language

12.8.1 Traditional methods: post-mortem, brain-injured people, electrical stimulation

The comparatively limited understanding we have of the neurological basis of language in the brain is the result of the application of a relatively small number of methods. The oldest method, that used by Broca himself, is the post-mortem examination of the brains of patients who had displayed language disorders while they were alive. The abnormalities he found in certain areas of their brains in post-mortems correlated with the language symptoms they displayed in life.

Another method involves observing the language of patients who have had brain operations. A person might require – because of an accident or a tumour, for example – the removal of a lobe of the brain (lobectomy) or even of an entire hemisphere (hemispherectomy). Then, too, the study of the language of living patients with severe brain damage caused by accidents or wartime injuries was and still is a useful method of investigation.

Yet another method, pioneered by Penfield in the 1950s, involves the electrical stimulation of the cerebral cortex in patients who are conscious during brain surgery. On being stimulated, patients would report, for example, that they remember childhood events or old songs. How to verify what the patient says about the past is a problem with this method. The use of this procedure has been very limited, since it is restricted to the open brain areas of persons who are undergoing surgery without the use of anaesthesia.

12.8.2 High-tech methods: CAT, PET, MRI, and ERPs

In recent years, revolutionary new methods have been developed that lend themselves nicely to the study of language and the brain. These involve powerful new techniques in imaging: CT or CAT (Computerized Axial Tomography), PET (Positron Emission Tomography), Magnetic Resonance Imaging (MRI) and Event-Related Potentials (ERPs). All of these techniques involve the brain as it is, without surgery or any other invasive procedure, and indicate the actual functioning of the brain in real time. As such they may be used to explore brain-functioning of normal persons as well as those with brain problems. (See Müller, 1996; Frackowiak, 2000; Cabesa and Kingstone, 2001, for extensive discussion of the current neuroimaging techniques and methods.)

12.8.3 Conclusion

It has only been in the past 40 years that brain exploration has been furthered by the development of technologically advanced methods. With such methods, our scientific knowledge of the brain and its functions has increased enormously, is still at a relatively primitive stage. The next decades of this new millennium will undoubtedly prove to be especially exciting in the development of technological methods in the discovery of the relations between brain and language.

References

Adams, M. J. (1994) *Beginning to Read*. Cambridge, MA: MIT Press.

Adelman, H. (1970) Learning to read in the classroom. *The Reading Teacher*, **2**, 28.

Akahane-Yamada, R., Tohkura, Y., Bradlow, A. R. and Pisoni, D. B. (1996) Does training in speech perception modify speech production? *Proceedings of the Fourth International Conference on Spoken Language Processing*. Philadelphia, PA., **2**, 606–9.

Albert, M. L. and Obler, L. K. (1978) *The Bilingual Brain: Neuropsychological and Neurolinguistic Aspects of Bilingualism*. New York: Academic Press.

Alexander, L. G. (1978) *Mainline Beginners*. London: Longman.

Andrews, V. and Bernstein-Ratner, N. (1987) *Patterns of Maternal and Paternal Response to Language-learners' Verbalization*. Paper presented at the American Speech and Hearing Association Convention, New Orleans.

Anthony, D. (1971) *Seeing Essential English*. Anaheim, CA: Educational Services Division, Anaheim Union High School District.

Antony, M. V. (1994) Against functionalist theories of consciousness. *Mind and Language*, **9**, 105–23.

Ardrey, R. (1970) *The Social Contract*. New York: Dell Publishing.

Ariniello, L. (2000) *Brain Plasticity, Language Processing and Reading*. [Online]. http://web.sfn.org/context/Publications/BrainBriefings.

Armstrong, D. M. (1968) *A Materialist Theory of Mind*. New York: Humanities Press.

Asher, J. (1966) The learning strategy of the total physical response: a review. *Modern Language Journal*, **50**, 79–84.

Asher, J. (1969) The total physical response approach to second language learning. *Modern Language Journal*, **53**, 133–9.

Asher, J. (1977) *Learning Another Language Through Actions: The Complete Teacher's Guidebook*. Los Gatos, CA: Sky Oaks Productions.

Asher, J. and Garcia, R. (1969) The optimal age to learn a foreign language. *Modern Language Journal*, **53**, 334–41.

Asher, J., Kusudo, J. A. and De La Torre, R. (1974) Learning a second language through commands: the second field test. *Modern Language Journal*, **58**, 24–32.

Ashton-Warner, S. (1963) *Teacher*. New York: Simon & Schuster.

Askov, M., Otto, W. and Smith, R. (1972) Assessment of the de-Hirsch predictive index test of reading failure. In R. Aukerman (ed.), *Some Persistent Questions on Beginning Reading*. Newark, DE: International Reading Association.

Au, T. K. (1983) Chinese and English counterfactuals: the Sapir–Whorf hypothesis revisited. *Cognition*, **15**, 155–87.

Bain, B. and Yu, A. (1980) Cognitive consequences of raising children bilingually: one parent, one language. *Canadian Journal of Psychology*, **34**, 4, 304–13.

Bancroft, W. J. (1978) The Lozanov method and its American adaptations. *Modern Language Journal*, **62**, 4, 167–75.

Bates, E. (1979) *The Emergence of Symbols: Cognition and Communication in Infancy*. New York: Academic Press.

References

Bates, E. and MacWhinney, B. (1982) Functionalist approaches to grammar. In E. Wanner and L. R. Gleitman (eds), *Language Acquisition: The State of the Art*. Cambridge: Cambridge University Press, pp. 173–218.

Bates, E., Thal, D. and Janowsky, J. S. (1992) Early language development and its neural correlates. In I. Rapin and S. Segalowitz (eds), *Handbook of Neuropsychology, Vol. 6: Child Neurology*. Amsterdam: Elsevier, pp. 69–110.

Bavin, E. (1992) The acquisition of Walpiri as a first language. In D. I. Slobin (ed.), *The Crosslinguistic Study of Language Acquisition*, Vol. 3. Hillsdale, NJ: Lawrence Erlbaum Associates, pp. 309–71.

Beckermann, A., Flohr, H. and Kim, J. (eds) (1992) *Emergentism or Reduction*. Berlin: De Gruyter.

Beeman, M. (1993) Semantic processing in the right hemisphere may contribute to drawing inferences from discourse. *Brain and Language*, **44**, 80–120.

Beeman, M. (1998) Coarse semantic coding and discourse comprehension. In M. Beeman and C. Chiarello (eds), *Right Hemisphere Language Comprehension: Perspective from Cognitive Neuroscience*. Mahwah, NJ: Lawrence Erlbaum Associates, pp. 255–84.

Beeman, M. and Chiarello, C. (eds) (1998) *Right Hemisphere Language Comprehension: Perspective from Cognitive Neuroscience*. Mahwah, NJ: Lawrence Erlbaum Associates.

Bell, A. G. (1883) Upon a method of teaching language to a very young congenitally deaf child. *American Annals of the Deaf and Dumb*, **28**, 3, 124–39.

Bellugi, U. and Fischer, S. (1972) A comparison of sign language and spoken language. *Cognition*, **1**, 173–200.

Bellugi, U., Wang, P. P. and Jernigan, T. L. (1994) Williams syndrome: an unusual neuropsychological profile. In S. Broman and J. Grafman (eds), *A Typical Cognitive Deficit in Developmental Disorders*. Hillsdale, NJ: Lawrence Erlbaum Associates, pp. 23–56.

Benson, D. F. and Patten, D. H. (1967) The use of radioactive isotopes in the localization of aphasia-producing lesions. *Cortex*, **3**, 258–71.

Benzaquen, J., Gagnon, R., Hunse, C. and Foreman, J. (1990) The intrauterine sound environment of the human fetus during labor. *American Journal of Obstetrics and Gynecology*, **163**, 484–90.

Bereiter, C. and Engelmann, S. (1966) *Teaching Disadvantaged Children in the Preschool*. Englewood Cliffs, NJ: Prentice Hall.

Berkeley, G. (1710/1952) *A Treatise Concerning Principles of Human Knowledge*. Chicago: Encyclopaedia Britannica.

Berko-Gleason, J. (1975) Fathers and other strangers: men's speech to young children. *Georgetown University Roundtable on Language and Linguistics*. Washington, DC: Georgetown University Press.

Bernstein, B. (1960) Language and social class. *British Journal of Sociology*, **11**, 271–6.

Bernstein, B. (1961) Social structure, language, and learning. *Educational Research*, **3**, 163–76.

Bernstein-Ratner, N. (1988) Patterns of parental vocabulary selection in speech to very young children. *Journal of Child Language*, **15**, 481–92.

Bever, T. G. (1970) The cognitive basis for linguistic structures. In J. R. Hayes (ed.), *Cognition and the Development of Language*. New York: Wiley, pp. 279–362.

Bialystok, E. (1979) An analytical view of second language competence: a model and some evidence. *Modern Language Journal*, **63**, 257–62.

Bialystok, E. (1981) Some evidence for the integrity and interaction of two knowledge sources. In R. Anderson (ed.), *New Dimensions in Second Language Acquisition Research*. Rowley, MA: Newbury House, pp. 62–74.

Bialystok, E. (2004) The impact of bilingualism on language and literacy development. In T. K. Bhatia and W. C. Ritchie (eds), *The Handbook of Bilingualism*. Malde, MA: Blackwell.

Bickerton, D. (1990) *Language and Species*. Chicago: University of Chicago Press.

Biegelow, E. (1934) School progress of underage children. *Elementary School Journal*, **35**, 186–92.

Birdsong, D. (1992) Ultimate attainment in second language acquisition. *Language*, **68**, 706–55.

Birdsong, D. and Molis, M. (2001) On the evidence for maturational constraints in second language acquisition. *Journal of Memory and Language*, **44**, 235–249.

Bishop, C. (1964) Transfer effects of word and letter training in reading. *Journal of Verbal Learning and Verbal Behavior*, **3**, 215–21.

Block, N. (1978) Troubles with functionalism. In C. W. Savage (ed.), *Perception and Cognition: Issues in the Philosophy of Science*. Minneapolis: University of Minnesota Press, pp. 261–325.

Bloom, A. H. (1981) *The Linguistic Shaping of Thought: A Study of the Impact of Language on Thinking in China and the West*. Hillsdale, NJ: Lawrence Erlbaum Associates.

Bloom, L. (1970) *Language Development: Form and Function in Emerging Grammars*. Cambridge, MA: MIT Press.

Bloom, L. (1973) *One Word at a Time: The Use of Single Word Utterances Before Syntax*. The Hague: Mouton.

Bloom, L., Lifter, K. and Hafitz, J. (1980) The semantics of verbs and the development of verb inflections in child language. *Language*, **56**, 386–412.

Bloom, L., Merkin, S. and Wootten, J. (1982) Wh-Questions: linguistic factors that contribute to the sequence of acquisition. *Child Development*, **53**, 1084–92.

Bloomfield, L. (1942/1961) Teaching children to read. In L. Bloomfield and C. L. Barnhart (eds), *Let's Read*. Detroit: Wayne State University Press, 1961. (Original work published in 1942.)

Blount, B. G. (1972) Parental speech and language acquisition: some Luo and Samoan examples. *Anthropological Linguistics*, **14**, 119–30.

Bochner, J. H. and Albertini, J. A. (1988) Language varieties in the deaf population and their acquisition by children and adults. In M. Strong (ed.), *Language Learning and Deafness*. Cambridge: Cambridge University Press, pp. 3–48.

Bollenbacher, J. (1959) Murphy-Durrell reading readiness test. In O. Buros (ed.), *Fifth Mental Measurement Yearbook*. Highland Park, NJ: Gryphen Press, pp. 778–9.

Bongaerts, T., Planken, B. and Schils, E. (1995) Can late learners attain a native accent in a foreign language? A test of the critical period hypothesis. In D. Singleton and Z. Lengyel (eds), *The Age Factor in Second Language Acquisition*. Clevedon, UK: Multilingual Matters, pp. 30–50.

Bongaerts, T., van Summeren, C., Planken, B. and Schils, E. (1997) Age and ultimate attainment in the pronunciation of a foreign language. *Studies in Second Language Acquisition*, **19**, 447–65.

Bonvillian, J. D., Orlansky, M. D. and Novack, L. L. (1983) Developmental milestones: sign language acquisition and motor development. *Child Development*, **54**, 6, 1435–45.

Bostwick, M. (1999) *A Study of an Elementary English Language Immersion School in Japan*. Unpublished doctoral dissertation, Temple University, Philadelphia.

References

Botha, R. P. (1989) *Challenging Chomsky: The Generative Garden Game*. Oxford: Basil Blackwell.

Braine, M. D. S. (1963) The ontogeny of English phrase structure: the first phase. *Language*, **39**, 1–13.

Braine, M. D. S. (1971) The acquisition of language in infant and child. In C. Reed (ed.), *The Learning of Language*. New York: Appleton-Century-Crofts, pp. 7–96.

Braine, M. D. S. (1976) Children's first word combinations. *Monographs of the Society for Research in Child Development*, **41**, 1. Chicago: University of Chicago Press.

Braine, M. D. S. (1992) What sort of innate structure is needed to 'bootstrap' into syntax? *Cognition*, **45**, 77–100.

Brandt, M. E. (1974) *Reading Readiness Redefined*. Unpublished MA thesis, University of California: San Francisco.

Brannon, E. M. and Terrace, H. S. (1998) Ordering of the numerosities 1 to 9 by monkeys. *Science*, **282**, 746–9.

Braun, C. (1977) Experience: the basis for communication skills development. In C. Braun and V. Froese (eds), *An Experience-Based Approach to Language and Reading*. Baltimore, London, Tokyo: University Park Press, pp. 3–18.

Brinton, D. M., Snow, M. A. and Wesche, M. B. (1989) *Content-Based Second Language Instruction*. New York: Newbury House.

Brooks, N. (1964) *Language and Language Learning*. New York: Harcourt Brace & World.

Brown, H. D. (1987) *Principles of Language Learning and Teaching*, 2nd edn. Englewood Cliffs, NJ: Prentice Hall.

Brown, R. (1973) *A First Language: The Early Stages*. Cambridge: Cambridge University Press.

Brown, R. and Bellugi, U. (1964) Three processes in the child's acquisition of syntax. *Harvard Educational Review*, **34**, 133–51.

Brown, R., Cazden, C. and Bellugi, U. (1969) The child's grammar from 1 to 3. In J. P. Hill (ed.), *Minnesota Symposia on Child Psychology, vol. II*. Minneapolis: University of Minnesota Press, pp. 28–73.

Brown, R. and Hanlon, C. (1970) Derivational complexity and order of acquisition in child speech. In J. R. Hayes (ed.), *Cognition and the Development of Language*. New York: Wiley, pp. 11–53.

Brown, R. and Lenneberg, E. H. (1954) A study in language and cognition. *Journal of Abnormal and Social Psychology*, **49**, 454–62.

Brownell, H. H. (1988) Appreciation of metaphoric and connotative word meaning by brain-damaged patients. In C. Chiarello (ed.), *Right Hemisphere Contributions to Lexical Semantics*. New York: Springer-Verlag, pp. 19–31.

Brownell, H. and Martino, G. (1998) Deficits in inference and social cognition: the effects of right hemisphere brain damage on discourse. In M. Beeman and C. Chiarello (eds), *Right Hemisphere Language Comprehension: Perspective from Cognitive Neuroscience*. Mahwah, NJ: Lawrence Erlbaum Associates, pp. 309–28.

Bruce, R. V. (1973) *Bell: Alexander Graham Bell and the Conquest of Solitude*. Ithaca: Cornell University Press.

Bruck, M., Lambert, W. and Tucker, G. (1976) Cognitive and attitudinal consequences of bilingual schooling: the St Lambert project through grade six. *International Journal of Psycholinguistics*, **6**, 13–33.

Brumfit, C. J. and Johnson, K. (eds) (1979) *The Communicative Approach to Language Teaching*. Oxford: Oxford University Press.

Byrne, B. (1991) Experimental analysis of the child's discovery of the alphabetic principle. In L. Rieben and C. A. Perfetti (eds), *Learning to Read: Basic Research and its Implications*. Hillsdale, NJ: Lawrence Erlbaum Associates, pp. 75–84.

Byrne, B. (1992) Studies in the acquisition procedure for reading: rationale, hypotheses, and data. In P. Gough, L. C. Ehri and R. Treiman (eds), *Reading Acquisition*. Hillsdale, NJ: Lawrence Erlbaum Associates, pp. 1–34.

Cabesa, R. and Kingstone, A. (eds) (2001) *Handbook on Functional Neuroimaging of Cognition*. Cambridge, MA: MIT Press.

Candland, D. K. (1993) *Feral Children and Clever Animals: Reflections on Human Nature*. New York: Oxford University Press.

Caprez, G., Sinclair-de-Zwart, H. and Studer, B. (1971) Enwicklung der Passiveform im Schweizerdeutschen. *Archives de Psychologie*, **41**, 23–52.

Carroll, J. B. (ed.) (1956) *Language, Thought, and Reality: Selected Writings of Benjamin Lee Whorf*. Cambridge, MA: MIT Press.

Casasanto, D. (2005) Crying 'Whorf'. *Science*, **307**, 1721–2.

Cattell, J. M. (1885) Ueber der Zeit der Erkennung und Bennenung von Schrifzeichen, Bildern und Farben. *Philosophische Studien*, **2**, 635–50.

Cazden, C. (1970) Children's questions: their form, functions, and roles in education. *Young Children*, March, 202–20.

Chalmers, D. J. (1996) *The Conscious Mind: In Search of a Fundamental Theory*. Oxford: Oxford University Press.

Chalmers, D. J. (1997) An exchange with David Chalmers. In J. R. Searle (1997), *The Mystery of Consciousness*. New York: The New York Review of Books.

Chastain, K. (1971) The audio-lingual habit theory versus the cognitive-code learning theory: some theoretical considerations. In R. C. Lugton and C. H. Heinle (eds), *Toward a Cognitive Approach to Second-Language Acquisition*. Philadelphia: The Center for Curriculum Development, pp. 111–21.

Cheney, D. L. and Seyfarth, R. M. (1982) How vervet monkeys perceive their grunts: field playback experiments. *Animal Behaviour*, **30**, 739–51.

Cheney, D. L. and Seyfarth, R. M. (1990) *How Monkeys see the World: Inside the Mind of Another Species*. Chicago: Chicago University Press.

Cheydleur, F. (1932) An experiment in adult learning of French at the Madison, Wisconsin Vocational School. *Journal of Educational Research*, **4**, 259–75.

Chiarello, C. and Beeman, M. (1998) Introduction to the cognitive neuroscience of right hemisphere language comprehension. In M. Beeman and C. Chiarello (eds), *Right Hemisphere Language Comprehension: Perspective from Cognitive Neuroscience*. Mahwah, NJ: Lawrence Erlbaum Associates, pp. ix–xii.

Chihara, T. and Oller, J. (1978) Attitudes and attained proficiency in EFL: a sociolinguistic study of adult Japanese speakers. *Language Learning*, **28**, 55–68.

Chomsky, N. (1955) The logical structure of linguistic theory. Ph.D. dissertation (Microfilm). Cambridge, MA: MIT Library.

Chomsky, N. (1957) *Syntactic Structures*. The Hague: Mouton.

Chomsky, N. (1959) Review of Skinner's Verbal Behavior. *Language*, **35**, 26–58.

Chomsky, N. (1962) Explanatory models in linguistics. In E. Nagel, P. Suppes and A. Tarski (eds), *Logic, Methodology, and Philosophy of Science*. Stanford, CA: Stanford University Press.

Chomsky, N. (1965) *Aspects of the Theory of Syntax*. Cambridge, MA: MIT Press.

Chomsky, N. (1966) *Cartesian Linguistics*. New York: Harper & Row.

Chomsky, N. (1967a) Recent contributions to the theory of innate ideas. *Synthese*, **17**, 2–11.

References

Chomsky, N. (1967b) The formal nature of language. In E. Lenneberg, *Biological Foundations of Language*. New York: Wiley, pp. 397–442. Also in N. Chomsky (1972), *Language and Mind* (enlarged edn). New York: Harcourt Brace Jovanovich.

Chomsky, N. (1968) *Language and Mind*. New York: Harcourt Brace Jovanovich.

Chomsky, N. (1975) *Conditions on Rules of Grammar*. Article based on lectures presented at the Linguistic Institute, University of South Florida. Also in N. Chomsky (1977), *Essays on form and Interpretation*. New York: North-Holland, pp. 163–210.

Chomsky, N. (1980a) Discussion of Putnam's comments. In M. Piattelli-Palmarini (ed.), *Language and Learning: The Debate Between Jean Piaget and Noam Chomsky*. Cambridge, MA: Harvard University Press, pp. 310–24.

Chomsky, N. (1980b) *Rules and Representations*. New York: Columbia University Press.

Chomsky, N. (1980c) On cognitive structures and their development: a reply to Piaget. In M. Piattelli-Palmarini (ed.), *Language and Learning: The Debate Between Jean Piaget and Noam Chomsky*. Cambridge, MA: Harvard University Press, pp. 35–52.

Chomsky, N. (1981a) *Lectures on Government and Binding*. Dordrecht, Netherlands: Foris Publications.

Chomsky, N. (1981b) Principles and parameters in syntactic theory. In N. Hornstein and D. Lighthood (eds), *Explanation in Linguistics: The Logical Problem of Language Acquisition*. London: Longman, pp. 32–75.

Chomsky, N. (1986) *Knowledge of Language: Its Nature, Origin and Use*. New York: Praeger.

Chomsky, N. (1988) *Language and Problems of Knowledge*. Cambridge, MA: MIT Press.

Chomsky, N. (1991) Linguistics and adjacent field: a personal view. In A. Kasher (ed.), *The Chomskyan Turn*. Oxford: Basil Blackwell, pp. 3–25.

Chomsky, N. (1995) *The Minimalist Program*. Cambridge, MA: MIT Press.

Chomsky, N. (2000) *New Horizons in the Study of Language and Mind*. Cambridge: Cambridge University Press.

Clark, E. V. and Barron, B. (1988) A thrower-button or a button-thrower? Children's judgements of grammatical and ungrammatical compound nouns. *Linguistics*, **26**, 3–19.

Clark, E. V. and Hecht, B. F. (1983) Comprehension, production, and language acquisition. *Annual Review of Psychology*, **34**, 325–49.

Cohen, A. (1998) *Strategies in Learning and Using a Second Language*. London: Longman.

Comenius (Jan Amos Komensky) (1568) *Didactica magna*. (1896, 1967) *The Great Didactic of John Amos Comenius* (in English). New York: Russell & Russell.

Conrad, R. (1979) *The Deaf School Child: Language and Cognitive Functions*. London: Harper & Row.

Corder, S. (1981) *Error Analysis and Interlanguage*. Oxford: Oxford University Press.

Coulmas, F. (1989) *The Writing Systems of the World*. Oxford: Blackwell.

Coulson, S., King, J. W. and Kutas, M. (1998) ERPs and domain specificity: beating a straw horse. *Language and Cognitive Processes*, **13**, 653–72.

Cowart, W. (1994) Anchoring and grammar effects in judgments of sentence acceptability. *Perceptual and Motor Skills*, **79**, 1171–1182.

Cowart, W., Smith-Pertersen, G. A. and Fowler, S. (1998) Equivocal evidence on field-dependence effects in sentence judgments. *Perceptual and Motor Skills*, **87**, 1091–1102.

Crane, T. (1995) The mental causation debate. *Proceedings of the Aristotelian Society,* Supplementary Vol., **69**, 211–36.

Cromer, R. F. (1980) Empirical evidence in support of non-empiricist theories of mind. *Behavioral and Brain Sciences,* **3**, 16–18.

Crookes, G. and Schmidt, R. (1991) Motivation: reopening the research agenda. *Language Learning,* **41**, 4, 469–512.

Cross, T. G. (1977) Mothers' speech adjustments: the contributions of selected child listener variables. In C. E. Snow and C. A. Ferguson (eds), *Talking to Children: Language Input and Acquisition.* Cambridge: Cambridge University Press, pp. 151–88.

Crystal, D. (1987) *Cambridge Encyclopedia of Language.* Cambridge: Cambridge University Press.

Cunningham, P. M. (2003) What research says about teaching phonics. In L. M. Morrow, L. B. Gambrell and M. Pressley (eds), *Best Practices in Literacy Instruction.* New York, London: The Guilford Press, pp. 65–86.

Curran, C. A. (1972) *Counseling-Learning: A Whole-Person Model for Education.* New York: Grune & Stratton.

Curran, C. A. (1976) *Counseling-Learning in Second Language.* Apple River, IL: Apple River Press.

Curtiss, S. (1977) *A Psycholinguistic Study of a Modern-Day Wild Child.* New York: Academic Press.

Curtiss, S. (1981) Dissociation between language and cognition: cases and implications. *Journal of Autism and Developmental Disorders,* **11**, 15–30.

Curtiss, S. (1989) The independence and task-specificity of language. In A. Bornstein and J. Bruner (eds), *Interaction in Human Development.* Hillsdale, NJ: Lawrence Erlbaum Associates, pp. 105–37.

Curtiss, S., Fromkin, V., Krashen, S., Rigler, D. and Rigler, M. (1974) The linguistic development of Genie. *Language,* **50**, 528–54.

Darian, S. (1972) *English as a Foreign Language: History, Development, and Methods of Teaching.* Norman, OK: University of Oklahoma Press.

Dean, C. (1939) Predicting first grade reading achievements. *Elementary School Journal,* **33**, 609–16.

de Boysson-Bardies, B., Sagart, L. and Durand, C. (1984) Discernible differences in the babbling of infants according to target language. *Journal of Child Language,* **11**, 1–16.

DeCasper, A. and Fifer, W. P. (1980) On human bonding: newborns prefer their mothers' voices. *Science,* **208**, 1174–6.

Demuth, K. (1989) Maturation and the acquisition of the Sesotho passive. *Language,* **65**, 56–80.

Demuth, K. (1990) Subject, topic and Sesotho passive. *Journal of Child Language,* **17**, 67–84.

Dennett, D. (1978) *Brainstorms.* Montgomery, VT: Bradford Books.

DePaulo, B. M. and Bonvillian, D. D. (1978) The effect on language development of the special characteristics of speech addressed to children. *Journal of Psycholinguistic Research,* **7**, 189–211.

Descartes, R. (1641) *Meditations on First Philosophy.* Chicago: Encyclopaedia Britannica (1952).

Dickson, U. E. (1923) *Mental Tests and the Classroom Teacher.* New York: World Book.

Dik, S. C. (1991) Functional grammar. In F. G. Droste and J. E. Joseph (eds), *Linguistic Theory and Grammatical Description.* Amsterdam: John Benjamins, pp. 247–74.

References

Doman, G. (1964) *How to Teach your Baby to Read*. New York: Random House.

Dörnyei, Z. (2003) Attitudes, orientations, and motivations in language learning: advance in theory, research, and applications. *Language Learning*, **53**, 1, 3–32.

Drach, K. M. (1969) The language of the parent: a pilot study. In *The Structure of Linguistic Input to Children*. Language Behavior Research Laboratory, Working Paper No. 14, University of California, Berkeley.

Dretske, F. (1981) *Knowledge and the Flow of Information*. Cambridge, MA: MIT Press.

Drozd, K. F. (1995) Child English pre-sentential negation as metalinguistic exclamatory sentence negation. *Journal of Child Language*, **22**, 583–610.

Dulay, H., Burt, M. and Krashen, S. (1982) *Language Two*. Oxford: Oxford University Press.

Dunn, S. S. (1953) Murphy-Durrell reading readiness test. In O. Buros (ed.), *Fifth Mental Measurement Yearbook*. Highland Park, NJ: Gryphen Press, p. 779.

Durkin, D. (1970) A language arts program for pre-first grade children: two-year achievement report. *Reading Research Quarterly*, **5**, 534–65.

Edwards, J. V. (2004) Foundations of bilingualism. In T. K. Bhatia and W. C. Ritchie (eds), *The Handbook of Bilingualism*. Malde, MA: Blackwell.

Ehri, L. C. (1991) Learning to read and spell words. In L. Rieben and C. A. Perfetti (eds), *Learning to Read: Basic Research and its Implications*. Hillsdale, NJ: Lawrence Erlbaum Associates, pp. 57–73.

Eldredge, J. L. and Baird, J. E. (1996) Phonemic awareness training works better than whole language instruction for teaching first graders how to write. *Reading Research and Instruction*, **35**, 193–208.

Elliot, A. J. (1981) *Child Language*. Cambridge: Cambridge University Press.

Ellis, R. (1994) *The Study of Second-Language Acquisition*. Oxford: Oxford University Press.

Ely, D. P. (1995) Trends and issues in educational technology. In G. T. Anglin (ed.), *Instructional Technology: Past, Present and Future*. Englewood, Colorado: Libraries Unlimited, pp. 34–58.

Emmorey, K. (1991) Repetition priming with aspect and agreement morphology in American Sign Language. *Journal of Psycholinguistic Research*, **20**, 365–88.

Ewing, A. and Ewing, E. C. (1964) *Teaching Deaf Children to Talk*. Manchester: Manchester University Press.

Faerch, C. and Kasper, G. (1983) *Strategies in Interlanguage Communication*. London: Longman.

Fathman, A. (1978) ESL and EFL learning: Similar or dissimilar? In C. Blatchford and J. Schachter (eds), *On TESOL*. Washington, DC: TESOL, pp. 213–23.

Feez, S. (1998) *Text-Based Syllabus Design*. Sydney: National Centre for English Teaching and Research.

Feigl, H. (1958) The mental and the physical. *Minnesota Studies in the Philosophy of Science*, **2**, 370–497.

Feldman, H. M. (1994) Language development after early unilateral brain injury: a replication study. In H. Trager-Flusberg (ed.), *Constraints on Language Acquisition*. Hillsdale, NJ: Lawrence Erlbaum Associates, pp. 75–90.

Feldman, H. M., Holland, A. L., Kemp, S. S. and Janosky, J. E. (1992) Language development after unilateral brain injury. *Brain and Language*, **42**, 89–102.

Felix, S. (1976) Wh-pronouns and second language acquisition. *Linguistische Berichte*, **44**, 52–64.

Ferguson, C. A. (1964) Baby talk in six languages. *American Anthropologist*, **66**, 103–14.

Ferguson, C. A. (1977) Baby talk as a simplified register. In C. E. Snow and C. A. Ferguson (eds), *Talking to Children: Language Input and Acquisition*. New York: Cambridge University Press, pp. 209–35.

Ferguson, C. A. and Garnica, O. K. (1975) Theories of phonological development. In E. H. Lenneberg and E. Lenneberg (eds), *Foundations of Language Development: A Multidisciplinary Approach*, Vol. 1. New York: Academic Press, pp. 153–80.

Fitch, W. T., Hauser, M. D. and Chomsky, N. (2005) The evolution of the language faculty: clarifications and implications. *Cognition*, in press. [Online, 19 August, 2005] www.wjh.harvard.edu/~mnklab/publications/languagespeech/EvolLangFac_Cognition.pdf

Fletcher-Flinn, C. M. and Thompson, G. B. (2000) Learning to read with underdeveloped phonemic awareness but lexicalized phonological recoding: a case study of a 3-year-old. *Cognition*, **74**, 177–208.

Flynn, S. and Martohardjono, G. (1994) Mapping from the initial state to the final state: the separation of universal principles and language-specific properties. In B. Lust, M. Suner and J. Whitman (eds), *Syntactic Theory and First Language Acquisition: Cross-linguistic Perspectives*, Vol. 1. Hillsdale, NJ: Lawrence Erlbaum, pp. 319–35.

Fodor, J. A. (1976) *The Language of Thought*. Sussex: Harvester Press.

Fodor, J. A. (1980) Methodological solipsism considered as a research strategy in cognitive psychology. *Behavioral and Brain Sciences*, **3**, 9–16.

Fodor, J. A., Bever, T. G. and Garrett, M. F. (1974) *The Psychology of Language*. New York: McGraw-Hill.

Foorman, B. R., Fletcher, J. M., Francis, D. J., Schatschneider, C. and Mehta, P. (1998) The role of instruction in learning to read: preventing leading failure in at-risk children. *Journal of Educational Psychology*, **90**, 37–55.

Foster, P. and Skehan, P. (1996) The influence of planning on performance in task-based learning. *Studies in Second Language Acquisition*, **18**, 299–324.

Fourcin, A. J. (1975) Language development in the absence of expressive speech. In E. H. Lenneberg and E. Lenneberg (eds), *Foundations of Language Development: A Multidisciplinary Approach*, Vol. 1. New York: Academic Press, pp. 263–8.

Fouts, R. S. (1973) Acquisition and testing of gestural signs in four young chimpanzees. *Science*, **180**, 978–80.

Fouts, R. S. (1983a) Chimpanzee language and elephant tails: a theoretical synthesis. In J. de Luce and H. T. Wilder (eds), *Language in Primates*. New York: Springer-Verlag, pp. 63–75.

Fouts, R. S. (1983b) Signs of the apes, songs of the whales. WGBH Boston: NOVA Videotape.

Fouts, R. S., Fouts, D. H. and van Cantfort, T. E. (1989) The infant Loulis learns signs from cross-fostered chimpanzees. In R. A. Gardner, B. T. Gardner and T. E. van Cantfort (eds), *Teaching Sign Language to Chimpanzees*. Albany, NY: State University of New York Press, pp. 293–307.

Fouts, R. S. and Mills, S. T. (1997) *Next of Kin: My Conversations with Chimpanzees*. New York: William Morrow & Company.

Fowler, A. E., Gelman, R. and Gleitman, L. R. (1994) The course of language learning in children with Down Syndrome. In H. Trager-Flusberg (ed.), *Constraints in Language Acquisition*. Hillsdale, NJ: Lawrence Erlbaum Associates, pp. 91–140.

Fowler, W. (1962) Teaching a two-year-old to read. *Genetic Psychology Monographs*, **66**, 181–283.

References

Frackowiak, R. S. J. (2000) Imaging neuroscience: system-level studies of physiology and anatomy of human cognition. In A. Maratz, Y. Miyashita and W. O'Neil (eds), *Image, Language, Brain*. Cambridge, MA: MIT Press, pp. 165–81.

Frank, P. (1953) *Einstein, his Life and Times*. New York: Knopf. Quotation appears in S. I. Hayakawa (ed.) (1954), *Language, Meaning and Maturity*. New York: Harper & Row.

Freeman, H. D., Cantalupo, C. and Hopkins, W. D. (2004) Asymmetries in the hippocampus and amygdala of chimpanzees (Pan troglodytes). *Behavioral Neuroscience*, **118**, 6, 1460–5.

Fries, C. C. (1952) *The Structure of English*. New York: Harcourt, Brace & World.

Fromkin, V., Krashen, S., Curtiss, S., Rigler, D. and Rigler, M. (1974) The development of language in Genie: a case of language beyond the critical period. *Brain and Language*, **1**, 87–107.

Furness, W. H. (1916) Observations on the mentality of chimpanzees and orangutans. *Proceedings of the American Philosophical Society*, Philadelphia, **55**, 281–90.

Furrow, D., Nelson, K. and Benedict, H. (1979) Mothers' speech to children and syntactic development: some simple relationships. *Journal of Child Language*, **6**, 423–42.

Furth, H. (1966) *Thinking Without Language*. New York: Free Press.

Furth, H. (1971) Linguistic deficiency and thinking: research with deaf subjects, 1964–1969. *Psychological Bulletin*, **76**, 58–72.

Gallaudet Research Institute (1985) *Gallaudet Research Institute Newsletter*. Washington, DC: Gallaudet College.

Galloway, L. M. and Scarcella, R. (1982) Cerebral organization in adult second language acquisition: is the right hemisphere more involved? *Brain and Language*, **16**, 56–60.

Gannon, P. J., Holloway, R. L., Broadfield, D. C. and Braun, A. R. (1998) Asymmetry of chimpanzee planum temporale: humanlike pattern of Wernicke's brain language area homolog. *Science*, **279**, 220–2.

Gardner, B. T. and Gardner, R. A. (1975) Evidence for sentence constituents in the early utterances of child and chimpanzee. *Journal of Experimental Psychology: General*, **104**, 244–67.

Gardner, R. A. (1985) *Social Psychology and Second Language Learning: The Role of Attitudes and Motivation*. London: Edward Arnold.

Gardner, R. A. and Gardner, B. T. (1969) Teaching sign language to a chimpanzee. *Science*, **165**, 664–72.

Garnica, O. K. (1977a) Some prosodic characteristics of speech to young children. *Working Papers in Linguistics*, No. 22. Ohio: Ohio State University.

Garnica, O. K. (1977b) Some prosodic and paralinguistic features of speech to young children. In C. E. Snow and C. A. Ferguson (eds), *Talking to Children: Language Input and Acquisition*. New York: Cambridge University Press, pp. 63–8.

Gates, A. I. (1928) *New Methods in Primary Reading*. New York: Teachers College, Columbia University.

Gates, A. I. and Bond, G. (1936) Reading readiness: a study of factors determining success or failure in beginning reading. *Teachers College Record*, **37**, 679–85.

Gates, A. I. and MacGinitie, W. (1968) *Readiness Skills (Teacher's Manual)*. New York: Macmillan.

Genesee, F. (1987) *Learning Through Two Languages: Studies of Immersion and Bilingual Education*. Cambridge, MA: Newbury House.

Genesee, F., Hamers, J., Lambert, W. E., Mononen, L., Seitz, M. and Stark, R. (1978) Language processing in bilinguals. *Brain and Language*, **5**, 1–12.

Genie: Secrets of a Wild Child. NOVA Videotape, USA, October 18, 1994.

Geschwind, N. and Levitsky, W. (1968) Human brain: left-right asymmetries in temporal speech region. *Science*, **161**, 186–7.

Gibson, E. J. and Levin, H. (1975) *The Psychology of Reading.* Cambridge, MA: MIT Press.

Gipper, H. (1979) Is there a linguistic relativity principle? On the verification of the Sapir-Whorf hypothesis. *Indiana*, **5**, 1–14.

Glass, P., Bulas, D. I., Wagner, A. E., Rajasinham, S. R., Civitello, L. A. and Coffman, C. E. (1998) Pattern of neuropsychological deficit at age five years following neonatal unilateral brain injury. *Brain and Language*, **63**, 346–56.

Gleitman, L. R., Newport, E. L. and Gleitman, H. (1984) The current status of the motherese hypothesis. *Journal of Child Language*, **11**, 43–79.

Goddard, H. H. (1917) Mental tests and the immigrant. *Journal of Delinquency*, **2**, 243–77.

Goldin-Meadow, S. and Mylander, C. (1998) Spontaneous sign systems created by deaf children in two cultures. *Nature*, **391**, 279–81.

Golinkoff, R. M. and Hirsch-Pasek, K. (1995) Reinterpreting children's sentence comprehension: toward a new framework. In P. Fletcher and B. MacWhinney (eds), *The Handbook of Child Language*. Cambridge, MA: Blackwell, pp. 430–61.

Gomez-Tortosa, E., Martin, E. M., Gaviria, M., Charbel, F. and Ausman, J. I. (1995) Selective deficit in one language in a bilingual patient following surgery in the left perisylvian area. *Brain and Language*, **48**, 320–5.

Goodglass, H. (1993) *Understanding Aphasia.* San Diego: Academic Press.

Goodman, N. (1973) *Fact, Fiction and Forecast*, 2nd edn. Indianapolis: Bobbs-Merrill.

Gordon, P. (2004) Numerical cognition without words: evidence from Amazonia. *Science*, **305**, 496–503.

Gordon, P. (2005) Response [to Gordon]. *Science*, **307**, 1722.

Gordon, D. P. and Zatorre, R. J. (1981) A right-ear advantage for dichotic listening in bilingual children. *Brain and Language*, **13**, 389–96.

Gosch, A., Stading, G. and Pankau, R. (1994) Linguistic abilities in children with Williams-Beuren syndrome. *American Journal of Medical Genetics*, **52**, 291–6.

Goswami, U. (2002) Early phonological development and the acquisition of literacy. In S. B. Newman and D. K. Dickinson (eds), *Handbook of Early Literacy Research*. New York, London: The Guilford Press, pp. 111–25.

Goswami, U. and Bryant, P. (1990) *Phonological Skills and Learning to Read.* Hillsdale, NJ: Lawrence Erlbaum Associates.

Gough, P. B. and Juel, C. (1991) The first stages of word recognition. In L. Rieben and C. A. Perfetti (eds), *Learning to Read: Basic Research and its Implications*. Hillsdale, NJ: Lawrence Erlbaum Associates, pp. 47–56.

Gouin, F. (1880) *L'art d'enseigner et d'étudier les langues.* Paris: Libraire Fischbacher. English version (1892): *The Art of Teaching and Studying Languages.* London: Philip.

Gray, W. (1948) *On their Own in Reading.* Chicago: Scott Foresman.

Greenfield, P. M. and Savage-Rumbaugh, E. S. (1990) Grammatical combination in Pan paniscus: processes of learning and invention in the evolution and development of language. In S. T. Parker and K. R. Gibson (eds), *Language and Intelligence in Monkeys and Apes*. Cambridge: Cambridge University Press, pp. 540–78.

References

Greenfield, P. M. and Smith, J. H. (1976) *The Structure of Communication in Early Language Development*. New York: Academic Press.

Gregg, K. (1984) Krashen's Monitor and Occam's Razor. *Applied Linguistics*, **5**, 79–100.

Grégoire, A. (1937) *L'apprentissage du Langage: les deux Premières Années*. Libraire E. Droz: Paris.

Griffin, D. R. (1992) *Animal Minds*. Chicago: University of Chicago Press.

Grossen, B. (1997) *A Synthesis of Research on Reading from the National Institute of Child Health and Human Development*. [Online]. http://www.nrrf.orgsynthesis_research.htm.

Gur'ianova, N. V. (1998) *Sovremennaia Lingvisticheskaia Kontseptsiia N. Khomskogo* (Modern linguistic theory of N. Chomsky). Ph.D. dissertation, Ul'ianovsk, Russia.

Hagoort, P., Brown, C. and van Groothusen, J. (1993) The syntactic positive shift (SPS) as an ERP measure of syntactic processing. *Language and Cognitive Processes*, **8**, 439–83.

Hailman, J. P., Ficken, M. S. and Ficken, R. W. (1985) The 'chick-a-dee' call of Parus atricapillus: a recombinant system of animal communication compared with written English. *Semiotica*, **56**, 191–224.

Half Brain Girl 'Fluent in Two Languages'. (2002) [Online]. BBC News. http://news.bbc.co.uk/1/hi/health/2004175.stm.

Halper, A. S. and Cherney, L. R. (2004) Right hemisphere stroke: group and individual performance trends on word list recall and recognition. *Brain and Language*, **91**, 166–7.

Halpern, D. F. and Coren, S. (1991) Handedness and life span. *New England Journal of Medicine*, **324**, 998.

Hammond, R. (1988) Accuracy versus communicative competency: the acquisition of grammar in the second language classroom. *Hispania*, **71**, 408–17.

Harley, B. and Doug, H. (1997) Language aptitude and second language proficiency in classroom learners of different starting ages. *Studies in Second Language Acquisition*, **19**, 3, 379–400.

Harris, J. (1998) *Design Tools for Internet-Supported Classroom*. Alexandria, VA: Association for Supervision and Curriculum Development.

Hauser, M. D. (1996) *The Evolution of Communication*. Cambridge, MA: MIT Press.

Hauser, M., Chomsky, N. and Fitch, W. T. (2002) The faculty of language: what is it, who has it, and how did it evolve? *Science*, **298**, 1569–79.

Hauser, M. D., Newport, E. L. and Aslin, R. N. (2001) Segmentation of the speech stream in a non-human primate: Statistical learning in cotton-top tamarins. *Cognition*, **78**, 3, B53–B64.

Hayes, C. (1951) *The Ape in our House*. New York: Random House.

Heider, E. R. (1972) Universals in color naming and memory. *Journal of Experimental Psychology*, **93**, 10–20.

Henley, N. M. and Kramarae, C. (1991) Gender, power, and miscommunication. In N. Coupland, H. Giles and H. Wiemann (eds), *'Miscommunication' and Problematic Talk*. Newbury Park: Sage, pp. 18–43.

Herman, L. M. and Forestell, P. H. (1985) Reporting presence or absence of named objects by a language-trained dolphin. *Neuroscience and Behavioral Reviews*, **9**, 667–81.

Herman, L. M., Kuczaj II, S. A. and Holder, M. D. (1993) Responses to anomalous gestural sequences by a language-trained dolphin: evidence for processing of semantic relations and syntactic information. *Journal of Experimental Psychology: General*, **122**, 2, 184–94.

Herman, L. M., Richards, D. G. and Wolz, J. P. (1984) Comprehension of sentences by bottlenosed dolphins. *Cognition*, **16**, 129–219.

Herman, L. M. and Wolz, J. P. (1984) Vocal mimicry of computer-generated sounds and vocal labeling of objects by a bottlenosed dolphin, Tursiops truncatus. *Journal of Comparative Psychology*, **98**, 1, 10–28.

Hillyard, S. A. and Picton, T. W. (1987) Electrophysiology of cognition. In F. Plum (ed.), *Handbook of Physiology, Section 1: Neurophysiology*. New York: American Physiological Society, pp. 519–84.

Hino, N. (1988) Yakudoku: Japan's dominant tradition in foreign language learning. *JALT Journal*, **10**, 45–55.

Hirsch-Pasek, K. and Golinkoff, R. M. (1991) Language comprehension: a new look at some old themes. In N. A. Krasnegor, D. M. Rumbaugh, R. L. Schiefelbusch and M. Studdert-Kennedy (eds), *Biological and Behavioral Determinants of Language Development*. Hillsdale, NJ: Lawrence Erlbaum Associates, pp. 301–20.

Hirsch-Pasek, K. and Golinkoff, R. M. (1993) Skeletal supports for grammatical learning: what the infant brings to the language learning task. In C. K. Rovee-Collier (ed.), *Advances in Infancy Research*, Vol. 10. Norwood, NJ: Ablex, pp. 299–338.

Hladek, E. and Edwards, H. (1984) A comparison of mother-father speech in the naturalistic home environment. *Journal of Psycholinguistic Research*, **13**, 321–32.

Hobson, J. (1959) Lee-Clark reading readiness test. In O. Buros (ed.), *Fifth Mental Easurement Yearbook*. Highland Park, NJ: Gryphen Press.

Holder, M. D., Herman, L. M. and Kuczaj II, S. A. (1993) A bottlenosed dolphin's responses to anomalous sequences expressed within an artificial gestural language. In H. Roitblat, L. M. Herman and P. E. Nachtigall (eds), *Language and Communication: Comparative Perspectives*. Hillsdale, NJ: Lawrence Erlbaum Associates, pp. 444–55.

Holme, R. (2004) *Mind, Metaphor, and Language Teaching*. New York: Pallgrave Macmillan.

Holmes, M. C. (1927) Investigation of Reading Readiness of First Grade Entrants. *Childhood Education*, **3**, 215–21.

Horgan, D. (1978) The development of the full passive. *Journal of Child Language*, **5**, 65–80.

Hough, M. S. (1990) Narrative comprehension in adults with right and left hemisphere brain-damage: theme organization. *Brain and Language*, **38**, 253–77.

Householder, F. (1952) Review of methods in structural linguistics. *International Journal of American Linguistics*, **18**, 260–8.

Houston, D., Santelmann, L. and Jusczyk, P. (2004) English-learning infants' segmentation of trisyllabic words from fluent speech. *Language and Cognitive Processes*, **19**, 1, 97–136.

Hoyte, K. J., Kim, A., Brownell, H. and Wingfield, A. (2004) Effects of right hemisphere brain injury on the use of components of prosody for syntactic comprehension. *Brain and Language*, **91**, 168–9.

Huey, E. B. (1968) *The Psychology and Pedagogy of Reading*. Cambridge, MA: MIT Press. (Original work published in 1908 by Macmillan, New York.)

Hume, D. (1748) *An Inquiry Concerning Human Understanding*. Chicago: Encyclopaedia Britannica (1952).

References

Huttenlocher, J. (1974) The origins of language comprehension. In R. L. Solso (ed.), *Theories in Cognitive Psychology: The Loyola Symposium*. Potomac, MD: Lawrence Erlbaum Associates, pp. 331–68.

Imura, T. (1940) Shitsugoshoo ni okeru shikkoosei shoojoo. (Apraxic symptoms in aphasia II.) *Seishin Shinkeigaku Zasshi* (Psychiatrica et Neurologica Japonica) **44**, 393–426. Cited in M. Paradis, H. Hagiwara and N. Hildebrandt (1985), *Neurolinguistic Aspects of the Japanese Writing System*. New York: Academic Press, pp. 84–5.

Ingram, D. (1974) The relationship between comprehension and production. In R. L. Schiefelbusch and L. L. Lloyd (eds), *Language Perspectives: Acquisition, Retardation, and Intervention*. Baltimore: University Park Press, pp. 313–34.

Ingram, D. (1989) *First Language Acquisition: Method, Description, and Explanation*. Cambridge: Cambridge University Press.

Itard, J.-M.-G. (1932) *The Wild Boy of Aveyron* (G. Humphrey and M. Humphrey, trans.). New York: Century.

Jackendoff, R. (1993) *Patterns in the Mind: Language and Human Nature*. Hemel Hempstead: Harvester Wheatsheaf.

Jakobson, R. (1968) *Child Language, Aphasia, and Phonological Universals*. The Hague: Mouton.

Jeffrey, W. E. and Samuels, S. J. (1967) Effect of method of reading training on initial learning and transfer. *Journal of Verbal Learning and Verbal Behavior*, **6**, 354–8.

Jensema, C. (1975) *The Relationship Between Academic Achievement and the Demographic Characteristics of Hearing-impaired Children and Youth*. Washington, DC: Gallaudet College, Office of Demographic Studies.

Jesperson, O. (1933) *Essentials of English Grammar*. Alabama: University of Alabama Press.

Johnson, J. and Newport, E. (1989) Critical period effects in second language learning: the influence of maturational state on the acquisition of English as a second language. *Cognitive Psychology*, **21**, 60–99.

Jones, P. (1995) Contradictions and unanswered questions in the Genie case: a fresh look at the linguistic evidence. *Language and Communication*, **15**, 3, 261–80.

Jones, N. (2000) Quick thinking. *New Scientist*, **168**, 2260, 18.

Junque, C., Vendrell, P. and Vendrell, J. (1995) Differential impairments and specific phenomena in 50 Catalan-Spanish bilingual aphasic patients. In M. Paradis (ed.), *Aspects of Bilingual Aphasia*. Oxford: Pergamon.

Jusczyk, P. W. and Hohne, E. A. (1997) Infants' memory for spoken words. *Science*, **277**, 1984–6.

Kaminski, J., Call, J. and Fischer, J. (2004) Word learning in a domestic dog: evidence for 'Fast Mapping'. *Science*, **304**, 1682–3.

Kaplan, J. A., Brownell, H. H., Jacobs, J. R. and Gardner, H. (1990) The effects of right hemisphere damage on the pragmatic interpretation of conversational remarks. *Brain and Language*, **38**, 315–33.

Karanth, P. (2003) *Cross-linguistic Study of Acquired Reading Disorders: Implications for Reading Models, Disorders, Acquisition and Teaching*. New York: Kluwer Academic/Plenum Publishers.

Karanth, P. and Rangmani, G. N. (1988) Crossed aphasia in multilinguals. *Brain and Language*, **34**, 169–80.

Kasper, G. and Kellerman, E. (1997) *Communication Strategies*. London: Longman.

Kawai, N. and Matsuzawa, T. (2000) Numerical memory span in a chimpanzee. *Nature*, **403**, 39–40.

Kay, P. and McDaniel, C. K. (1978) The linguistic significance of the meanings of basic color terms. *Language*, **54**, 610–46.

Keller, H. (1903/1996) *The Story of My Life*. New York: Collier Macmillan International. Originally published in 1903 by Doubleday.

Kellogg, W. N. (1968) Communication and language in the home-reared chimpanzee. *Science*, **162**, 423–7.

Kellogg, W. N. and Kellogg, L. A. (1933) *The Ape and the Child: A Study of Environmental Influence upon Early Behaviour*. New York: McGraw-Hill.

Kelly, L. (1969) *Centuries of Language Teaching*. Rowley, MA: Newbury House.

Kemler-Nelson, D. G., Hirsch-Pasek, K., Jusczyk, P. W. and Cassidy, K. W. (1989) How the prosodic cues in motherese might assist language learning. *Journal of Child Language*, **16**, 55–68.

Kent, R. D. and Bauer, H. R. (1985) Vocalizations of one-year-olds. *Journal of Child Language*, **12**, 491–526.

Kess, J. F. (1992) *Psycholinguistics: Psychology, Linguistics, and the Study of Natural Language*. Amsterdam: John Benjamins.

Kidd, M. (1997) Obstacles to the implementation of CALL in the curriculum. In P. Liddel (ed.), *FLEAT III. Foreign Language Education and Technology. Proceedings of the Third Conference*. University of Victoria, B.C.: Language Centre, pp. 187–98.

Kimura, D. (1961) Cerebral dominance and the perception of verbal stimuli. *Canadian Journal of Psychology*, **15**, 166–71.

Kirkham, N. Z., Slemmer, J. A. and Johnson, S. P. (2002) Visual statistical learning in infancy: evidence for a domain general learning mechanism. *Cognition*, **83**, 2, 335–42.

Kite, Y. and Steinberg, D. D. (1979) Rougakkou koutobu 3 gakunen seito no hatsuwa nouryoku no kenkyuu. (The speech ability of Japanese deaf persons and hearing persons, and hearing persons' rating of their intelligence and attractiveness.) *Roo Kyooiku Kagaku* (Japanese Journal of Educational Research of the Deaf), **21**, 4, 181–7.

Klar, A. (1999) *A Gene for Handedness*. United Press International, Cambridge, MA.

Klima, E. S. and Bellugi, U. (1966) Syntactic regularities in the speech of children. In J. Lyons and R. J. Wales (eds), *Psycholinguistic Papers*. Edinburgh: Edinburgh University Press, pp. 183–208.

Klima, E. S. and Bellugi, U. (1979) *The Signs of Language*. Cambridge, MA: Harvard University Press.

Kobashigawa, B. (1969) Repetitions in a mother's speech to her child. In *The Structure of Linguistic Input to Children*. Language Behavior Research Laboratory, Working Paper No. 14, University of California, Berkeley.

Kolers, P. (1970) Three stages of reading. In H. Levin and J. Williams (eds), *Basic Studies on Reading*. New York: Basic Books.

Korzybski, A. (1933) *Science and Sanity: An Introduction to Non-Aristotelian Systems and General Semantics*, 4th edn, 1958. Lakeville, CT: The International Non-Aristotelian Publishing Co.

Krashen, S. D. (1973) Lateralization, language learning, and the critical period: some new evidence. *Language Learning*, **23**, 63–74.

Krashen, S. D. (1982) *Principles and Practice in Second Language Acquisition*. Oxford: Pergamon.

Krashen, S. D. and Pon, P. (1975) An error analysis of an advanced ESL learner: the importance of the Monitor. *Working Papers on Bilingualism*, **7**, 125–9.

References

Krashen, S. D. and Scarcella, R. (1978) On routines and patterns in language acquisition and performance. *Language Learning*, **28**, 283–300.

Krashen, S. D. and Terrell, T. D. (1983) *The Natural Approach: Language Acquisition in the Classroom*. Oxford: Pergamon.

Kuhl, P. K. and Meltzoff, A. N. (1988) Speech as an intermodal object of perception. In A. Yonas (ed.), *Perceptual Development in Infancy. Minnesota Symposia on Child Psychology*, Vol. 20. Hillsdale, NJ: Lawrence Erlbaum Associates, pp. 235–66.

Kuroda, S.-Y. (1973) Where epistemology, style, and grammar meet: a case study from Japanese. In S. Anderson and P. Kiparsky (eds), *Festschrift for Morris Halle*. New York: Holt, pp. 377–91.

Kutas, M. and Hillyard, S. A. (1980) Reading senseless sentences: brain potentials reflect semantic incongruity. *Science*, **207**, 203–5.

Labov, W. (1970) The logic of non-standard English. In J. Alatis (ed.), *Report of the Twentieth Annual Round Table Meeting on Linguistics and Language*. Washington, DC: Georgetown University Press, pp. 30–87.

Lahey, M., Liebergott, J., Chesnick, M., Menyuk, P. and Adams, J. (1992) Variability in children's use of grammatical morphemes. *Applied Psycholinguistics*, **13**, 373–98.

Lakoff, G. (1987) *Women, Fire, and Dangerous Things: What Categories Reveal About the Mind*. Chicago: University of Chicago Press.

Lakoff, G. and Johnson, M. (1980) *Metaphors We Live By*. Chicago: University of Chicago Press.

Lakoff, R. (1975) *Language and Women's Place*. New York: Harper & Row.

Lamm, O. and Epstein, R. (1999) Left-handedness and achievements in foreign language studies. *Brain and Language*, **70**, 504–17.

Lane, H. (1976) *The Wild Boy of Aveyron*. Cambridge, MA: Harvard University Press.

Lane, H. S. and Baker, D. (1974) Reading achievement of the deaf: another look. *Volta Review*, **76**, 489–99.

Langacker, R. W. (1991) Cognitive grammar. In F. G. Droste and J. E. Joseph (eds), *Linguistic Theory and Grammatical Description*. Amsterdam: John Benjamins, pp. 275–306.

Lantz, D. (1963) *Color Naming and Color Recognition: A Study in the Psychology of Language*. Doctoral dissertation, Harvard University.

Lapkin, S., Swain, M. and Shapson, S. (1990) French immersion research agenda for the 90s. *Canadian Modern Language Review*, **46**, 638–74.

Laurillard, D. (1993) *Rethinking University Teaching: A Framework for the Effective Use of Educational Technology*. London: Routledge.

Law, G. (1995) Ideologies of English language education in Japan. *JALT Journal*, **17**, 213–24.

Lecanuet, J.-P., Granier-Deferre, C. and Busnel, M. C. (1989) Differential fetal auditory reactiveness as a function of stimulus characteristics and state. *Seminars in Perinatology*, **13**, 421–9.

Legerstee, M. (1990) Infants use multimodal information to imitate speech sounds. *Infant Behavior and Development*, **13**, 343–54.

Lenhoff, H. M., Wang, P. P., Greenberg, F. and Bellugi, U. (1997) Williams syndrome and the brain. *Scientific American*, December, 42–7.

Lenneberg, E. H. (1962) Understanding language without the ability to speak: a case report. *Journal of Abnormal Social Psychology*, **65**, 419–25.

Lenneberg, E. H. (1967) *Biological Foundations of Language*. New York: Wiley.

Lenneberg, E. H. (1972) Prerequisites for language acquisition by the deaf. In T. I. O'Rourke (ed.), *Psycholinguistics and Total Communication: The State of the Art. American Annals of the Deaf* (Monograph).

Lenneberg, E. H., Rebelsky, F. G. and Nichols, I. A. (1965) The vocalization of infants born to deaf and hearing parents. *Human Development*, **8**, 23–37.

Leopold, W. F. (1947) *Speech Development of a Bilingual Child: A Linguist's Record, Vol. 2: Sound Learning in the First Two Years*. Evanston, IL: Northwestern University Press.

Leopold, W. F. (1953) Patterning in children's language learning. *Language Learning*, **5**, 1–14.

Levorato, M. and Cacciari, C. (1995) The effects of different tasks on the comprehension and production of idioms in children. *Journal of Experimental Psychology*, **60**, 2, 261–81.

Lewis, D. (1980) Mad pain and Martian pain. In N. Block (ed.), *Readings in the Philosophy of Psychology*, Vol. 1. Cambridge, MA: MIT Press, pp. 216–22.

Lieberman, A. M. (1957) Some results of research on speech perception. *Journal of the Acoustic Society of America*, **29**, 117–23.

Lieberman, P. (1967) *Intonation, Perception, and Language*. Cambridge, MA: MIT Press.

Lightbown, P. (1978) Question form and question function in the speech of young French L2 learners. In M. Paradis (ed.), *Aspects of Bilingualism*. Columbia, SC: Hornbeam, pp. 21–43.

Lilly, J. C. (1962) Vocal behavior of the bottlenose dolphin. *Proceedings of the American Philosophical Society*, **106**, 520–9.

Lilly, J. C. (1965) Vocal mimicry in Tursiops: ability to match numbers and durations of human vocal bursts. *Science*, **147**, 300–10.

Limber, J. (1973) The genesis of complex sentences. In T. Moore (ed.), *Cognitive Development and the Acquisition of Language*. New York: Academic Press, pp. 169–85.

Locke, J. (1690) *An Essay Concerning Human Understanding*, Book III, ch. ii, sect. 1 (Great books of the Western World). Chicago: Encyclopaedia Britannica (1952).

Locke, J. L. (1993) *The Child's Path to Spoken Language*. Cambridge, MA: Harvard University Press.

Lou, M. (1988) The history of language use in the education of the deaf in the United States. In M. Strong (ed.), *Language Learning and Deafness*. Cambridge: Cambridge University Press, pp. 75–98.

Lyon, J. (1996) *Becoming Bilingual: Language Acquisition in a Bilingual Community*. Clevedon, UK: Multilingual Matters.

Mack, M. A. (1986) A study of semantic and syntactic processing in monolinguals and fluent early bilinguals. *Journal of Psycholinguistic Research*, **15**, 463–88.

Malotki, E. (1985) *Television Programme: The Mind's Language*. Station WNET New York.

Maloney, J. C. (1987) *The Mundane Matter of the Mental Language*. Cambridge: Cambridge University Press.

Malson, L. (1972) *Wolf Children and the Problem of Human Nature – With the Complete Text of the Wild Boy of Aveyron*. New York: Monthly Review.

Mann, V. A. (1991) Phonological abilities: effective predictors of future reading ability. In L. Rieben and C. A. Perfetti (eds), *Learning to Read: Basic Research and its Implications*. Hillsdale, NJ: Lawrence Erlbaum Associates, pp. 121–33.

Maratsos, M. P., Kuczaj, S. A., Fox, D. and Chalkley, M. A. (1979) Some empirical studies in the acquisition of transformational relations: passives, negatives and the past tense. In W. A. Collins (ed.), *Children's Language and Communication: The*

Minnesota Symposium on Child Psychology, Vol. 12. Hillsdale, NJ: Lawrence Erlbaum Associates, pp. 1–45.

Markus, G. F., Vijayan, S., Bandi Rao, S. and Vishton, P. M. (1999) Rule learning by seven-month-old infants. *Science*, **283**, 77–80.

Martin, L. (1986) Eskimo words for snow: a case study in genesis and decay of an anthropological example. *American Anthropologist*, **88**, 418–23.

Martin, R. and Freedman, M. (2001) Short-term retention of lexical-semantic representations: Implications for speech production. *Memory*, **9**, 261–80.

Martin, R. and He, T. (2004) Semantic short-term memory and its role in sentence processing: A replication. *Brain and Language*, **89**, 76–82.

Mason, M. K. (1942) Learning to speak after six and one-half years of silence. *Journal of Speech and Hearing Disorders*, **7**, 4, 295–304.

Masur, E. G. (1995) Infants' early verbal imitation and their later lexical development. *Merrill Palmer Quarterly*, **41**, 286–396.

Matsui, S. (2000) The relevance of the native language in foreign language acquisition: the critical period hypothesis for foreign language pronunciation. Unpublished doctoral dissertation, University of Texas, Austin.

Mayberry, R. and Fischer, S. D. (1989) Looking through phonological shape to lexical meaning: the bottleneck of non-native sign language processing. *Memory and Cognition*, **17**, 740–54.

Mayberry, R. I. and Lock, E. (2003) Age constraints on first versus second language acquisition: Evidence for linguistic plasticity and epigenesis. *Brain and Language*, **87**, 369–84.

McGuinness, D., McGuinness, C. and Donohue, J. (1995) Phonological training and the alphabet principle: evidence for reciprocal causality. *Reading Research Quarterly*, **30**, 830–52.

McLaughlin, B. (1978) The Monitor model: some methodological considerations. *Language Learning*, **28**, 309–32.

McLaughlin, B. (1987) *Theories of Second-Language Learning*. London: Edward Arnold.

McLaughlin, B. (1992) The rise and fall of British emergentism. In A. Beckermann, H. Flohr and J. Kim (eds), *Emergence or reduction*. Berlin: De Gruyter, pp. 49–73.

McNeill, D. (1970) *The Acquisition of Language: The Study of Developmental Psycholinguistics*. New York: Harper & Row.

McNeill, D. (1987) *Psycholinguistics: A New Approach*. New York: Harper & Row.

McNeill, D. and McNeill, N. B. (1968) What does a child mean when he says 'no'? In E. Zale (ed.), *Language and Language Behavior*. New York: Appleton-Century-Crofts, pp. 51–62.

Meadow, K. (1966) *The Effects of Early Manual Communication and Family Climate on the Deaf Child's Early Development*. Unpublished doctoral dissertation, University of California, Berkeley.

Meadow, K. (1980) *Deafness and Child Development*. London: Arnold.

Miles, H. L. (1983) Apes and language: the search for communicative competence. In J. De Luce and H. T. Wilder (eds), *Language in Primates: Perspectives and Implications*. New York: Springer-Verlag, pp. 43–61.

Miles, H. L. (1990) The cognitive foundations for reference in a signing orangutan. In S. T. Parker and K. R. Gibson (eds), *Language and Intelligence in Monkeys and Apes: Comparative Developmental Perspectives*. Cambridge: Cambridge University Press, pp. 511–39.

Mill, J. (1829) *Analysis of the Phenomena of the Human Mind*. New York: A. M. Kelley (1967).

Mill, J. S. (1843) *A System of Logic, Ratiocinative and Inductive, Being a Corrective View of the Principles of Evidence and the Methods of Scientific Investigation*, 8th edn. London: Longman, Green and Co. (1930).

Mohan, B. (1986) *Language and Content*. Reading, MA: Addison Wesley.

Morgan, C. L. (1923) *Emergent Evolution*. London: William & Northgate.

Morphett, M. C. and Washburne, C. (1931) When should children begin to read? *Elementary School Journal*, **31**, 496–503.

Moskowitz, B. A. (1978) The acquisition of language. *Scientific American*, November, 92–108.

Mowrer, O. H. (1960) *Learning Theory and the Symbolic Processes*. New York: Wiley.

Moya, K. L., Benowitz, L. I., Levine, D. N. and Finklestein, S. (1986) Covariant deficits in visuospatial abilities and recall of verbal narrative after right hemisphere stroke. *Cortex*, **22**, 381–97.

Müller, R.-A. (1996) Innateness, autonomy, universality? Neurological approaches to language. *Behavioral and Brain Sciences*, **19**, 611–75.

Murdoch, B. E., Whelan, B.-M., Theodoros, D. G. and Cahill, L. (2004) A subcortical chain of command involved in the regulation of linguistic processes? *Brain and Language*, **91**, 175–6.

Murray, A. D., Johnson, J. and Peters, J. (1990) Fine-tuning of utterance length to preverbal infants: effects on later language development. *Journal of Child Language*, **17**, 511–25.

Nagata, H. (1988) The relativity of linguistic intuition: the effect of repetition on grammaticality judgments. *Journal of Psycholinguistic Research*, **17**, 1–17.

Nagata, H. (1989a) Judgments of sentence grammaticality with differentiation and enrichment strategies. *Perceptual and Motor Skills*, **68**, 463–9.

Nagata, H. (1989b) Judgments of sentence grammaticality and field-dependence of subjects. *Perceptual and Motor Skills*, **69**, 739–47.

Nagata, H. (1992) Anchoring effects in judging grammaticality of sentences. *Perceptual and Motor Skills*, **75**, 159–64.

Nagata, H. (1995a) On-line and off-line reflexive resolution in Japanese logophoric sentences. *Journal of Psycholinguistic Research*, **24**, 205–29.

Nagata, H. (1995b) Off-line reflexive resolution in parsing Japanese logophoric sentences: An extension. *Perceptual and Motor Skills*, **81**, 128–30.

Nagata, H. (1997a) Anchoring effects in judging grammaticality of sentences violating the subjacency condition. *Psychologia*, **40**, 163–71.

Nagata, H. (1997b) An assimilation effect in judging the grammaticality of sentences violating the subjacency condition. *Perceptual and Motor Skills*, **84**, 755–67.

Nagata, H. (2001) Judgments of grammaticality of Japanese bitransitive sentences with a differing number of arguments. *Perceptual and Motor Skills*, **92**, 997–1005.

Nagata, H. (2003a) Judgments of grammaticality of Japanese sentences violating the principle of Full Interpretation. *Journal of Psycholinguistic Research*, **32**, 693–709.

Nagata, H. (2003b) Judgments of grammaticality of sentences violating the principle of Full Interpretation: a further exploration. *Perceptual and Motor Skills*, **97**, 477–82.

Nagata, H. (2004) Faulty Japanese sentences are judged more grammatical when punctuation is used: negative implications for Chomsky's principle of Full Interpretation. *Perceptual and Motor Skills*, **99**, 325–36.

Nagata, H. (2005) The role of emphasis and argument order in the judgments of grammaticality of Japanese bitransitive sentences violating Chomsky's principle of Full Interpretation. *Psychologia*, **48**, (in press).

Nagata H. and Bain, B. (2000) Judgments of grammaticality of sentences with differing number of arguments: a comparison of English and Japanese speakers. *Perceptual and Motor Skills*, **91**, 503–11.

Nakazima, S. (1962) A comparative study of the speech developments of Japanese and American English in childhood. *Studies in Phonology*, **2**, 27–39.

Nation, I. S. P. (1990) *Teaching and Learning Vocabulary*. Boston: Heinle & Heinle.

National Reading Panel (2000) *Report of the National Reading Panel: Teaching Children to Read*. Washington, DC: National Institute of Child Health and Human Development. [Online]. http://www.nichd.nih.gov/publications/nrp/smallbook.htm.

Neufeld, G. (1978) On the acquisition of prosodic and articulatory features in adult language learning. *Canadian Modern Language Review*, **34**, 163–74.

Newport, E. L. (1975) *Motherese: The Speech of Mothers to Young Children. Technical Report No. 52*. Center for Human Information Processing, University of California, San Diego.

Newport, E. L. (1976) Motherese: the speech of mothers to young children. In N. J. Castellan, D. Pisoni and G. Potts (eds), *Cognitive Theory*. New York: Wiley, pp. 177–210.

Newport, E. L. (1990) Maturational constraints on language learning. *Cognitive Science*, **14**, 11–28.

Newport, E. L., Gleitman, H. and Gleitman, L. (1977) Mother, I'd rather do it myself: some effects and non-effects of maternal speech style. In C. Snow & C. Ferguson (eds), *Talking to Children: Input and Acquisition*. New York: Academic Press, pp. 109–49.

Newport, E. L. and Supalla, T. (1980) Clues from the acquisition of signed and spoken language. In U. Bellugi and M. Studdert-Kennedy (eds), *Signed and Spoken Language: Biological Constraints on Linguistic Form*. Weinheim: Verlag Chemie.

Niyekawa-Howard, A. (1972) The current status of the linguistic relativity hypothesis. *Working Papers in Linguistics*, University of Hawaii, **42**, 1–30.

Nolan, C. (1981) *Dam-burst of Dreams*. Athens, OH: Ohio University Press.

Nolan, C. (1988) *Under the Eye of the Clock*. London: Pan Books.

Nunan, D. (1989) *Designing Tasks for the Communicative Classroom*. New York: Cambridge University Press.

Nwokah, E. E. (1987) Maidese vs. Motherese: is the language input of child and adult caregivers similar? *Language and Speech*, **30**, 213–37.

Oller, D. K. and Eilers, R. E. (1982) Similarity of babbling in Spanish- and English-learning babies. *Journal of Child Language*, **9**, 565–77.

Oller, J., Baca, L. and Vigil, F. (1978) Attitudes and attained proficiency in ESL: a sociolinguistic study of Mexican-Americans in the Southwest. *TESOL Quarterly*, **11**, 173–83.

Oller, J., Hudson, A. and Liu, P. (1977) Attitudes and attained proficiency in ESL: a sociolinguistic study of native speakers of Chinese in the United States. *Language Learning*, **27**, 1–27.

Olsen, S. (1980) Foreign language departments and Computer-Assisted Instruction: a survey. *Modern Language Journal*, **64**, 82–96.

O'Malley, J. M. and Chamot, A. U. (1990) *Learning Strategies in Second Language Acquisition*. Cambridge: Cambridge University Press.

Osgood, C. E. (1953) *Method and Theory in Experimental Psychology*. New York: Oxford University Press.

Osgood, C. E. (1971) Where do sentences come from? In D. D. Steinberg and L. A. Jakobovits (eds), *Semantics: An Interdisciplinary Reader in Philosophy, Linguistics, and Psychology*. New York: Cambridge University Press, pp. 497–529.

Osgood, C. E. (1980) *Lectures on Language Performance*. New York: Springer-Verlag.

Osgood, C. E., Suci, G. J. and Tannenbaum, P. H. (1957) *The Measurement of Meaning*. Urbana, IL: University of Illinois Press.

Oxford, R. (1990) *Language Learning Strategies: What Every Teacher Should Know*. New York: Newbury House.

Oxford, R. (1996) *Language Learning Strategies Around the World: Cross-Cultural Perspectives* (Technical Report No. 13). Honolulu: Second Language Teaching and Curriculum Center, University of Hawaii at Manoa.

Oyama, S. (1976) A sensitive period in the acquisition of a non-native phonological system. *Journal of Psycholinguistic Research*, **5**, 261–85.

Palmer, H. (1922) *The Principles of Language-study*. London: George G. Harrup. Reprinted (1964), London: Oxford University Press.

Palmer, H. and Palmer, D. (1925) *English Through Actions*. Reprinted (1959), London: Longman, Green and Co.

Paradis, M. (1977) Bilingualism and aphasia. In H. Whitaker and H. A. Whitaker (eds), *Studies in Neurolinguistics*, Vol. 3. New York: Academic Press, pp. 65–121.

Paradis, M. and Goldblum, M.-C. (1989) Selective crossed aphasia in a trilingual aphasic patient followed by reciprocal antagonism. *Brain and Language*, **36**, 62–75.

Paradis, M. (2003) Differential use of cerebral mechanisms in bilinguals. In M. T. Banich and M. Mack (eds), *Mind, Brain, and Language*. Mahwah, NJ: Laurence Erlbaum Associates, pp. 352–71.

Paradis, M. (2004) *A Neurolinguistic Theory of Bilingualism*. Amsterdam: John Benjamins.

Patel, A. D., Gibson, E., Ratner, J., Besson, M. and Holcomb, P. J. (1998) Processing syntactic relations in language and music: an event-related potential study. *Journal of Cognitive Neuroscience*, **10**, 717–33.

Patkowski, M. (1980) The sensitive period for the acquisition of syntax in a second language. *Language Learning*, **30**, 440–72.

Patterson, F. G. (1978a) Conversations with a gorilla. *National Geographic*, **154**, 4, 438–65.

Patterson, F. G. (1978b) The gestures of a gorilla: language acquisition in another pongid. *Brain and Language*, **5**, 72–97.

Patterson, F. G. and Linden, E. (1981) *The Education of Koko*. New York: Holt, Rinehart & Winston.

Paul, R. and Alforde, S. (1993) Grammatical morpheme acquisition in 4-year-olds with normal, impaired, and late-developing language. *Journal of Speech and Hearing Research*, **36**, 1271–5.

Peal, E. and Lambert, W. (1962) The relationship of bilingualism to intelligence. *Psychological Monographs*, **76**, 27, 1–23.

Pepperberg, I. M. (1987) Acquisition of the same/different concept by an African grey parrot (Psittacus erithacus): learning with respect to color, shape, and material. *Animal Learning & Behavior*, **15**, 423–32.

Pepperberg, I. M. (1993) Cognition and communication in an African grey parrot (Psittacus erithacus): studies on a nonhuman, nonprimate, nonmammalian subject. In H. Roitblat, L. M. Herman and P. E. Nachtigall (eds), *Language and*

Communication: Comparative Perspectives. Hillsdale, NJ: Lawrence Erlbaum Associates, pp. 21–48.

Pepperberg, I. M. and Kozak, F. A. (1986) Object permanence in the African grey parrot (Psittacus erithacus). *Animal Learning & Behavior*, **14**, 322–30.

Perani, D., Abutalebi, J., Paulesu, E., Brambati, S., Scifo, P., Cappa, S. F. and Fazio, F. (2003) The role of age acquisition and language usage in early, high-proficient bilinguals: an fMRI study during verbal fluency. *Human Brain Mapping*, **19**, 170–82.

Perfetti, C. A. (1991) Representation problem in reading acquisition. In L. Rieben and C. A. Perfetti (eds), *Learning to Read: Basic Research and its Implications*. Hillsdale, NJ: Lawrence Erlbaum Associates, pp. 33–44.

Perfetti, C. A. and Rieben, L. (1991) Introduction. In L. Rieben and C. A. Perfetti (eds), *Learning to Read: Basic Research and its Implications*. Hillsdale, NJ: Lawrence Erlbaum Associates, pp. vii–xi.

Pestalozzi, J. H. (1801/1898) *Wie Gertrude ihre Kinder lehrnt (How Gertrude Teaches her Children)*. London: George Allen & Unwin.

Petitto, L. A. and Marentette, P. F. (1991) Babbling in the manual mode: evidence for the ontogeny of language. *Science*, **251**, 1493–6.

Philips, S. U., Steele, S. and Tanz, C. (eds) (1987) *Language, Gender and Sex in Comparative Perspective*. Cambridge: Cambridge University Press.

Phillips, J. R. (1973) Syntax and vocabulary or mothers' speech to young children: age and sex comparisons. *Child Development*, **44**, 182–5.

Piaget, J. (1955) *The Language and Thought of the Child*. Cleveland, OH: World.

Piaget, J. (1968) Quantification, conservation, and nativism. *Science*, **162**, 976–9.

Piaget, J. and Inhelder, B. (1969) *The Psychology of the Child*. New York: Basic Books.

Piattelli-Palmarini (ed.) (1980) *Language and Learning: The Debate Between Jean Piaget and Noam Chomsky*. Cambridge, MA: Harvard University Press.

Pica, P., Lemer, C., Izard, V., Dehaene, S. (2004) Exact and approximate arithmetic in an Amazonian idigene group. *Science*, **306**, 499–503.

Pica, T. (1994) Research on negotiation: what does it reveal about second language learning, conditions, processes, outcomes? *Language Learning*, **44**, 493–527.

Picard, A. (2004) Bilingual older adults found to stay sharper longer. *Globe and Mail*, June 14, A2.

Pike, K. L. (1954) *Language in Relation to a Unified Theory of the Structure of Human Behavior*. Glendale, CA: Summer Institute of Linguistics.

Pine, J. M. (1994) The language of primary caregivers. In C. Gallaway and B. J. Richards (eds), *Input and Interaction in Language Acquisition*. Cambridge: Cambridge University Press, pp. 15–37.

Pinker, S. (1984) *Language Learnability and Language Development*. Cambridge, MA: Harvard University Press.

Pinker, S. (1994) *The Language Instinct*. New York: William Morrow.

Pinker, S. (2002) *The Blank Slate: The Modern Denial of Human Nature*. New York: Viking.

Pinker, S. and Bloom, P. (1990) Natural language and natural selection. *Behavioral and Brain Sciences*, **13**, 707–84.

Pinker, S. and Jackendoff, R. (2005) The faculty of language: What's Special about it? *Cognition*, **95**, 210–36.

Poizner, H., Klima, E. S. and Bellugi, U. (1989) *What the Hands Reveal About the Brain*. Cambridge, MA: MIT Press.

Politzer, R. and Weiss, L. (1969) Developmental aspects of auditory discrimination, echo response and recall. *Modern Language Journal*, **53**, 75–85.

Posner, M. I. (2001) Cognitive neuroscience: the synthesis of mind and brain. In E. Dupoux (ed.), *Language, Brain and Cognitive Development*. Cambridge, MA: MIT Press, pp. 403–16.

Premack, D. (1970) A functional analysis of language. *Journal of Experimental Analysis of Behavior*, **14**, 107–25.

Premack, D. (1971) Language in the chimpanzee? *Science*, **172**, 808–22.

Premack, D. (1976) *Intelligence in Ape and Man*. Hillsdale, NJ: Lawrence Erlbaum Associates.

Premack, D. and Premack, A. (2005) Evolution versus invention. *Science*, **307**, 673.

Preston, D. (1989) *Sociolinguistics and Second Language Acquisition*. Oxford: Blackwell.

Pual, R. and Alforde, S. (1993) Grammatical morpheme acquisition in 4-year-olds with normal, impaired, and late-developing language. *Journal of Speech and Hearing Research*, **36**, 1271–5.

Putnam, H. (1967) The 'innateness hypothesis' and explanatory models in linguistics. *Synthese*, **17**, 12–22.

Putnam, H. (1980) What is innate and why: comments on the debate. In M. Piattelli-Palmarini (ed.), *Language and Learning: The Debate Between Jean Piaget and Noam Chomsky*. Cambridge, MA: Harvard University Press, pp. 287–309.

Pye, C. (1983) *Mayan Motherese: An Ethnography of Quiche Mayan Speech to Young Children*. Unpublished manuscript.

Quigley, S. and Paul, P. (1986) A perspective on academic achievement. In D. Luterman (ed.), *Deafness in Perspective*. San Diego: College-Hill Press, pp. 55–86.

Quine, W. V. O. (1960) *Word and Object*. Cambridge, MA: MIT Press.

Reich, P. A. (1986) *Language Development*. Englewood Cliffs, NJ: Prentice Hall.

Richards, J. and Rodgers, T. (2001) *Approaches and Methods in Language Teaching*. Cambridge: Cambridge University Press.

Rieben, L. and Perfetti, C. A. (eds) (1991) *Learning to Read: Basic Research and its Implications*. Hillsdale, NJ: Lawrence Erlbaum Associates.

Ringbom, H. (1978) The influence of the mother tongue on the translation of lexical items. *Interlanguage Studies Bulletin*, **3**, 80–101.

Robertson, D. (1999) Proof that we see colors with our tongue. *New York Times* article appearing in the *Asahi Evening News*, 3–4 April.

Robinson, P. (1996) Learning simple and complex second language rules under implicit, incidental, rule-search, and instructed conditions. *Studies in Second Language Acquisition*, **18**, 27–67.

Rosen, H. J., Petersen, S. E., Linenweber, M. R, Snyder, A. Z., White, D. A., Chapman, L., Dromerick, A. W., Fiez, J. A. and Corbetta, M. (2000) Neural correlates of recovery from aphasia after damage to left inferior frontal cortex. *Neurology*, **55**, 1883–94.

Rosenbaum, P. (1967) *The Grammar of English Predicate Constructions*. Cambridge, MA: MIT Press.

Rousseau, J. J. (1780/1964) *Émile ou de l'éducation*. Paris: Garnier Frères.

Rubin, J. (1981) The study of cognitive processes in second language learning. *Applied Linguistics*, **2**, 117–31.

Rumbaugh, D. (1977) *Language Learning by a Chimpanzee: The LANA Project*. New York: Academic Press.

References

Ryle, G. (1949) *The Concept of Mind*. London: Hutchinson.

Rymer, R. (1993) *Genie: A Scientific Tragedy*. New York: Harper Collins.

Sachs, J., Brown, R. and Salerno, R. A. (1976) Adults' speech to children. In W. von Raffler-Engel and Y. Lebrun (eds), *Baby Talk and Infant Speech*. Amsterdam: Swets & Zeitlinger, pp. 240–5.

Sachs, J. S. and Truswell, L. (1976) Comprehension of two-word instructions by children in the one-word stage. *Papers and Reports on Child Language Development* (Department of Linguistics, Stanford University), **12**, 212–20.

Sachs, J. S. and Truswell, L. (1978) Comprehension of two-word instructions by children in the one-word stage. *Journal of Child Language*, **5**, 17–24.

Saer, D. J. (1922) An inquiry into the effect of bilingualism upon the intelligence of young children. *Journal of Experimental Pedagogy*, **6**, 232–40 and 266–74.

Saer, D. J. (1923) The effects of bilingualism on intelligence. *British Journal of Psychology*, **14**, 25–38.

Salive, M. E., Guralnik, J. M. and Glynn, R. J. (1993) Left-handedness and mortality. *American Journal of Public Health*, **83**, 265–7.

Sapir, E. (1921) *Language: An Introduction to the Study of Speech*. New York: Harcourt, Brace & World.

Sapir, E. (1929) The status of linguistics as a science. *Language*, **5**, 207–14.

Sasanuma, S. (1994) Neuropsychology of reading: universal and language-specific features of reading impairment. In P. Bertelson, P. Eelen and G. d'Ydewalle (eds), *International Perspectives on Psychological Science, Vol. 1: Leading Themes*. Hove, UK: Lawrence Erlbaum Associates, pp. 105–25.

Sauveur, L. (1878) *The Natural Method: Introduction to the Teaching of Ancient Languages*. New York: Holt.

Savage-Rumbaugh, E. S., McDonald, K., Sevcik, R. A., Hopkins, W. D. and Rubert, E. (1986) Spontaneous symbol acquisition and communicative use by pygmy chimpanzees (Pan paniscus). *Journal of Experimental Psychology: General*, **115**, 211–35.

Savage-Rumbaugh, E. S. and Rumbaugh, D. M. (1978) Symbolization, language, and chimpanzees: a theoretical reevaluation based on initial language acquisition processes in four young Pan troglodytes. *Brain and Language*, **6**, 265–300.

Savage-Rumbaugh, E. S., Shanker, S. and Taylor, T. (1998) *Apes, Language and the Human Mind*. Oxford: Oxford University Press.

Scarborough, H. (2002) Connecting early language and literacy to later reading (dis)abilities: evidence, theory and practice. In S. B. Newman and D. K. Dickinson (eds), *Handbook of Early Literacy Research*. The Guilford Press: New York, London, pp. 97–110.

Scarcella, R. and Higa, C. (1981) Input, negotiation and age differences in second language acquisition. *Language Learning*, **31**, 409–37.

Schaler, S. (1991) *A Man Without Words*. New York: Simon & Schuster.

Schlesinger, I. M. (1982) *Steps to Language: Toward a Theory of Language Acquisition*. Hillsdale, NJ: Lawrence Erlbaum Associates.

Schmidt, R. (1995) Consciousness and foreign language learning: a tutorial on the role of attention and awareness in learning. In R. Schmidt (ed.), *Attention and Awareness in Foreign Language Learning*. Honolulu: University of Hawaii Press, pp. 1–63.

Schulwitz, B. S. (1977) The teacher: fostering interest and achievement. In L. Ollila (ed.), *The Kindergarten Child and Reading*. Newark, DE: International Reading Association, pp. 40–55.

Scollon, R. (1976) *Conversations with a One Year Old: A Case Study of the Development Foundation of Syntax.* Honolulu: University of Hawaii Press.

Scouten, E. (1963) The place of the Rochester Method in American education of the deaf. *Report of the Proceedings of the International Congress on Education of the Deaf,* pp. 429–33.

Scouten, E. (1967) The Rochester Method, an oral-multisensory approach for instructing pre-lingually deaf children. *American Annals of the Deaf,* **112**, 50–5.

Scovel, T. (1978) The effect of affect on foreign language learning: a review of the anxiety research. *Language Learning,* **28**, 129–42.

Scovel, T. (1988) *A Time to Speak: A Psycholinguistic Inquiry into the Critical Period for Human Speech.* Rowley, MA: Newbury House.

Searle, J. R. (1997) *The Mystery of Consciousness.* New York: The New York Review of Books.

Sebastián-Gallés, N. and Bosch, L. (2001) On becoming and being bilingual. In E. Dupoux (ed.), *Language, Brain, and Cognitive Development.* Cambridge, MA: The MIT Press, pp. 379–93.

Seitz, S. and Stewart, C. (1975) Imitations and expansions: some developmental aspects of mother-child communications. *Developmental Psychology,* **11**, 763–8.

Seyfarth, R. M., Cheney, D. L. and Marler, P. (1980) Monkey responses to three different alarm calls: evidence of predator classification and semantic communication. *Science,* **210**, 801–3.

Shankweiler, D., Palumbo, L. C., Ni, W., Mencl, W. E., Fulbright, R., Pugh, K. R., Constable, R. T., Harris, K. S., Kollia, B. and Van Dyke, J. (2004) Unexpected recovery of language function after massive left-hemisphere infarct: Coordinated psycholinguistic and neuroimaging studies. *Brain and Language,* **91**, 181–2.

Shattuck, R. (1981) *The Forbidden Experiment: The Story of the Wild Boy of Aveyron.* New York: Washington Square Press.

Shatz, M. and Gelman, R. (1973) The development of communication skills: modifications in the speech of young children as a function of the listener. *Monographs of the Society on Research in Child Development,* **5**, Serial No. 152, 1–37.

Shaywitz, S. E. (1996) Dyslexia. *Scientific American,* November, 78–84.

Shoemaker, S. (1975) Functionalism and qualia. *Philosophical Studies,* **27**, 291–315.

Silberman, H. F. (1964) *Exploratory Research on a Beginning Reading Program.* Santa Monica, CA: System Development Corp.

Singh, J. A. L. and Zingg, R. M. (1942) *Wolf Children and Feral Man.* New York: Harper.

Siple, P. and Fischer, S. D. (eds) (1990) *Theoretical Issues in Sign Language Research.* Chicago: University of Chicago Press.

Sjoholm, K. (1979). Do Finns and Swedish-speaking Finns use different strategies in the learning of English as a foreign language? In R. Palmberg (ed.), *Perception and Production of English: Papers on Interlanguage.* AFTIL Vol. 6 (Dept. of English, Abō Akademi, Finland), pp. 89–119.

Skailand, D. B. (1971) *A Comparison of Four Language Units in Teaching Beginning Reading.* Berkeley, CA: Far West Laboratory for Educational Research and Development.

Skehan, P. (1989) *Individual Differences in Second-language Learning.* London: Edward Arnold.

Skehan, P. (1998) *A Cognitive Approach to Language Learning.* Oxford: Oxford University Press.

Skinner, B. F. (1957) *Verbal Behavior.* New York: Appleton-Century-Crofts.

References

Skinner, B. F. (1964) Behaviorism at fifty. In T. W. Wann (ed.), *Behaviorism and Phenomenology*. Chicago: University of Chicago Press, pp. 79–97.

Skinner, B. F. (1971) *Humanistic Behaviorism. The Humanist*, May–June, 35.

Slapkin, S., Swain, M. and Shapson, S. (1990). French immersion research agenda for the 90s. *Canadian Modern Language Review*, **46**, 4, 638–74.

Slobin, D. I. (1975) On the nature of talk in children. In E. H. Lenneberg and E. Lenneberg (eds), *Foundations of Language Development: A Multidisciplinary Approach*, Vol. 1. New York: Wiley, pp. 283–98.

Smart, J. J. C. (1959) Sensations and brain processes. *Philosophical Review*, **68**, 141–56.

Smith, A. and Sugar, O. (1975) Development of above normal language and intelligence 21 years after left hemispherectomy. *Neurology*, **25**, 813–18.

Smith, F. (1982) *Understanding Reading*. New York: CBS Publishing.

Smith, M. E. (1933) The influence of age, sex and situation on the frequency, form and function of questions asked by preschool children. *Child Development*, **4**, 201–13.

Smith, M. E. (1939) Some light on the problem of bilingualism as found from a study of the progress in mastery of English among pre-school children of non-American ancestry in Hawaii. *Genetic Psychology Monographs*, **21**, 119–284.

Smith, S. M., Brown, H. O., Toman, J. E. P. and Goodman, L. S. (1947) The lack of cerebral effects of d-tubocurarine. *Anæsthesiology*, **8**, 1–14.

Sniezek, J. A. and Jazwinski, C. H. (1986) Gender bias in English: in search of fair language. *Journal of Applied Social Psychology*, **16**, 642–62.

Snow, C. and Hoefnagel-Hohle, M. (1978) The critical age for language acquisition: evidence from second-language learning. *Child Development*, **49**, 1114–28.

Snow, C. E. (1972) Mothers' speech to children learning language. *Child Development*, **43**, 549–65.

Snow, C. E., Arlmann-Rupp, A., Hassing, Y., Jobse, J., Jooksen, J. and Vorster, J. (1976) Mothers' speech in three social classes. *Journal of Psycholinguistic Research*, **5**, 1–20.

Snowden, C. T. (1993) Linguistic phenomenon in the natural communication of animals. In H. Roitblat, L. M. Herman and P. E. Nachtigall (eds), *Language and Communication: Comparative Perspectives*. Hillsdale, NJ: Lawrence Erlbaum Associates, pp. 175–94.

Soares, C. (1982) Converging evidence for left hemisphere language lateralization in bilinguals. *Neuropsychologia*, **20**, 653–9.

Söderbergh, R. (1971) *Reading in Early Childhood*. Stockholm: Almquist and Wiksell. (Reprinted by Georgetown University Press, Washington, DC, 1977.)

Söderbergh, R. (1976) *Learning to Read Between Two and Five: Some Observations on Normal Hearing and Deaf Children*. Stockholm Universitet, Instituten for Nordiska Spraak (Preprint No. 12).

Solomon, A. (1994) Defiantly deaf. *New York Times Magazine*, 28 August, pp. 38ff.

Specter, M. (1999) The dangerous philosopher. *The New Yorker*, 6 September, 46–55.

Sperry, R. W. (1969) A modified concept of consciousness. *Psychological Review*, **76**, 532–6.

Sperry, R. W. (1982) Some effects of disconnecting the cerebral hemispheres. *Science*, **217**, 1223–6.

Sprache, E. and Sprache, G. (1969) *Reading in the Elementary School*. Boston: Allyn & Bacon.

Staats, A. (1968) *Learning, Language, and Cognition*. New York: Holt, Rinehart & Winston.

Staats, A. (1971) Linguistic-mentalistic theory versus an explanatory S-R learning theory of language development. In D. I. Slobin (ed.), *The Ontogenesis of Grammar*. New York: Academic Press, pp. 103–50.

Stark, R. E. and McGregor, K. K. (1997) Follow-up study of a right- and a left-hemispherectomized child: implications for localization and impairment of language in children. *Brain and Language*, **60**, 222–42.

Steinberg, D. D. (1969) Natural class, complementary distribution, and speech perception. *Journal of Experimental Psychology*, **79**, 195–202.

Steinberg, D. D. (1975) Chomsky: from formalism to mentalism and psychological invalidity. *Glossa*, **9**, 218–252.

Steinberg, D. D. (1976) Competence, performance and the psychological invalidity of Chomsky's grammar. *Synthese*, **32**, 373–86.

Steinberg, D. D. (1980) *Teaching Reading to Nursery School Children: Final Report* (Grant No. G007903113). Washington, DC: Office of Education, US Department of Education.

Steinberg, D. D. (1981) *Kinouhou ni yoru kana no dokuji gakushuu* (Learning to read syllable *kana* symbols by induction). *Dokusho Kagaku* (Science of Reading – Japan), **25**, 59–69.

Steinberg, D. D. (1982) *Psycholinguistics: Language, Mind and World*. London: Longman.

Steinberg, D. D. (1984) Psycholinguistics: the writing system as a native language for the deaf. *Annual Review of Applied Linguistics*, **5**, 4, 36–45.

Steinberg, D. D. (1993) *An Introduction to Psycholinguistics*. London: Longman.

Steinberg, D. D. (1999) The anti-mentalistic skeletons in Chomsky's closet make psychological fiction of his grammars. In S. Embleton, J. E. Joseph and H.-J. Niederehe, *The Emergence of the Modern Language Sciences, Vol. 1: Historiographical Perspectives*. Amsterdam/Philadelphia: John Benjamins, pp. 267–82.

Steinberg, D. D. and Chen, S.-R. (1980) *Aru 3 sai kenchou a ji no yomi no gakushuu* (A 3-year-old child learns to read: the illustration of fundamental reading principles). *Dokusho Kagaku* (Science of Reading – Japan) **24**, 134–41. Also, in English, in *Working Papers in Linguistics* (University of Hawaii), 1980, **12**, 77–91.

Steinberg, D. D., Harada, M., Tashiro, M. and Yamada, A. (1982) *Issai no sentensei chookaku shoogaiji-no mojigengo shuutoku* (A 1-year-old Japanese congenitally deaf child learns written language). *Chookaku Shoogai* (Auditory Disorders – Japan), **376**, 7, 22–46, and **377**, 8, 16–29.

Steinberg, D. D. and Harper, H. (1983) Teaching written language as a first language to a deaf boy. In F. Coulmas and K. Ehlich (eds), *Writing in Focus*. The Hague: Mouton, pp. 327–54.

Steinberg, D. D. and Koono, R. (1981) English words are easier to learn than letters. *Dokusho Kagaku* (Science of Reading – Japan), **25**, 3, 85–95. Also, in English, in *Working Papers in Linguistics* (University of Hawaii), 1979, **9**, 3, 115–17.

Steinberg, D. D., Kushimoto, K., Tatara, N. and Orisaka, R. (1979). Words are easier to learn than letters. *Working Papers in Linguistics*, University of Hawaii, **11**, 121–32.

Steinberg, D. D., Nagata, H. and Aline, D. P. (2001) *Psycholinguistic: Language, Mind and World*, 2nd edn. London: Longman.

Steinberg, D. D. and Sakoda, K. (1982) *Hoikuen 2 saiji no yomi no shidou* (Teaching 2-year-olds to read in a pre-school). *Dokusho Kagaku* (Science of Reading – Japan), **26**, 3, 115–30.

References

Steinberg, D. D. and Steinberg, M. T. (1975) Reading before speaking. *Visible Language*, **9**, 197–224.

Steinberg, D. D. and Tanaka, M. (1989) *Ni sai kara doowa ga yomeru* (Reading from 2 years of age). Tokyo: Goma Shobo.

Steinberg, D. D. and Xi, J. (1989) *Liang sui you er ke yue du* (Two-year-olds can read: teach your child to read). Tianjin: Tianjin Peoples Publishing House.

Steinberg, D. D. and Yamada, J. (1978–9) Are whole word *kanji* easier to learn than syllable kana? *Reading Research Quarterly*, **14**, 1, 88–99.

Steinberg, D. D. and Yamada, J. (1980) Shoji nouryoku hattatsu ni kansuru kisotekikenkyuu (The ability of young children to write). *Kyooiku Shinrigaku Kenkyuu* (Japanese Journal of Educational Psychology), **28**, 4, 46–54.

Steinberg, D. D., Yamada, J., Nakano, Y., Hirakawa, S. and Kanemoto, S. (1977) Meaning and the learning of kanji and kana. *Hiroshima Forum for Psychology*, **4**, 15–24.

Steinberg, D. D., Yoshida, K. and Yagi, R. (1985) *1 saiji oyobi 2 saiji ni taisuru katei deno yomi no shidou* (Teaching reading to 1- and 2-year-olds at home). *Dokusho Kagaku* (Science of Reading – Japan), **29**, 1–17.

Stemmer, B. and Joanette, Y. (1998) The interpretation of narrative discourse of brain-damaged individuals within the framework of a multilevel discourse model. In M. Beeman and C. Chiarello (eds), *Right Hemisphere Language Comprehension: Perspective from Cognitive Neuroscience*. Mahwah, NJ: Lawrence Erlbaum Associates, pp. 329–48.

Stoel-Gammon, C. and Cooper, J. A. (1984) Patterns of early lexical and phonological development. *Journal of Child Language*, **11**, 247–71.

Stokoe, W. C., Casterline D. C. and Croneberg, C. G. (1965) *A Dictionary of American Sign Language on Linguistic Principles*. Washington, DC: Gallaudet College Press.

Stoller, F. (1997) Project work: a means to promote language and content. *English Teaching Forum*, **35**, 4, 2–9.

Strong, M. (1988) A bilingual approach to the education of young deaf children: ASL and English. In M. Strong (ed.), *Language Learning and Deafness*. Cambridge: Cambridge University Press, pp. 113–29.

Stryker, S. and Leaver, B. (1993) *Content-Based Instruction in Foreign Language Education*. Washington, DC: Georgetown University Press.

Supalla, S. J. (1990) Manually Coded English: the modality question in signed language development. In P. Siple and S. D. Fischer (eds), *Theoretical Issues in Sign Language Research*, Vol. 2. Chicago: University of Chicago Press, pp. 85–109.

Sussman, H. M., Franklin, P. and Simon, T. (1982) Bilingual speech: bilateral control? *Brain and Language*, **15**, 125–42.

Suzuki, S. and Notoya, M. (1984) Teaching written language to deaf infants and preschoolers. *Topics in Language Disorders*, **3**, 10–16.

Suzuki, T. (1984) *Words in Context*. Tokyo: Kodansha International.

Tabors, P. and Snow, C. (1994) English as a second language in preschool programs. In F. Genesee (ed.), *Educating Second Language Children: The Whole Child, the Whole Curriculum, the Whole Community*. Cambridge: Cambridge University Press.

Tahta, S., Wood, M. and Loewenthal, K. (1981) Age changes in the ability to replicate foreign pronunciation and intonation. *Language and Speech*, **24**, 363–72.

Tarone, E. and Swain, M. (1995) A sociolinguistic perspective on second language use in immersion classrooms. *Modern Language Journal*, **79**, 166–79.

Taylor, I. and Taylor, M. (1995) *Writing and Literacy in Chinese, Korean and Japanese*. Amsterdam: John Benjamins.

Teale, W., Sulzby, E. and Farr, M. (eds) (1986) *Emergent Literacy: Writing and Reading.* Westport, CT: Greenwood Publishing Group, Inc.

Terman, L. M. (1918) An experiment in infant education. *Journal of Applied Psychology,* **23**, 219–28.

Terrace, H. S. (1979a) Is problem-solving language? *Journal of Experimental Behavior,* **31**, 161–75.

Terrace, H. S. (1979b) *Nim: A Chimpanzee Who Learned Sign Language.* New York: Knopf.

Terrace, H. S. (1983) *Signs of the Apes, Songs of the Whales.* WGBH Boston: NOVA videotape.

Terrace, H. S., Petitio, L. A., Sanders, R. J. and Bever, T. G. (1979) Can an ape create a sentence? *Science,* **206**, 891–900.

Terrell, T. D. (1977) A natural approach to second language acquisition and learning. *Modern Language Journal,* **61**, 325–36.

Terrell, T. D. (1982) The natural approach to language teaching: an update. *Modern Language Journal,* **66**, 121–32.

The Boy With Half a Brain. (2000) [Online]. BBC News. http://news.bbc.co.uk/1/low/health/880478.stm.

The Man With Two Brains. (2000) [Online]. BBC News. http://news.bbc.co.uk/1/low/health/870311.stm.

Thompson, E. (1991) Foreign accents revisited: the English pronunciation of Russian immigrants. *Language Learning,* **41**, 177–204.

Thorndike, E. L. (1928) *Adult Learning.* New York: Macmillan.

Thorndike, E. L. (1932) *The Fundamentals of Learning.* New York: Teachers College, Columbia University.

Tincoff, R. and Jusczyk, P. W. (1999) Some beginnings of word comprehension in 6-month-olds. *Psychological Science,* **10**, 172–5.

Titone, R. (1968) *Teaching Foreign Languages: An Historical Sketch.* Washington, DC: Georgetown University Press.

Todd, P. H. III (1972) *Learning to Talk with Delayed Exposure to Speech.* Unpublished doctoral dissertation, University of California, Berkeley.

Tomasello, M. (2000) Do young children have adult syntactic competence? *Cognition,* **74**, 209–53.

Tomasello, M. (2003) *Constructing a Language. A Usage-Based Theory of Language Acquisition.* Cambridge, MA: Harvard University Press.

Tonkova-Yampol'skaya, R. V. (1969) Development of speech intonation in infants during the first two years of life. *Soviet Psychology,* **7**, 48–54.

Traweek, D. and Berninger, V. W. (1997) Comparisons of beginning literacy programs: alternative paths to the same learning outcome. *Learning Disability Quarterly,* **20**, 160–8.

Tulving, E. (1983) *Elements of Episodic Memory.* Oxford: Oxford University Press.

Twaddell, W. (1935) On defining the phoneme. In M. Joos (ed.) (1957), *Reading in Linguistics.* Washington, DC: American Council of Learned Societies, Reprinted as *Readings in Linguistics,* I. Chicago: Chicago University Press, pp. 55–79.

Tyack, D. and Ingram, D. (1977) Children's production and comprehension of questions. *Journal of Child Language,* **4**, 211–24.

US Supreme Court Reports (1922) October Term, Meyer v. Nebraska, pp. 392–403.

Vaid, J. (1987) Visual field asymmetries for rhyme and syntactic category judgements in monolinguals and fluent and early and late bilinguals. *Brain and Language,* **30**, 263–77.

van Wagenen (1933–58) *Reading Readiness Scales*. Van Wagenen Psycho-Educational Research Laboratories: Minneapolis.

Vanlancker-Sidtis, D. (2004) When only the right hemisphere is left: studies in language and communication. *Brain and Language*, **91**, 199–211.

van Wuijtswinkel, K. (1994) *Critical Period Effects on the Acquisition of Grammatical Competence in a Second Language*. Unpublished Master's thesis, University of Nijmegen, The Netherlands.

Varadi, T. (1983) Strategies of target language learner communication: message adjustment. In C. Faerch and G. Kasper (eds), *Strategies in Interlanguage Communication*. London: Longman, pp. 79–99.

Vargha-Khadem, F., Carr, L. J., Isaacs, E., Brett, E., Adams, C. and Mishkin, M. (1997) Onset of speech after left hemispherectomy in a nine-year-old boy. *Brain*, **120**, 159–82.

Velten, H. V. (1943) The growth of phonemic and lexical patterns in infant language. *Language*, **19**, 281–92.

Vihman, M. M., Macken, M. A., Miller, R., Simmons, H. and Miller, J. (1985) From babbling to speech: a re-assessment of the continuity issue. *Language*, **61**, 397–445.

von Humboldt, W. (1836) *Über die Verschiedenheit des menschlichen Sprachbaues und ihren Einflus auf die geistige Entwickelung des Menschengeschlects* (Linguistic variability and intellectual development). Coral Gables, FL: University of Miami Press (1971).

Vygotsky, L. S. (1934/1962) *Thought and Language*. Cambridge, MA: MIT Press.

Wada, J. A., Clarke, R. and Hamm, A. (1975) Cerebral hemispheric asymmetry in humans. *Archives of Neurology*, **32**, 239–46.

Walters, J. and Zatorre, R. J. (1978) Laterality differences for word identification in bilinguals. *Brain and Language*, **6**, 158–67.

Wanner, E. (1980) The ATN and the sausage machine: which one is baloney? *Cognition*, **8**, 209–25.

Watson, J. (1924) *Behaviorism*. New York: Norton.

Wells, G. (1978) What makes for successful language development? In R. Campbell and P. Smith (eds), *Recent Advances in the Psychology of Language*. New York: Plenum, pp. 449–69.

Wenden, A. and Rubin, J. (1987) *Learner Strategies in Language Learning*. New York: Prentice Hall.

White, L. and Genesee, F. (1996) How native is near-native? The issue of ultimate attainment in adult second language acquisition. *Second Language Research*, **12**, 3, 233–65.

Widdowson, H. G. (1978) *Teaching English as Communication*. Oxford: Oxford University Press.

Wilkins, D. A. (1972) *The Linguistic and Situational Content of the Common Core in a Unit/Credit System*. Strasbourg: Council of Europe.

Wilkins, D. A. (1976) *Notional Syllabuses*. Oxford: Oxford University Press.

Williams, S. (1968) *Bilingual Experiences of a Deaf Child*. ERIC Document Reproduction Service No. ED 030 092.

Wilson, K. and Norman, C. A. (1998) Differences in word recognition based on approach to reading instruction. *Alberta Journal of Educational Research*, **44**, 221–30.

Witkin, H. A. and Goodenough, D. R. (1977) Field dependence and interpersonal behavior. *Psychological Bulletin*, **84**, 661–89.

Witkin, H. A. and Goodenough, D. R. (1981) *Cognitive Style: Essence and Origin – Field Dependence and Independence*. New York: International Universities Press.

Witkin, H. A., Goodenough, D. R. and Oltman, P. K. (1979) Psychological differentiation: Current status. *Journal of Personality and Social Psychology*, **37**, 1127–45.

Wittelson, S. F. and Pallie, W. (1973) Left hemisphere specialization for language in the newborn. *Brain*, **96**, 641–6.

Witty, P. and Kopel, D. (1936) Preventing reading disability: the reading readiness factor. *Educational Administration and Supervision*, **28**, 401–18.

Wuillemin, D., Richardson, B. and Lynch, J. (1994) Right hemisphere involvement in processing later-learned language in multilinguals. *Brain and Language*, **46**, 620–36.

Yalden, J. (1983) *The Communicative Syllabus: Evolution, Design and Implementation*. Oxford: Pergamon.

Yamada, J. (1997) *Learning and Information Processing of Kanji and Kana*. Hiroshima: Keisuisha.

Yamada, J. E. (1990) *A Case for the Modularity of Language*. Cambridge, MA: Bradford Books/MIT Press.

Yashima, T., Zenuk-Nishide, L. and Shimizu, K. (2004) The influence of attitudes and affect on willingness to communicate and second language communication. *Language Learning*, **54**, 1, 119–52.

Yeoman, E. (1996) The meaning of meaning: affective engagement and dialogue in a second language. *Canadian Modern Language Review*, **52**, 596–610.

Yeon, S.-H. (2003) Perception of English palatal codas by Korean speakers of English. [Online]. *Journal of Pan-Pacific Association of Applied Linguistics*, **7**.

Zatorre, R. J. (1989) On the representation of multiple languages in the brain: old problems and new directions. *Brain and Language*, **36**, 127–47.

Author Index

Subject Index